THE GOOD INTENT

Ruth Anderson Phillips, circa 1907
Photo courtesy of the Phillips Family Collection

THE GOOD INTENT
The Story and Heritage of a Fresno Family

JOHN RENNING PHILLIPS

MAGNOLIA GROUP PRESS
2007

CONTENTS

PART I

PART II

For My Father

*   *   *

In Memoriam

John Pressley Phillips
(July 18, 1891 – September 10, 1954)

Ruth Anderson Phillips
(May 23, 1897 – March 28, 1995)

*   *   *

Believing that the fundamental principles of Christianity and the Golden Rule are essential for real success in life, I have endeavored to make a practical application of them in my life and practice. While one is naturally disappointed at times, yet I am persuaded that in its last analysis it pays.

We are helped by helping others,
If we give, we always get.
Seeing others as our brothers
Is life's safest, surest bet.

If we give what men are needing,
It will help us in the end,
And we can't just help succeeding
In the game of life, my friend.

David Pressley Anderson
(July 15, 1868 – January 3, 1949)

PART I

I. INTRODUCTION

This is the story and heritage of my father's parents, John and
Ruth Phillips of Fresno, California. Although they were
rather well known within their social circle in Fresno and
elsewhere from the 1920s until my grandmother passed away in
1995, little has ever been written about them in the newspaper or
elsewhere. Since my father and his sister Mary Walker Phillips
are perhaps the last of our family to live in Fresno, I feel that the
time is right to present their story, and to preserve their heritage
for posterity.

Most of the families were originally from England, Scotland
and Ireland. My grandparents were related, but not as we might
have thought. My assumption has always been that they were
related through the Pressley family, for the name Pressley
appears in both of their families. As this book will explain, if
they were related within the Pressley family, the common
ancestor must have lived in Scotland well before our first Pressly
families immigrated to South Carolina. Rather, their more recent
common ancestors are the patriot David Adams Jr. and his wife
Ann Chaplin. As a result, my grandparents were third cousins,
once removed.

One group of Presslys[1] came to South Carolina on the ship
The Good Intent in 1734 with the Witherspoons. These are the
ancestors of my great-great-grandfather John Gotea Pressley,
despite the fact that it is David Pressley Anderson's family who
are related to these Witherspoon immigrants. (*Note: Two*

different lines of my ancestors bore this very similar surname. Each believes its spelling was the correct one.) As this book will discuss, the Pressly ancestors of David Pressley Anderson immigrated to Charleston, South Carolina in 1767 and did not first go to Williamsburg District as has been previously surmised.

The Presslys and Witherspoons were not the first American immigrants in our family. In fact, there were many before, including William Collins who arrived in Virginia Colony in 1635, Nathaniel Adams who received a land grant in Weymouth, Massachusetts in 1642, John Chaplin in 1662, Rev. William Screven sometime before 1674, Thomas Lynch in 1677, Sir Nathaniel Johnson in 1679 and Paul Grimball in 1682.

This is the first edition of a book I hope to update periodically. I am grateful for the help of others, especially John B. Kent of Baton Rouge, Louisiana and Peter B. Miazza of Jackson, Mississippi for their assistance in helping me trace my Phillips ancestry. I am particularly indebted to my great-great-grandfather Judge John Gotea Pressley for documenting his Pressly, Brockinton[2], Burckmyer and Gotea families, and to my father's third cousin Bruce Tognazzini[3] for his acumen in compiling these family roots and extending the ancestry back even further. I am also particularly indebted to my aunt Martha for archiving many of the John Gotea Pressley and William Walker Phillips papers.

Any errors in this book are wholly my responsibility for I have relied upon the research of others with respect to the rest of the extended family and hope to correct any errors in later editions.   Although each chapter number corresponds to a generation (e.g., my great-grandparents are in chapter four), I have at times collapsed some earlier family generations within a chapter when it seemed to me appropriate to do so.

I decided to write this book on May 23, 2007, the 110th anniversary of my grandmother's birth, as a gift for my father William David Phillips, named for both of his grandfathers, on the occasion of his eightieth birthday on November 13, 2007. This is the culmination of three years of research on my part towards a better understanding of our Phillips ancestry, combined with an untold amount of research performed by others. These include Janyce Anderson, who has traced our Anderson and Wilson families, and Mary Collins Landin, who researched our Collins and Willis families.

We all have a family story to tell. As my father would no doubt acknowledge, we have a wonderful heritage.   I am delighted that, with the help of others, I am able to offer much of our family tradition here for the first time in print.

John Renning Phillips
New York City
September 23, 2007

II. RUTH ANDERSON PHILLIPS

My father's parents were very popular in Fresno, California. This was despite a city population of about 45,000 in 1920, the decade in which they moved to town from my great-grandfather's River Ranch on the Old Friant Road.

I knew my grandmother Ruth Anderson Phillips from as far back as I can remember until she passed away, a little less than two months before her 98th birthday, on March 28, 1995. I suppose I knew her thirty years, which is longer than many people have the privilege of knowing a grandparent.

Ruth was born in Santa Rosa, California, the daughter of David Pressley Anderson and Mattie L. Reid, on May 23, 1897, exactly 110 years to the day before I decided to write this book.

She enrolled in the class of 1919[4] at U. C. Berkeley where she was a member of the Gamma Phi Beta sorority[5]. She then moved to Fresno when she married my grandfather in 1918. Together they lived at the River Ranch[6] and on January 20, 1920, their daughter, my aunt Martha Elizabeth Phillips was born. Martha passed away in 1994.

Following her birth, my grandparents moved to Dixon, California where my grandfather established an experimental dairy ranch in conjunction with the California Agriculture College, today known as U. C. Davis. Following this, they returned to Fresno and raised John Pressley Phillips, Jr., born on February 11, 1921 (and who died tragically[7] at Stanford University on October 1, 1941); Mary Walker Phillips, who was born on November 23, 1923 and who currently resides in Fresno; and my father, William David Phillips, who was born on November 13, 1927 and who lives in Fresno as well.

I called my grandmother "Hoo Hoo." Instead of ringing the door bell at my parents' home, she had the habit of opening the front door a little bit and chiming "hoo hoo..." in the way people today might call "yoo hoo, over here..." I was probably about three at the time, and the name stuck.

Hoo Hoo lived for music and the arts. Invariably, her radio was set to KMJ FM, the McClatchy FM radio station devoted to classical music in Fresno. Until I was twelve and discovered a more flamboyant and bespectacled pianist from London who shared my first name as his last, this was the only music I knew.

She joined the Fresno Musical Club in 1929 and was a member for sixty-six years. I accompanied her to many Fresno Musical Club and Fresno Philharmonic Orchestra concerts in Fresno and often, her home was the chosen venue for the after-concert artist parties. Opera soprano Beverly Sills, who recently passed away, was one of the many famous artists I remember coming to her home.

Today there is a bench outside of the Fresno Art Museum[8] named for her with the words "Ruth Anderson Phillips Celebrating A Lifetime Of Music and Art."

Also, the piano bench used by the Fresno Philharmonic Orchestra is named for her, which is proper because, in her day, she was a fine pianist.

Ruth Anderson Phillips Bench at the Fresno Art Museum
"Celebrating a Lifetime of Music and Art"
Photo courtesy of Brandon Drake, Registrar, Fresno Art Museum

My grandmother was an extremely generous person with her time and concern for the causes she deemed important. Like most grandparents, she spoiled me just a little bit, but mostly she was simply proud of me and wished me the best. She always enjoyed our visits in her sun room with the old stove fireplace in the corner. I remember wanting to spend time with her from as early as when I was old enough to get around on my own; first by bicycle, later by car and eventually when living elsewhere, by airplane.

Everything she did was done so tastefully, whether it was the simple present she wrapped for someone so nicely with fine thick paper and string, or the beautiful decorations she bought for her home at Gump's in San Francisco. When I was young, all I would hear about was how she was going to "Gump's" and I couldn't figure out why I couldn't go to "the dump" with her. Later, when I lived in San Francisco, I learned what all the fuss was about.

Mrs. Levon Kemalyan, Mrs. Klenner F. Sharp
and Mrs. John P. Phillips, April 18, 1965
© 2007 THE FRESNO BEE

I'll never forget the wonderful dinners at her house, with all the guests dressed so nicely and always so kind to me. For many years, she had a cook for these special occasions named Mrs. McCaulley who was, no doubt, older than she was and probably grateful for the work. Dinner at her house was always a special treat and my favorite was the leg of lamb she served, always with rice and onion gravy, peas and mint jelly.

I could never understand the fascination with rice, served even at Thanksgiving and Christmas. Rice was, of course, a plantation crop in South Carolina, the English Colony where so many of my grandparents' families were from. Little did I know when I was young that I was the beneficiary of a 250-year-old "family tradition."

At the dinner table she kept a large brown bell at the top of her placemat at the head of the table. Mrs. McCaulley made the most delicious little round biscuits, split in half and buttered on the inside, and they were only a bell's ring away.

That bell also served to remind everyone at the table who was in charge. My father might have sat at the other end of the dining table, but there was never any doubt in anyone's mind that Hoo Hoo was truly the "Chairman of The Board."

It was also at her home, on evenings such as these, when I started to come to understand just how respected she was in Fresno. She had so many friends. At times, during her many house parties, they would overflow her relatively large living room at the home she built in 1970, located at 518 East Saginaw Way at Wilson Avenue. This home would later become known within the family as "Hoo Hoo's Hacienda."

While her new house was being built, we all flew to "the islands" of Hawaii to spend Christmas in 1970. I loved the experience so much that to this day Hawaii holds a special place in my heart. Now, whenever I arrive in Hawaii and smell the orchids at the Honolulu airport, I'm instantly reminded of my first visit to "the islands" on that family trip. I remember spending Christmas day that year at the Hana Maui Ranch, riding a galloping horse on the ranch property to an open-air venue where they served us steak and eggs for breakfast. The whole experience was magical.

On the way over to Hawaii, we spent the night at "The Metropolitan Club" in San Francisco before our flight the next day on Pan Am. I distinctly recall the joy of eating breakfast in bed at my grandmother's club and I'm sure such experiences hastened my interest in city life.

In 1977 my grandmother turned eighty. During that year, I was a *Fresno Bee* paper boy and delivered papers to everyone in my neighborhood, including our family friends Karl and Doris Falk. The experience was hard; I had to get up every morning at 5:00 a.m. to be done by 7:00 a.m. in order to get to school on time. However, the experience enabled me to be able to use my own money to buy my grandmother a birthday present. I took the bus downtown to Warner's Jewelers in the Fulton Mall and purchased for my grandmother a beautiful silver tray which I had engraved, "Happy Birthday Hoo Hoo" with the date of her eightieth birthday, May 23, 1977. When she opened her present at our family home, she nearly was in tears over my heart-felt gesture. Sixteen years later she returned it to me and my bride, engraved with our wedding date.

Later that year, around the time of my 15th birthday, she told me how she had read in *The Fresno Bee* that Elton John, the famous singer and songwriter she knew I admired, was retiring from show business. Nevertheless, it was around this time that I started to write piano music as well, and my grandmother proudly told her friends that I was busy "composing."

During the 1970s Hoo Hoo had a black woman named Estelle who came to work for her several days a week. I suppose Estelle washed her clothes and did light housekeeping. She was a wonderful woman and was always especially kind to me. This was a point in time when it was, I suppose, still acceptable for a relatively well-off white woman in Fresno to directly employ a black woman of relatively poor means. I was a boy at the time and thought nothing of it. Estelle was like family to me, and in the world I knew, as far as I was concerned, she adored me as much as my grandmother's friends. It never bothered me that Estelle always ate in the kitchen when the family gathered around the dinner table. This was how it was. Yet, unlike some women of her day, my grandmother would share lunch with Estelle in her sunroom. No doubt they enjoyed each other's company.

I remember the summer evenings, when we would join my grandmother for dinner. She would often serve an aspic salad over butter lettuce, followed by the main meal which, if not leg of lamb, might have been pot roast, ham or just about anything else one can serve with rice and peas. If dessert was not a chocolate potato cake, a "chocolate watermelon," which was a form of steamed chocolate cake, or (my personal favorite) her chocolate bread pudding, we would retire on hot summer evenings to her large deck off the living room for fresh peaches and ice cream. The still evening air following a hot summer day in Fresno is matched only by the new morning air of the next day.

I remember those summer days in the mid-1970s, getting up early and riding my bicycle over to my grandmother's house at around 7 a.m. Aunt Mary and I would ride our bicycles up and down Wilson Avenue and return by 8 a.m., at which point we would have a breakfast of cooked apricots, yogurt and coffee on the porch off her bedroom. My grandmother would then join us, and we would start our day just about every summer morning this way. The sprinklers were still on at this hour, watering the ivy down below, and Fresno, during typically hot summer months, was still very cool and tranquil. After breakfast, I would leave Aunt Mary to her projects, which around this time included her 1977 book *Knitting*. Since the early 1960s, Mary lived in Greenwich Village, New York, but always spent two months every summer and several weeks every Christmas in Fresno, staying at my grandmother's house.

On the rare occasions when we would have a family dinner out at a restaurant, there were only two choices: Casa Canales[9] and Estrada's. Estrada's Spanish Kitchen was started by Louisa Estrada in Visalia in 1914, and her children started Estrada's restaurants all over California. Her daughter Cruz Estrada brought the restaurant to Fresno in 1917, operating their establishment out of an old house on the east side of Blackstone Avenue about two blocks north of Belmont Avenue. I so often remember going there with my family and invariably meeting up with family friends. The food was not really Mexican nor was it really Spanish either. It was really a unique "early California" cuisine. In my opinion, their specialty was their tostada which we called their "hot salad," made from a crisp corn tortilla topped with refried beans and shredded iceberg lettuce, tossed in oil and vinegar dressing, and finished with a hot sauce. We always wanted it "sizzling," meaning that the tortilla was very hot which made the salad on top sizzle. This specialty combined with their homemade tortilla chips, their enchiladas, cheese macaroni, chili relleno and fried chicken made this restaurant a Fresno tradition. When President George H. W. Bush came to Fresno, they took him for lunch at Estrada's. Unfortunately, the restaurant is gone now. I can't begin to say how much I miss the atmosphere of the old house, the great food, the company, and the special treatment we all received. In the bar area there was a mural painting by Mary Ponsart in which Joan Jertberg Russell and her two young sons can be found in one scene.

Hoo Hoo's home at 518 East Saginaw Way was built by architect John Mathias of Tiburon, California who is credited with the design of the walkway in front of the mid-1970s development of Tiburon condominiums at the edge of the waterfront. On a relatively small lot, he built her a marvelous 3-level home, designed for entertaining, with a span of ivy on both sides of the front of the house. Aunt Martha's room was downstairs behind the garage, and the entire lower floor was covered with faux brick.

The main part of the house was on the half-level. As one climbed the stairs, the floors on this level were completely dark hardwood. The living room was to the left, and the sunroom was to the right. Entering the living room, one found a large oriental carpet her father-in-law William Walker Phillips purchased in Egypt in 1910. Behind was a large bookshelf, which extended to the ceiling filled with books. Hoo Hoo loved to read. Within the living room, and to the left next to the large glass doors leading out to the deck, sat two old Vicksburg chairs with mahogany wood and yellow cotton fabric. The sofa in the middle faced two McGuire chairs which were separated by a large Chinese red box purchased at Gump's. The fireplace, in the middle to the right, separated a modern oil painting, on the left, by Freddy Albert[10] and icons, on the right, probably of Greek origin. On the left was an old-fashioned buffet and hutch. Towards the rear was the Steinway piano, which I now own. She had purchased it during the height of the Depression, much to her immediate remorse. When she confessed in tears to my grandfather that she had bought the piano, he was only too supportive, despite the circumstances of the times. To the right of the piano was the dining room, where we spent many evenings, decorated in light yellow wallpaper and Chinese lamps. To the right of this was the kitchen which was designed to allow any refuse to be dropped down to the trash cans below. To the right of the kitchen was the infamous sunroom. There my grandmother kept her desk and watched her television which was to the right of the old fire stove. Adjoining this level was her large deck, the length of the living room, complete with an olive tree planted in the middle. Adjacent to the dining room was a screened porch.

Upstairs on the third level, her large bedroom was just in front of the top of the stairs; to the left was my aunt Mary's bedroom. All of this was connected by a third-level deck which provided porches adjacent to both my grandmother's and my aunt's bedroom.

During the early 1980s I was away at college, although I did return to Fresno for a couple of years in the mid to late 1980s. By that point, Hoo Hoo was slowing down and the dinner parties were becoming less frequent.

In 1989 I was living in San Francisco and survived the earthquake of that year. In fact, I had been in the Marina District at the time and witnessed the collapse of a building one block behind me. Because my own apartment near Golden Gate Park was damaged, I ended up spending the next month with Aunt Martha who was always especially kind to me. Following the earthquake, I became her neighbor when I took an apartment at Broadway and Laguna.

About a year later, while my grandmother was visiting San Francisco, she, Aunt Martha and I were invited to have lunch at the home of Mr. and Mrs. Warren Mohr who lived nearby in Pacific Heights. They served us lunch on the most exquisite and valuable Chinese plates that were apparently the single copy of what now resides in a Chinese museum. The other set had apparently belonged to a Chinese emperor. We were all very impressed. My grandmother, who loved and collected oriental art, pretended that she was going to take some plates home with her which drew much laughter around the table.

Mr. Mohr was also a collector of books about Charles Darwin and he showed me his extensive collection. During lunch at his house, he mentioned his intention to donate all of them very soon to the Huntington Library, a place I was familiar with from my Occidental College days.

The other interesting comment I remember from that luncheon was how they were the godparents of Neil Young's wife Pegi Morton. I remember how much Mrs. Mohr said she enjoyed Neil's company but just wished "he would get a good hair cut." Neil told Mr. Mohr around that time that the new record album he had just recorded was his best in years.

One Thanksgiving, perhaps a couple of years later, my grandmother came up to San Francisco and organized Thanksgiving Dinner for all of us including me, my fiancé, my aunt Martha, my cousin and her boyfriend, and Dixon Heise[11], my third cousin once removed. We celebrated Thanksgiving that year at Harris' Restaurant on Van Ness at Pacific. They gave us the best round table available and my grandmother chose the seating positions, with me (of course) to her right so that I might sit on the side of her "good ear."

Painter Maynard Dixon and my grandfather were second cousins. Dixon Heise was also a second cousin once removed to Maynard. Richard Lawrence Dixon and Julia Rebecca Phillips Dixon, who was my great-great-grandfather's sister, had several children including Harry St. John Dixon, who was Maynard's father, and Edward Turner Dixon, whose daughter Julia Dixon married Arthur Roy Heise (the parents of Edward Dixon Heise). Dixon's twin brother, Arthur Roy Heise, Jr., was my aunt Martha's first husband and her third cousin. He was killed in World War II shortly after they were married.

E. Dixon Heise
Photo from U. C. Berkeley's *Blue and Gold*, 1938

In December 1991, I held my engagement party at Dixon Heise's beautiful full-floor apartment in San Francisco. Throughout the next ten years we shared many lunches and dinners, whether at the Pacific Union Club in San Francisco where he was a member (and hoped I might someday join) or on his many visits to London, where I was living in the late 1990s.

His uncle was Arthur Towne of Blake, Moffitt and Towne. This pioneer company, started in 1855, was a large and well-known manufacturer and distributor of paper products which was sold to Kimberly-Clark about twenty years ago. The Townes did not have any children and Dixon, following the death of his twin brother Roy, was their only heir. The Townes owned the gorgeous full floor apartment where my engagement party was held at Pacific and Webster Streets in San Francisco. Dixon never married, and after he passed away on February 23, 2006 at the age of 89, he left a $14 million bequest to the University of California, San Francisco (UCSF) which has endowed the E. Dixon Heise Distinguished Professorship in Oncology.

I recently contacted Dan Riley, Senior Director of Gift Planning at University of California, San Francisco and he explained to me[12] how Dixon's extraordinarily generous bequest came about:

> Dixon, over a span of twenty-five years, made a number of very generous gifts to UCSF, including several life-income gifts, i.e., charitable remainder trust gifts and charitable gift annuities. He was a graduate of the University of California (UC Berkeley), but chose to make his major gifts here. I believe that his initial connection to UCSF was the result of his life-long friendship with Dr. Herbert C. Moffitt, Jr., who practiced medicine in San Francisco and was on clinical faculty here. As you no doubt are aware, Dixon was Vice President and Corporate Secretary of Blake, Moffitt and Towne, so there was that family connection with Dr. Moffitt as well. Plus, Dixon and Dr. Moffitt were both members of the Pacific Union Club. While Dr. Moffitt may have been responsible for introducing Dixon to UCSF, he grew closer to us and our mission of medical education, research, patient care, and community service with each additional gift he made.

I was living in San Francisco in the early 1990s and this Thanksgiving Dinner was one of the last few trips I remember my grandmother making to the city. It's unfortunate, as I look back on it, that we didn't get to spend more time together in San Francisco. She knew the city very well and remembered going to Neiman Marcus with her mother as a child. I only wish I could have had the opportunity for her to show me the city she knew.

I'm sure that my grandmother's longevity was in part due to the fact that she simply enjoyed walking. Every morning and afternoon, she would walk to the end of Wilson Avenue and back, a total distance of about four miles. She continued this daily regimen right up until she broke her hip in 1994. Prior to that she was very active, always coming and going here and there. The French bakery at Fig Garden Village around that time was the local social "club," and I'm sure she went there often to see people she knew.

In earlier days she would drive me to Fig Garden Village but would always park a good long walking distance from the Foodland supermarket. Ever since the 1973 "energy crisis," she felt it was her patriotic duty to do her part and help conserve fuel.

This probably accounted for why, in a large house, only her sunroom was warmed by the old stove fireplace.

She was driving her car as late as 1993 until she had a little mishap and drove through an intersection at Ashlan Avenue and Van Ness Boulevard. She apparently did not see the other car approaching at what was by then no longer a four-way stop. There was an accident but, thankfully, no one was harmed.

Nevertheless, it fell to my father to rein in a very independent woman. She was very bent out of shape for a while when my father took away her car keys. From then on she started calling my father "Boolie," the name of a character from the 1989 film "Driving Miss Daisy" which she enjoyed (Boolie was Miss Daisy's son who hired a driver for his mother). My father did his part, taking her wherever and whenever she needed to go somewhere. I was living and working in San Francisco at the time, but had I been living in Fresno, I would have gladly done my part as well.

Her daughter Martha died in the fall of 1994, and we had lunch together at a restaurant in San Francisco after the memorial service.   That was probably the last time I had a good conversation with her despite the circumstances. It was also her last trip to San Francisco or anywhere outside of Fresno. By Thanksgiving she had broken her hip and was becoming quieter. She was also beginning to sleep more and more. By Christmas my father was spending many hours with her, just being a good son and helping in any way he could.

I went to see her sometime in early 1995, and she had been sleeping nearly round the clock. My father took me to her bedroom while she was sleeping; he whispered to her, "John is here." She opened her eyes as I kissed her on the cheek and was clearly delighted to see me. A moment later, as I started to talk to her, she fell back asleep. I knew then that unfortunately, this was perhaps the last I'd see of my dear grandmother. My father later told me that this was the only time she had opened her eyes that day. I suppose that what little energy she had left on that day was reserved just for me.

How proud she would have been of me had she known that about a year later I would be living in London. She would have been anxious to hear from me and to learn of my exploits. In turn, I would have sent her gifts from Harrods or any little thing from London. After all, it was in a bedroom at her home at 410 Van Ness[13] in Fresno, that I remember learning the nursery rhyme "London Bridge Is Falling Down." How odd it was that a year after she passed away, I found myself working at No. 1 London Bridge, London. The view from my office window was of London Bridge itself.

When Hoo Hoo passed away on March 28, 1995, it was Roger Tatarian, the retired Vice President and Editor in Chief of United Press International, who wrote a wonderful piece about her in the April 2, 1995 edition of *The Fresno Bee*, just three months before he died:

"Ruth Phillips' legacy merits remembrances"

Ruth Phillips died the other day at the age of 97 and it is important not to permit her contribution to the cultural life of this community to go unrecorded.

Ruth Anderson Phillips had been a resident of Fresno since 1918 and, until her health began failing a year or two ago, she was deeply involved in the city's artistic life as a member or officer of the Fresno Musical Club and the Fresno Art Museum.

At 97, Ruth Phillips was a link with the era when Fresno audiences filled the old White Theater on Broadway to hear such world famed artists as Ernestine Schumann-Heink, Alma Gluck, Fritz Kreisler, Amelita Galli-Curci and Luisa Tetrazzini. A Fresno that was only a fraction of its present size was able to attract such luminaries because of the dedication of the Fresno Musical Club.

Grand entertainers

She joined the Musical Club in 1929 and as a member, director or its president in later years participated in arranging appearances of such artists as Marian Anderson, John Charles Thomas, Giovanni Martinelli, Arthur Rubinstein, Leontyne Price, Ellie Ameling and a host of others.

It is perhaps no longer in fashion to refer to women of great standing in a community as "great ladies" but people who knew Ruth Phillips and others like her will agree that no other characterization can do them justice.

Ruth Phillips was Old Fresno at its best - soft-spoken, urbane, gracious and equally dedicated to raising a family of two sons and two daughters, and to doing her part to add to the amenities of the city where she lived. She came here from Santa Rosa in 1918 as the bride of John Pressley Phillips, a fruit packer and shipper. He died in 1954.

Like many of her generation, Ruth Phillips rarely if ever left home without gloves - usually white ones. In her early years in Fresno, a Japanese parasol in summer was standard equipment for ladies walking downtown to shop on J Street, later Fulton, or K Street, now Van Ness. Others may have discontinued the habit of wearing gloves before venturing out of doors, but not Ruth Phillips.   Even on her briefest shopping excursions, she was reluctant to be seen without gloves.

She took daily walks with great regularity. Well after her 90th birthday she was a familiar sight to others who favored the shaded streets of Old Fig Garden for their daily strolls. She loved driving, too. In 1924, her husband acquired a tan, two-door Dodge sedan equipped with disc wheels, and it was a car she never forgot. She drove much more sophisticated cars well into her 80s but that old Dodge remained her all-time favorite.

A giving person

Ruth Phillips was responsible for innumerable acts of kindness both to people she knew and to many she did not. She was generous in her donations to charities and scholarships, and was always solicitous about the health of friends. She was firmly convinced that a floating island pudding or beef tea was a greater restorative than anything invented in a pharmaceutical laboratory and was quick to deliver one or the other when she heard a friend was ill.

She was for many years on the board of the Fresno Art Museum and in 1991 was honored with a Horizon Award by the Fresno Arts Council. She followed other civic affairs with great interest and was proud of her service on the Fresno County grand jury.

Hers was not a life without adversity. Not only her husband, but a son and daughter preceded her in death, and in the Depression years, when the family business struggled to keep afloat, she did her share in the fruit packing sheds.

To say that Ruth Phillips was quiet and soft-spoken is not to say she was reticent to speak out when necessary or that she lacked a spirit of adventure. Back in the days when movie theaters offered prizes to patrons holding lucky tickets, she heard that the drawing for a bicycle was to be held at the Wilson Theater on the same night she was giving a small dinner party. She slipped away from her guests for a brief while, got herself down to the Wilson - and came home riding the bicycle.

Decisive action

In the 1950s, while the family lived at 410 Van Ness, in the area south of City College, some of the old sycamore trees along the street were designated to be cut down. When city crews, saws in hand, approached the Phillips residence, she rushed out, placed herself in front of her tree, stood the crews off and went down to City Hall and got the order rescinded.

Mostly, though, she did what she did quietly and without fuss, with the style and grace characteristic of very "great ladies." It was our good fortune as a community to have had her in our midst for the many years that we did.

Roger Tatarian, a native Fresnan, is professor emeritus of journalism at California State University, Fresno. He worked for 34 years for United Press International, culminating his career as editor. His column appears Sunday. © THE FRESNO BEE 2007.

At her memorial service on April 8, 1995, old family friend James McClatchy, who loved my grandmother since childhood had this to say:

What can we say when somebody so loved, so universally loved, is no longer with us?

Ruth had a rich life of friendships with innumerable people, of all walks of life. She was loving and caring with all of them. I saw this many times over the years since our friendship began when I was just two years old. It might be surprising to think of a friendship between a two-year-old and a mature woman, but Ruth was the kind of person who extended friendship in all circumstances and she extended friendship to me from the beginning.

Ruth was a part of my family's life --- I can't remember anything in my life that precedes Ruth. I was 2 when my parents moved to Fresno and bought a house on Yosemite Avenue next to a vacant lot. On the other side of the vacant lot was the Phillips home.

So Ruth and John Sr. soon were visiting with my parents and they became fast friends. As the years went by, other children arrived and became friends. "Brud," as John the son was known, and I were buddies. We dug caves in the vacant lot and rode our tricycles on the sidewalk.

John Pressley Phillips, Jr. and James McClatchy
Fresno, California circa 1926
Photo courtesy of the Phillips Family Collection

Our families vacationed together. We camped in tents at Giant Forest and our families developed bonds that grow through that kind of shared happiness. One of the prized mementos for both our families was a photo of Brud and myself, about 4 or 5 years old, dressed in fireman's hats, standing in front of our toy fire wagon. I saw that photo again on the wall of Ruth's room only a few weeks ago.

In all those years, Ruth was a solid rock of support for my mother, helping my mother through her personal tragedies and stresses as my mother helped her. You all know Ruth's extraordinary ability to be supportive and understanding --- a tower of strength, always in a gentle and loving way.

For 70 years they gave each other total trust, support for each other and intimacy of experiences, understanding and caring, and all those other qualities that are so real but so hard to measure or describe. Ruth was my mother's closest friend, but also a very dear, close friend to me. And Ruth also extended her friendship to my wife Susan who quickly became very much attached to Ruth.

Ruth gave this care and attention to so many people all her long life. To all people, not just family intimates.

She bore her own griefs with grace and courage, never letting her sorrows infect other people. Brud died in a meaningless, tragic accident when we were at Stanford together, and I had to phone his parents with the news[14]. I will never forget her cry of disbelief. Later as we shared this experience, she did her utmost to relieve me of the pain and anguish I felt.

I don't know anybody who could better be described as a great lady --- generous, supportive, reaching out, open-minded, thoughtful, with boundless energy, steadfast, wise, clear-minded about values in life and what she was doing. She was modest as it should be defined. She never sought the limelight or advantage for herself --- she found her rewards in helping others.   An extraordinary person who gave her love and strength to countless people, and who in turn was loved by everybody who knew her.

Roger Tatarian expressed these thoughts very sensitively in a recent column, which reached many more people than we have here who feel as we do.

I always felt blessed with the gift of her affection when we were together. It was totally disarming, genuine and open, a most wonderful quality. Ruth enriched and elevated the lives of all who came into contact with her. We extend our condolences to her family as we honor the memory of this extraordinarily loving person whose compassion for others was unlimited.

James McClatchy was a close friend of my father's brother John Jr. who was called "Brud," while James' brother C. K. McClatchy was about the same age as my father. I knew Mr. McClatchy as well. I remember the private dinner party his mother Phebe Conley gave for him at her home on Huntington Boulevard, a beautiful old house with character, like so many of those older large homes on that street. My grandmother and I were the only guests. At this occasion in 1980 I met his sons, William and Carlos, who were great fun to spend an evening with. During dinner, Mr. McClatchy announced his engagement to Susan. A few years later we all celebrated Mrs. Conley's birthday at my grandmother's house, and I distinctly recall the poem William wrote which he read for his grandmother. I remember being very impressed because I had never done that myself for my grandmother. Now I wish I had.

Another multi-generational family relationship formed in those early days in Fresno and which continues to this day, started with my grandparents' friendship with Judge and Mrs. Gilbert H. Jertberg in the 1920s.

Judge Jertberg was a Stanford-educated Fresno lawyer who, having served three years on the Federal District Court for Southern California, was elevated by President Dwight D. Eisenhower to the United States Court of Appeals for the Ninth Circuit in 1958. Unfortunately, my grandfather only knew him as a Fresno lawyer and didn't live to see him become a federal judge. In 1954 he handled my grandfather's estate.

In 1958 there were just several dozen Federal Appeals Court judges in the United States, junior only to the nine justices on the Supreme Court. Judge Jertberg, a close personal friend of Earl Warren, took senior status on the bench at the age of 70 in 1967 but continued to work a full caseload until his last illness and death in 1973. I remember the day clearly; my father informed me at breakfast that his dear friend and "partner" Judge Jertberg had passed away.

Mrs. Henrietta Burns Jertberg taught all subjects in grades one to twelve in a one-room schoolhouse near Fresno during the First World War. She married Gilbert Jertberg in 1922 and worked as a musician for hire (piano and violin) in the Fresno area. Later, she was First Violinist for the Fresno Civic Symphony between the wars. She was associated with the Fresno Musical Club, the Monday Club, and other organizations in the company and friendship of my grandmother. At Christmas in 1973 Mrs. Jertberg gave me a framed photo of Judge Jertberg which I still have. Her gift meant a great deal to me, for he was like the paternal grandfather I didn't have and I missed him.

Their daughter Joan, a close friend of my aunt Mary, attended Stanford and married Fresno lawyer and sculptor T. Newton "Newt" Russell, who also went to Stanford.   Joan has always been wonderful to me, and I remember, as a child, helping her bake raisin bread up at the Jertberg and Russell cabin at Huntington Lake.

Her husband Newt was a real renaissance man.   He and his partners built a robust law firm of the highest reputation with a statewide tax and business practice.   Thomas, Snell, Jamison, Russell and Asperger set the standard for the Central Valley for several decades, with the sophistication and clients of "big city" firms.   A disciplined lawyer who also had enormous creative drive, he became a respected sculptor, working mostly with native river granite to create a magnificent body of work.   Some pieces are monumental in scale.   He conceived, designed or built many of the devices and methods needed to drill, carve, shape and connect stones weighing up to several hundred pounds each. Today his work can be found in many public and private collections.

Newt was looking forward to the day that I too would become a father, and lived just long enough to learn of my daughter Matilda's birth.

T. Newton ("Newt") Russell (1918-2001)
Newt is using his own invented tools to hoist river granite into place.
Photo circa 2000 by James Newton Russell
Photo courtesy of the Russell Family Collection

I knew the Jertbergs when they lived in their beautiful old adobe house at 3917 North Wilson Avenue, across from my grandmother's house on Saginaw. Judge Jertberg was very kind to me, once pulling a nickel from behind my ear, and always happy to see me when I rang his doorbell. When I was a little older, he once invited me to come visit his office and court room.

We exchanged letters in the same way he did with my father when he was the same age. My father would send my letters "First Class" which I think humored the Judge. They were after all "partners;" they had a special handshake invented when my father was a boy. I now share this special partner's greeting with his grandsons.

I came to know the two Jertberg grandsons in the late 1960s when our families spent summers together in nearby cabins at Huntington Lake. They, of course, knew me when I was very little. We became very dear friends, brothers in fact; one grandson served as my best man at my wedding in Finland while the other stood by me at my blessing ceremony in San Francisco. Our friendship, or "partnership" as we sometimes call it, continues to this day with my close relationship with the three Jertberg great-grandchildren, all of whom I knew as babies and for whom I feel a great deal of affection.

The Honorable Gilbert H. Jertberg (1897-1973)
Photo courtesy of the Russell Family Collection

John Pressley Phillips (1891-1954)
Photo courtesy of the Phillips Family Collection

III. JOHN PRESSLEY PHILLIPS

My grandfather John Pressley Phillips died before I was born so I never had the pleasure of knowing him. He was born in Santa Rosa on July 18, 1891, the son of William Walker Phillips and Elizabeth B. Pressley.

My grandfather graduated from Fresno Technical High School in 1909 and enrolled at U. C. Berkeley for the class of 1913. In March 1910, he took a train with his parents to New York and a steamer to Europe where they eventually toured the Mediterranean, including Egypt where the family was photographed on camels in front of the pyramids.

After he returned to Berkeley where he was a member of the Chi Phi fraternity[15], he suffered a burst appendix and was hospitalized for several months. Worse, the University would not let him return because of their strict physical education requirement that he could not handle. Today it seems inconceivable that a university would reject a student for such a reason, but such were the conditions of the day.

In 1911 he returned from Berkeley to Fresno and managed his father's River Ranch on the old Friant Road, turning it into a dairy ranch. Two years after his mother passed away, he married my grandmother Ruth in 1918. Following a five-week honeymoon trip to the Midwest and to the East Coast (including Niagara Falls), they returned via Chicago where John purchased a carload of registered Holstein cows for the ranch he planned to turn into a dairy farm.

Together they lived on the ranch for about two years. Fortunately, my grandmother was spared the job of cooking for all of the ranch hands. There was a cook named "Tori" who helped in this regard and my great-grandfather recalled how he helped Tori's husband secure her entry into the United States from Japan.

After my aunt Martha was born at the River Ranch on January 20, 1920, my grandparents moved to Dixon, California where John established an experimental dairy ranch in conjunction with the California Agriculture College, today known as U. C. Davis. Following this, my grandparents returned to Fresno and settled in a new home on Yosemite Avenue. Their new home, separated by an empty lot, was next door to the home of C. K. and Phebe McClatchy.

These two families became multi-generational best friends before my grandparents bought the house at 410 Van Ness in 1931. During these years, my father's brother John Pressley Phillips Jr. was born on February 11, 1921, followed by his sister Mary Walker Phillips[16] who was born on November 23, 1923, and my father who was born on November 13, 1927.

Martha Elizabeth Phillips (1920-1994)
Fresno, California circa 1940
Photo courtesy of the Phillips Family Collection

John Pressley Phillips, Jr. (1921-1941)
Stanford University circa 1940
Photo courtesy of the Phillips Family Collection

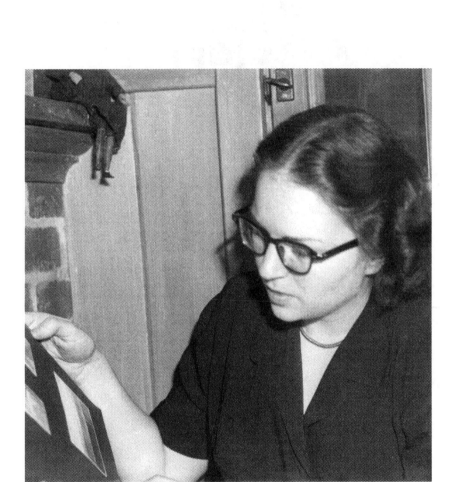

Mary Walker Phillips (1923-   )
Fresno, California circa 1940s
Photo courtesy of the Phillips Family Collection

William David Phillips (1927-   )
Fresno, California circa 1940s
Photo courtesy of the Phillips Family Collection

John joined Federal Fruit Distributors in 1923, starting
initially as a field man, and soon was made a minority partner,
contracting with the growers for their crops. During the twenty-
nine years he was with the company, he would often drive 150
miles per day to visit the various growers during harvest time,

which, of course, was during the middle of summer. This was before automobiles had air conditioning, although the idea of putting air conditioning in cars did catch on in the 1950s. In 1930, the packing house had twenty-five employees, and by mid-August of that year they had packed forty-four train car loads made up of about one-third plums, one-third grapes and one-third peaches. By 1942 C. E. Harding was President and Treasurer, and my grandfather was Vice President and Secretary.

Federal Fruit Distributors, Fresno, California
Fruit Crate Label, circa 1940s

Federal Fruit Distributors, Fresno, California
Fruit Crate Label, circa 1940s

During those days, my father's whole family, with the exception of his sister Mary (who was often sick as a child), would work in the packing house during the summer packing season. Since the family was busy packing fruit in the summers, this meant that they as a family did not have the opportunity to enjoy a typical summer family vacation.

John, like his father before him, was on the Chapter Governing Board of St. James Episcopal Parish and was instrumental in bringing Dean Malloch to the Cathedral. Malloch Elementary School in Fresno was named after the Dean.

My father has often described my grandfather affectionately as "a real gentleman." My father remembers how his father always came home at dinner time, even if he sometimes had to return to the packing house afterwards. When he would get home, he would take a bath, put on a coat and tie and come downstairs to join the rest of the family at the dinner table. He was the type of man who felt that if my grandmother had worked so hard to prepare a wonderful meal, the least he could do was to make himself look presentable for dinner.

Joan Jertberg Russell was a close friend of Aunt Mary. She remembers how they used to play jacks or dig for clay in the nearby ditch as children. She also remembers the little cardboard fruit boxes that she and Aunt Mary assembled on the front porch for which my grandmother paid each girl a nickel (considered a lot of money by young children at the time). She further remembers my grandfather on evenings when the Jertbergs went to have dinner at my grandparents' house at 410 Van Ness. She recalls him coming down the stairs into the living room looking very happy, clasping his hands in anticipation of dinner with friends. Joan says my grandfather was very affable and friendly. She also remembers how she saw her father, Gilbert Jertberg, and my grandfather talking outside the house on the lawn one afternoon. Gilbert later told Joan that my grandfather mentioned that he had enjoyed a very prosperous year.

Unfortunately, my grandfather became ill and retired from the packing house in 1952. During these years, my father was living in Oakland and Aunt Martha was living in San Francisco. My aunt Mary stayed in Fresno and helped Hoo Hoo care for him.   Tragically, he passed away just two years later on September 10, 1954, at the early age of 63.

Considering that my grandfather's father, William, lived to be 83, how sad it is that my grandfather did not live to reach a similar age. If he had, I would have had the opportunity to know him until I was perhaps about eleven, at least long enough to remember him in the way I remember Judge Jertberg.

When I think of my two paternal great-grandfathers, both pioneers who came to California in 1870, I realize that what both men shared in common in the early days of California was a work ethic combined with faith, as well as an interest in banking, ranching and politics.

When David Pressley Anderson came out to California from South Carolina, he went to work in a dentist's office initially to perform the dentist's bookkeeping.   Later he apprenticed to become a dentist, joined with the dentist in a dental partnership and became very successful.   He then invested in and became a director of the Santa Rosa Building and Loan Association in 1894.   For two years beginning in 1925, he served in the California State Legislature.

Likewise, my other great-grandfather William Walker Phillips, who was about 17 years older, came out to California in the same year from Mississippi. After establishing a successful store in Centerville, he was offered the opportunity to start a new bank in Fresno.

Like David, William also enjoyed politics. In 1894 he ran as a Democrat for a position as a Railroad Commissioner. Twenty years later, he also hoped to run as a Republican for California State Treasurer, an office his grandfather held in Mississippi about eighty years earlier.   Unfortunately, this was during the time of the Progressive "Bull Moose" party of Teddy Roosevelt who split with the Republican Party.   As a result, not a single

Republican was chosen as a candidate for State Treasurer in the 1914 California election.   Although he did not win, William then ran for a Republican seat in the House of Representatives in 1916.

Even more amazingly, the local newspaper reported that he was tipped in 1892 by local Democrats to be the Fresno Democratic choice for Governor of California in the state election to be held two years later in 1894.   An official nomination, however, did not materialize.   Considering that the winner of the 1914 race for State Treasurer did eventually become governor, it is interesting to me that he very well could have become governor had he been nominated and won in that election.

William Walker Phillips (1851-1935)
Photo courtesy of the Phillips Family Collection

IV. WILLIAM WALKER PHILLIPS AND DAVID PRESSLEY ANDERSON

WILLIAM WALKER PHILLIPS

William Walker Phillips, my grandfather's father, was born in Yazoo City, Mississippi on July 21, 1851. He lost his father, Seaborn Moses Collins Phillips, in 1861 at the start of the Civil War when he was just 9 years old. After this tragedy, he and the family moved to Madisonville, Mississippi about forty miles away where his mother's family, the Walkers, owned a plantation.

One of his earliest memories was the Presidential Election of 1860, no doubt a closely watched race in Madisonville. The family was Democratic and voted for John C. Breckinridge who ran on a pro-slavery platform.

South Carolina had promised to secede from the Union if Lincoln were elected in 1860, and Mississippi was sure to follow. Many people, including my Phillips family, migrated from South Carolina to Mississippi in its territory days and in later years.

Abraham Lincoln seemed like an unlikely presidential candidate. He was a former Congressman who ran an unsuccessful bid for Senator from Illinois in 1858, prompted by the Supreme Court's "Dred Scott Decision" of the prior year. That decision ruled that people of African origin, whether or not they were slaves, could never be citizens of the United States.

He famously debated Stephan A. Douglas, arguing:

A house divided against itself cannot stand. I believe that the government cannot last as long as America is half slave and half free. I do not expect the Union to fall apart - the house to fall. I do expect that it will become either all one thing or all the other - either all slave or all free. Either the people against slavery will stop it forever, or it will become lawful in all the states, old and new, north and south alike.

The final Lincoln-Douglas debate of 1858 took place in Alton, Illinois. The location of that debate is a place I've seen many times on my numerous trips to Illinois while Judge Jertberg's grandson was a circuit court judge in Jerseyville, Illinois. The South, in no uncertain terms, took these words to mean a guarantee that if Lincoln were elected President in 1860, he would both preserve the union and end slavery. The Southern economy depended upon slavery and this was an unacceptable prospect. The man from Illinois, a Northern state, could therefore not be trusted.

What seems clear to me is that the South would have ultimately required more and more labor over time to fuel their economy, meaning the immigration of more and more slaves, a prospect abhorrent to many in the Northern states. The South was probably on borrowed time by 1860, and had Lincoln not been elected, it would have probably only pushed the inevitable end of slavery back by four to eight more years at the very most. Eventually, they would have had to own up to a policy that, although accepted at the time, was morally repugnant and doomed to fail.

During the Civil War, "the Federals" or as young William's family called them, "the Yankees," captured some towns in the area where he grew up. As a result, supplies were scarce and the good old days of prosperity in Mississippi, which he never really was old enough to know, were over.

William, or "Billy" as he was sometimes called, attended public schools until he was 13 (which was probably around 1864), while the Civil War went. During this time, candles were not available so they had to make them out of tallow which was equally hard to obtain. Young William often had to study at night by the glimmer of lighted pine knots, or he would lie on his stomach before the fire. Such were the conditions in which he tried to educate himself during the Civil War.

Eventually, the family ran out of the supplies which were no longer available locally. William went with his aunt to try to secure some "provisions" from a store they knew of in Vicksburg. After traveling the 65 miles to get there, they discovered that the store had closed up; "the Yankees" had captured the city. Needless to say, they were very disappointed.

After the war, with his father dead and the local economy shattered, William, as the oldest living child, had to help support his mother and younger siblings. With this in mind, he managed to secure a job in a store about eight miles away in Canton, owned by Mr. J. B. Otto. William was paid twenty dollars a month as well as room and board.

A year later, around 1867, William became ill and had to give up his job. Around that time, former Confederate President Jefferson Davis and his nephew General Joseph R. Davis, who were returning home from prison, came through Canton on their way home to Beauvoir House, his home in Biloxi, Mississippi. This home and presidential library suffered tremendous damage during Hurricane Katrina in 2005. The cost of repairs to the house total $4.1 million of which the federal government will contribute $2.5 million. Trustees of the house and library are currently seeking $1.6 million from the public.

Beauvoir
Before Hurricane Katrina of 2005
Photo courtesy of the Jefferson Davis Home and Presidential Library

Mr. Otto had some fine French brandy in his cellar, and asked William to "go down in the cellar and bring up two quart bottles and take them up to the hotel and present one to the President, and one to the General with my compliments and best wishes."

William was delighted with the task for he knew that his father and Jefferson Davis were close friends. In fact, his father also knew President Zachary Taylor, for he had been a Lieutenant Colonel of Jefferson Davis' Regiment in the Mexican-American War of 1846 to 1847 under the command of Major General Zachary Taylor.

The Mexican-American War started when the Mexicans attacked some American troops along the southern Texas border on April 25, 1846, a year after the United States annexed Texas, despite Texas being an independent republic for ten years. Some think that the United States provoked the war through the annexation of Texas and, more deliberately, by placing an army at the opening of the Rio Grande. Others believe that President

James K. Polk forced Mexico into war in order to seize California and the Southwest.

Regardless, on May 13, 1846, war was declared with Mexico and ended about 16 months later when the United States occupied Mexico City on September 14, 1847.

California gained its own independence from Mexico on June 14, 1846 and was known briefly as the "California Republic." However, the revolt in California, which took place in Sonoma, was made by men unaware of the declaration of war a month earlier. Less than a month later, on July 9, 1846, California was annexed to the United States[17].

A peace treaty was signed on February 2, 1848 at Guadalupe Hidalgo which not only recognized the U.S. annexation of Texas, but also ceded California and New Mexico (including all the present-day states of the Southwest) to the United States. California became a free state on September 9, 1850[18].

After William was well enough to work again, his step uncle Rhesa Hatcher (William's grandmother Sarah Phillips' son from a prior marriage to Rhesa Hatcher Sr.) helped him obtain a job in Jackson, Mississippi as a page in the Mississippi State Legislature (circa 1867-1868) over the application of many other boys seeking a similar position. As William later described it:

> Of course, I was delighted for it paid three dollars per day, and my uncle would not accept any pay for my board – his reason for so doing was that he and I had made an agreement some years before that if I did not take a drink of liquor, chew tobacco, or smoke until I was twenty-one years of age that he would give me a fine horse and a good bridle and saddle as my reward.
>
> Well he said, "Will, the War has broke me and I have no horses on my plantation and I know I will not be able to carry out my bargain with you, so I will make good as best I can and not charge you a cent for your room and board. I told him that I had kept my promise up to that time and would surely keep it until I was twenty-one. I did keep the promise, and have kept the most of my life for I have never used tobacco in any form. I could not thank him enough for his kindness and generosity, and have ever felt grateful to him, for it enabled me to send all but a few dollars to my mother every month.

Step uncle Rhesa later became the Mayor of Jackson, Mississippi briefly in 1869 and again from 1871-1872. Rhesa Hatcher died before 1880 in Jackson, Mississippi.

After about four months, the legislative session adjourned and William learned of a school for the children of Civil War veterans in Lauderdale, about fifty miles from Jackson.

After arriving at the school circa 1868, he discovered that his own text books in Philosophy, Latin, Greek, and Geometry were too advanced for the regular classes. Worse, he learned that the school was self-supporting, meaning that he would have to work in the field clearing land for the spring planting. The teacher proposed that he would tutor William at night.

This proved to be too much. He was exhausted in the evening, the food was very poor and often he went to bed feeling hungry. Yet he was expected to have the energy after a hard day's work to study his lessons following a tutoring session. One morning after a big breakfast, he hopped the fence and left, thus ending his formal education when he was about 16 years of age.

William then tried to find a job in Vicksburg, Mississippi. The war was over but jobs were still very scarce in circa 1868. William called on a family friend in Vicksburg, Mr. H. C. Lampkin, who served in William's father's regiment as a private. Mr. Lampkin, who at one time lived in Yazoo City, took an interest in William and let him stay with the family for a couple of weeks while he looked for work.

One morning, while they walked together down Mulberry Street in Vicksburg, Mr. Lampkin noticed that a new company was opening up. William told him that he'd already inquired and that there were not any positions available. Mr. Lampkin insisted that they go over anyway. Sure enough, thanks to Mr. Lampkin's prodding, William was told to come to work the next morning, and that he would be paid thirty dollars a month including a room but unfortunately without board.

As a result, William lived on a diet of bread and ham for several months, and he kept a strict account of his expenses. Doing so, he managed to save fifteen dollars every month, or half his income, which he dutifully sent to his mother to help the family. He did have some very kind help however.

An old black woman named Angeline, who, before the war, had belonged to his mother, was by now living in Vicksburg. She had nursed him when he was a child, and had somehow heard he was in town. Angeline came to see him, and when she saw how William was struggling, she insisted on doing his laundry every week without charge. She cooked his ham and once in a while would even bring him a blackberry pie which he said tasted "awfully good." Such was the kind nature of his family's former slave. I take this as strong evidence of her loyalty towards his family following the war, a clear indication in my mind of kind treatment towards her by my family. There were bonds there that didn't just end with emancipation.

Shortly after being hired by this new company, business picked up with Mr. Lampkin's firm Lampkin and Egleston. Mr. Lampkin offered William a job for forty dollars a month, including room, and this time, including board as well.

Lampkin and Egleston in circa 1869 was a business which shipped cotton from railroad train yards to the steam ships which ran between Vicksburg and New Orleans. At times, William spent forty straight days managing the shipment of cotton to the The Robert E. Lee, The Frank Purgond, The Billie Lee, and The Natchez, all of which were ships he considered to be "floating palaces." Mark Twain wrote a book called *Life on the Mississippi*, published in 1883, which paints a picture of life in this region and these "floating palaces." Twain also writes in this book about the great race of 1870 between The Natchez and The Robert E. Lee from Carrollton, New Orleans to St. Louis.

Steamships in Vicksburg
after the Civil War
Illustration by Wallace Morgan, 1917

At the end of a work day he went to the Lampkin and Egleston office, made out his Bill of Lading, took it to the boat, and was always invited by the captain or clerk to stay and have dinner. He never refused the fine dinners they served.

Later, William suffered an attack of "bilious fever," (stomach flu), the result, he said, "of eating too much ice cream at a friend's dinner" and "came near dying." Mr. Lampkin's sister, "Miss Savannah," took care of him as if he were her own son. Two weeks later he was able to return home to Madisonville, although very weak and concerned that his frequent illnesses were turning into a chronic problem. For the next six months, he was too weak to do anything and was generally very discouraged about his future.

Eventually William thought about his uncle Richard Lawrence Dixon who, by late 1870, was living at "Refuge," also known as the "Alabama Settlement," in Madera, California about 20 miles from present-day Fresno. In 1848 Uncle Richard had been a guardian of William's uncles Hadley Brandon Phillips and

James A. J. Phillips. The Dixon family (which included his aunt,
Julia Rebecca Phillips Dixon, the wife of Judge Richard
Lawrence Dixon) had moved to California with his sister Laura.

William decided to write to his cousin Harry St. John Dixon,
Judge Dixon's son, to ask if he knew of any positions which
might be available in California and if so, could he send some
money to help him make the trip? William received a quick
reply.

Harry found William a job at a new store opening up in
Centerville, California and sent William a draft written on a New
York bank for $250.00 to help him buy a train ticket. Centerville
is located 18 miles east of downtown Fresno.

In spite of his poor health and weak condition, he packed a
carpet sack and, with a blanket, he headed to California. The
train trip to Stockton took nine days with William sleeping coiled
up in his seat with his blanket over him.

While visiting the Weber Hotel in Stockton, he overheard
some people talking about the "Alabama Settlement." William
realized that they must be from there. One of the two men, Mr.
Zach Hall, did live there and apparently was his sister Laura's
boyfriend at the time.

In 1870 the railroad had only been completed as far as
Modesto, California, which was about eighty miles from the
"Alabama Settlement." Mr. Hall asked William how he planned
to get there, pointing out that the only stage coach from Stockton
ran to Millerton, which was still forty miles away from where he
was going.

Mr. Hall then offered to lend him his horse, bridle, and saddle
to ride the eighty miles, but the horse was twelve miles from
Stockton at Dr. Ashe's ranch.

William gladly accepted his offer, and Mr. Hall gave him an
order for the foreman at the ranch to deliver the horse, bridle and
saddle. At this point, he had only six dollars left to get himself to
the "Alabama Settlement," so he went to a livery stable and
asked the owner what he would charge to take him out to the
Ashe Ranch.

The owner of the livery stable wanted four dollars which he
could not afford. William then went back to the hotel, collected

his carpet sack and blankets, asked for directions to the Ashe ranch, and walked six miles before becoming tired. Spending the night in Knights Landing outside of Stockton, the next morning he walked the remaining six miles to the Ashe Ranch.

Upon arrival, William presented his order for the horse to the foremen. When William asked about the saddle and bridle, the foreman said that they were at the other ranch, some twenty miles away!

Undeterred, they fashioned a bridle out of baling rope, and after throwing his blanket over the horse, the foreman gave William a lift. With sheer grit, off he went to the "Alabama Settlement," and the home the Dixon family called "Refuge" some sixty-eight miles away.

William spent the first night at McSwain's Ferry on the Merced River. After an early breakfast, he passed a blacksmith's shop. There, to his delight, he found an old saddle tree which he managed to buy for one dollar. With a piece of baling rope he tied the tree on, threw his blankets over it, and felt "well fixed" for the remainder of his ride.

William arrived at his Aunt Julia and Uncle Richard's new California ranch home in Madera at 2:00 p.m. on New Year's Day, 1871, more than a year before the first house was built in Fresno. However, everyone was out visiting friends on New Year's Day, so the family cook prepared a meal for him. At about 5:00 p.m. the whole family returned to give him a joyous welcome to California.

The ride, however, was very hard; William was worn out and needed to go to bed. His Aunt Julia, whom he called "Aunt Beckey," sent for her doctor who came to see him. The doctor put him on a diet to gain weight saying it would take at least a month to get well enough to work. William didn't want to lose his job, so his cousin Edward Dixon[19] went to Centerville to take his place until he was able to work.

Richard Lawrence Dixon's family moved to the "Fresno Plains" in 1870 and bought their land and house from Captain Hussey near the Mordecai family's "Alabama Colony," and as other Southern families settled into the area, the colony became part of the "Alabama Settlement," a Confederate outpost in early central California.

Earlier, Julia and Richard's sons, Harry and Jimmy, came out to California looking for property. The Mordecais, who were from Virginia, first moved to Raleigh, North Carolina after the war. In August 1868, the Mordecais bought their Madera property from Dr. R. P. Ashe who had bought 17,000 acres from Mr. Friedlander. The Mordecais paid $2.50 per acre for what they originally called the Mordecai-Devereux Ranch. It was in Millerton that the Dixon boys met George Washington Mordecai, from whom they learned about the Settlement in Madera.

When the Dixons moved to California in 1870, Judge Dixon decided to call his new home and land "Refuge." Their daughter, Louise Hunter Dixon, married George Washington Mordecai in 1876. In those days, the nearest communities with a store were Millerton and Firebaugh. Fresno County, however, was established in 1856 and recently celebrated its 150th Sesquicentennial in 2006.

Julia Rebecca Phillips Dixon
Maynard Dixon's grandmother
My great-grandfather's "Aunt Beckey"
Sister of Seaborn Moses Collins Phillips
Photo courtesy of Brooke Wissler

Judge Richard Lawrence Dixon
Husband of Julia Rebecca Phillips
My great-grandfather's uncle
From the estate of E. Dixon Heise
Photo courtesy of Brooke Wissler

Millerton, California in 1870
Photo courtesy of the Fresno Historical Society Archives

In 1880 the Dixons sold Refuge and its 2,000 acres to their new son-in-law George Washington Mordecai. The property remains in the Mordecai family to this day. George and Louise had a daughter named Louise Mordecai, affectionately known in her family as "Ouidy," whom I met at the occasion of her 100th birthday celebration at Refuge on January 19, 1980. She was my grandfather's second cousin and my second cousin twice removed. She had lived at Refuge her entire life.

Louise Hunter Dixon in 1870
Memphis, Tennessee, the night before moving to California

Louise Mordecai (1880-1980)
Photo courtesy of Brooke Wissler

On February 1, 1871, William rode over to Centerville with a friend and went to work at the store of E. Jacob. Dr. W. L. Graves, an old army doctor and surgeon, was practicing medicine in Centerville, and William went to see him. After a month of the doctor's medicine, William was entirely well. Dr. Graves eventually married William's sister Laurentina, who was called Laura.

In the fall of 1872 William's mother, Emily Cushman Walker Phillips, moved with her four younger sons from Madisonville, Mississippi to Centerville, California. Her daughter Laura had come to California with the Dixon family in 1870. The war had left the family without much in the way of financial means, and as a result, Emily became a teacher. Her son Dixon assisted by teaching mathematics, although he was not yet fifteen years of age at the time.

In 1873 William's brothers Burris and Dixon planted the first cotton crop of 40 acres on the bottom lands of the Kings River in Tulare County. They were then fourteen and fifteen years of age respectively. The machinery needed to harvest their crop was too expensive, and as a result, their fine 450 pounds to the acre crop was not profitable. In 1874 they grew an experimental crop on the uplands of Tulare County for G. H. Eggers, but it failed as well for lack of enough water. In 1874 the family moved to Fresno, and Dixon worked as a painter and carpenter.

Dixon L. Phillips was one of Fresno's first school teachers. In the fall of 1877 he attended one term of school at White River, and, after successfully passing an examination before the County Board of Education, he received a certificate to teach in the California public schools. He was still under nineteen years of age at the time.

Securing his certificate in March 1878, he used this as a stepping-stone to the law, teaching in winter and studying during the summer with Sayle, Tupper & Tupper, of Fresno.

Dixon was admitted to practice law in the Thirteenth District Court on June 16, 1879. He opened his first office at Centerville in July, 1880, and was appointed Deputy District Attorney under W. D. Grady.

A year later in 1881, Dixon Phillips moved to Hanford and married Miss Florence C. Miller, the daughter of Theodore Miller, a prominent California lawyer and Mary Louise "Bama"

Johnson.   Twice he was appointed District Attorney of Tulare County.

James Jackson Phillips was born in about 1856, and I have not found any reference as to whether he ever moved to the Fresno area with his family.   In Dixon's obituary in 1933, only one brother, William, is mentioned suggesting that he was by 1933 no longer alive.

Burris R. Phillips, another of William's younger brothers, was born on January 12, 1857 in Yazoo City, Mississippi.   He was employed as clerk in the Kutner-Goldstein store in Fresno, remaining with them more than two years. He then went to San Francisco and took a course of study in Heald's Business College.   In 1880 Burris married Sarah Rogers in Hanford, the daughter of John E. Rogers, a pioneer of the Mussel Slough region of Tulare County who raised workhorses. Burris then worked in farming near Hanford until 1883, when he went to Oregon and Washington Territory and worked for the Oregon Railway & Navigation Company, returning to Tulare County in 1885, and continuing farming. In 1887 Burris then worked in the lumber business in Selma, as manager for D. B. Stevens, and in 1888 he secured a position in the United States Internal Revenue Department as a gauger and storekeeper from Los Angeles to San Francisco, holding this position until 1890. In that year he bought the business of the Fresno Transfer Company from Bradshaw & Dodge, where he continued to work through 1892[20]. This was the only such company in Fresno, with representative messengers on incoming trains. As stated previously, only one brother, William, is mentioned in Dixon's obituary in 1933, suggesting that Burris might have passed away before that year.

The youngest brother was Seaborn Moses Phillips, Jr. who was born on August 2, 1860. After arriving in Centerville, he left California in 1881 to explore the western states but returned to Fresno in 1883.   He then joined Woldenberg & Foster as a bookkeeper. *The Fresno Republican*, on May 10, 1884 reported that someone overheard a store customer remark, "Tilly, you can get five prizes at Mose Phillips' store for a quarter. Why not get one there?" Seaborn Moses Phillips, Jr. died in Napa, California on September 16, 1887 at the age of 27 and is buried at the

Mountain View Cemetery in Fresno. He was married to Mary
Theodora "Mollie" Miller, the sister of Dixon L. Phillips' wife
Florence C. Miller. In 1889 his widow Molly, who once lived in
the San Francisco Bay Area and taught piano, went to work for
the County Recorder's Office.

Mary Theodora "Mollie" Miller Phillips
Wife of Seaborn Moses Phillips, Jr. circa 1890s
Photo courtesy of Nancy Eldred Williams

After two and a half of years of working in the Centerville
store of E. Jacob circa 1871-1873, William was hired by a new

store, this time in Fresno, founded in 1874 by Adolph Kutner, who came to Fresno from Reno, and Samuel Goldstein, who came to Fresno from Sacramento. By this point, the two-year-old town of Fresno had a population of only about 200.

Fresno, circa 1874
Mariposa Street looking away from the site of the first courthouse
Photo from *Imperial Fresno*, published in 1897

Fresno, circa 1875
Mariposa Street looking towards the first courthouse
Photo courtesy of the Fresno Historical Society Archives

The twenty-five by sixty-foot store was called Kutner-Goldstein and Co., and he clerked from 1874-1876. The store offered dry goods, carpets, curtains, and wallpaper. William made the decision to leave Centerville for the new town of Fresno because he knew that since Fresno was located on a railroad line, the prospects for Fresno were greater than those for Centerville. The Central (Southern) Pacific Railroad decided to build a station in Fresno in 1872, and with all due appreciation to Leland Stanford, the town which would soon surround "Fresno Station" was born. By 1874 the town of Millerton was abandoned.

Kutner-Goldstein & Co., circa 1875
Photo courtesy of the Fresno Historical Society Archives

He made the right decision. The new Fresno store was a success and, as a reward for his hard work, Kutner and Goldstein offered to make him a partner in a new store if he could find a good place to start one. William selected Centerville because, at the time, Fresno was still too small to support two stores and nearby Millerton had been abandoned.

In 1875, a book titled *The Patrons of Husbandry of the Pacific Coast* was published[21] which listed William as the secretary of Garretson Grange, No. 132, located in Centerville (Kings River), Fresno County.

On July 1, 1877, he rented a store in Centerville and commenced business as a co-owner with a small stock of goods. Over the course of four and a half years, William saw the new store generate $30,000 in profits at a time when Fresno County's overall population was still less than 10,000.

Two boys on a Kutner-Goldstein delivery wagon, circa 1890
Photo courtesy of the California Genealogy and History Room of the
Fresno Public Library

On October 7, 1880, William married Elizabeth B. Pressley, the Santa Rosa daughter of Judge John Gotea Pressley. She was born in 1854 in Kingstree, South Carolina. They met while Judge Pressley was holding court in Fresno.

The Fresno Republican wrote on October 9, 1880:

> Our enterprising young mercantile friend of Centerville, W. W. Phillips was this week married to a young lady of Santa Rosa. His business interests will undoubtedly increase and his host of friends become more numerous, by reason of his new departure. We join the throng in wishing the young couple a joyous life and abundant prosperity.

As the Centerville store prospered, the owners, including William, prospered. In 1882 Kutner and Goldstein decided to invest the store's profits into a new bank, to be called the "Farmers Bank," and they wanted William to run it for them.

William was very surprised by the generous offer but told them that he knew nothing about the banking business. "You are a good bookkeeper, you know the values of land, and you know the people, and you know who to trust," they told him. "You can learn the business in a week."

The Farmers Bank was incorporated on March 8, 1882 with a capital stock of $100,000, of which $50,000 was paid in. William sold his half interest to Kutner-Goldstein and Co. in the Centerville store for $15,000 which allowed him to purchase 150 shares of the new bank.

William then contacted his new father-in-law, Judge Pressley in Santa Rosa, to ask if he could arrange for him to spend a couple of weeks at the Santa Rosa bank to learn about their business methods.

The week of March 11, 1882, *The Santa Rosa Republican* wrote: "W. W. Phillips, of Fresno, son-in-law of Judge Pressley, is here preparing himself under the tuition of George Noonan and John Overton, of the Savings Bank, for cashier of a bank which he and others are soon going to open in Fresno City."

After a couple of weeks, he learned their bookkeeping system and the new bank in Fresno was started in earnest. In that same year, William was one of the members of the Fresno Hook and Ladder Co., the volunteer fire department organized in February 1877. *The Fresno Bee*, in an article printed on October 23, 1933, mentioned that William was one of the original 25 charter members, and assisted Leopold Gundelfinger in raising the initial

$500 to purchase the truck, ladders and equipment. On October 31, 1883, a third fire department was created, known as Fresno Alert No. 1 with William as the treasurer.

The Fresno Hook and Ladder Company, circa 1877
Mr. Leopold (Lee) Gundelfinger, the fire chief, is seated in the center of the front row of this photograph. The other fire fighters starting in the back row from left to right are: Charles Wainwright, John Elam, Lephonso Burks, Harry Rea, Charles DeLong, Louis Einstein, Charles Overholzer, and N. D. Gilbert. The front row from left to right are: Fred Kramer, George Strine, Frank Tadlock, Steve Spano, John Dwyer, William. Lawrenson, Lee Gundelfinger (chief), Will Silvers, John Welsh, William H. McKenzie, Andrew Basso and John Boyle.
Photo courtesy of the California Genealogy and History Room of the Fresno Public Library

In 1882 Dr. W. L. Graves moved from Centerville to Fresno with his family, and William convinced him to buy some stock in the new bank and help him run it. Dr. Graves was made Vice President and remained with the bank for about two years.

On July 1, 1882, *The Fresno Republican* reported that William was elected Chief Councilor of a new insurance society:

CHOSEN FRIENDS - This is the name of an insurance society that operates something after the manner of the A. O. U. W., the Legion of Honor, etc., and is now numbered among the fraternal organizations of Fresno. Harmony Council was instituted Thursday evening by Deputy Grand Councilor Alex Rothenstein of San Francisco, with twenty-eight charter members.

In 1884 Dr. Graves and his wife Laura, William's sister, moved to Tennessee but returned to California in 1885 and made their home in Los Angeles. William's mother Emily died at their Los Angeles home on May 20, 1907.

The bank was phenomenally successful and, when Dr. Graves left, William was made Vice President as well as Manager. His salary was increased as well.

On March 7, 1885, *The Fresno Republican* reported: "W. W. Phillips returned on Saturday night's train from his trip to the World's Fair and visit with friends in the South." The World's Fair that year was held in New Orleans, and this trip may have been the last time William visited Mississippi.

Published on August 10, 1886, the *Report of the Bank Commissioners of the Sate of California* wrote:

> The Farmers Bank of Fresno is located in Fresno, about two hundred miles from San Francisco by rail. Fresno is the center of a very rich and successful fruit-growing district. Land can be had at twenty to fifty dollars per acre. The freight charges for moving crop to market is three dollars and sixty cents per ton. The cash receipts per month at the railroad office in this town averages, one month with another, forty thousand dollars. This enormous tax takes nearly all that is made of profits by the producers in the Fresno district. The population of Fresno is about three thousand five hundred, and its vote at the last election was nine hundred. The bank is conducted carefully and with good judgment. Fifty thousand dollars of the capital came from the earnings of the bank, and the shareholders have also been paid a handsome dividend on the capital invested.

In 1887 William tried to persuade the city of Fresno to buy at least three more street lights to help the gas company make ends meet.

On February 24, 1888, *The Daily Republican* reported:

The Main Line
Fresno Wants a Competing Line of Railroad
And is Willing To Pay For It
Committee of Ten Citizens Selected to Talk Business
to the Paige-Wilbur-Paulsell Company

In response to the call for a mass meeting, published in these columns yesterday morning, a mass meeting was held at the opera-house[22] last night to secure to Fresno the main line of the Paige-Wilbur-Paulsell Railroad, now building from Antioch to Rogers via White's Bridge in this county. On motion of W. D. Grady, W. W. Phillips, cashier of the Farmers Bank, was chosen president of the meeting, and before taking the chair Mr. Phillips briefly stated the objects of the meeting, and invited H. C. Warner, J. L. Tait, Louis Einstein and C. G. Sayle to accept seats on the stage as vice-presidents. A. M. Drew[23] was elected secretary.

W. D. Grady made a few remarks, and called on T. C. White to give such information as he could with regard to railroad now building down the west side of the valley.

Mr. White stated that the object of the San Francisco and San Joaquin Valley Railroad was to get the shortest possible route from Mojave to San Francisco; that the Atlantic and Pacific would float the bonds of the new company. He thought it would be difficult for Fresno to obtain the main line, but that a branch might be secured through proper effort; that the managers of the road had made a proposition at one time to build a branch into Fresno if the people would subscribe one hundred and fifty thousand dollars, payable when Fresno had secured terminal shipping facilities.

Professor J. M. Martin followed Mr. White, and spoke to the point. He favored securing the main line, but was not in favor of assisting to build a plug road, and advocated the reserving of our forces for a main line.

F. H. Short spoke to the question, saying he thought a right of way could be secured without difficulty. Our city needs the main line, and can better afford to give the company two hundred and fifty thousand dollars for it than one dollar for a branch. We must have the main line.

Mr. Hughes said Mr. Paige's interest was to have the road run south, and not come through Fresno, as he (Paige) owns thousands of acres of land along the line of the proposed route. Did the stockholders know this? Did they care whether the road was built to accommodate the business of large communities or for the benefit of one or two men who occupied official positions of influence? Fresno's interests as a community should certainly outweigh those of Mr. Paige or any other individual. Mr. Tait was of the opinion that the united effort of our people would secure the main line. Would do all in his power to accomplish the result. Mr. White thought Mr. Paige was in favor of the main line coming to Fresno.

Mr. Louis Einstein said he had lately talked with some of the S. F. & S. J. V. Railroad Company, but they thought there was not money enough to bring the road through Fresno.

Mr. Sayle thought it was not worthwhile to appoint a committee. Thought the better way would be to instruct the secretary to "write to the Paige-Wilbur-Paulsell company for their terms for the main line." Mr. Tait thought the road could not afford to leave Fresno out and would come in with a branch anyhow.

Mr. S. N. Griffith moved that a committee of ten be appointed to go to San Francisco, interview the railroad company, ask them plainly how much money it will take to have the main line built through Fresno, and to employ every honorable means to secure the main line. The motion was carried, and the following well known citizens were chosen to serve on the committee: W. W. Phillips, S. N. Griffith. C. G. Sayle, J. L. Tait, W. D. Grady, J. P. Vincent, Professor J. M. Martin, F. G. Berry, T. E. Hughes, T. C. White, F. H. Short and H. C. Warner.

The people of Fresno are now ready to act, and we trust that the railroad folks will show an equal willingness to do business upon business principles from the word go. This city is going to have a competing line of railroad and if we cannot have the Paige-Wilbur-Paulsell road we are going to have another. This is the decision of the community, and *THE REPUBLICAN* rejoices.

On November 9, 1888, *The Fresno Republican* reported:

Several days ago a man calling himself Harry Cavanaugh, who has loafed around this city and put in his time gambling for some days past, went to Visalia to try his luck there. He got broke in Visalia and from there went to Lemoore and going to Frank Vail's saloon he gave him a bundle of what appeared to be bank checks which he asked Vail to put in the safe for him until morning. This Vail did, Cavanaugh calling particular attention to one of the checks which was for $600 and which he claimed was signed by W. W. Phillips of the Farmers Bank here. The name on the check read W. M. Fillips, however, but Vail only knowing Mr. Phillips by reputation as manager of the bank here, was not aware how he spelled his name. Again the check was drawn on the First National Bank here and not on the Farmers Bank. We are informed that Cavanaugh told Mr. Vail that he had deposited the amount of money called for in the check and had taken the check so he could use it if he wanted it.

Cavanaugh commenced playing cards and losing as usual until his ready cash was exhausted. He then went to Mr. Vail and endorsing the $600 check, drew $40 on it, then $60, then $100, and finally the whole amount. The next day Cavanaugh left the town, and Thursday Mr. Vail arrived here with the check, only to have it handed back with the polite "no funds, and never had any deposited here." Mr. Vail was sure there was some mistake, asked for Mr. Phillips, the banker, and when he was told that gentleman spelled his name Phillips, and not Fillips, the gentleman from Lemoore realized that he had purchased $600 worth of experience that could be wrapped up in a very small bundle.

He at once returned home to find Cavanaugh but failed and then telegraphed to Constable Fraser here to arrest the man if he showed up. The officer found Cavanaugh on the streets yesterday and jailed him. It was reported that the prisoner is a farmer living on the west side, but we are informed that it is the prisoner's brother who is the farmer. At any rate, whether a farmer or not, he takes matters very much like a man who had been in jail before and also one who knew how to escape some of the consequences of his acts. At first he claimed that he was drunk when the check was made and passed, but afterwards he said, "I'm no forger. I'm too smart for that. Fillips is not W. W. Phillips the banker."

"What if you said it was, though?" was asked.

"Well, that wouldn't be forgery, would it?"

He will be taken to Lemoore for trial.

On November 16, 1888, *The Fresno Weekly Republican* reported:

W. W. Phillips' Latest Purchase

On yesterday, Mr. W. W. Phillips, Vice-President and General Manager of the Farmers Bank, purchased the building operated by the Elite Saloon, having a frontage of twenty-five feet on Mariposa, and depth of 65 feet, for $16,000. The Farmers Bank purchased the building adjoining the Elite and extending to the corner, some time ago, and will shortly tear it down and erect an elegant and costly brick block in its stead. It is probable Mr. Phillips will make his building conform, in front at least, with the new block, thus making one of the largest and by far the most imposing structure in the city. On Monday of next week, the work of excavating for the foundation of the Phillips block, which is to be built on I Street almost opposite to the new Griffith block, will be commenced, and no time will be lost in completing the structure. Mr. Phillips is one of Fresno's enterprising citizens and he proposes to practice what he preaches in regard to building, as he does in other things. The new Phillips block will be a beauty.

SEMI-ANNUAL REPORT OF THE

FARMERS BANK OF FRESNO.

[Incorporated March 8, 1882.]

Showing its Financial Condition on the morning of January 1, 1889, as sworn to by the Officers of the Bank.

LEWIS LEACH, President. JOHN REICHMAN, Cashier.

Resources.	Amount.	Liabilities.	Amount.
Bank premises	$19,004 35	Capital paid in coin	$160,000 00
County warrants	3,160 07	Profit and loss	48,172 66
Loans on real estate	101,606 53	Due depositors	347,288 01
Loans on personal security	264,710 20		
Money on hand	68,720 69		
Due from banks and bankers	50,899 33		
Furniture and fixtures	1,800 00		
Expenses	13,560 81		
Other assets (interest accrued on current loans)	15,790 77		
Total resources	$555,460 67	Total liabilities	$555,460 67

DETAILS.

The amount of capital stock is $200,000; amount subscribed is $200,000; amount paid in coin is $160,000. The total number of shares of stock issued is 2,000 shares; the amount paid on each share of stock is $80.

The names of the Directors, and number of shares of stock held by each, are as follows:

A. Kutner .... 440 shares.   Alex. Goldstein .... 20 shares.
W. W. Phillips .... 280 shares.   C. H. Norris .... 10 shares.
Lewis Leach .... 60 shares.
Total number of shares held by the Directors is .... 810 shares.

LOANS ON REAL ESTATE BY COUNTIES.

Name of County.	Amount Loaned.	Market Value.
Fresno	$101,606 53	$250,000 00

AMOUNT LOANED ON OTHER SECURITIES.

Description of Securities.	Amount Loaned.	Value of Securities.
Loans on grain in warehouse	$16,207 92	$20,000 00

170   BANK COMMISSIONERS' REPORT.

BANK COMMISSIONERS' REPORT TO THE ATTORNEY-GENERAL.

Statement showing Financial Condition of the Farmers Bank, doing business at Fresno, County of Fresno, on the twentieth day of October, 1889, at the close of business.

Resources.	Amount.	Liabilities.	Amount.
Bank premises	$18,000 00	Capital paid up.................	$160,000 00
Other real estate	4,000 00	Due depositors	327,050 59
Invested in warrants	2,475 35	Interest collected	13,754 25
Loans and discounts...........	385,772 41	Rents, exchange, etc.	4,552 98
Cash balance	57,844 53	Profit and loss.................	3,974 00
Due from banks and bankers.	30,219 49		
Furniture, fixtures, etc........	1,800 00		
Expenses, taxes, etc...........	9,220 04		
Total resources...............	$509,331 82	Total liabilities	$509,331 82

Semi-Annual Report of the Farmers Bank of Fresno
As of January 1, 1889
Report of the Board of Bank Commissioners of the State of California

William continued to own 15% of the bank, and by July 1, 1889, he held 300 of the 2,000 total shares issued.

In 1889 street cars were installed in Fresno, and the bank was ready for a brand new building which was to be built in that year. My great-grandfather took his young son William Walker Phillips, Jr. to Santa Rosa and, returning via San Francisco, he purchased all of the new furniture and fixtures for the bank's new building at Mariposa and "I" Street ("I" Street is today known as Broadway Plaza).

William Walker Phillips, Jr., who was born on April 30, 1884, died on March 11, 1900 at the age of 15 when my grandfather was 8 years old.

The bank building was designed by San Francisco architect W. H. Armitage, born in England in 1861 and the son of John Armitage, a large manufacturer in Sheffield. The building was constructed of granite and pressed brick[24].

Reporting on an enthusiastic meeting of the Democrats in Fresno County, *The Fresno Weekly Republican* noted on May 30, 1890 that William was on the "resolutions" committee. "W. W. Phillips, the banker, responded to an earnest call. He also advised harmony in the party and spoke of the attitude of the Democrats on the silver bill which he said was in the interests of the people, and he said that the sentiment of the Democratic Party was that silver should be remonetized[25]."

At the convention, the same paper reported, "Reel B. Terry was elected by acclamation delegate at large, and the following nine were nominated from which the remaining four were to be selected: Herman Lew, Gillum Baley, E. J. Griffith, William H. Dwyer, W. D. Grady, W. W. Phillips, R. P. Mace, George Rupert and A. Bernhard. W. D. Grady, W. W. Phillips, William H. Dwyer and E. J. Griffith were elected."

On June 13, 1890, *The Fresno Republican* reported:

STONEWALL JACKSON CAMP.
Ex-Confederate Veterans Organize a Society in Fresno.

The ex-confederate veterans, who banqueted themselves at the Hughes hotel last Thursday night, have signed the following agreement, which speaks for itself:

"We, the undersigned, hereby organize ourselves into a camp to be known as Stonewall Jackson Camp of confederate veterans of the county of Fresno, for the social intercourse of its a members, by a meeting at least once a year, on the 26th day of April of each year hereafter, and for the promotion of American patriotism and charity to the destitute of our comrades and their widows and orphans."

Dr. H. St. George Hopkins, Thomas Reel, J. G. Rance of Virginia, Colonel H. S. Dixon[26], W. W. Phillips, J. H. Sample, of Mississippi; C. C. Harris, Ike Walton, L. B. McWhirter, J. W. Reece, J. Wilkerson, of Tennessee; D. J. McConnell, J. S. Bedford, M. Farley, of Alabama; Dr. Meyers, P. LeBlanc, of Louisiana; Thomas P. Ryan, Preston Brooks, Reuben Goins (colored), of South Carolina; J. W. Dumas, of Texas; Martin Elder, B. B. Bronaugh, E. D. Edwards, of Missouri.

Of the foregoing, W. W. Phillips, Preston Brooks and L. B. McWhirter are not veterans, but the sons of veterans.

On June 26, 1890, William wrote a letter, signed Vice President and Manager, from the Farmers Bank to Mr. Baldwin informing him of monies owed on account of a lawsuit.

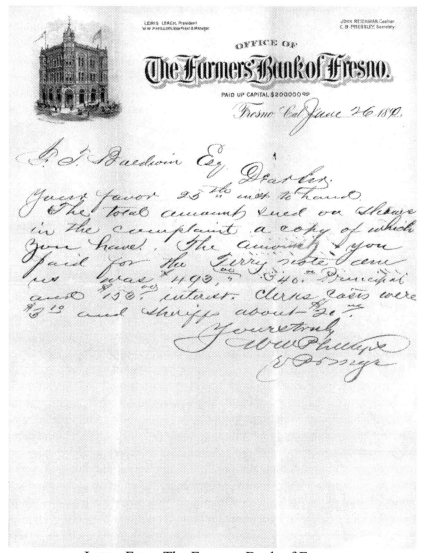

Letter From The Farmers Bank of Fresno
From W. W. Phillips, Vice President and Manager
Photo courtesy of the Fresno Historical Society Archives

On October 17, 1890, under a headline which read, "A Pleasant Party - A Reception at the Residence of W. W. Phillips," *The Fresno Weekly Republican* reported: "On Monday evening W. W. Phillips entertained a party of ladies and gentlemen, comprising Mr. and Mrs. Herman Eggers, Mr. and Mrs. C. B.

Pressley[27], Miss Mayriach of Alameda, Mr. and Mrs. W. More Young, Thomas H. Lynch and Fred B. Dexter. A pleasant evening was spent."

The Farmers Bank (on the right) circa 1890s

The Farmers Bank (on the right) circa 1890s
Photos courtesy of the California Genealogy and History Room of the
Fresno Public Library and the Fresno Historical Society Archives

In 1890 William was part of a committee of five dedicated to promoting baseball in Fresno. The Fresno club wanted to join the state league and William had gone to San Francisco to find out how to best accomplish this. Like the others on the committee, he subscribed for five dollars per month to help preserve the current team until a permanent organization would be formed. By this point, William was quite involved with numerous civic, business and community interests, promoting the location of a Baptist Academy in Fresno in 1890. In earlier years his mother Emily had organized concerts to raise funds for the first Southern Methodist Church in Fresno.

The newspapers of the day frequently reported which parties he and his wife Elizabeth gave or attended, such as the "progressive euchre" party they held in 1891, the year my grandfather was born.

William attended the "Bankers Association" meeting, held in Los Angeles from March 11-13, 1891, where he presented a paper. At this meeting, the California Bankers Association was formed, and William was chosen to be a member of the executive council and would serve a three-year term. Members included 150 of the 246 banks in California at the time. The enthusiastic delegation from San Francisco organized a visit to Stanford University where they met Governor and Mrs. Stanford which was followed by a banquet at the Palace Hotel in San Francisco. The convention of 1893 was to have been held in Fresno, but with the panic of that year, the bankers all decided to stay put and concentrate on business at hand. The California Bankers Association continues to this day. Member banks in 2007 currently hold more than $2.7 trillion in assets and loans in excess of $1.5 trillion.

On June 7, 2007, I contacted the California Bankers Association to inquire whether they might have a copy of William's speech he gave when he was only 39 years of age. The next day, Curtis Paullins, Vice President for Customer Management of the California Bankers Association graciously sent me a copy of the *Proceedings of the California Bankers Association, Held at Los Angeles, March 11, 12 and 13, 1891*.

On page 24, the following was printed:

A paper was next read by W. W. Phillips, of Fresno, entitled:

GRATUITOUS WORKS DONE BY BANKS

Upon this subject much may be said, but I shall not attempt to enumerate the many things done by Banks without compensation.

Were I to ask the many bankers present for their individual experiences in this kind of work, no doubt we should all be much surprised.

I shall point out what I consider the most important items of this gratuitous work done. For instance, I do not believe that a banking institution in the State gets sufficient pay for the collections it makes. In many cases it gets no pay at all. As an illustration of this fact, a bank receives a sight draft, drawn on a merchant with exchange who happens not to be a client of that particular bank. The collection clerk after registering the collection, starts out to collect it.

Possibly he has made two visits before he has found the merchant in his office. The merchant upon examination of the draft, declines to pay, for the reason that he does not pay exchange, as he gets that free of charge at the bank with which he has his account.

The collection is returned after the two repeated efforts to collect, with the reason of non-payment, the bank being loser the time of its collection clerk, postage and stationery.

And again, how many collections are received, and an effort made to collect, and finally returned unpaid at the bank's expense.

Now if it is proper to charge for those collected, why should it not be proper to make a charge for those uncollected? If the bank has performed its duty, it has made an earnest and strenuous effort to make the collection. In fact, more actual work has been done than in the collection of those which were promptly paid.

For this work a proper charge should be made, otherwise at the end of the year the bank has lost money in the collection business.

A promissory note is left by a client for collection; it is usually one of the doubtful kind and no doubt the holder has exhausted his individual powers to collect. To hand it to an attorney would cost him ten percent of the amount of the note but his banker will make the collection for a nominal fee, possibly not charge him anything at all.

If he is charged more than one or two dollars for collecting a note of one thousand dollars, he complains, and thinks it too much. There should be some regular charge for services of this kind, equitable and fair.

Collections of checks received from the San Francisco banks and correspondents are made for nothing.

Why should this be so? I have never had a satisfactory reason given.

It cannot be argued the city correspondent does similar service without remuneration, as such work is not in proportion; besides, the city bank has the benefit of the deposit of all sums collected, and no interest allowed on credit balances.

I think it within the power and one of the duties of this Convention to consider these matters, and if possible to arrive at some method of correcting this condition of affairs. I think it a proper time to call a halt on the gratuitous work done by Banks.

On April 25, 1891, President Benjamin Harrison visited Fresno. William was on the reception committee, as reported by Charles Hedges in his book *Speeches of Benjamin Harrison*[28]:

A crowd of 10,000 greeted the party at Fresno; upward of 1,000 school children were present, led by Professors Heaton, Sturges and Sheldon. The Committee of Reception consisted of Mayor S. H. Cole, Dr. Chester A. Rowell, F. G. Berry, Dr. A. J. Pedlar, Dr. St. George Hopkins, W. W. Phillips, I. N. Pattison, Louis Einstein, Nathan W. Moodey, C. W. De Long, and J. C. Herrington. Atlanta Post, G. A. R., Capt. Fred Banta, Commander, also Company C., National Guard, Capt. M. W. Muller, and Company F, Capt. C. Chisholm, participated in the reception. A number of handsome floral designs and other mementos were presented to the several members of the party.

Dr. Rowell delivered the welcoming address. President Harrison, responding, said:

"My fellow citizens – it is altogether impossible for me to reach with my voice the vast concourse of friends. I can only say that I am profoundly grateful for this enthusiastic greeting. I receive with great satisfaction the memento you have given me of the vast products of this most fertile and happy valley. I shall carry it with me to Washington as a reminder of a scene that will never fade from my memory. It is very pleasant to know that all these pursuits that so much engage your thoughts and so industriously employ your time have not turned your minds away from the love of the flag and of those institutions which spread their secure power over all of your homes. What is it that makes the scattered homes of our people secure?   There is no policeman at the door; there is no guard to accompany us as we move across this great continent. You and I are in the safekeeping of the law and of the affection and regard of all of our people. Each respects the rights of the other. I am glad to receive this manifestation of your respect. I am glad to drink in this morning with this sunshine and this sweet balmy air a new impulse to public duty, a new love for the Union and flag. It is a matter of great regret that I can return in such a small measure your affectionate greeting. I wish it were possible I could greet each one of you personally, that it were possible in some way other than in words to testify to you my grateful sense of your good will." [Cheers.]

Shortly after noon on the same day, President Benjamin Harrison visited Merced where he was introduced to a large crowd by Chairman E. T. Dixon[29].

Less than three months later on July 18, 1891, my grandfather John Pressley Phillips was born, named for his maternal grandfather John Gotea Pressley.

On February 2, 1892, *The Fresno Morning Republican* reported:

RAILROAD CONVENTION
To be Held at Bakersfield Today.
FRESNO WILL BE REPRESENTED
The County Will Work for a More Direct Line to
Tidewater at Port Harford.

Recently a committee consisting of Messrs. O. J. Woodward, W. W. Phillips, Fulton G. Berry, T. C. White and H. D. Colson was appointed to represent this county at the railroad convention to be held at Bakersfield today. The object of the convention is for the counties interested to devise ways and means of building a railroad from Bakersfield to Port Harford. Of the members appointed to represent Fresno only Messrs. H. D. Colson and W. W. Phillips expressed their intention of going. They left on the 5 p.m. train last evening.

There is not much reason to believe that this county will go into throes of enthusiasm over the project in its present shape. Most of Fresno's people fail to understand the advantage to Fresno of its people being able to reach tidewater via Bakersfield, though they acknowledge very freely that Bakersfield would benefit thereby. The distance from the latter city to Port Harford is about eighty-six miles, and from Fresno to Bakersfield 108 miles. Now as in a direct line Port Harford is only some 116 miles from this city, the wisdom of increasing it to nearly 200 miles is doubted by those who believe the eastern terminus should be Fresno.

Delegates are expected at Bakersfield from San Luis Obispo and Tulare counties besides Fresno. The citizens of Bakersfield will give the visitors a cordial reception, a banquet being one of the features.

The Fresno Morning Republican wrote on July 29, 1892:

The outlook for the financial market in Fresno is brighter than it has been for some time past. W. W. Phillips of the Farmers Bank said to a *Republican* writer yesterday that the market is improving on account of the beginning of an active movement in cereals and the fact that the receipts from fruit are beginning to come in. The excellent market for fruit at remunerative prices to the grower has greatly strengthened the financial prospects.

Around this time, William became active in politics as well. In 1892 William was elected a delegate for the Democratic National Convention. He was very proud to attend the convention in Chicago and was an enthusiastic supporter of Grover Cleveland's bid for a return to the White House.

On April 29, 1892, *The Fresno Weekly Republican* reported within a longer article, "Now this ticket has a very great significance, as well as an important bearing on the fight for delegate to the Democratic National Convention which is being waged in this county between the friends of W. W. Phillips and A. B. Butler. It is said that Phillips wants the county to instruct its delegates for Cleveland, while on the other hand Butler's friends want an uninstructed delegation."

On May 6, 1892, *The Fresno Weekly Republican* wrote, "The Third Ward Democratic Club has elected the following named gentlemen to the county convention: W. W. Phillips, S. B. Wright, O. M. Thompson, W. Ellery, C. C. Elliot, E. Riggins, M. J. Murray, O. J. Meade, A. Lucas and N. N. Berbora. The delegates were pledged to throw the weight of their influence in favor of the nomination of ex-President Cleveland."

In the same paper, within a story about "Discontent Among County Democrats," *The Fresno Weekly Republican* wrote:

> The only ward in the city whose people have had the courage to oppose the Triangle and its methods is the first. In that ward there is a set of delegates to the county convention nominated by the Triangle and a set nominated by the democrats. Of course the latter ticket can easily win if the decent Democrats turn out in their full numerical strength. The primary in that ward will be the test of the sincerity of the anti-Triangle men. Another ward which has shown some sign of desiring to unload the Triangle is the third. This is due to some extent to W. W. Phillips, I hear.
>
> Mentioning Phillips reminds me that that gentleman has abandoned his nonchalant air and is actively presenting his claims to be elected as a delegate to the Democratic National Convention. He was disposed at first to let the people decide between Butler and himself without any special effort to influence the result, but the intervention of some ungrateful friends in Butler's behalf has put Phillips on his mettle, and this, together with the earnest solicitation of his friends, has decided Mr. Phillips to make a

vigorous fight. Phillips is a strong Cleveland man and believes in an instructed delegation from California, which alone would make him the favored candidate. Butler, to the contrary, does not believe in an instructed delegation, sharing the views of his friends, W. D. English, M. F. Tarpey and W. W. Foote, on this point.

In an article subtitled "The Fight For or Against an Instructed Delegation - What Delegates Say," *The Fresno Daily Republican* on May 17, 1892 wrote in part:

A rumor prevailed last evening that there was a disposition on the part of some of the Fresno County delegation to sacrifice W. W. Phillips for A. B. Butler. It is said several of them went among the other delegates with the statement that they were making a fight merely for Butler and that Phillips would be dropped willingly enough if his candidacy jeopardized Butler's. The friends of Phillips were highly indignant when they heard of this.

Senator Goucher was asked concerning the matter, but stated that there was nothing in the rumor, and that it had been started by the Tulare people who were anxious to get a man from their locality, E. Jacobs, the place. It is a fact, however, that several of Phillips' friends put faith in the report, and not a few delegates have the impression that Phillips is a mere stepping stone to make Butler's ascent easier.

Later in the same article, *The Fresno Daily Republican* continued:

Considerable interest was taken in the local fight last night. W. W. Phillips informed a reporter that he had been promised the support of several counties in this district, and that he was reasonably confident of being elected from this end of the district. He did not think that his candidacy would interfere in any way with A. B. Butler's candidacy as a delegate at large, and he did not believe that there was any truth in the report that he would be sacrificed by Butler's friends on the altar of Butler's ambition.

On May 20, 1892, *The Fresno Weekly Republican* reported:

Reel B. Terry, who had for the last three weeks openly declared on the streets and elsewhere that he was opposed to Cleveland and that he and his political associates were for Hill first, last and all the time, introduced the following resolution: "Resolved, That the delegates to be elected by this convention to the Democratic state convention be and they are hereby instructed to cast the vote of Fresno County for A. B. Butler for delegate at large and for W. W. Phillips from this district."

In the same article under the general title "Cleveland Wins - The Hill Triangle Outfit Surrender Unconditionally," *The Fresno Weekly Republican* wrote:

PHILLIPS WINS.

W. H. McKenzie and W. W. Phillips were placed in nomination for endorsement as delegate from the district to the national convention. A vote was taken and resulted in favor of Phillips with 163 ½ votes to 49 for McKenzie. Before the vote was completed a motion was made to declare the nomination of Mr. Phillips unanimous but as there were a dozen vehement noes the roll call was concluded with the above result. The convention then adjourned until 10 o'clock this morning.

Also, in the same article with the subtitle "Goucher Spoke From the Fullness of His Heart and Created a Laughable Sensation," Sen. Goucher said during his speech:

"Gentlemen of the convention, I know from the lips of Billy Phillips and from the lips of A. B. Butler that both are as strong and enthusiastic and earnest Hill men as any men in the country." This open, frank, but unintended declaration of Mr. Goucher's innermost convictions set the house in a roar. Brother Ferguson of the *Expositor* lay back in his chair and broke three legs off it, and Mr. Terry bowed his head in his hands and silently wept and prayed, and Mr. Goucher, with a despairing look at *THE REPUBLICAN* reporter, seized a glass of water and without waiting to blow the foam from the top drained it to the dregs. It was several minutes before order was restored, and Mr. Goucher, issuing like the fabled Phoenix from his own ashes, proceeded:

"Gentlemen of the convention, I have discovered that the tower of mesmerism that springs from Mr. Cosgrave's eyes has influenced me. *THE FRESNO REPUBLICAN* will again have chance in the ring. [Laughter.] It will say in the morning that from force of habit I endorsed the candidacy of David Bennett Hill. I will say that I personally heard from Messrs. Phillips and Butler that they are Cleveland men."

CALIFORNIA.

AT LARGE.

District.		District.	
W. W. Foote.		J. V. Coleman.	
S. M. White.		A. B. Butler.	
1st	C. W. Taylor.	5th	L. A. Whitehurst.
	T. L. Thompson.		T. F. Barry.
2nd	Russ Stephens.	6th	J. D. Carr.
	W. S. McGee.		Geo. S. Patton.
3rd	F. J. Moffitt.	7th	H. W. Patton.
	L. W. Buck.		W. W. Phillips.
4th	J. F. Sullivan.		
	Jos. Clark.		

From The *Official Proceedings*[30]
of the National Democratic Convention, held in Chicago, Ill.
June 21st, 22nd and 23rd, 1892

On July 15, 1892, *The Fresno Weekly Republican* carried a large story about "Pilgrim Phillips" returning from the windy city, "looking as bright as a newly-coined eagle."

"I had an elegant time," he told the reporter. "I was fortunate in that I secured a room through our correspondent having to pay only $4 a day; most of the others had to pay $6 and $7 a day for a room alone. The New Yorkers were particularly angry on account of this imposition and were loud in their complaints. The World's Fair commission has taken the matter up, with a view to prevent the same state of affairs during the exposition. The Wigwam, where we met, had miserable accommodations, the roof leaking like a sieve, when it rained. The city also showed its inability to entertain properly a very large number of visitors. To illustrate the enterprise of the Chicagoans, take the matter of tickets of admission to the convention. Each delegate was allowed five; the rest, some eighteen or nineteen thousand, were sold, some of them as high as $20 each. Of course, the California delegation was solid for Cleveland; there was no opportunity for that portion of the delegation that favored Hill to do anything for him. Cleveland being nominated on the first ballot, there was no chance for combinations or anything of that kind."

A little taste of the political atmosphere must have rubbed off on him, because by fall, there was talk of him running for California Governor, presumably in the 1894 election. On September 30, 1892, *The Fresno Weekly Republican* wrote:

It is somewhat surprising that the Democratic papers in this county can find gubernatorial timber nowhere but in Butler's vineyard. They have often stated that it is time this valley were recognized in connection with the governorship, but seem themselves to be able to recognize no one as available for this exalted place but A. B. Butler. I have often done injustice to Mr. Butler's many excellent qualities of purse and mind, but nevertheless take the liberty of believing there are other Democrats here as worthy as Mr. Butler of the Democratic nomination for governor, should Fresno get that magnificent plum. What turned my thoughts into this channel was the remembrance of a conversation I had some time ago with a Democrat on this matter. He mentioned W. W. Phillips in particular as fit in every way to be the party's standard bearer, believing him preferable in many respects to even Mr. Butler. Phillips has many friends, and should the fates decree that Fresno Democrats shall have the proud privilege of naming the Democratic candidate for governor Phillips will make a formidable rival to Butler.

On October 7, 1892, *The Fresno Weekly Republican* referred to William as "Butler's rival for the Democratic nomination for governor." The same day's paper also reported:

A DINNER PARTY
Given To A Number Of Friends
W. W. Phillips gave a dinner to a few friends at his residence on Thursday evening. It was a masterpiece of culinary art and very much enjoyed by the guests. The evening was spent in a very interesting manner in the discussion of politics and the telling of innocent little anecdotes.

There were present Hon. Olin Wellborn, John P. Irish, Judge S. A. Holmes, J. W. Ferguson, W. L. Ashe, J. M. Meclure, Michael Tarpey, J. E. Baker, Hon. G. W. Mordecai[31], John Reichman, and Judge M. K. Harris.

And again on November 18, 1892, *The Fresno Weekly Republican* reported how "both rival candidates for the Democratic nomination for governor, A. B. Butler and W. W. Phillips" attended the chrysanthemum fete given by the ladies of the St. James guild.

That same year, a book entitled *The Memorial and Biographical History of the Counties of Fresno, Tulare and Kern, California* was published in Chicago by the Lewis Publishing Company. They wrote:

> In this rapidly developing country of ours where opportunities for all are equal make swifter strides toward prosperity than others, and their wonderful success may be attributed to natural ability and tact combined with resolute will and persistent determination to succeed. The subject of this sketch is one whose business career is worthy of note. Mr. Phillips is today one of the youngest bank officers in the State of California; and the phenomenal success he has achieved during the years of his residence here justly entitle him to honorable mention in this volume. He helped to establish the Fresno Ice Works in 1874; was instrumental in organizing, and is now director of, the Fresno Gas Light Company; was the first secretary of the Fair Ground Association; is at present a director of the Fresno Water Company, and has an interest in the Fresno Bonded Warehouse. Mr. Phillips possesses many pleasing traits of character, and his amiable qualities have won for him a large circle of friends.

In December 1892 a new tariff bill was to be introduced in Congress. The raisin growers in Fresno, fearful that the tariff on raisins would be lowered and thereby jeopardize their young industry, called a mass meeting of the growers in Fresno. At that meeting, they decided to send a group to Washington to meet the Ways and Means Committee whose duty it was to formulate a tariff bill, and to present to them their best arguments for not reducing the tariff on raisins.

The issue of tariff laws has always been political and still is. What helps some hurts others. At this point in time, tariffs provided the single-most important source of federal revenue, and so a reduction in the tariff would mean that the revenue would have to come from somewhere else.

The meeting selected William, Mr. T. C. White, and a Mr. McGovern of New York to represent them. They raised $1,000 to cover all of their expenses, and reached Washington in time to make their arguments before the Committee. They were partially successful, and were happy with the result of their efforts.

The Ways and Means Committee also called on President Cleveland. In December 1892 Cleveland was not yet President for the second time. If William met with Cleveland before March 4, 1893, he would have met with Cleveland as a private citizen. William wrote in 1932:

> I remember telling him that, as a clerk five or six years before[32], I had sold Spanish raisins at 50¢ per pound, but since the California farmer had begun to produce them in large quantities, that the price of California raisins could be bought at 25¢ per pound, meaning, of course, the choicest variety. He was in entire sympathy with our cause. Mr. Cleveland made a great President, and I was glad to have met him.

The manuscript division of the Library of Congress reports that unfortunately the name "W. W. Phillips" is not noted in the correspondence index of the finding guide to the Grover Cleveland Papers. A simple explanation might be that he met with Cleveland while he was a private citizen and there was not any additional official correspondence.

Additionally, the Center for Legislative Archives at the United States National Archives and Records Administration reports that few Congressional hearings were recorded or printed until the early 20th century. A name index for this period does not reveal any listing for either W. W. Phillips or T. C. White.

The Center's holdings include petitions submitted to the Ways and Means Committee by category, but nothing for raisins. There is a box number HR52A-H24.19 for "and various subjects," but in a spot check nothing was found.

President Grover Cleveland (1837-1908)
Photo courtesy of the Library of Congress Prints & Photographs

President Cleveland was a Democrat, and it was the Democrats who were against the high tariffs who put him back in the White House (he was by then the 24th President having uniquely also previously been the 22nd President). The severe depression of 1893 turned the tide on the Democratic Party and their Wilson-Gorman Tariff Act of 1894, which proposed to lower the overall tariff rates from 50% to 42%.

Bowing to the Republicans, who feared the new resulting taxation that a reduction in the tariff might bring, President Cleveland vetoed the bill, but not because of views from people like William; far from it. In fact, he vetoed the legislation because it contained far too many protection provisions for specific local industries of the very type my great-grandfather talked to him about[33]. Regardless, Cleveland remained a great man as far as William was concerned, for the tariff on raisins was not lowered.

William's family in Mississippi was Democratic, and so was William at this point. However, with the emerging agricultural industry of Fresno, which had to compete then as it does today with foreign produce, William began to espouse the views of the Republicans who, at the time, were in favor of maintaining high tariffs, which also provided the ancillary benefit of preventing any need for an "income tax."

From my own personal experience of having spent much time in Hawaii and having visited the 'Iolani Palace, I learned about the overthrow of Queen Lili'uokalani and the establishment of a provisional government in Hawaii at the behest of American sugar importers who were angry about having to pay high tariffs on foreign sugar. They reasoned that if Hawaii were made a part of the United States territory, no tariff would be placed upon Hawaiian sugar, thereby lowering their purchasing cost.

The Queen had, of course, known President Cleveland; they exchanged portraits. She thought for sure he would rectify the situation once he learned the facts. In a controversy that continues to this day, Cleveland ultimately dropped support for reinstating the Queen and diplomatic relations with the new Republic of Hawaii was declared on July 4, 1894. Four years later, Hawaii was annexed to the United States. This, no doubt, pleased the sugar importers, for Hawaiian sugar would no longer be the subject of a tariff.

On February 10, 1893, *The Fresno Weekly Republican* reported:

INTEREST GROWING
In the Monterey & Fresno Railroad.
BUSINESS MEN HOLD A MEETING
The Project is Thoroughly Discussed – A Good Suggestion by M. Theo Kearney.

A number of prominent business men met at the Hughes Hotel yesterday morning to consider the proposed tidewater railroad from Fresno to Monterey and to take steps that will further the enterprise. The interest in the project is increasing, our business men beginning to realize the importance of such a road, and yesterday's meeting has given it a stimulus that will be productive of good results.

W. W. Phillips was elected chairman of the meeting. After stating its objectives briefly, Mr. Phillips spoke of the various advantages that would accrue to Fresno if it were made the eastern terminus of the road. He did not believe that all enterprise was dead in Fresno, and was of the opinion that $50,000 could be raised here as Fresno's share of the required bonus.

After Mr. Phillips had finished, M. Theo Kearney was asked for his views on the subject. He said that, while in New York about two weeks ago, he met a man who was endeavoring to work up a railroad scheme for the purpose of providing the San Joaquin valley with an outlet. This man was trying to negotiate the sale of bonds to a trust company. Asked what subscriptions had been given, the man answered none, and the company would negotiate no further with him. Mr. Kearney related this incident to emphasize the necessity of being able to show that the people along any proposed road are interested in it.

Mr. Kearney stated that what the bond buyers desired to know was whether the people wanted the road and would patronize it. A large number of subscribers cause them to consider a scheme with great favor. The more subscribers the better. If $50,000 were raised in subscriptions of $1 each so much the better. A trust company with millions back of it doesn't care much for a $50,000 subscription as such, but it does care for that sum as an expression of the feeling of the people toward an enterprise.

It was suggested by Mr. Kearney that the bankers of this city act as trustees for the subscribers to the bonus for the Monterey & Fresno Railroad, and that they pay the money to the railroad, as such trustees, when the road is completed and in operation, independently of the Southern Pacific company. Furthermore, the subscriptions and the value of the rights of way should be made a part of the bonded indebtedness of the company, with the understanding that they would have to be paid along with the other bonds should the road in any way fall into the hands of the Southern Pacific.

If the Monterey road itself agrees to pay back the subscriptions if the road passes into the hands of the Southern Pacific, that agreement might not amount to anything if the road becomes bankrupt, and therefore not be able to redeem its promise. By making the subscriptions a part of the bonded indebtedness, the subscribers would be certain of getting back their money if the road should ever pass into the hands of the Southern Pacific.

Two things should be done immediately by the people of this valley, continued Mr. Kearney: one of them is to organize the raisin industry and the other to build a competing railroad to Tidewater.   If the raisin men could be led to see that with reasonable freight rates they would realize as much for raisins at 3 cents per pound as they do now at 6, every owner of a twenty acre vineyard would favor the road. The speaker concluded by saying that the fruit company in New York wanted to get a road independent of the Southern Pacific, and assurance must be given Colonel Jones that the people wanted the road, so that when he goes to New York he will have no difficulty in selling the bonds.

Fulton G. Berry thought the quickest way to raise the $50,000 would be for twenty-five men to subscribe $2,000 each.   Mr. Kearney repeated that a large number of small subscriptions would be better than a few-large ones.

Chairman Phillips then broached the matter of right of way. It was his opinion that property owners in the city and suburbs would not give the rights of way for the road to cross their lots.   He thought this difficulty might he settled by the city trustees allowing the road to come in on one of the streets on the west side of the Southern Pacific track.

Mr. Kearney suggested that perhaps the supervisors would allow the road to follow California Avenue for ten miles west of the city, and after that there would be no trouble in securing the right of way.

O. J. Woodward, T. C. White and W. W. Phillips were elected a committee to wait upon the board of supervisors of this county and the trustees of this city, and invite them to attend the mass meeting on Saturday evening at 7:30 o'clock, in Kutner Hall. It was also decided by those present that all interested in the project should do their best to secure a large attendance at this meeting.

M. Theo Kearney, A. J. Wiener and Thomas E. Hughes were appointed a committee to secure the co-operation of the press of this city in the matter of making the mass meeting on Saturday evening a success. T. C. White and O. L. Walter were chosen to furnish music for the occasion. T. C. White made a suggestion that meetings be held in the colonies in order to get the farmers and vineyardists interested. If they did not want to subscribe they should pledge themselves to patronize the road. Mr. Kearney thought it would only be necessary to put the project before the people in its proper light in order to get them to put their shoulders to the wheel. After a little more general discussion the meeting adjourned.

Everything will be done to make the mass meeting next Saturday evening a grand success. It is hoped that every one interested in the project and capable of lending it a helping hand will be present. Speakers thoroughly informed on all matters in connection with the road will address the meeting, and Colonel Jones will also talk. Mr. Kearney, by the way, has raised his subscription to $5,000 and Fulton G. Berry his to $2,000.

On February 14, 1893, *The Fresno Morning Republican* reported:

ON TO MONTEREY.
FIVE THOUSAND DOLLARS
CONTRIBUTED YESTERDAY.
W. W. Phillips Gives his Opinion
Regarding Silurianism in Fresno.

The finance committee appointed at the last mass meeting in behalf of the Monterey & Fresno Railroad went on a collecting tour yesterday afternoon, and in about three hours collected a little more than $4,000, the most of which was subscribed in small sums.

W. W. Phillips was asked by a *REPUBLICAN* reporter yesterday as to his opinion of the prospects of the road being built. He said:

"It seems to me that the property owners of this town are not awake to the real importance of building this road, the terminal facilities which it will offer will be of great benefit to the producers especially. In fact they will be benefited more than any other class of people. If the property owners of this county are not the people to aid and encourage this enterprise who are? We cannot call upon the working classes, because although they also will be benefited they cannot afford to subscribe anything. If the people of Fresno will not take hold of this thing what will they take hold of?

"If the county is divided and Madera made the county seat there is a strong probability in the failure of Fresno to do her part, that the road may go to Madera. The people of this town are not alive to their personal interests it they don't encourage this enterprise all that they can.

"If Fresno's proportion of the bonus is not raised to pay the first interest on the bonds of this road as they desire it will certainly fall through. Can it be possible that the people of Fresno who have the name and reputation abroad as a broad-gauged, liberal and progressive community will sit down and allow this opportunity to escape them at this time.

"A good deal has been said about the Pollasky road, especially to the effect that the people had been gulled (duped) on that project. But the men who put up their money for the right of way, etc., on this road have not uttered one word of complaint. They say that they are enjoying more than value received for every dollar they put up."

On February 17, 1893, *The Fresno Weekly Republican* listed those who contributed to the bonus for the establishment of the Monterey & Fresno Railway. The following contributed $1,000: O. J. Woodward, C. L. Walter, W. W. Phillips, Alex Gordon, C. L. Morrill, T. E. Hughes, W. H. McKenzie, F. G. Berry, First National Bank and J. R. White. Other names within the long list include E. J. Bullard, $500, C. G. Sayle, $250 and C. B. Shaver, $250.

On March 12, 1893, *The Fresno Morning Republican* wrote, "Another delightful affair, given the same evening, was a dinner at W. W. Phillips'. It was, like all dinners given by Mr. Phillips, irreproachable – unless some of my friends wish to find fault because no ladies were present. But the eternal woman must be omitted now and then. There were present Judge S. A. Holmes,

Judge M. K. Harris, J.L., Messrs. J. O. Rue, John Reichman, H. C. Tupper, W. D. Tupper, Robert Perrin. After dinner the guests amused themselves with cards and billiards."

On April 27, 1893, William and Elizabeth's daughter Julia B. Phillips was born in Fresno. Tragically, she died on January 5, 1898 at the age of four.

On June 15, 1893, *The Fresno Morning Republican* reported a fraud which involved The Farmers Bank:

CLEVER FORGERIES
TWO SAN FRANCISCO BANKS MADE VICTIMS.
A Draft Issued by the Farmers Bank
Raised From $38 to $3800

The following dispatch from San Francisco gives the particulars of one the cleverest forgeries that have been detected in California for many years:

San Francisco, June 14 - Two cases of forgery to the extent of $9300, done on May 13th, were discovered here this morning. On that day a check was drawn on the Bank of Butte County in Chico on the London and San Francisco bank for $5500, was paid; on the same day a check for $3800 was drawn by the Farmers Bank of Fresno on the London-Paris-American bank, was paid. When the discrepancies were discovered in the accounts of the different banks, it was found that the checks had been raised respectively from $55 and $38. The work was done with great skill, the peculiar feature being that so accurately were the names of different cashiers formed that they themselves failed to detect the imitation. Detectives are at work on the case.

W. W. Phillips of the Farmers Bank told a *REPUBLICAN* reporter last night that the check for $38 was issued by the bank on May 10th to George Clark, probably a fictitious name. The name "George Clark" was written on the back of the check, together with the forged signature of John Reichman, cashier.

The check when presented to the San Francisco bank for payment was neatly perforated for $3800, evidently with a duplicate of the bank perforator. Then the check was restamped, the whole work being done so well that the fraud was discovered only after the careful examination by experts.

"In all cases where we issue checks," said Mr. Phillips, "the holders of which must be identified, we have always taken pains to write a letter to the bank stating that we hold his certificate of deposit, etc., and we never identified anybody by simply writing our name on the back of the check. Mr. Reichman would not go the trouble of doing this in the case of so small an amount as $38 because the person could carry the money in his pocket to San Francisco, and if such a request had been made of him he would have refused to issue the draft to the applicant."

"The San Francisco bank will have to stand the loss of what it paid in excess of $38."

On December 8, 1893, *The Fresno Morning Republican* reported:

THE FARMERS BANK.
A President Elected to Succeed Dr. Leach, Resigned.

At a meeting of the directors of the Farmers Bank Wednesday evening Dr. Lewis Leach, president of the bank since its organization, resigned his position and also retired from the board of directors. A. Kutner was elected president, and George R. Glenn, director.

The retirement of Dr. Leach is very much regretted by the stockholders, but his practice and other business demanded so much of his time that he finally decided to resign his position in the institution he has done so much to popularize.

His successor is the senior member of the firm of Kutner-Goldstein company. Mr. Kutner has been connected with the bank since its organization, and possesses rare business acumen. His career of prosperity will no doubt be continued under his presidency. Mr. Glenn, the new director, is a capitalist and a shrewd financier.

It is rumored that other changes will occur the first of the year. One of these is the retirement of W. W. Phillips, manager of the bank, who contemplates going into business for himself. Alex Gordon, one of the directors, it is said will also withdraw, his private business requiring all his attention. It is believed Alex Goldstein, of the Kutner-Goldstein company, may succeed Mr. Phillips.

On February 9, 1894, *The Fresno Weekly Republican* reported about a meeting of raisin growers which took place at Kutner Hall the previous day. There was much concern about the "depressed condition of raisin and fruit growing," and the best way to maintain prices. D. T. Fowler was elected chairman and William was elected secretary.

The same day, the same paper reported "W. W. Phillips vs. James Karnes; report of T. L. Reed, receiver, read; order to strike out personal expenses; receiver allowed $5 per day; report approved; judgment ordered for $1,669.08 and costs, and $130 attorney's fees."

After nearly twelve years with the Farmers Bank, William retired in 1894, and bought the River Ranch on the Old Friant Road. William enjoyed the outdoor aspects of looking after the property and became a successful rancher.

On April 22, 1894, *The Fresno Morning Republican* wrote: "W. W. Phillips has purchased the Williams ranch on the San Joaquin river, twelve miles north of Fresno for $16,500. This bargain is considered an excellent one for Mr. Phillips."

On June 8, 1894, *The Fresno Weekly Republican* reported:

THE RAISIN MEETING
Members of the Committee Confer With Packers.

Yesterday morning at the Hughes there was held a meeting of raisin committee, and packers, to discuss the raisin question and to confer with regard to grading, packing and marketing raisins.

The raisin growers' committee was represented by W. W. Phillips, Carroll Ghent, Dr. Baker, F. H. Rowell and W. H. Hodgkin. W. W. Phillips presided and Carroll Ghent was secretary.

A committee of five consisting of E. G. Chaddock, W. M. Griffin, A. N. Taylor of Hanford, J. H. Kelley and William Forsyth was appointed to decide upon a uniform system of packing. This committee will report at a meeting to be held a week from next Friday. An attempt will also be made to formulate some plan of f. o. b. sales.

W. W. Phillips, W. M. Griffin and A. B. Butler were appointed a committee to wait upon the proper railroad officials for the purpose of obtaining more favorable rates. All the packers of the county are invited to attend the next meeting.

On June 10, 1894, *The Fresno Morning Republican* printed a story about how my great-grandfather made a very smart investment in the River Ranch.

DOES FARMING PAY?
A Banker Who Believes It Is
Better Than Government Bonds.

W. W. Phillips, the banker, certainly knew what he was about when he purchased the Williams fruit farm on the San Joaquin River for $16,000. He has already sold his fruit crop for this season for $4,000, the purchaser to do the picking, and has made a lease of the farm for the ensuing three years for a cash rental of $5,000 per year, aggregating $15,000. In addition to the fruit he has on the farm ninety acres of alfalfa, which will produce this year about six tons per acre, which will probably be worth in the market $10 per ton. From this source, then, $5,400. The following returns are in sight:

Fruit sold on trees:	$ 4,000
Alfalfa:	$ 5,400
Cash rental for the years '95, '96, '97	$15,000
Total	$21,000

The basis of the rental above would represent 10 per cent per annum on an investment, of $50,000. It would he hard to find a better investment for $16,000 in any county or during any kind of times.

On June 29, 1894, *The Fresno Weekly Republican* reported, "W. W. Phillips has returned from a trip to Stockton where he went to visit his family."

A month later on August 24, 1894, *The Fresno Weekly Republican* reported that "W. W. Phillips went to San Francisco yesterday noon to attend the Democratic State Convention, to which he is a delegate."

William was also campaigning in 1894 for a position as a Railroad Commissioner, a tricky proposition for any Fresno candidate who ultimately wished to safe-guard the interests of the local growers against a very powerful interest, the railroad. For sure, this was a political "hot potato." William campaigned with

James Budd who became California's governor in 1895 and William T. Jetter who likewise became one of two lieutenant governors in 1895.

The Fresno Weekly Republican wrote on September 28, 1894:

Democratic Guns at Bakersfield

Bakersfield - September 21 - After a large procession this evening, Jetter, Phillips and Budd addressed a large outdoor assemblage. Jetter said that to vote for Estee was to vote for the Southern Pacific Company. Phillips made all kinds of promises if elected. Budd followed with a great effort to refute Estee's speech on state expenditures.

Governor James Budd with personal assistant Kate Acock
Photo circa 1895-1899 courtesy of the California State Capitol

On October 12, 1894, *The Fresno Weekly Republican* wrote an editorial about the politics behind the race for Railroad Commissioner:

RAILROAD COMMISSIONERS.

The evening journal says that no one has accused Mayor W. R. Clark of Stockton, Republican nominee for railroad commissioner, "of being anti-railroad except for revenue." So far as our information goes the *Expositor* has no more ground for making such a charge than *THE REPUBLICAN* would have for making a similar charge against W. W. Phillips, the Democratic nominee.

No man can say that either one of these candidates are "anti-railroad" until they have been tried. If there be any foundation for the *Expositor's* insinuation that there are people who know Mr. Clark who believe that he will not do his duty if elected, the same can be said of Mr. Phillips with absolute truthfulness. No one is better informed than the *Expositor* in regard to the number of Democrats in Fresno who do not expect any unusual benefits in the event of Mr. Phillips' election. Because of this fact it does not necessarily follow that Mr. Phillips will not do his duty should he become a member of the railroad commission, nor do these opinions give *THE REPUBLICAN* license to say that he will not.

This paper does not propose to promise the voters of this valley that Mr. Clark will relieve them from the unjust burdens which are imposed upon them, for it does not know that he will do so, nor does it, because there are considerable numbers of Mr. Phillips' fellow Democrats who doubt his sincerity, propose to say that he will not keep his promises. That sort of thing is all right for a scurrilous and irresponsible partisan organ, but it is not in line with the policy of this paper.

Of the two candidates Mr. Clark is the one who has a public record, and we are reliably informed that he has been instrumental in securing the enforcement of municipal regulations in Stockton that were decidedly opposed by the Southern Pacific company. His record, therefore, is in his favor. Mr. Phillips has never been put to the test in any public capacity, and must therefore be judged entirely by the estimate placed upon him by those who know him in his private business relations. In this respect *THE REPUBLICAN* has no more excuse for attacking him than the *Expositor* has for assailing Mayor Clark[34]. Probably the worst thing that can be said of Mr. Phillips as a candidate for railroad commissioner is that he apparently has the support of the *Expositor*.

In an article titled "Jim Budd's Turn," the same day's paper mentioned: "Chairman McMullin next introduced W. W. Phillips of Fresno, whom Mr. Budd had significantly referred to as 'a ladies' man.' Mr. Phillips made some seasonable remarks, which were well received."

In 1894 my great-grandfather did not run for Governor, but he was a delegate to the California State Convention and ran as a Democrat for a position as a Railroad Commissioner for the third district. On November 16, 1894, the voters chose a Republican for Railroad Commissioner.   After the panic of 1893, the Democrats fell out of favor, and it is not surprising that a Republican won this race. Additionally, William R. Clark was the alleged choice of the railroad. My great-grandfather did pick up 40,210 votes however, and as a result, he became known throughout the state. Had William gained 10,089 more votes, he would have won this election and had he not acted in the interests of the Fresno growers, he might have harmed his future political chances. As they say, things sometimes work out for the best.

Aaron Bretz	People's Party	31.5%
William R. Clark	Republican	35.9%
H. L. Kuns	Prohibition	3.8%
W. W. Phillips	Democratic	28.7%

On February 1, 1895, *The Fresno Weekly Republican* reported: "Ernest Vincent is learning engineering at the W. W. Phillips ranch. Mr. Phillips is having a large reservoir made for irrigating his orchard. Mr. Phillips is putting a stationary 30 horse power boiler and engine to pump water from a well to irrigate his fine fruit and alfalfa ranch."

On June 14, 1895, *The Fresno Weekly Republican* reported: "At the annual school election for trustee Mrs. W. W. Phillips was elected for three years. W. W. Phillips has a splendid property interest in the district and Mrs. Phillips feels and manifests a deep interest in the education of their three children."

Within five years, William and his wife "Miss Bettie" would have only one child left, my grandfather.

On September 7, 1895, *The Daily Evening News* of Modesto reported:

> *The Visalia Times*, in speaking of railroad commissioner Clark says:
>
> > *The Fresno Republican* is making frantic appeals to Commissioner Clark to stand by the people, but their appeals carry the painful consciousness that they will go unheeded. Now, we ask in all sincerity why should Commissioner Clark abandon the railroad at this juncture? His position was as well understood before election as after. That he was nominated at the bidding of the Southern Pacific is an open and notorious fact. It was just as open and notorious before election as since. During the election Clark could not be induced to get on a public platform or state his intentions in any straightforward, unequivocal way. The railroad gave him its undisguised support at the polls, as it did in the convention. Yet the *Republican* supported him and the people elected him. What right have they or the *Republican* to complain of him now? The voters of this district endorsed Commissioner Clark's candidacy and the means and influences which produced it. He was nominated by a boss at the behest of the Southern Pacific. It was a nomination ratified at the polls by the people. From that day till this no person of good common sense has expected other than that Clark would stand by the interests of the corporation and neglect those of the people. It will always be thus so long as newspapers and voters denounce the railroad in editorials and resolutions and then give the lie to their professions by electing the tools of the railroad to office in obedience to partisan prejudice. When the voters sacrifice their own financial interests on the altar of mistaken party loyalty they have no one to blame but themselves. In what are they entitled to sympathy if they go on year after year permitting themselves to be buncoed with their eyes open?
> >
> > *The Fresno Republican* pretended to believe in the face of the facts that Dr. Clark would be a friend of the people. It is an intelligent newspaper, and we must vindicate its perspicacity at the expense of its sincerity. No doubt it is sincerely opposed to the railroad's exactions and domination in politics, but it

inconsistently surrenders its convictions on these points to party loyalty. That it does so under protest does not improve the situation. Its partisan prejudice will not permit it to pursue its opposition to the railroad further than the doors of a Republican convention. But the *Republican* is less to blame than the farmers and shippers of the San Joaquin Valley. They have suffered more at the hands of the railroad than anyone else. Yet note how they have licked the hands that smote them and bitten those who defended them! With this unimpeachable record before them they defeated W. W. Foote for re-election and elected the notorious Jim Rea, the undisguised candidate of the Southern Pacific. When four years in office had proved the worst that was charged against him, he was re-nominated and re-elected over Lawrence Archer, a man of pure character and high intellect who had for years, in and out of the legislature, opposed the exactions and political aggressions of the railroad monopoly. Did not the voters, by the most signal and only efficacious method at their disposal, condemn Foote and endorse Rea? Why blame politicians and newspapers for supporting railroad candidates and schemers when the people themselves give emphatic approval at the polls to those very candidates and schemers? Was not Rea abundantly justified in pursuing the same course during his second term that he pursued during his first? If the voters were deceived the first time they were assuredly not deceived the second time. They deliberately endorsed Rea, with his record before them, by a largely increased majority over a man of stainless character and unimpeachable record.

In the last campaign, W. W. Phillips was nominated on a platform containing a specific pledge to reduce transportation rates. He was a business man of excellent reputation and undeniable capacity. For many years a resident and property owner of the San Joaquin Valley, he was intimately acquainted with the needs and conditions of this section. He was endorsed by the Traffic Association, a non-partisan organization of merchants and shippers, organized to fight for lower freight rates. In every considerable town of the district he publicly announced his adhesion to the Democratic pledge and the pledge of the Traffic Association. Clark took no pledges and gave no assurances; he was the avowed railroad candidate. How did the farmers and shippers of this valley treat these two men on election day? They gave the railroad candidate a

majority[35].   In the strong Republican county of Alameda,
where the Traffic Association's influence was large, Clark
received a bare majority – less than 300.   In the San Joaquin
Valley where, if popular professions are sincere, Phillips
should have received an overwhelming vote, he was actually in
the minority.

These are the things that disgust and discourage men who
are consistently and honestly opposed to the abuses practiced
on the public for the transportation monopoly.   They deter men
from espousing the cause of the people and encourage the self-
seeking politicians who court the favor and domination of the
railway monopoly.   Just so long as politicians understand that
wearing the railroad livery involves no danger of defeat, just so
long will all attempts to curb the greed and arrogance of the
corporation prove abortive.   The people must first be sincere
and true to themselves before they can hope or expect
politicians and office holders to be faithful.   Why should the
selection of members of the railroad commission which has
neither political power nor patronage, be dictated by partisan
affiliation?   The sole office of the commission is to regulate a
business arrangement between the public and the transportation
companies.   The commission has naught to do with political
issues and has no official relation with the policies which
divide the voters into parties.   Its members should be fair-
minded, intelligent and experienced business men with the will
and courage to do justice to all parties concerned.   But partisan
politics has made the commission a house of refuge for rogues
and demagogues; and the people are to blame for it.

Victorian Era View From The Courthouse
Photo courtesy of the Fresno Historical Society Archives

On March 13, 1896, *The Fresno Weekly Republican* reported:

GRADY'S RAISIN CASE IS BROUGHT AGAINST
THE CUTTING COMPANY
He Claims That The Returns To Him Were
False and Fraudulent.

W. D. Grady has brought suit, in behalf of his son W. M. Grady, to quiet title to the Magnolia Vineyard, situated eight miles west of Fresno. It appears that W. W. Phillips, by virtue of a $2,000 mortgage on the vineyard, held in trust. Phillips made a contract with Cutting Packing Company for the assignment of last year's raisin crop. This was the raisin crop of eighty-four tons which Mr. Grady referred to in his speech before the Hundred Thousand Club on Monday evening. The returns showed that Grady through Phillips, was indebted to the commission firm in the sum of $803 and according to the contract, Mr. Grady says is a lien upon the vineyard. He now brings suit to set aside the contract between Phillips and the commission firm. "The Cutting Company will have to give me an accounting upon the sale of my raisin crop when the case is brought into court," said Mr. Grady to a

Republican reporter yesterday. "I intend to make it an interesting case. I claim that the Cutting Company defrauded me in their weights, charges for wastage, freight, etc., and that their returns to the effect that the crop only averaged 1 cent net, are false and fraudulent. Upon these grounds I will ask the court to declare the contract null and void." The plaintiff will be represented by Walter D. Tupper and George B. Graham.

That same day, March 13, 1896, *The Fresno Weekly Republican* also reported:

The Fresno County Horticultural Society organized yesterday with thirty-three members. The meeting was called to order by W. W. Phillips in the room of the Chamber of Commerce. He stated the objects of the proposed society in substance as follows:

"To advise with and educate one another in the best methods of cultivating, pruning and curing fruits and for the further purpose of how best to market them; To act as a unit so as to better the condition of this great industry; To use our best efforts in inducing San Francisco capital to erect a fruit canning establishment in Fresno, thus creating a demand for green fruits at home to say nothing of the immense benefits afforded our wage earners in Fresno. If by hearty cooperation we can bring about a unanimous agreement not to consign our dried fruit to the eastern commission merchant, this society will not have been organized in vain[36]. I believe, gentlemen this society can accomplish a great deal under the laws laid down for our mutual good and I hope to have the hearty support of every grower in the county to the desired end."

If 2,000 tons of suitable fruit for canning purposes can be guaranteed at a stipulated price, it is probable the cannery will be established. W. W. Phillips was appointed on the committee of one to correspond with the San Francisco parties.

The following resolution was passed by a unanimous vote:

Whereas the county of Fresno in one of the largest fruit growing counties in the State of California and

Whereas the fruit industry of this state is in great danger of becoming demoralized in the near future through lack of organization, mutual understanding and concentration of interests of the fruit growers, be it

Resolved that for the purpose of uniting the interests of the growers of Fresno County, and of obtaining and disseminating useful information with reference to planting, growing, curing and marketing deciduous and all other tree fruits, we immediately organize a permanent horticultural society in Fresno County.

The following, bylaws were adopted:

This association shall be known as the Fresno County Horticultural Society. Its object shall be to unite and promote in every possible way the interest of the horticulturists of Fresno County.

Its officers shall consist of a president, vice president, treasurer and secretary who shall serve without compensation. Its principal place of meeting and business shall be in the city of Fresno. Every horticulturist of Fresno County may become a member of this association by being proposed for membership at any meeting, and shall be entitled to all the privileges thereof after receiving a majority of all members present and signing these bylaws. There shall be no dues of any kind connected with membership, the expenses of this association shall be paid by voluntary subscription.

This association shall hold regular monthly meetings on the first Saturday of each month at 2 p.m., in Fresno city. Special meetings may be called by the president and secretary at any time or place within this county provided three day notice be given in the Fresno daily papers. The officers shall be elected annually on the first Saturday of April each year. The duties of the officers shall be the customary duties of the respective offices. Six members shall constitute a quorum. Any of the foregoing articles may be amended by a majority vote at any regular meeting of the association or at a special meeting if called for that purpose.

The sentiment of the society was strongly against consigning dried fruit to eastern brokers to sell on commission. The next meeting will be held on the first Saturday in April at 2 p.m. and the subject for discussion will be "Marketing Fruit."

The permanent officers are W. W. Phillips, president, B. C. Hutchinson vice-president, O. B. Olufs, secretary and treasurer.

Col. H. Trevelyan was invited to address the meeting on his plan of selling raisins. He complied and explained the method which he believed would meet the requirements of this case. It was the same as this paper published over his signature a few days ago.

Following are the charter members of the society and the number of acres of fruit owned by each: O. B. Olufs 80 acres, W. W Phillips 150 acres, O. N. Freman, 60 acres... [W. W. Phillips held the largest amount of total acreage amongst the 33 members].

The Fresno Republican reported on April 5, 1896 that William wanted a vacant seat on the Board of Supervisors:

> Mr. Phillips resides on the San Joaquin River, in the Second District. He is actively at work, and it is said that a macadamized road out of Blackstone Avenue from the city to the river has already been promised.

On April 15, 1896, *The Fresno Republican* reported:

> Members of the Fresno Horticultural Society discussed the possibility of raising $2,500 as an inducement to the Tenney Cannery of San Francisco to move its plant to Fresno. W. W. Phillips, who presided over the meeting, said $1,500 had been assured and $1,000 more is needed to bring the business to Fresno.

On April 30, 1896, he announced in *The Fresno Republican* that the Horticultural Society, of which he was President, would be held on May 2nd at 11 o'clock a.m. instead of the customary 2 p.m.

The Fresno Weekly Republican reported the following superior court proceeding on May 1, 1896: "W. M. Grady vs. W. W. Phillips; motion to dissolve injunction taken under advisement."

On May 15, 1896, *The Fresno Weekly Republican* wrote about the last meeting of the season of The Wednesday Club:

> ...one of the most prominent organizations of ladies in the city. It holds weekly meetings devoted to the study of literature. The club gives two social events every year, the 'annual' in the middle of the year and the 'optional.' These have always been very enjoyable.

The article continued:

> Progressive salmagundi was the principal entertainment. The games were played with great interest and were highly enjoyed.

At this party, William's wife Elizabeth won the ladies' "booby prize."

In 1897 the 184-page souvenir *Imperial Fresno* was published by *The Fresno Republican* with photographs and a description of the bank. "Its management," they wrote: "was marked by great conservatism from the very commencement, and it rapidly gained the confidence of the business world." The souvenir described the 1889 bank building as a stately and ornate structure:

> No convenience or precaution of modern bank buildings was omitted. The fire-proof and burglar-proof vaults and the safe-deposit boxes are of the very best style, and the furniture of the bank is of the most elegant description. The officials of the bank take pride in the truthful statement that during the severe panic of 1893, when other banks were resorting to every legal method of gaining time in which to realize on securities, the Farmers Bank pursued the even course of daily business and promptly met every demand of depositors, even on time or interest-bearing certificates. Nothing could speak more forcibly of the soundness of its business management.

The Farmers Bank of Fresno
From the 1897 souvenir, *Imperial Fresno*

On January 21, 1897, *The Fresno Weekly Republican* reported the following real estate transaction:

> W. D. Bowen et al to W. W. Phillips, all right, title and interest in and to that portion of ne ¼ of Section 5 lying north and east of the San Joaquin Valley Railroad, t 13, r 21; $10.
>
> W. W. Phillips to W. D. Bowen et al, all right, title and interest in and to that portion of Section 5 lying south and west of the San Joaquin Valley Railroad, t 13, r 21; $10.

On March 7, 1897, *The Fresno Morning Republican* reported, "W. W. Phillips and wife are here from San Francisco. Mr. Phillips is now in the commission business in the metropolis, but still retains his extensive interests here."

An article in *The Fresno Weekly Republican* on March 12, 1897 discussed how the Board of Supervisors would help the county and "stand by the raisin growers" through an appropriation to help secure a higher duty on Zaute Currants. The article claimed *The Expositor* was critical of the plan to send a delegation to Washington "to satisfy a private grudge and make a political play." They wrote:

> In 1893, when the raisin situation in regard to national legislation was very much the same as it is now, T. C. White and W. W. Phillips were sent to Washington to secure proper protection for the industry. Both were Democrats, but no one thought of making a political issue of the matter. In fact it was regarded as entirely appropriate that Democrats should be sent to Washington, for it was a Democratic administration and both houses of congress were Democratic. Republicans as well as Democrats contributed to the fund to defray the expenses of these gentlemen who made a successful fight and received all the credit they deserved for their efforts.
>
> Mr. White was seen by a *REPUBLICAN* reporter last night, and he stated in answer to a question that if he were a member of the Board of Supervisors he would do exactly as the present members have done if the same condition prevailed. He said in substance that everything depended upon the raisin industry. Even the welfare of the man who raised apples in the foothills depended more or less upon the welfare of the raisin industry. If the latter

was in a prosperous condition the foothill apple grower would find a ready local market for his product. If not he would suffer with the raisin grower. Mr. White is too intelligent a man to take a partisan view of this matter, and the same may be said of Mr. Phillips who aided him in his excellent work at Washington four years ago.

On April 18, 1897, *The Fresno Morning Republican* printed the following story which illustrated the character of W. D. Grady:

GRADY'S CASE A FARCE
His Examination Is Held At Last.
Denies He Bit The Man's Ear
He "Wasn't Within Biting Distance" – The Case
Taken Under Advisement.

A joke of huge proportions was enacted yesterday afternoon in department 3 of the Police Court. An appreciative audience winced and smiled as the details of the screaming farce followed one another, until the hero of the merry jest, W. D. Grady, and his fellow jokers allowed Acting Police Judge Carroll to bring down the curtain and put out the lights.

Even the presence in court of William Schaefer, whose left ear was bitten off by Grady on the night of January 19th, did not interrupt the success of the farce that has been almost three months in preparation. The positive testimony of three witnesses who saw Grady chew Schaefer's ear, was also powerless to mar the symmetry of the joke. The testimony availed nothing against the mirth-provoking words and acts of the humorous defendant, the attorney and even the judge. It seemed a fitting end of Grady's record-breaking performance of sixteen continuances and his unequalled exemplification of what can be done with a full-grown Police Court "pull." There will be another case on Monday, but it will lack interest because it has been foreshadowed. Judge Carroll has promised to announce on Monday the result of his deliberations on the amusing events of yesterday.

Prosecuting attorney O'Callaghan, suddenly deserted by the special attorney for the prosecution, was unprepared, but the serious character of Schaefer's charge could not be entirely supported. Mr. Schaefer took the witness stand and told in his own way, though seriously hampered by the sustained objections of defendant's counsel, how Grady had, without provocation, bitten off a portion of Schaefer's ear.

William Munch, steward of the Orpheum Theater[37], testified that he had seen Grady bite off a portion of the waiter's ear. Henry Comers, a waiter, and E. M. Koesner, leader of the Orpheum orchestra, also witnessed Grady's act. The testimony against Grady was corroborated by other witnesses. Then the real fun began.

As its first witness, the defense called John Hogan. He said he was present when the trouble occurred, but did not see the ear-biting act.

W. W. Phillips, who knew Grady in Fresno, said he had witnessed the encounter from a distance and could not tell one contestant from the other.

H. G. Stevens, who has drawn $30 from the treasury as witness fees and mileage in this case, confessed to an entire lack of knowledge concerning the affair. He was with Mr. Phillips at the time of the fight and has attended court regularly ever since. Each time he appeared in court he received $6.50; of this amount $5 was for mileage from Napa, where he does not live, and $1.50 was for fees allowed by law as a witness from another county.

To make his defense complete, Grady took the stand, and related to the court how he had knocked down two waiters, one with the right hand and the other with the left, and had then threatened to "bite the head and neck off any one that interfered with him." He declared, however, that he "never was within biting distance of Schaefer," and that he could not account for that gentleman's loss of an ear.

Messrs. Foote and Levy declared themselves satisfied with their case, and were willing to submit it without argument. They referred rather contemptuously to the poor showing made by the prosecution, and intimated their belief that the judge would not hesitate for a moment in giving their client his freedom.

Mr. O'Callaghan apologized for himself and asked for a continuance, on the ground that time was necessary for him to prepare a logical argument. The judge agreed to give O'Callaghan until Tuesday. Foote and Levy objected, and the judge reversed himself and denied O'Callaghan an opportunity to present arguments. The prosecuting attorney began another statement, but the judge cut it short by announcing that he would render his decision next Monday, Messrs. Foote and Levy laughed, Grady laughed, the audience laughed, and the joke was over.

But Schaefer, the poor waiter, after suffering from a serious wound, must go through life without his ear, disfigured and distressed, which isn't so great a joke. The law calls these ear-bitings mayhem, and sends men who have not a police court pull to state prison for the offense. On Monday the people will know whether Justice Carroll intends to jest with the law still further and submit to the "pull" of the man-biter.

In W. D. Grady's obituary published in the *The Fresno Morning Republican* on October 13, 1923, he was described as having attained a wide reputation as an able attorney and "at one time proved before a court and jury that a man had bitten off his own ear."

On August 27, 1897, *The Fresno Weekly Republican* wrote:

Grady to Sell His Vineyard

Judge Webb of the superior court granted the petition of W. D. Grady to sell the real estate of Walter M. Grady, his son, of whom he is guardian. The property in question is the north half of the northeast quarter of section 13, township 14, range 18 and consists of 80 acres. The land is at present in control of W. W. Phillips, who foreclosed a mortgage on it.   The petitioner asked to be allowed to sell the vineyard so that he could realize about $500 above the encumbrances in behalf of his ward. The vineyard is about eight miles west of Fresno.

Bill Coate, a teacher in Madera, California (who organized a student project to transcribe the diaries of George Washington Mordecai, his wife Louise Hunter Dixon Mordecai, and their life on the Fresno Plains at Refuge) has written about Refuge, the Dixons and W. D. Grady.

In an article printed in *The Madera Tribune* on March 15, 2005 entitled "Richard Lawrence Dixon Suffered a Grave Injustice" and republished on August 15, 2006 as "Dixon Gave No Insult and Took None," he wrote about W. D. Grady who was considered "the new lawyer in town" after R. L. Dixon. A portion is printed here.

In the meantime, Fresno had attracted another lawyer, Walter D. Grady. He came to town, rented an office and hung out his shingle. Clever, fearless and arrogant, he troubled himself but little with that elusive thing called ethics.

Aghast, conservative members of the local bar watched Grady confuse witnesses, abuse opponents, and from time to time defy the judge. It didn't take a soothsayer to foretell a dismal future for the new lawyer, given the fact that Richard Lawrence Dixon was on the scene.

One day, Dixon and his son, Harry, had the misfortune of having to tend to business in Grady's office. As the twosome walked across the street, little Rebecca Dixon[38], Harry's daughter, trailed them. She had dropped into her father's office on her way home from school. Years later she recalled an incident that was the talk of the legal community for years to come.

In Rebecca's words, "I used to go to the office to walk home with Father. There was a shyster lawyer in the growing town by the name of Grady. There was some sort of dirty legal business afoot, and Grady was handling it.

"Father, accompanied by Grandfather, left his office, walked across the street, and climbed the steps to Grady's office with me tagging along. Grady rose from his seat and half-crouched behind his desk, obviously afraid. I remember the relaxed and perfect dignity, the great force, the contempt with which Father tossed some legal papers at Grady and turned and walked out."

Grady's relief was only temporary, because as Harry left, his father remained. Quickly a quarrel ensued between Grady and the old gentleman. If the young lawyer thought he could intimidate his elder, he was sadly mistaken. Although he had reached the age of 75, Richard Lawrence Dixon walked around the desk, grabbed the younger man by the scruff of the neck and kicked him down a flight of stairs and out into the street. So worked up was Dixon that he borrowed a whip from one of the buggies tethered in front of the buildings and proceeded to chase Grady in and out of the carriages. It was a hilarious sight and brought onlookers for blocks around.

No one knows to what extent anything but Grady's pride was injured on that day, but it is clear that the populace of Fresno was pleased. As Rebecca recorded in her diary, "For these deeds of valor, the delighted citizens presented him (Richard Lawrence Dixon) with an inscribed, gold-handled cane." © 2007 The Madera Tribune and William S. Coate.

On January 8, 1898, *The Fresno Morning Republican* opined that since Governor Budd would undoubtedly appoint a Democrat to the vacancy on the Board of Railroad Commissioners, "it would be entirely proper that the job be given to W. W. Phillips, who was the choice of the Democrats of this District in the last election and is now resident of the district in which the vacancy occurred."

On January 23, 1898, *The Fresno Morning Republican* reported:

A GOOD DEMOCRAT
Phillips Did Not Suit Budd
He Will Not Be a Railroad Commissioner
Is Not Pleased Because The Position of Fresno Democrats
Was Misrepresented

W. W. Phillips, for many years a banker in Fresno, is down from San Francisco looking after his business interests in this county. Mr. Phillips has withdrawn from the race for appointment as Railroad Commissioner and in the future his time will entirely be taken up in managing his produce commission business and with a new line of steamships between San Francisco and Dawson City, Alaska. He is largely interested in the steamship, backed by W. C. Gates[39], a wealthy Klondike miner.

Mr. Phillips says that owing to his increasing business responsibilities he was compelled to withdraw as an aspirant for the place as Railroad Commissioner. He was pleased by the loyal support given him by the Democratic party of Fresno and said to a *REPUBLICAN* reporter yesterday:

"I wish to thank the Democratic County Central Committee for its endorsement of me for appointment by Governor Budd as Railroad Commissioner. I was with the Fresno Democrats for over twenty years and took an active part in building up the party. While here I attended nearly every state and national convention and it is pleasant to know that I have not been forgotten by my political friends, although now residing at a distance."

The Expositor has indirectly opposed Mr. Phillips' appointment by favoring that of James H. Barry of the *San Francisco Star*. Although Mr. Phillips did not ask for the paper's endorsement, he expected that it would voice the sentiments of the county Democracy and favor him.

"The *Expositor's* endorsement would have added little influence anyway," said Mr. Phillips, "and I do not care to discuss its peculiar action in opposing me when the party was on record in my favor.

"In the past I have contributed liberally to the Democratic state and county campaign funds and made the race for Railroad Commissioner four years ago. In that campaign, I was endorsed by the Traffic Association, the *Bulletin*, *Post* and *Examiner*. About two weeks ago Governor Budd, in responding to the positions in favor of my appointment, replied that he thought it would be a reflection on the people of the Second District to appoint a man who had made the race at the last election for railroad commissioner in the Third district. I think Budd will appoint Barry.

"I do not wish to be considered sore because Budd and the *Expositor* were against me, but desire to explain to my friends in Fresno that I am out of the race and desire to extend my heartfelt thanks for the endorsement of the county central committee and the loyalty of my friends."

Mr. Phillips here dropped politics and spoke of his new business venture.

"I am interested in two Alaska steamship lines," he said, "and intend to go to Boston in a few days to purchase a steamer for the company in which W. C. Gates, the Klondike miner is interested. We will go from Boston around the Horn to Skaguay and expect to take 600 passengers on the trip. The steamer will carry 1,200 tons of supplies.

"San Francisco is filled with people getting ready to make the rush for the Klondike. The Board of Trade estimates that fully 150,000 people will go to Alaska in the spring. It is expected that the northern gold fields will result in $50,000,000 worth of trade for California the present season.

"Every boat that can be pressed into use has been secured for the Alaska travel and next month the rush will commence. There will be sixty steamers on the Yukon the present season. Travel on the river will not be open until about July 1st and the river will be navigable for about four months. Last season only three steamers made the trip through.

"Potatoes, beans and other produce is going up on the account of the Alaskan demand. There are several factories in San Francisco where vegetables are dessicated for the use of prospectors.   The vegetables dry up so that seven pounds are reduced to one pound.

"W. C. Gates, known as 'Swift Water Bill,' struck it rich on the Klondike and to hear him talking of the wonderful wealth of the mines makes one think he is listening to a modern Monte Cristo.

"By the way, no matter where I may be I desire all the Fresno news and want the REPUBLICAN sent to me."

Advertisement in *The Fresno Republican*
which ran from February through March 1898

The 843-ton Dirigo was built in 1898 by P. Mathews, Grays Harbor, Washington for J. S. Kimball Company, San Francisco. In 1900 The Dirigo was purchased by the Alaska Steamship Company and sank on November 16, 1914 one hundred miles west of Cape Fairweather on a voyage from Cordova, Alaska to Seattle.

On January 28, 1898, *The Fresno Morning Republican* reported:

WILL NOT RESIGN.
Colonel Wright May be Placed on the Retired List.

Colonel S. S. Wright has returned from San Francisco, where he was engaged in making preparations to visit Alaska. He says that his trip to Alaska will not necessarily result in his retirement. He has no thought of resigning, as in a few months he will have served the time required to be eligible for the retired list.

Colonel Wright has not yet definitely decided when he will leave for Alaska, but he expects to be a member of the expedition sent out by the Alaska Transportation, Trading and Mining Company. W. W. Phillips is a director in this company.

On August 16, 1898, *The Fresno Weekly Republican* reported:

W. W. PHILLIPS' BAD LUCK
Bilked by Man Whom He Had Trusted.

The *San Francisco Chronicle* of Sunday contained the following account of a piece of bad fortune that befell W. W. Phillips, formerly of this city:

"W. W. Phillips of 401 California Street yesterday swore to a complaint in Police Court 1, charging J. B. Olsen with felony embezzlement. Phillips alleges that he gave Olsen. $1,600 with which to purchase city hall warrants, and that Olsen failed to make any return for the money. Olsen was until recently stenographer in Police Court. He lost his position by reason of his having been indicted for perjury by the grand jury, Olsen was arrested last night by Lieutenant Hanna, and, being unable to secure bail, was locked up in the city prison."

"Last June Phillips charged another man with the embezzlement of $2,000, which Phillips claimed to have given him for the purpose of buying salary warrants. That case was on trial before Police Judge Joachimsen yesterday and was continued until September."

On September 25, 1898, *The Fresno Morning Republican* reported within a lengthy article about state politics that William was in Seattle but due to return since his brother Dixon aspired to become a superior court judge:

> Smith has the happy ability of shoving himself forward. I understand he is now figuring in the contest for the superior judgeship in Kings County, made vacant by the death of Judge Justin Jacobs. The young man is working in the interest of Dixon L. Phillips. The aspirant is a brother of W. W. Phillips, now of San Francisco, who was a candidate for railroad commissioner on the Democratic ticket when Budd was running for Governor. They campaigned together and are close friends. It therefore looks as if Phillips had good chance for the Judgeship. Unfortunately, his brother is in Seattle at present, but his early return is looked for.
>
> It is reported that Phillips' friends are planning to influence the Governor through Sam Lenke, the manager of the *Call*. While the newspaper man is probably on friendly terms with Budd, it is not likely that he will interest himself in the Kings County fight.

On January 1, 1899, the Farmers Bank became a "national" bank and became known as the Farmers National Bank of Fresno. In that year they began to issue their own bank notes.

Farmers National Bank of Fresno, December 5, 1898

On March 17, 1899, *The Fresno Weekly Republican* reported that W. W. Phillips transferred to Elizabeth B. Phillips, parts of lots 27 and 28, block 84, in the city of Fresno.

Elizabeth B. Pressley Phillips (1854-1916)
Photo courtesy of the Phillips Family Collection

On June 27, 1899, *The Fresno Morning Republican* reported:

W. W. Phillips yesterday began suit in the superior court against W. M. Grady and W. D. Grady, his guardian, to quiet title to the n ½ of the ne ¼ of section 13, township 14, range 18. The plaintiff claims that in June 1896, he advanced to the California Savings and Loan Society, $3,500 in payment of a foreclosure judgment obtained by that corporation against the property in question. In return for the $3,500, Grady gave Phillips a deed to the property with the understanding that he, Grady, might redeem it at any time within two years. This the defendant failed to do, and the plaintiff therefore asks that an absolute deed to the property be granted him by decree of court. The real estate in question is the well known Magnolia Vineyard, nine miles west of this city. It was at one time one of the best improved pieces of land in the county, but of late has been neglected.

The Magnolia Vineyard was described in 1892 as owned by Walter Drane Grady, containing 400 acres of raisins and 4,000 acres of wheat. The vineyard alone at the time was valued at $150,000, with income from the grain and raisins valued at about $40,000 per year.

On August 3, 1899, *The Fresno Weekly Republican* reported:

THE GRADY SUIT
The Defendants Filed Their Answer Yesterday.

In the suit of W. W. Phillips against W. M. Grady and W. D. Grady, his guardian the defendants yesterday filed their answer to the plaintiff's complaint. They deny that Phillips has any interest in the property described in the complaint. It is admitted that he loaned Grady $2,000 to pay off the mortgage on the property held by the California Savings and Loan Society but the statute of limitations is a bar to action for the recovery of this amount. The defendants also demur to the complaint filed by Phillips on the ground that it does not state facts sufficient to constitute a cause for action.

W. D. Grady, individually, files a disclaimer in the case. He denies that he has or claims any interest to the property described in the complaint. C. C. Merriam is attorney for W. M. Grady.

William appears on the list of donors found in the cornerstone of the 1901 St. James Episcopal Church.

The Farmers National Bank of Fresno, 1904
Pictured from left to right: J. A. Phillips, Herbert Levy,
Ivan C. McIndoo[40], Henry Korn and Ralph Beardon.
Photo courtesy of Robert Boro

The person standing on the left is identified as "J. A. Phillips" in this 1904 candid photograph within the interior of the Farmers National Bank of Fresno. I am unaware of anyone in our family who meets this description. However, interestingly, the third gentleman, Ivan C. McIndoo, was the original owner of the family home at 410 Van Ness purchased by William's son John in 1931.

In 1905 a company proposed building a million dollar sugar processing factory in Fresno. On September 17, 1905, *The Fresno Morning Republican* reported that William made a short address to the Chamber of Commerce on the profits of beet growing, which he had observed in visits to sugar fields in the southern part of the state. "Diversity of crops," he said, "is a crying need in this county, and the present proposition is too big to be neglected."

On September 19, 1905, *The Fresno Morning Republican* reported that a mass meeting took place at the Chamber of Commerce. A company wanted to process sugar in Fresno and asked the farmers to grow beets. William suggested that a committee of three be sent to Oxnard to learn about the industry and report back to the farmers. He said farmers would be more likely to believe statements if made by men from among themselves. William then made a motion that President Hobbs appoint such a committee and the motion was carried.

Two days later, *The Fresno Morning Republican* reported:

W. W. Phillips, George Roeding[41], Wiley M. Giffen and W. F. Chandler were yesterday appointed by President Hobbs as the members of the committee to visit Oxnard and other beet-sugar districts, to investigate the question of sugar profits from the farmers' standpoint. All the members have signified their acceptance except Mr. Roeding, who may be too busy to go! He will be strongly urged to assent by the other members of the committee. The committee will leave for the sugar districts this morning, and will return in time to report to the meeting next Thursday.

On September 28, the report by the committee, including W. W. Phillips, W. F. Chandler, W. M. Giffen and H. V. Rudy was discussed at a mass meeting of interested growers.

On the same day, September 28, 1905, *The Fresno Republican* posted the following small advertisement: "I WILL PAY $25 reward for information regarding to poisoning of my big black Newfoundland dog. Mrs. W. W. Phillips, 1407 M Street." This location at the corner of "M" and Tuolumne Streets was just a short walk from the bank.

On October 15, 1905, *The Fresno Morning Republican* reported:

The first anniversary dinner of the Sequoia Club was held last night in the banquet room of the club in the Forsythe building, and as usual when the members of that club get together there was a royal good time, and much good fellowship. Three score members and guests sat down to the banquet table and ate of the things named on the menu card - Blue Points on half shell, consomme de volialle aux quenelles, terrapin a la Maryland, and other dishes as attractive - and drank of the drinks - sauterne, zinfandel and champagne.

The table was in the shape of a horseshoe and the decorations were red. Stories were told and good-natured jokes and josh were passed about until the banquet dishes were cleared away and the smokes passed around.

Then came the toasts, every one of which was good. M. F. Tarpey, with his usual flow of wit, presided as toastmaster. Toasts were responded to by V. H. M. MacLymont, president of the Sequoia club, L. K. Rogers of the Las Palmas vineyard; Judge M. K. Harris, F. E. Cook, A. L. Hobbs, Dr. J. D. Davidson, Dr. J. B. Maupin, W. A. Sutherland, W. W. Phillips and L. O. Stephens.

On October 17, 1905, *The Fresno Morning Republican* offered a glimpse of a nice party organized for William's sister Laura:

Mr. and Mrs. W. W. Phillips entertained very charmingly at dinner and cards afterwards last night in honor of Mr. Phillips' sister, Mrs. W. L. Graves of Los Angeles. Mrs. Graves has been much feted during her short visit to Fresno and well does she deserve such flattering attentions, for she is a most interesting woman and extremely popular in the southern city, where she is a prominent society and club woman. Mrs. Graves holds a very warm spot in her heart for her Fresno friends, and they find her visits altogether too brief, and too infrequent. The affair last night was of the usual hospitable kind always to be met with in this cordial household. The decorations of the table were in roses and smilax simply arranged, the handsome toilettes of the ladies adding brilliancy to the scene. In the games of "500" following, General Muller[42] easily carried off first honors.

The guests with Mrs. Graves were: Mr. and Mrs. W. D. Coates, Dr. and Mrs. J. D. Davidson, Mr. and Mrs. Frank Short, General and Mrs. Muller, Collis Emmons.

Mrs. Graves will be the guest of honor at a luncheon today with Mrs. Frank Short as hostess and will leave tonight.

On October 18, 1905, *The Fresno Morning Republican* reported:

Mrs. Frank Short was hostess yesterday at a most attractive card luncheon complimentary to Mrs. W. L. Graves of Los Angeles, who concluded a week's visit with Mr. and Mrs. W. W. Phillips yesterday, when she left for the south. The morning from 10 o'clock until luncheon time was devoted to the fascinations of 500 and then the guests sat down to an exquisitely appointed luncheon table. In the center upon a center piece of beautiful lace was arranged a quantity of pink roses and the name cards bore the rose decoration. With the hostess at table were: Mesdames W. L. Graves, Everett Ames of Oakland, W. W. Phillips, Henry Avila, J. D. Davidson, M. W. Muller, DeWitt Gray, Frank Gray, F. M. Romain, L. L. Cory, Fred Dodd, E. E. Manheim, T. W. Patterson, Emory Donahoo.

Mrs. T. W. Patterson carried off first honors in the game and received a handsome vase of art glass as a prize. Mrs. Graves made the most lone hands and was rewarded with a berry spoon of artistic design.

On October 21, 1905, *The Fresno Morning Republican* wrote, "The Alpha Whist club met yesterday for the first time this season with the president, C. L. Walters. The reunion was a delightful one and every member was in her place. Mrs. W. L. Graves, has come up from Hanford where she has been attending her brother, Dixon L. Phillips, for a brief return visit with Mr. and Mrs. W. W. Phillips, was a guest of the afternoon."

On the letterhead of the Shaver Lake Fishing Club with "Headquarters: 1003 J Street, Fresno, Cal." and which contained a photograph of the members in front of the clubhouse, William wrote a typed letter on April 6, 1906 to Governor George C. Pardee, received by the Governor the next day:

My Dear Governor:

The annual outing of the Shaver Lake Fishing Club will commence on the 1st day of May. I wish to remind you that you are an honorary member of this club and that you will be very derelict in your duty, politically and socially, if you do not attend this outing with us. You will remember you promised me while at

Santa Rosa last December that you would come if you possibly could do so and the Club very much hopes that you can find it convenient to be with us. We anticipate a very large and happy time.

Permit me to say that this Club is a very influential one, comprising the most genial spirits in our city, and that we suggest that it might not come amiss to combine a little business with your pleasure in looking after your political fences in this County. I do not believe that our friend Frank Short will run against you and I suggested to him a few days ago that it would be well to make a combination with you and in case of your not being able to secure the nomination to make a fight for Short. You have a great many political friends here, who with Short out of the field, you will be able to secure the delegation from this County. In a quiet way I am doing all I can for you and wish you success.

Again hoping that you will be with us and trusting to hear from you very soon, I am,

Very truly yours,

W. W. Phillips

P.S. Your friend Gen. M. W. Muller concurs in the above letter and wished to be kindly remembered and says to be sure and come. W. W. P.

Shaver Lake Fishing Club

HEADQUARTERS: 1003 J STREET

Fresno, Cal.,

G. C. P.#2.

In a quiet way I am doing all I can for you and wish you success.

Again hoping that you will be with us and trusting to hear

from you very soon, I am,

Very truly yours,

W. W. Phillips

Your friend Gen. M. W. Muller concurs in the above letter and

d to be kindly remembered and says to be sure and come.

W. W. P.

Portion of letter From W. W. Phillips to Gov. George C. Pardee

April 6, 1906

Courtesy of the Bancroft Library, U. C. Berkeley, used with permission

On April 12, 1906, on letterhead from the Byron Hot Springs Resort, William wrote a second letter longhand in reply to the Governor which was received the following day:

Gov. Geo C. Pardee
My Dear Sir,

Yours of the 9th inst. was forwarded me here where I am recruiting for the trip to Shaver Lake.

I appreciate your position of trying to make a good Governor for the people and at the same time trying to have some enjoyments in life as you go along.

I am glad to know that you can be with us on the 3rd and should anything interfere to delay you please wire me from San Diego say on the 30th so I can arrange to have some of the members of the Club to go up with you.

I may possibly wait over for you myself, that will depend upon circumstances, as I am Commissary of the Club and will have to

look after the "issuer" man. The Stage leaves Fresno at 5 a.m. every day and arrives at the Lake at 5 p.m. the same day. I know that the members will be delighted to have you with us. I return home next Sunday and will inform the members of your coming.
Very truly yours,
W. W. Phillips

According to an article published in *The Fresno Bee* on April 13, 1937, the Shaver Lake Fishing Club, founded by General Muller, celebrated its 34th anniversary, suggesting that the club was formed in April 1903. An original group of eight members served as an advance team, who headed up to the lake to make all the necessary preparations for two-week stays by their invited guests. When the guests did arrive, they found sleeping tents plus two large army tents, one of which served as a dining room and the other which served as an assembly room. The chef from the Hughes Hotel would serve elegant meals in his white chef's cap and culinary aprons. C. B. Shaver built the first clubhouse in about 1904.

On April 18, 1906, San Francisco experienced a major earthquake which caused the death of some of my Santa Rosa family members. William was in San Francisco that day for the opening of the opera season, and along with other people from Fresno, camped out in Golden Gate Park while Chinatown was on fire. Along with others, including O. J. Woodward, he returned home that evening on the train. M. Theo Kearney was staying at The St. Francis Hotel and, after being awoken by the earthquake, he suffered a mild heart attack from fright. Mr. Kearney, who had plans to build a castle-like "Chateau Fresno" on his property in Fresno, died a month later on May 27, 1906 and left his entire estate to the University of California in the hope that it would one day become a university campus. Despite this opportunity, 100 years have passed and Fresno still does not have a UC campus.

On May 3, 1906, Governor George C. Pardee presumably arrived at the Shaver Lake Fishing Club, although arguably his plans may have been derailed by the San Francisco Earthquake. William also invited his cousin Harry's son, Maynard Dixon, to Shaver as well. In 1906 Maynard painted a very unusual painting of Shaver Lake and dedicated it in the lower left corner "To Cousin Willie and Cousin Bettie." This painting is now owned by my father and, to my knowledge, has never been exhibited.

William was first elected to the vestry of St. James Episcopal Church on May 21, 1906. He became Senior Warden in 1910 when St. James sent the proposal to the Bishop to become a pro-cathedral (which it became in 1911), and served as Senior Warden through 1916. St. James Episcopal Cathedral in Fresno, where I was confirmed, has in their records: "William also served on Fresno's first Board of Education and was a member of the Masonic Order."

Although this is the only reference to William having been a Mason, it must be noted that during the festivities of the commencement of construction of the courthouse in 1874, under the direction of the Masonic Order, Emily Phillips, William's mother played the organ and sang in the choir.

On September 5, 1906, *The Fresno Morning Republican* reported an explosion at the Calwa Winery while William's brother Burris was inside. They wrote:

> Gauger B. R. Phillips who had arrived only the night before from Hanford, was in the fortifying room in consultation with Special Agent Lemmy of the Internal Revenue Department. They started for a door immediately after the explosion, which brought a shower of dust and debris down upon them. At the door they were stopped by the falling of a huge water spout that came near striking them. Seeing that the air was full of flying boards and pieces of brick, they drew back into the fortifying room and remained there until it was safe to venture out. Mr. Phillips states that the explosion was followed by two minor crashes. His theory of the cause of the fire is that gases ignited from spontaneous combustion, due to the high temperature of the room.

On October 6, 1906, *The Fresno Morning Republican* reported:

TAXPAYERS LEAGUE SPONSORED BY
REAL ESTATE BOARD
W. W. Phillips and Judge M. K. Harris Give Cases of
Extravagance on Part of the Supervisors - The Judge No Longer
Thinks All Public Officials Are Honest - Unprofitable to Own
Property in Fresno With the High Taxes - Extravagance of
Supervisors Must Be Checked - Building Castles for Paupers.

The first steps toward the organization of a Taxpayers League, designed to watch the expenditure of public moneys by the Board of Supervisors of Fresno County and to take legal steps to stop what is deemed to be the extravagant use of these moneys, was taken last night at the regular meeting of the Fresno Realty Board. The Realty Board decided by a unanimous vote to stand sponsor for the movement and a committee was appointed to draw up a constitution of the new organization.

W. W. Phillips and Judge M. K. Harris, who have been prominently identified with the movement, made addresses last night and the statement was made by both these gentlemen that the organization will find plenty to do when once started. Mr. Phillips presented some figures gathered from the tax rolls of the county showing how much it has cost the taxpayers of the county to run during the past year and declared that they have nothing to show for the expenditure of this sum of money.

President DeWitt Gray of the Realty Board, called last night's meeting to order and introduced Mr. Phillips as the first speaker. Mr. Phillips outlined the new movement in brief and told of its purpose and the need for such an organization. "We are now paying a tax of 2 cents," said Mr. Phillips, "and this does not include the school taxes. Now, we don't want to criticize the actions of our Board of Supervisors, but if this organization is formed, we can act in an advisory capacity to the board. Instances can be cited where the public money was expended recklessly. Take for example the building of the county hospital. It started out with a contract for $40,000 and before the building was finished it cost the county $130,000. This was taken out of our year's tax rate when it should have been taken out of money collected from a bond issue.

"Then again, look at our roads. They are in very poor condition. The work that has been done on them in the past few years is simply repair work. They have no foundations. It would be a good plan to have an election at a general election to vote on the proposition of a bond issue for roads. The money expended annually at the present time on repairs would more than pay the interest as such a bond issue.

"The Board of Supervisors propose to build an almshouse. They tell us that it will cost $30,000, but it will likely cost the county $50,000 before they are through with it. There has been an increase of $1,800,000 in the assessed valuation of the county property this year and still we have a higher tax rate. The Board of Supervisors have this money promised already for they seem to know where it is to be expended. If there is any attempt to expend this money lavishly maybe the Taxpayers League can stop it by advising with the board against it. If not we can do as we have done in the past, take our case to the courts. We won the case against the supervisors when they proposed to expend an enormous sum of money to fix up the courthouse park and we can win again.

"There is no reason why I, who was active in the courthouse case, should have to bear the odium of such a movement and the labor. There is no reason why any individual citizen should have to bear this responsibility. If we organize a Taxpayers League we can have funds for this purpose and we can pay our attorneys and take the case to the courts as a unit. There is one thing that we can be thankful for, and that is that the courts of this country are ever ready to listen to the taxpayers in questions of the expenditure of public moneys. The increase in the tax rate of this county should bring a cry of protest from every taxpayer in the county."

Mr. Phillips then read a statement of how much the county government has cost for the fiscal year just finished. His figures, he said, were collected at the auditor's office. [The paper then listed the figures reported by William.]

"What do we get for the expenditure of this money?" asked Mr. Phillips. We have no roads to speak of. The roads of the County are not oiled, except just outside the city. There is not a single member of the Board of Supervisors who is a road expert. The supervisors have no knowledge of how to build a proper road. Is there no limit to this sort of thing? I have been waiting for the time when prosperity in this county would make for a lower tax rate. I think that the limit has been reached now. Sonoma County has about the same amount of taxable property as Fresno County and has a lower tax rate. They have good roads there, too. It's about time that the taxpayers of this county began to wake up and take the thing into their own hands." [Judge M. K, Harris then made a similar speech].

On motion of DeWitt Gray, Mr. Phillips was appointed chairman of a committee of three to prepare a constitution for the Taxpayers League. Mr. Phillips was empowered to appoint two other members of the Realty Board to act with him and appointed J. M. Collier and F. M. Chittenden. The constitution will be prepared and acted upon by the Realty Board in the near future.

When it is finally adopted, a campaign will be made in all parts of the county for members and funds provided with which to carry on the work of the league.

The Fresno Morning Republican reported on October 9, 1906:

NEW LEAGUE AFTER CITY
Tax Payers League to Investigate City Government.
Meeting of Committee On Organization Called for
Today - Large Membership promised

That the proposed Taxpayers League will investigate the expenditures of city as well as county funds is the statement of W. W. Phillips, who has been prominently identified with the movement and who is chairman of the committee which will draw up the constitution of the new organization.

"We do not intend to confine ourselves to the county government by any means," said Mr. Phillips last night, "but we shall look after the city officials as well. It is as common for city officials to practice dishonesty as it is for county officials and we would not be justified in confining our attention to the county government.

"I am not conversant with the affairs of the city government enough at this time to state whether or not I think that there are any extravagances in the present administration, but if anyone thinks that there are we will have an organization that will look into the matter for him and prosecute the case if there is any truth in his suspicions."

The committee appointed at the last meeting of the Realty Federation to draw up a constitution for the new body will have its first meeting today. The constitution will be presented to the

Realty Board at its next meeting and after its adoption a campaign for membership will be started. "I have had a great many people volunteer to come into the organization," said Mr. Phillips last night, "and we will have a very large membership."

On November 3, 1906, *The Fresno Morning Republican* reported, "Miss Phillips of Hanford, daughter of Mr. and Mrs. Dixon Phillips, is visiting her aunt and uncle, Mr. and Mrs. W. W. Phillips this week."

On November 18, 1906, *The Fresno Morning Republican* reported: "Miss Gotea Dozier of Oakland is visiting her aunt and uncle Mr. and Mrs. W. W. Phillips, for a few weeks. Yesterday, Mr. and Mrs. Phillips, with Miss Dozier and Dr. David Anderson, a cousin of Mrs. Phillips, from Santa Rosa, drove to Sanger for a day's visit with Dr. and Mrs. C. B. Pressley[43]."

In 1906 William served as Foreman on the Grand Jury. Apparently, this made some people nervous. As *The Fresno Morning Republican* reported on November 22, 1906:

There is evidence that the promised activity of the newly impaneled grand jury has put a number of people to thinking. In fact there is considerable trepidation with regard to what may happen should a careful investigation be made of public expenditures along the county road funds. In particular, a story spread abroad yesterday afternoon that attempts would be made to discredit the standing of the grand jury in advance, by attacking its members, especially its foreman, W. W. Phillips.

Some enemies of the latter gentleman discovered that Mr. Phillips some time ago gave a deed to his wife to his ranch on the San Joaquin River. They jumped to the conclusion that they might show that one of the main organizers of the Taxpayers League and the foreman of the new grand jury was not a taxpayer himself and had falsely represented himself as such on the impanelment of the latter body. An investigation of the books in the Recorder's Office confirmed the story about the transfer of the River Ranch to Mrs. Phillips.

Mr. Phillips was very indignant when he heard about this proposition. "I should think I am a taxpayer," he said. "Just a few days ago I paid in several hundred dollars to the Tax Collectors Office. It is true I deeded the River Ranch to my wife, but I own in my own name two ranches, one in the Fort Washington school district and the other near Sanger. I also have owned in my own name for several years a building on I street, 50 by 150 feet in dimension."

On November 24, 1906, *The Fresno Morning Republican* reported about William's certainty of graft within the county over the cost of roads work:

The Board of Supervisors yesterday allowed seventy-five of the bills turned in by Supervisor Burleigh's district for work upon the roads of the district during the last two months. The total amount of the bills allowed yesterday is $3,973.73. The bills were allowed by the county lawmakers only after obtaining a written opinion from Deputy District Attorney Kauke that the bills are legal claims against the county.

When informed last night that the supervisors had allowed some of the Burleigh bills, Foreman Phillips of the grand jury stated that that body would call for the bills in question and make an investigation. He intimated that a fund would be raised by the Taxpayers League to prosecute the guilty men if any fraud has been committed in this transaction. Mr. Phillips also intimated that indictments might follow the deliberations of the county in inquisitorial body.

Phillips Certain of Graft.

When informed last night that the supervisors had passed some of Burleigh's notorious bills, Foreman Phillips of the grand jury said that the body would call on the auditor for the bills and make an investigation of the legality of the bills. If it is found that there is any question as to the genuineness of any bills, the Taxpayers League will be called upon to furnish a fund for the looking up of evidence that may lead to indictments of several persons who it is alleged, have turned in bills for work that they did not do.

"This sort of thing is very hard to get at," said Mr. Phillips last night. "As I understand it the bills are not itemized and it is almost impossible to get any evidence of fraud in any particular instance. Of course, if anyone knows that the county has been defrauded in any instance by the bills paid today, it is his duty to appear before the grand jury and let us know the facts. But if we can get on the trail of any fraud, I shall call upon the officials of the Taxpayers League to furnish the funds with which to make a thorough

investigation of the charges that have been so frequently made in
the last few weeks, and no guilty man will escape. The matter will
be thoroughly gone into. In San Francisco they have a fund raised
by a few public spirited citizens and detectives have been
employed to ferret out the graft. I am certain that there is graft in
Fresno County and if we can get the money to investigate it, we
may have some indictments here."

In a separate article from the same day's paper, *The Fresno
Morning Republican* reported:

> After spending the entire day in a minute examination of the
> plans before the supervisors for the construction of the proposed
> almshouse the grand jury yesterday announced their approval of
> the project and through their foreman, W. W. Phillips, officially
> warned the supervisors not to exceed the limit of $30,000 provided
> for in the tax levy for the almshouse.
>
> The members of the grand jury expressed the opinion that from
> what they had seen in their visit to the county poorfarm day before
> yesterday there is a great need of an almshouse in the county and
> that if the structure would not cost the county several times what
> the specifications called for it will be a good thing for this county.
>
> In reporting the result of the day's investigations to the
> supervisors yesterday afternoon, Foreman Phillips said: "The
> grand jury fully approves of the idea of building an almshouse, but
> we warn you however, to keep within the limit of the amount set
> aside by this board for the building and to see to it that there will
> not be bills of extras so that the cost will not exceed $30,000. We
> have examined the plans and any action that you may take in
> regard to their acceptance will meet with the approval of the grand
> jury. We have a preference as to plans, but will not express that
> unless the board desires."

On December 20, 1906, *The Fresno Morning Republican*
wrote a lengthy story titled, "County Salary Question Considered
By Officials." Within the lengthy story, they wrote about a
meeting which took place:

> After some informal discussions while the men were gathering,
> W. W. Phillips was elected chairman of the meeting. "I appreciate
> the honor you do me, gentlemen," he said, "in choosing me to

preside tonight. I feel this the more so, because I understand, I think, the importance of the work of determining some of the financial questions that now confront the county legislators. I regret the necessity that has kept a number of the members of the executive committee of the Taxpayers League away from this meeting tonight.

"The matter of the salaries that shall be fixed by the Fresno representatives in the next legislature in the county government bill they propose to introduce is extremely important. Some salaries should possibly be lower than they are at present. Others should be higher. In the course of my duties as foreman of the grand jury I have noticed some positions that are certainly underpaid. In particular I might mention the position of cashier and chief deputy in the office of the tax collector. Only $100 a month is paid at present, when I should think that for a man who handles as much money as he does and carries the responsibility, $150 would be much more just. Then again, the chief deputy in the office of the assessor gets but $80 from the county. It should be higher.

"We should give special attention to the office of the assessor. This is the basis of all the county financial system, for upon the good work of the assessor depends the amount of taxes that are paid in and the justice of relative assessments. It certainly is a fright the way the assessments have been made the last few years. The personal property assessment has been ridiculously low. It amounted to less than $200,000, while there are $8,000,000 in the banks of this city.

"There is not a single corporation franchise tax in this county that is assessed, as far as I have been able to discover. We have immense corporations here that pay big revenues, and which in other counties of the state would pay a good tax. The gas company pays no tax here, and we pay $1.25 a thousand for the gas, while in Los Angeles, the company pays a franchise tax, and the people have gas for 65 cents.

"The taxation of merchandise in this city is a farce. Not a tenth of the valuation of the property is taxed. You see big dray horses that some of these stores have on the street, worth at least $400 a span, and valued on the assessor's books at $15 apiece. At the same time farmers have to pay on an assessment of $40 apiece for scrubby horses.

"There is not a bit of doubt in my mind that if the assessments on property valuations in this county were to be equitably made, there would not be one-tenth the complaint there is now regarding the assessments, and at the same time we would not have to pay more than $1.50 on the hundred. I recognize that some changes should be made in the law. For instance it is perfectly natural for men to feel that they are overtaxed should they turn in money statements. Suppose a man has $1,000 in the bank and a $1,000 lot. The money is assessed for $1,000, while the lot in assessed for, say, $600. As near as possible all the tax should be paid equitably.

"But there is no question that the salary of the assessor is too low. In my personal opinion, a good man for that office should demand about $4,000, or if he receives commissions, $3,000. There is room at the present time (I make no accusations) for graft in the way of the collection of personal property tax in advance from property owners that have plenty of real estate as security. The law does not contemplate that any such thing should be done. There are firms in this city that so pay, as do also Miller & Lux, and possibly others.

"Finally, the pay of the justices and constables should be on a salary basis. I am informed that at the present time the justice of the peace in this city has been drawing as much from the county treasury as the salary of both Superior judges amounts to. The law, of course, does not contemplate anything of the sort. Just what these salaries should be the Taxpayers League has not cared to say. We think that the fixing of salaries is entirely within the jurisdiction of our legislators, two of whom are themselves lawyers. We recognize the fact that the cost of living has increased, and that the duties required of many of these officers has increased. The matter is now before you gentlemen for consideration."

Later, in the same article, *The Fresno Morning Republican* wrote:

Mr. Phillips, on the other hand, thought the supervisors should give more of their time to the inspection of bills, and less to road work. In fact, he was in favor of not having the road work in charge of supervisors any more but giving it in charge of two or three commissioners, who should let the building of all new roads by contract. He pointed out that nearly a half of the expense of carrying on the county government is due to money spent on roads.

Road Funds for Corruption.

"I understand," he said, "that charges are made that money is spent freely for road work that is really used to influence elections. I am not making these charges myself. I do not have to, for the members of the board make them against each other. But there are certainly some big leaks in this roads business, and they should be stopped."

The article also mentioned that "Mr. Phillips pointed out that the pay of jurors $2 a day, is inadequate for those that come from a distance to serve in court."

On December 28, 1906, *The Fresno Morning Republican* reported how William's brother Burris narrowly escaped being killed five years previously:

The examination for insanity of Gus Itter, who created considerable excitement Wednesday morning at the county hospital and later on Ventura Avenue by going on a rampage with little clothes on his body, was held yesterday before Judge Murphy of Inyo County, sitting for Judge Church. Dr. G. L. Long conducted the medical part of the examination. The testimony showed that Itter was of a destructive nature and when he had imbibed too much port and sherry would not hesitate to take a shot at a person. The fact was brought out that Itter had formerly been employed at the Eggers and other vineyards near Fresno, and had been in the habit of drinking large quantities of wine and brandy each day. He drank about two and a half gallons of port wine and one-half a gallon of brandy each day for months at a time, and occasionally would get crazy drunk and go on a rampage.

In 1901 while Itter was employed at the Eggers vineyard east of this city, he went on one of his sprees and fired two shots at Burris Phillips. The two shots missed their mark, fortunately for Phillips, and Itter afterwards served four years in the state penitentiary at San Quentin for his offense. Superintendent Joseph H. Bland of the county hospital testified that Itter was generally of a depressed and melancholy nature while in the institution, except in his periods of violence; that he appeared to be depressed, and constantly studying over something, which he could not understand. In the course of the testimony it was also brought out that Itter was committed to the Stockton Insane asylum in 1899 and spent six weeks at that Institution, being then discharged as cured.

Itter was declared yesterday to be insane and was ordered committed again to the Stockton asylum. He will be taken to that institution this morning.

William was on the Board of Directors of the Alaska United Copper Exploration Company, according to an advertisement in *The Washington Post* on March 24, 1907. The advertisement referred to him as "Hon. W. W. Phillips of Fresno."

On November 10, 1907, *The Fresno Morning Republican* reported how William and Elizabeth entertained Julia Dixon[44] with twenty-seven guests for an impromptu and informal dinner:

> Mr. and Mrs. W. W. Phillips entertained some young people and a few young married people at cards last evening complimentary to their young cousin Miss Julia Dixon of Merced, who is their guest. The briefness of Miss Dixon's visit made it imperative to give something quite impromptu and informal, but the Phillips' hospitality is equal to any emergency and their informal gatherings are quite as jolly and the welcome just as warm as in their more formal entertainments. In fact the latch string to their door is always out and one may always be assured of finding a cordial welcome within. Some very handsome chrysanthemums graced the rooms and in the dining room a buffet supper was served, the table looking most lovely in decoration of white flowers and smilax.
>
> Among those asked to meet this charming visitor were Mr. and Mrs. W. J. Cleary, Mr. and Mrs. Arthur Anderson, Misses Lillian Dunn, Elsie Smith, Eugenia Miller, Adeline Thornton, Zoe Eden, Aimee Newman, Imo Dickinson, Mattie and Sadie Lowden, Helen Sprague of Visalia, Messrs. James Gearbart, Butler Minor, Fred McKenzie, Emil Gundelfinger, J. C. Kuster, Jack Sprague, John Hutchinson, A. W. Goodfellow, Clarence Edwards, Will Holmes, Russell Ritchie, Dan Brown, W. A. Veith.

On November 15, 1907, *The Fresno Morning Republican* reported about a dinner party which included Julia Dixon, George Mordecai, Mr. and Mrs. C. B. Shaver[45] and Fulton G. Berry[46]:

> Mr. and Mrs. William Walker Phillips entertained with a very enchanting little dinner last night covers being laid for twelve. The Phillips' dinners are noted for their jollity and pleasant informality

which seems characteristic of the Southern hostess of which Mrs. Phillips is a delightful type. The table was a picturesque vision in delicate pink chrysanthemums and autumn leaves. Those seated at the table with Mr. and Mrs. Phillips were: Mr. and Mrs. C. B. Shaver, Mr. and Mrs. Harvey Swift, Miss Nellie Borden, Miss Maud Muller, Miss Julia Dixon of Merced, Messrs. Fulton G. Berry, Collis H. Emmons, George Mordecai of Madera.

On November 29, 1907, *The Fresno Morning Republican* reported: "Mr. and Mrs. Dixon L. Phillips of Hanford were Thanksgiving Day guests of the former's brother and his wife, Mr. and Mrs. W. W. Phillips. They will remain over the weekend, the party being augmented tomorrow, by Mr. and Mrs. Dallas of Merced, who are coming down for the Elks' Memorial Service at the Barton[47] on Sunday, and will be guests under the hospitable Phillips roof-tree during their stay."

On December 2, 1907, *The Fresno Morning Republican* made mention of the fact that William was on the committee in charge of memorial exercises of the Fresno Lodge No. 439, of the Benevolent Protective Order of Elks. The memorial service held that day was to honor Elks members who had passed away between 1901 and 1907.

The Fresno Morning Republican reported on December 14, 1907: "W. W. and E. B. Phillips have mortgaged to Alice F. Williams for $3,000 for one year eight lots in block 2 of Miller and Northcraft addition. A deed by William G. and Mildred Uridge conveyed the lots to Phillips."

On December 28, 1907, *The Fresno Morning Republican* reported, "Mrs. W. W. Phillips has gone to Santa Rosa, where she was summoned to the bedside of her mother, who is most seriously ill." Two days later, on December 30, 1907, Elizabeth's mother Julia Caroline Burckmyer Pressley passed away.

On November 28, 1909, *The Fresno Morning Republican* reported:

The North Park Bridge Club, composed of members from this fashionable residence section, has renewed its meetings for the season, the club holding its first affair with Mr. and Mrs. W. L.

Coates. The meetings are to be fortnightly, the next one being with Mr. and Mrs. W. W. Phillips next Saturday night.

The members of this cozy little organization include Mr. and Mrs. Coates, Mr. and Mrs. W. W. Phillips, Mr. and Mrs. Herbert Miles, Mr. and Mrs. M. B. Harris, Mr. and Mrs. S. L. Strother, Mr. and Mrs. F. E. Hansen.

On April 5, 1908, *The Oakland Tribune* reported:

VINE INDUSTRY TO BE PROTECTED

Rev. Harvey S. Hanson Talks on Temperance Versus Prohibition.

FRESNO, April 4. - At a mass meeting of vine growers held today in the Barton Opera House, M. F. Tarpey was chosen as chairman ex-officio of a committee of five to effect permanent organization, the object being the protection of the industry. The other members of the committee will be announced later.

A committee consisting of W. W. Phillips, V. H. M. McLymont, A. W. Goodfellow, Judge C. C. Goodwin, W. D. Basingame, W. T. Mattingly and Frank Helm was appointed on resolutions. Tarpey suggested that offices for the collection and dissemination of statistics pertaining to the vine industry of the state should be maintained in the principal towns.

Rev. Harvey S. Hanson, an Episcopal clergyman, argued in favor of temperance versus prohibition, alleging that if a man is prevented from drinking he will crave liquor all the more. Rev. Duncan Wallace of the Cumberland Presbyterian Church said he believed in giving the wine men a chance to make good the assertion that the use of wine instead of strong drink will further the end of temperance. He cautioned the wine men not to become entangled with the saloon question, stating that in his opinion the open saloon is doomed, and rightly so. Both pastors were loudly applauded.

Late this afternoon the mass meeting of vineyardists appointed the following committee on permanent organization: M. F. Tarpey, chairman; L. R. Rogers, George P. Beveridge, Harvey Swift, William Forsythe, A. G. Wishon and O. J. Woodward, who are among the most prominent citizens in the county.

On December 4, 1908, *The Fresno Morning Republican* mentioned in an article about St. James Episcopal Church that

William was elected to the vestry during the annual parish meeting.

On November 4, 1909, *The Fresno Morning Republican* reported:

> TOBACCO GROWING IMPRESSES PHILLIPS
> Local Man Convinced That Plant Will Do
> Well in This Vicinity
>
> President W. W. Phillips of the Boosters Club has returned from Los Angeles where he inspected the plantations of Turkish tobacco now growing in the south. He found laborers at work harvesting the second crop of tobacco which had been planted last June. The Fresno man also found a warehouse filled with the highest quality Turkish tobacco and was informed that Fresno's land and climate were better adapted to growing the tobacco than in the south. It is stated that there the heavy fogs have a tendency to burn holes through the leaves of the tender plants. Mr. Phillips has been asked to become a member of the board of directors of the new local company being formed to grow tobacco and will probably accept. Headquarters are soon to be established here and plowing is to start in the near future at Clark's Valley in the Mount Campbell vicinity.

In 1910 William decided he could afford a trip to Europe and his son John and wife "Bettie" eagerly agreed to go. They took the train on March 10, 1910 to New York for a Mediterranean cruise, and had a lovely time, enjoying the experience immensely. While in Egypt, William and his son John were individually photographed in Bedouin costumes. All three in the family were also photographed on camels in front of the pyramids.

S.S. George Washington, circa 1915
© Mystic Seaport, Rosenfeld Collection, Mystic, CT
Photo used with permission

On their return trip home from Cherbourg, France, they sailed on a beautiful steamer called the S.S. George Washington[48] built just two years previously in 1908. One morning as William and his wife Bettie were "promenading" on the deck, Mrs. Grover Cleveland was pointed out to them.

William decided to introduce himself since he had met and supported her husband. While she was lying in her steamer chair, he left his wife Bettie in the Ladies Lounge and went over to ask her, "Are you Mrs. Cleveland?"

"Yes," she answered. William then told her his name, that he was a delegate at the Convention in Chicago and helped nominate her husband for President in 1892. President Cleveland had died nearly two years earlier.

William asked her if she had ever heard what Burke Cockran had said about her, after he had made a very eloquent speech against her husband's nomination, advocating instead for the nomination of David B. Hill. She said "no," she had not heard it. William then told her that when Mr. Cockran was informed that Mrs. Cleveland had heard over the wire all that he had said against her husband, his reply was, "had I known that, what nice things I would have said about Mrs. Cleveland." She was very pleased to hear the story and remarked, "he was capable of saying that and was a gallant gentleman."

She then asked William to introduce his wife, which he did. They were very pleased with their new acquaintance and William thought Mrs. Cleveland was "without question the handsomest lady that ever graced the White House."

Frances Folsom Cleveland (1864-1947)
Photo courtesy of the Library of Congress

That evening Mrs. Cleveland brought her two daughters and introduced them as well. William danced with both and found them to be "good dancers and very pleasant girls."

On June 18, 1912, *The Fresno Republican* reported: "W. W. Phillips, the president of the Fresno Chamber of Commerce, was to leave to inspect newly improved roads in the San Francisco area as part of a study intended to better the highways of this area."

On January 31, 1913, William went to a banquet held at the Hotel Fresno for the Shaver Lake Fishing Club which was established in 1903, the year after John S. Eastwood of the Pacific Light and Power Company selected Big Creek as the site for a power plant, following surveys made in 1884.

William Walker Phillips
seated in the center next to a man holding a fish
Shaver Lake Fishing Club, Shaver Lake, California, circa 1911-1913
Photo courtesy of the Shaver Lake Fishing Club

William Walker Phillips
(close-up from same photograph)

William Walker Phillips at the top of the stairs
Shaver Lake Fishing Club, Shaver Lake, California, circa 1911-1913
Photo courtesy of the Shaver Lake Fishing Club

Around 1904, C. B. Shaver constructed a club house which was reduced to kindling by the snow from the following winter. The membership was assessed, and a new more durable club house building and bunk house was then constructed.

During these days, the way to get to Shaver Lake was by stage coach. The group of doctors, dentists, lawyers and businessmen who gathered at 4:30 a.m. for the ride up to Shaver Lake presented themselves as a "disreputable bunch of bums. In their mountain clothes, they were a happy and hilarious gang, full of anticipation of the fun that awaited them at the lake." One member who was a judge and accused by another member of some misdemeanor replied, "this court recognizes no law above the Tollhouse," a phrase which forever characterized these annual summer outings.

Every year there was a competition to see who could catch the largest fish with the winner to receive a new fishing pole. General Muller had the reputation of being the worst fisherman of the bunch. Yet, one day while trolling on the lake, Muller pulled in a three pound trout. E. L. Chaddock pulled in a clearly smaller trout later the same afternoon. Chaddock seized upon the opportunity to play a little hoax on Muller. He had the chef pour army shot down the trout's throat until the fish weighed about an eighth of a pound more than Muller's. To Muller's utter disbelief and grave disappointment, Chaddock was declared the winner of the new fishing pole. Later in the evening, the chef came out and suddenly exposed the hoax revealing the army shot he had discovered in the belly of the trout to which General Muller let out a shriek of joy that shook the building when he realized that he was indeed that year's winner[49].

The location of the original club was on land that is now under lake water once the big dam at Shaver Lake was completed in 1927. The club then went dormant for a while until an 18-acre tract was set aside for the incorporated club members. A new clubhouse was built in about 1938 but was demolished in 1950. Since then, most families now have individual cabins and the clubhouse was never replaced.

William Walker Phillips at top right
Shaver Lake Fishing Club, Shaver Lake, California, circa 1911-1913
Photo courtesy of the Shaver Lake Fishing Club

William Walker Phillips, center
Club members without their hats
Shaver Lake Fishing Club, Shaver Lake, California, circa 1911-1913
Photo courtesy of the Shaver Lake Fishing Club

William Walker Phillips, center
Club members with their hats
Shaver Lake Fishing Club, Shaver Lake, California, circa 1911-1913
Photo courtesy of the Shaver Lake Fishing Club

William Walker Phillips, top left
Shaver Lake Fishing Club, Shaver Lake, California, circa 1911-1913
Photo courtesy of the Shaver Lake Fishing Club

In 1911, the Big Creek-San Joaquin Project began, one of the largest water power projects in the world and an engineering achievement matched only by the building of the Panama Canal in those days. Huntington Lake (named after Henry Huntington) and Shaver Lake (named after C. B. Shaver who created the Fresno Flume and Irrigation Company) were artificially created to generate hydroelectric power. The dam at Shaver Lake was completed in 1927, and by 1929, three lakes and six dams were created. Huntington founded the Pacific Electric Railway, centered in Los Angeles, and developed an extensive intercity transit system to transport citizens from his suburban housing developments to their jobs in the city. Huntington needed a massive amount of electric power, which Big Creek ultimately provided.

Huntington Lake as a community was created in 1913, with Cedar Crest built in 1923 and Lakeshore in 1924[50]. The old lodge at Lakeshore still stands but today is badly in need of repair. I certainly hope that this landmark for so many Fresno families will be spared. Generations in my family and the Jertberg family spent many evenings at the lodge for social gatherings and teen dances which continue to this day. Cedar Crest had an old movie projector outside by a camp fire where we generally saw the same film repeatedly, for example, the 1970 film, "A Man Called Horse," starring Richard Harris. The Cedar Crest owners still have the old projector, but spare parts are now hard to find.

Huntington Lake is an especially great sailing lake, and we spent many summers sailing around the island, past the dams, down to Lakeshore and back and stopping by different docks to visit with friends. As a young boy, I sailed a "Flipper" in the High Sierra Regatta held at Huntington Lake every July since 1953. I distinctly remember yelling "starboard" from my little Flipper to an enormous sailing yacht that hovered over me. They yielded, but it was the laugh of the regatta that year in the mid-1970s.

According to an article about the Shaver Lake Fishing Club that appeared in *The Fresno Bee Sports* on April 10, 1937: "The club was organized in 1903 when a group including General M. W. Muller, Dr. A. J. Pedlar, J. Ed Hughes and Judges M. K. Harris and W. D. Crichton drew up organization plans." The article continued: "The first outing was held under tents on the old site at the lake and a clubhouse was built and later went under water when the dam was constructed at the resort."

On June 19, 1913, the *Oakland Tribune* reported that 44 delegates from around the state of California met at the Hotel Del Coronado in San Diego to form the California Celebrations Committee to promote fairs throughout the state. M. F. Tarpey was the President and W. W. Phillips was a delegate from district five representing Madera, Merced and Fresno.

While President of the Fresno County Chamber of Commerce from 1912 to 1915, *The Fresno Morning Republican* reported on September 4, 1913 about the recent work of the Chamber for the benefit of its members. Of particular interest was the charge by the editor of *The Fresno Evening Herald* that the advertising funds spent by the Chamber of Commerce, particularly in favor of *Sunset Magazine*, were "wasted" and that newspaper advertising would have been cheaper. One board member took this to suggest that the board members had their hands in the tax-payers pockets. This board member responded by calling the editor a "liar and a scoundrel" and threatened to "punch his face in." *The Fresno Morning Republican* wrote:

PRESIDENT W. W. PHILLIPS REVIEWS WORK OF CHAMBER OF COMMERCE FOR COUNTY

Gentlemen of the Chamber of Commerce:

This being the first meeting of the board since our adjournment last June, I think it is incumbent upon me at this time to advise you of matters which have come up for action, but could not be taken up by the board, as nearly all of the members were away on their summer vacation.

The good roads petitions, after considerable hard work, were sufficient in names, to present to our board of supervisors, who received them in a friendly spirit, then referred them to the county clerk for verification.

Sufficient names could not be verified, as those securing the signatures had in several instances failed to have the signer place opposite his name his place of residence, though the column for that purpose was plainly printed on the petition. This of course necessitates additional signatures.

The district attorney now advises that the voting precinct of each signature should be put opposite the name, and expressed regret that he did not advise us of the necessity of doing so in the first instance. I have instructed our secretary to draw up new petitions indicating the residence, voting precinct and description of the realty holdings, and I would advise that we take some action at this time toward securing these signatures.

There is no question in my judgment that the people of this county desire permanent roads built, and will at the proper time give a hearty support to a bond issue.

In the diversion of the state highway matter, this chamber was waited upon by a committee representing the Chambers of Commerce at Selma and Kingsburg, and urged to use its best influence to defeat the proposed diversion, which, I am frank to say, would have done a great injustice to the people of these two towns, and would have put a burden of fifty or sixty thousand dollars upon our taxpayers, to accommodate the people of an adjoining county. Your president was urged to go before the State advisory board and protest against this injustice, which he did; and I am pleased to say that, the advisory board unanimously accepted our views in the matter and have ordered the highway built on the direct and most economical route; that is along the line of the Southern Pacific Railroad[51]. I hope that the action of your president in this matter meets with your approval.

In the matter of the proposed increase of internal revenue tax on brandies necessary to fortify our wines, this chamber was suddenly confronted with a question that was vital to the welfare of thousands of grape growers in this county, and we put ourselves in communication at once with our senators and representatives and members of the Senate Finance Committee, and protested against this tax as vigorously as we knew how.

Subsequently we called several meetings of the wine grape growers and wine manufacturers, which resulted in the sending of the Hon. M. F. Tarpey to Washington to plead against the injustice of this tax. Our latest information from Mr. Tarpey is that there is a strong probability that the Pomerene Amendment will be withdrawn.

No doubt you are aware that our chamber has been sharply criticized by those who have signally failed to secure a division of the county appropriation. A new tack was taken and a meeting was held by six gentlemen representing their several localities, for the purpose of forming a county development board. We were requested by the secretary of the Sanger Chamber of Commerce, and no one else, to send a representative to that meeting. As a quorum of the chamber was not in our county, and personally, its object not meeting with my approval, (for I believe its purposes were to supersede the work of this chamber). I did not attend. For the first time complaints were made that their several localities were not receiving their share of advertising. If anyone interested in this matter will go through the excellent booklet recently published by this chamber, he can see for himself how untrue the statement is. Never has a complaint been made to this body, for the simple reason that there were no just grounds for one.

Should our board of supervisors (who have the sole jurisdiction of this advertising fund) see fit to have this chamber take counsel or advice from any body of citizens, as to the best methods of handling this fund, I am quite sure no objection will be raised by this chamber. We shall pay no attention to carping criticism or unjust attacks, but will continue (at least until our term expires) to carry on the work of this chamber for the best interests of all the people of our county.

Let me assure you that our efforts in the past are duly appreciated, for I have had a great many people to assure me of their cordial support and high appreciation of our work. Your members of the advertising committee possibly do not know of the attacks made upon you by our evening paper. We have been told in several editorials that you did not know how to advertise, and "that you were too old to learn, and that you have frittered away 75 per cent of the funds." As this board shares with you in this attack, I wish to say, as the one who appointed you, that I have the same confidence in your ability now that I have always had, and I trust these foolish charges will not disturb you in the least in your future efforts.

We have a paying membership of 341 members, who contributed last year $4,640 as an additional fund for the publicity work of this chamber, and if, by chance, we have made more mention of the city of Fresno than was our due, (as charged by some of our critics) I trust when those critics read these figures they will agree that we were doing the fair thing in giving our city the prominence it has had in our literature.

DISTRIBUTION OF ADVERTISING FUND

Sunset Magazine	4,000.00
Maintenance San Francisco exhibit	300.00
Maintenance Oakland exhibit	67.50
County fair	33.75
State fair (won first prize)	800.00
Exhibit expense	92.00
Orange show (National) won second prize	300.00
Advertising Chicago Tribune	250.00
Advertising Little Farms Magazine	250.00
Advertising Republican	191.00
Duplicator	31.30
Additional advertising supplies	281.50
Total	6,597.05

The contract with Sunset Publishing Company noted above for $4,000 includes the following: 20,000 copies of a 64-page illustrated booklet advertising the county and the cities therein; 20,000 copies of a 6-page colonist folder; four-page illustrated articles in *Sunset*, *Pacific Monthly* and *Sunset Abroad*; privilege of maintaining exhibit in Pacific Electric Building at Los Angeles, with fruits preserved and jars furnished free of charge, and all expenses paid incident to the care and maintenance of the exhibit; personal representation at various eastern land shows, with the *Sunset* special lecture bureau service and at all eastern information bureaus, and the privilege of using 60,000 names received from eastern advertising.

This indicates that the money was well and profitably spent, and not merely frittered away.

Respectfully submitted.

W. W. Phillips,

President.

On September 16, 1913, *The Fresno Morning Republican* reported:

COMMERCE CHAMBER THANKS
BRANDY TAX WORKERS
Telegrams of Commendation Sent To
Washington By Officials
Senators, Congressmen and Special Lobbyists
Included In List

To show the appreciation of Fresno County for the throwing out of the Pomerene Amendment that proposed a tax of $1.10 a gallon on the brandy used in the fortification of sweet wines which was brought about by the work of the California congressmen and senators at Washington, aided by special committee sent East by the wine grape growers of this state, the Fresno County Chamber of Commerce sent a series of telegrams last night to them, commending those who were instrumental in having the measure thrown out, for the good work that they did.

These telegrams were sent by W. W. Phillips and William Robertson, respectively president and secretary of the Chamber of Commerce, from Sacramento, where they are in attendance of the state fair which is in session there.

Copies of the telegrams sent East were also sent in a special dispatch to *The Republican* for publication by W. W. Phillips.

The telegrams of commendation were as follows:

Senator Works, Washington, D. C.

Our people appreciate your interest in their behalf on tariff bill.
(Signed)
FRESNO COUNTY CHAMBER OF COMMERCE.
W. W. Phillips, President.
William Robertson, Sec'y.
(Same to Senator Perkins, Washington, D. C.)

Honorable Denver S. Church, Congress, Washington, D. C.

Our people are proud of your splendid fight and deeply
appreciate your manly courage and perseverance.   Nothing
succeeds like success if it does take hard work to win.   Kindly
convey our heart-felt appreciation to your colleagues of the House
and members of the Senate.
(Signed)
FRESNO COUNTY CHAMBER OF COMMERCE.
W. W. Phillips, President.
William Robertson, Sec'y.

Honorable J. C. Needham, Washington, D. C.

Our people appreciate your splendid self-denial and great work
in their behalf. Accept the thanks and the hope that your path may
be strewed with honor in the future as it has been in the past.
(Signed)
FRESNO COUNTY CHAMBER OF COMMERCE.
W. W. Phillips, President.
William Robertson, Sec'y.

Honorable Theodore Bell, Washington, D. C.

Please accept our thanks for your splendid work in our behalf
and kindly convey the same to our friends in the House and Senate.
California will never forget the great fight you made in its behalf.
(Signed)
FRESNO COUNTY CHAMBER OF COMMERCE.
W. W. Phillips, President.
William Robertson, Sec'y.

Honorable M. F. Tarpey, Washington D. C.

Please convey to our friends of the House and Senate the heartfelt thanks of the thousands of wine grape growers of California. Also of all its people for the splendid care of our interests and well-being and may God bless them all. Await you when you return.
(Signed)
FRESNO COUNTY CHAMBER OF COMMERCE.
W. W. Phillips, President.
William Robertson, Sec'y.

The Fresno Morning Republican reported on September 26, 1913 about a large public meeting for the organization of a "City Beautiful Committee" to consist of twenty-one members. William was reported to be on the nominating committee and was made chairman of the meeting, during which William suggested that there should be uniform tree-planting on the streets and further suggested that some streets needed to be renamed. Afterwards, William, as president of the Fresno County Chamber of Commerce announced a $20 prize for the best general plan for beautifying Fresno.

On October 7, 1913, the *Oakland Tribune* reported:

CARLOADS TO BE DISTRIBUTED FREE
California Land Show Exhibitors Determined
to Make Housewives Converts.

If the California housewife does not become a convert to the "California products only" doctrine after visiting the California Land Show and Home Industry Exhibition, which opens next Saturday at Eighth and Market streets, it will not be the fault of the farmers and manufacturers of the state, for carloads of products of all kinds will be distributed without stint among the visitors during the fifteen days of the progress of the show.

Fresno County, which is one of the large space holders at the show, will have as part of its exhibit a raisin seeder and packer[52], a wonderful machine which removes the seeds and packs in cartons without the touch of human hands. This machine will be in operation during the entire fifteen days, and the cartons will be given to the visitors free. There is no limit to the quantity of raisins to be given, and a carload has been arranged as a start.

W. W. Phillips, president of the Chamber of Commerce of Fresno, declares that the exhibit of that county will be the most unusual in plan and the most extensive ever arranged by any county, and he expects to capture all premiums and medals in the classes in which he enters. Secretary Robertson arrived yesterday at the grounds and the exhibit will be built in a few days; a score of carpenters and decorators having been engaged.

"Placer peaches" - five carloads of them will also be given away, and apples and other fruits and the luscious products of California soil will be liberally distributed among the visitors to the show. Manufacturers of California-made goods will be equally generous with their products, and the exhibition is expected to be the most convincing demonstration of the superiority of California products ever presented.

The interior of the great pavilion at Eighth and Market streets has been converted into a forest of redwood trees and hundreds of workmen are busily preparing for the opening next Saturday. The doors will be opened in the afternoon, but the formal opening, in which Governor Johnson and Mayor Rolph will participate, will be in the evening.

Fresno County Chamber of Commerce Exhibition
circa 1913
Photo courtesy of the California Genealogy and History Room
Fresno Public Library

On October 18, 1913, *The Fresno Morning Republican*
reported:

FRESNO MAY ENROLL IN NATIONAL C. OF C.
Four Directors Favor Alliance With
U. S. Chamber of Commerce
Representative Will Bear Endorsement to Phillips In S. F.

At a meeting late yesterday afternoon with four Chamber of
Commerce directors, John Lind, membership secretary of the
Chamber of Commerce of the U. S. A., with headquarters in
Washington, D. C., convinced the local men of the advisability of
enrolling the Fresno County organization in the national Chamber
of Commerce, with the result that a letter was penned to President
W. W. Phillips in San Francisco asking that Lind be given a
hearing and assuring Phillips that the proposition looked favorable
from this end.

Those present when Lind explained the plan yesterday were T.
E. Collins, D. J. Newman, Ralph Woodward and Bart Harvey.

The necessity of organization to secure the benefits of the
cooperation of leading business men all over the country was
pointed out by Mr. Lind in exposing the operations of the national
chamber. In California there are now the following members: San
Francisco, Los Angeles, Sacramento, Oakland, Santa Barbara, San
Diego, Santa Ana, Bakersfield, Pasadena and Riverside.

In the national organization every member has a vote, but none
more than ten votes. One vote is given for the first twenty-five
members afterward. There are at present 400 members in every
state in the union. Cost of membership would be about $15 a year
for the local organization.

The Chamber of Commerce of America is a league of business
organizations of the United States, including chambers of
commerce, boards of trade and national trade associations. Its
purposes, in brief, are as follows: To focus business sentiment for
business legislation; to make more available and more useful to
business men who work in the various bureaus at Washington; to
encourage and promote the organization of associations of business
men in all parts of the country, that they may act in concert in
promoting the nation's business, to study the work of existing
organizations and their value to trades and communities, to
advocate the standardization of association methods, and to
become the source of information with respect to new opportunities
for trade expansion, especially in foreign markets.

Each organization appoints a national councillor who serves as the connecting link between his organization and the national chamber.

The Chamber through its Washington office provides direct service to its members in response to requests for information and also through its publications. Its regular publication, *The Nation's Business*, is issued monthly; a general bulletin is issued weekly throughout the year, and a legislative bulletin, issued weekly during sessions of Congress, gives condensed information in regard to bills affecting commerce.

The members who met with representative Lind yesterday were convinced of the advantage to the local organization a membership would prove to be. Lind will see both Phillips and Secretary Robertson in San Francisco, and will probably sign up the local association.

On October 23, 1913, *The Fresno Morning Republican* reported:

MANY ATTEND LAND SHOW AT BAY
ON FRESNO DAY
Raisin Seeder Continues to Attract Hundreds of Visitors
"Grown In San Joaquin" Is Statement That Rang
From All Corners
(Special to The Republican)

SAN FRANCISCO, Oct. 22 - This was Fresno day at the Land show. Quite a number of Fresno people celebrated the occasion. The attendance today was one of the largest recorded, W. W. Phillips delivered an able address on Fresno County, which was enthusiastically received.

The raisin seeder has been kept busy in dealing out cartons of raisins to the crowds. Amusing incidents occasionally occur which add a comical side to the occasion. For instance two elderly women were each served with cartons and while they stood eating the raisins, one suddenly exclaimed to the other, "Why it is wonderful. Up to a few years ago people grew raisins, now they are making them by machinery."

"Grown in the San Joaquin Valley" was the statement that rang out from every corner of the pavilion today as the products of that fertile section were proudly exhibited. Fresno. Merced, Madera, Stanislaus, Tulare, San Joaquin and Kern counties participated in the celebration of the day, each with prize exhibits of different kinds.

Fruits of all kinds were given the visitors this evening by the several counties, Fresno making a specialty of its seedless and seeded raisins. Madera relied on its dried fruit, Merced on its sweet potatoes, while Kern county showed its mineral products. Stanislaus county augmented its campaign with 500 feet of "movies" taken from an aeroplane that hovered over its lands.

Among the Fresnans who attended are the following: Louis Einstein and wife, Edwin Einstein, George Kahler and wife, W. T. Hite, W. A. Frutiger, T. L. LaRue, C. T. Anderson, H. A. Kemp, W. E. Patterson and wife, J. S. Jones and wife, H. W. Swift, L. A. Nares, B. F. Shepherd, Sr., Emory Donahoo, Leon Levy[53], F. M. Hill, Frank Homan and wife, E. E. Webster and daughter, Mrs. A. E. Colquhoun, Myrtle Harrell, Dr. and Mrs. C. Farnham, Jake Blumingdale, Wm. Helm and wife, George Helm and wife, J. B. Johnson, John I. Pimentel, George C. Roeding, A. Sorenson and wife, R. Hargrave and wife, K. K. Rives, John Bonnar, Mrs. Robert Boot, W. W. Phillips, wife and son, J. H. Lewis, Miss Ella Scott, S. W. Morris and wife, Mrs. J. A. Stelhins and son.

On October 29, 1913, *The Fresno Morning Republican* reported:

C. OF C. OFFICIALS RETURN FROM LAND SHOW
Phillips and Robertson Say Fresno Display Great Success
Will Take Up Good Roads Petition At Meeting
This Afternoon

W. W. Phillips and William Robertson, respectively president and secretary of the Fresno County Chamber of Commerce, returned last night from San Francisco, where they had charge of the county exhibit at the California Land Show. Both men were very enthusiastic over the success of the show and say that Fresno County received many thousand dollars worth of advertising at an expenditure of but a few hundred dollars. Fresno County took ten gold medals, three silver, one bronze and five diplomas at the show, which was more than any other county received.

Over 45,000 two-ounce cartons of raisins were distributed to the visitors. They estimate that fully 300,000 people saw the Fresno booth, which was one of the most attractive in the building. The big drawing card at the local booth was a raisin seeder which was kept at work most of the time. A bevy of pretty girls put the raisins seeded by it into cartons and distributed them.

Both Robertson and Phillips came down last night so as to be in readiness for the meeting of the board of directors of the Fresno County Chamber of Commerce this afternoon. The first matter of importance which they intend to take up and put through will be the securing of the needed signatures of freeholders in the good roads petitions that are now in their hands.

The committee in charge of soliciting sufficient funds to carry out this work will commence the gathering of the money needed within a short time. It is their desire to have the money in time to get the number of signatures desired before the year is out.

W. W. Phillips had his arm fractured last Saturday in Oakland, when he fell as he was stepping from a streetcar that was in motion. While the wound is not considered serious, Phillips says that it will necessitate his carrying it in a sling for the next five weeks or so.

While Phillips was away on this trip, he made a visit to Los Angeles and attended some meetings there of the boosters clubs. He was much impressed by the lively spirit.

On July 20, 1914, *The Oakland Tribune* reported:

W. W. Phillips of Fresno, candidate for the Republican nomination for state treasurer, was in Oakland today, in the interests of his canvas for the office. Mr. Phillips says he finds conditions very favorable to his candidacy, which is straight Republican[54]. Mr. Phillips came to California in the early '70s. He commenced work as a clerk in a store and soon became a partner in the business. Having been successful as a merchant, he organized the Farmers Bank of Fresno, and was at the head of that institution as manager for twelve years. He is now a large fruit grower and dairyman. He is now serving his third term as president of the Fresno County Chamber of Commerce. In this work, he has been active in the settlement and upbuilding of his county. Since becoming a Republican in 1890[55], he has always supported its principles and policies from conscientious motives. Believing himself well qualified for the duties of state treasurer, he asks the Republicans of the state to place him on the ticket as their nominee. *The Fresno Herald* of his hometown has this to say about his aspirations: "W. W. Phillips, the lively and efficient president of the Fresno County Chamber of Commerce, has gone north in the interests of his candidacy for the position of State Treasurer. Phillips is eminently qualified in the essentials of energy, integrity and financial sagacity for the position to which he aspires. His biggest recommendation is the universal esteem and confidence in which he is held by his neighbors of Fresno County, where he has lived for more than forty years.

The same paper, *The Fresno Evening Herald*, which was published in Fresno from 1909 to 1924, now praised William yet less than a year earlier had suggested that he and the board members of the Fresno County Chamber of Commerce lacked sufficient experience in advertising. This short-lived newspaper was sold on a street-corner by writer William Saroyan when he was a boy.

Having known rough characters like W. D. Grady, and the fact that one of his own board members of the Fresno County Chamber of Commerce had threatened violence against the editor of the *Fresno Evening Herald*, I am impressed that the editor apparently never directly criticized William; less than a year later the editor was praising William as fit for the office of State Treasurer. The real testimony of William's solid standing in the community was his wife Bettie. She and her father, Judge John Gotea Pressley, were solid, upstanding Christian citizens and he must have reflected their good character as well.

I also find it interesting that the article fails to mention that William's grandfather, Judge James Phillips, Jr., was twice the State Treasurer of Mississippi. While it is possible that William didn't know about his grandfather's office, a more likely scenario is that in identifying with the Republicans, he might have been distancing himself from his southern Democratic roots.

On September 23, 1914, *The Fresno Morning Republican* reported, "Mrs. Arthur Chambers of San Francisco is a house guest of Mr. and Mrs. W. W. Phillips. Mrs. Chambers is well known here being the daughter of Harry S. Dixon, one of the pioneers of the county, and spent her childhood here. She is the sister of Maynard Dixon, the well known artist."

The same day's paper reported:

IMPORTANT MEETING OF CHAMBER TONIGHT
Robertson Returns From Sacramento With Fresno Display

A special meeting of the Fresno County Chamber of Commerce will be held tonight. It was called yesterday by the president, W. W. Phillips, and a number of important matters are to be attended to at this time. William Robertson, the secretary of the chamber, has been absent for the past few weeks in Sacramento attending the Fresno County exhibit there, but returned last night. Tonight he will make his report, and the chamber will then make their arrangements to make the same exhibit at the Fresno District Fair.

The prize money that was earned by the county at the state fair will be devoted to some good cause. The last prize money won by this county was turned over to the raisin growers to assist them in perfecting their organization.   President W. W. Phillips has some scheme for the use of the money that he is not at liberty to divulge until tonight.

The sum won amounts to considerably more than $1,000.

It has already been settled that President W. W. Phillips and Bart Harvey are to represent the Chamber at the California Inland Waterways Association's convention at Stockton Thursday, Friday and Saturday of this week, and tonight other delegates will be chosen. It is thought that a very strong representation will be made by the Chamber of Commerce, in order to make as good a showing as is to be made by the other organizations of the city.   Progress will also be reported on the good roads petitions.

The same day's paper further reported:

POSSIBLE REDUCTION OF SWEET WINE TAX
Phillips Thinks Rate Will Be Set at Ten Cents

"I think it probable that the proposed tax of 20 cents per gallon on sweet wines will be greatly reduced before congress will permit the war revenue bill to be passed," stated W. W. Phillips, president of the chamber of commerce yesterday. "We feel that we have no hope of completely defeating the tax especially since the President refused to receive the California delegation headed by Theodore Bell Monday, but a substantial reduction is certainly expected. The reduction should not make the gallon tax more than ten cents and may even be only half that amount. The situation is far from hopeless."

The following telegram was received yesterday afternoon by Congressman Church in answer to the protest wired by the Fresno County Chamber of Commerce:

Washington, D. C. September 21st, 1914
W. W. Phillips
President, Chamber of Commerce, Fresno, Calif.

We are doing everything possible to defeat the tax on dry and sweet wines - we understand fully the gravity of the situation, a hundred percent tax is fundamentally wrong.
DENVER S. CHURCH

The office of California State Treasurer had been occupied by three Republicans before this election, but after sixteen years, a member of the Progressive Party, Friend W. Richardson won on November 3, 1914. For whatever reasons, William's name does not appear "on the ticket" of that election and in fact no Republican is named.

Friend William Richardson	Progressive	78.3%
Albert S. Spaulding	Prohibition	9.7%
George W. Woodbey	Socialist	11.9%

A Quaker, William Richardson legally added the Quaker greeting to his name and after serving as the State Treasurer, he became Governor of California with Clement Calhoun Young serving as his Lt. Governor. C. C. Young, who eventually became Governor himself, was a close friend of my other paternal great-grandfather, David Pressley Anderson.

Had his name been on the ticket, surely he would have split the Progressive vote, but it's impossible to know whether he might have won. The fact that Friend William Richardson ultimately became Governor makes me pause to wonder, would William have become Governor had his name been "on the ticket" and had he won this election? Friend William Richardson, ironically, became the Governor as a Republican.

William's wife, my great-grandmother Elizabeth B. Pressley Phillips, passed away on March 16, 1916 at the age of 62. William called her "a good wife, a noble woman, and a splendid mother." During the last eight years of her life, she lived at 346 Van Ness[56] in Fresno. This house is now gone, perhaps removed during the time of the construction of Hwy 41. However, the house across the street at 345 Van Ness still stands.

Elizabeth B. Pressley Phillips (1854-1916)
Photo courtesy of the Phillips Family Collection

Her funeral service was conducted by the bishop and dean of St. James Episcopal Church. The Board of Directors of the

Fresno County Chamber of Commerce passed the following resolution:

Whereas, Mrs. W. W. Phillips, wife of our late president, has been called hence; and

Whereas, Mrs. Phillips was an honored member of this community, a woman of fine personality, high intelligence, a good wife and mother, and one who enjoyed the affectionate regard of a large number of our best citizens, therefore let it be

Resolved, that the members of the board of directors of the Fresno County Chamber of Commerce desire to express their heart-felt sympathy with the bereaved husband and son, and that the secretary be instructed to forward this resolution to Mr. Phillips, and that it be also recorded in the minutes of the Fresno County Chamber of Commerce.

Signed   JOHN A. NEU[57], President

Attest: WILLIAM ROBERTSON, Secretary

In 1916 a Republican Convention assembled and again selected William, this time as their candidate for Congress for the Seventh District.

No doubt, his opposition to the Pomerene Amendment to the Palmer Bill in 1913, promoted by the Democrats, indicates that his political views shifted towards the Republican Party, perhaps as early as 1898, in alliance with the growers of the San Joaquin Valley. The Palmer Bill, signed by President Wilson in 1919, introduced a 10% tax on the net profits of all industries which violated a child labor law. The law was ultimately struck down by the Supreme Court. Not until the Depression era, when adults were willing to work for a child's wage, were nationwide child labor laws eventually signed by President Roosevelt in 1938[58].

Being selected as a congressional candidate was an exciting surprise for him. He appreciated the honor very much and strongly campaigned for the seat.

On September 9, 1916, *The Fresno Morning Republican* reported:

BAKERSFIELD HOST W. W. PHILLIPS
Republican Candidate Promises to Help Oil Men

BAKERSFTELD, Sept. 8. - W. W. Phillips, candidate for Congress on the Republican ticket from the seventh district, was the guest at a reception and banquet here today. The reception was held in the Hotel Tegler in the afternoon and the banquet, held later was attended by about 100 men and women, prominent in social, business and political circles.

Phillips, in his talk at the banquet, pledged himself to work for the interests of the oil men of the district if he is elected to congress. He said that the Democrats had temporized with the oil men for a long time, and had put them off and put them off. He said that the oil men were entitled to remedial legislation and that he would pledge himself to work for this end.

Others who spoke briefly at the banquet were Col. T. H. Minor, A. W. Mason, Monroe Hochheimer and W. W. Kaye. It was decided at the banquet to authorize Col. Minor to appoint a committee of seven whose duty it would be to organize a permanent W. W. Phillips For Congress Club.

The Bakersfield Lodge of Elks has invited Phillips and his party to remain over till tomorrow evening to enjoy the special Admission Day exercises arranged by the members of the local lodge.

On September 11, 1916, *The Fresno Morning Republican* reported:

PHILLIPS CONFERS WITH OIL OPERATORS
Is Guest of Honor at Admission Day Exercises

BAKERSFIELD, Sept 10. - W. W. Phillips, Republican congressional nominee, was the guest of honor last evening at the Admission Day exercises in Elks' Hall. Mr. Phillips was well received by local Republicans, and he shook the hands of a very large number of voters, who pledged him support. The oil men here have shown deep interest in Mr. Phillips' candidacy. Phillips informed the oil men that he would work for their interests if he was elected to congress.

On September 13, 1916, *The Fresno Morning Republican* reported: "BAKERSFIELD, Sept. 12 – The Kern County Republican Central Committee was organized this morning at the courthouse, the meeting being entirely harmonious and resolutions were adopted endorsing the following candidacies: Hughes and Fairbanks; Hiram W. Johnson for United States senator; W. W. Phillips for Congress; W. C. Theile for Assemblyman."

On September 18, 1916, *The Fresno Morning Republican* reported:

PHILLIPS WILL GO TO MODESTO FAIR
Will Attend Cattle Show; to Make Address at
Merced Friday

W. W. Phillips, Republican candidate for Congress in the seventh district, will leave this morning to spend the afternoon and evening in Modesto at the Stanislaus County Fair. Phillips is interested in the cattle and dairy stock shows and is attending as a stockman and will not do any politics while on the trip. He will leave here this morning at 8 o'clock in his automobile and will be accompanied by his son, John Phillips, and Charles Fletcher.

Tuesday Phillips will motor back to Fresno and will make short stops at the cities between Modesto and Fresno. Friday Phillips will go to Merced to be present for Republican Day at the Merced Fair. Phillips will be one of the principal speakers.

On September 20, 1916, *The Fresno Morning Republican* reported:

GRAVES, FORMER FRESNAN DEAD
Nephew of W. W. Phillips Dies in Los Angeles;
Funeral Today

William L. Graves Jr., formerly a resident of this city, died Monday in Los Angeles according to word that W. W. Phillips, an uncle, received last night when he reached this city from a trip to Modesto. Graves was about 31 years of age. He left here twenty years ago with his father, Dr. W. L. Graves, to make his home in Los Angeles.

Phillips left last night for Los Angeles to attend the funeral, which will he held this morning. Phillips will return here Thursday morning.

The same day's paper also reported:

PHILLIPS IS BACK FROM MODESTO FAIR
Republican Congressional Candidate Will Be
in Merced Friday

W. W. Phillips, Republican candidate for Congress, returned last night from a trip up the San Joaquin Valley as far as Modesto, where he visited the Stanislaus county fair. Phillips and his son John Phillips and Charles Fletcher, left early Monday morning and motored to Modesto. They stayed in the Stanislaus County seat Monday afternoon. Short stops on the return trip were made in Ceres, Turlock, Livingston and Atwater. Phillips and party will return to Merced Friday, where the congressional candidate will be a speaker on the Republican Day program at the Merced County fair. The return trip will be started Saturday and a stop will be made in Madera, where Phillips will confer with the Republican leaders.

On September 23, 1916, *The Fresno Morning Republican* reported:

REPUBLICAN DAY IS FAIR FEATURE AT MERCED
W. W. Phillips Gives Talk to Large Crowd at Evening Program
Fair Closes Today With Children's Program and Good Roads Day

MERCED. Sept. 22. – Republicans ruled at the Merced County Fair today, this being "Republican Day." The political program for the event included speeches this evening by W. W. Phillips, Republican nominee for the House of Representatives, Dr. H. Kylberg, Republican candidate for the Assembly, and C. W. Fletcher.

On October 7, 1916, *The Fresno Morning Republican*
reported:

W.W. PHILLIPS IS OILFIELD SPEAKER
Candidate for Congress Says Administration Has Not Helped
(Special to The Republican.)

BAKERSFIELD, Oct. 6 – Clearing skies and sunshine greeted
W. W. Phillips, Republican nominee for Congress, in his campaign
speaking tour of the southern section of the Seventh Congressional
District, for the first time today since leaving Fresno last Tuesday
morning.

On his return to Bakersfield today from Fresno by train,
Phillips was met by A. W. Mason, chairman of the Republican
County Central Committee of Kern county, Boyce K. Fitzgerald,
secretary, W. W. Kaye, W. J. Schultz of Maricopa, H. H. Bell of
Taft and other prominent Republicans and Progressives of the
county. The party traveling in a motor car caravan left Bakersfield
at noon for the West Side oil fields.

The first stop was at Maricopa at 3 o'clock this afternoon. Oil
men and employees from all of the big leases in the vicinity
gathered on the main street of the little town where Phillips
speaking from a motor car addressed them. A crowd of several
hundred assembled at Taft where a similarly enthusiastic night
meeting was held at 9 o'clock tonight.

The greatest interest in the Phillips' meetings in the oil fields
lay in the prospect of action by the next Congress to give relief to
operators and owners of oil lands (which) through the passage of a
satisfactory oil lands leasing measure will protect investments and
exploration and development work that has been done on lands
affected by the Withdrawal Act of 1909[59].

"For almost twelve months now, the present administration has
had under consideration action that would help to straighten out the
perilous situation into which the oil industry of the Kern county
fields, particularly have been plunged," declared Phillips.

"The oil industry of the State has employed the best counsel
obtainable and enlisted the aid of a United States Senator and
others in Washington to obtain action. Committee hearings have
been held, conferences participated in, and from time to time
during these months, hope has been high in the breasts of all who
are so vitally concerned in the outcome that Congress would act.

"But what has been the result. From time to time there have
been   postponements,   delays   and   conflict   between   the

administration and the administrative policy of Secretary Daniels of the Navy department, until Congress adjourned without definite action to insure relief.   It is only another illustration of the vacillation and vexatious negative policy of the present administration.

"Congress lets the proposed legislation go over. An election is coming on.   Oil operators, in keeping with persons seeking readjustment of rural post office routes, the enforcement of the eight-to-one standard test for oranges, promised appropriations for much needed post office buildings and a host of other important matters, are told that if the Democratic Party can carry the next Congress, they are told that if a Democrat can be returned to the Seventh District, that then the procrastination will cease and action will take its place.

"But it appears to the reasoning voter of this district that this is merely a specious pretext upon which votes may be caught."

On October 8, 1916, *The Fresno Morning Republican* quoted William's opponent, incumbent Denver S. Church, as he spoke before a large crowd in Tulare: "One of the best laws enacted by the Wilson Administration is the income tax measure, which was approved October 3, 1913, during the special session of the Sixty-third Congress. It provides that a tax shall be levied upon the annual income of a single person which exceeds $3,000 per year and upon a married person which exceeds $4,000, the tax rate increasing at a ratio directly proportionate to the amount of income."

On October 9, 1916, *The Fresno Morning Republican* reported:

SPEAKING CAMPAIGN OF WEEK ARRANGED
Candidates for Congress Map Out Tour for Vote Making
W. W. Phillips, candidate for Congress from the Seventh Congressional District on the Republican ticket, will spend practically all of this week in Fresno County, the dates of which are to be fixed today by the Republican County Central Committee. He returned yesterday after an interesting trip through the west side oil fields of Kern County.   Next Saturday he will speak at Chowchilla, on the anniversary of the fourth year of the

establishment of that district.   An all day celebration is being arranged by the people of Chowchilla, a barbecue and general entertainment being planned. Phillips will speak here in the afternoon and in the evening he will address the residents of Madera.

Congressman Denver S. Church leaves this morning for the northwest side of the San Joaquin Valley. This afternoon he will speak at Dos Palos and in the evening at Los Banos. Tomorrow afternoon he will talk at Gustine and tomorrow evening at Newman.

The same day's paper also reported:

PHILLIPS' TOUR OF OIL DISIRICT
Cordial Greeting Given to Republican Nominee
in Kern County.

BAKERSFIELD. Oct. 8. - W. W. Phillips, Republican nominee for Congress, put in one of the busiest days of the campaign thus far yesterday. Leaving Taft where he made three speeches, last night the nominee struck out on a busy schedule that took him straight up the West Side oil fields, taking in Fellows, where he met many voters at 9 o'clock, McKittrick at 11 a. m., Reward at noon, Belridge at 2 p.m., Lost Hills at 4 p.m., Wasco at 6:30 p.m. The total distance covered was more than 90 miles, and it was late when the party traveling in two machines, reached Bakersfield, but the sentiment was unanimous that it was one of the most profitable days experienced.

It was through heavy showers and part way over slippery, muddy roads that the party reached Taft at 6 o'clock Friday night. Taft, the metropolis of the West Side oil fields, turned out a crowd of upwards of 100. It surrounded the entrance of the hotel in the main street and listened attentively for 30 minutes while Phillips spoke from his motor car. His talk was demoted principally to the question of relief legislation for the oil interests affected by the Withdrawal Act of 1909. The Republican nominee was introduced by H. H. Bell of Taft, an attorney and member of the Kern County Republican Central Committee. Applause at the close of his talk was enthusiastic. Phillips spoke earnestly and was convincing in manner. He showed a fighting spirit that is developing a spirited aggressiveness as the itinerary lengthens.

Just for good measure and to wind up a busy day, Phillips talked to two large audiences at two motion picture theaters in Taft.

He spoke on the oil remedial legislation, the tariff and flayed the Democratic administration for its failure to make good in its platform promise to reduce the high cost of living.

Saturday's schedule was largely a hand-to-hand meeting with the oil land owners. The superintendents of the big leases, drillers, tool dressers and employees generally.

"I promised after being nominated to carry the story of Democratic failure of the last four years into every corner of this district, and I'm living up to that promise," Phillips declared to a crowd at Belridge.

"Go to it Billy," shouted a man in the audience, "you're setting a hot pace."

On October 10, 1916, *The Fresno Morning Republican* reported:

WILL TOUR HOME COUNTY THIS WEEK
Phillips Will Speak at Fowler Tonight;
Auto Parties Go Along

A visit to the towns of his home county will be made this week by W. W. Phillips, Republican candidate for Congress from the Seventh district. Starting tonight with Fowler, Phillips will hold meetings nightly at the following places in the order named: Reedley, Sanger, Clovis. The last week of the campaign will find Phillips touring the rest of the business centers in the county, Kerman, Tranquility, Coalinga, Selma and Kingsburg.

A number of friends of the Republican congressional candidate will meet this evening in front of the Republican headquarters in J Street, to accompany the nominee by auto to the Fowler Hall. Accompanying them will be a brass band and a number of entertainers. Fireworks will also be part of the political meetings scheduled for this county during the week.

Phillips returned this week from a hard campaign in Kern County and a few northern points where he was enthusiastically received.

On October 12, 1916, *The Fresno Morning Republican* reported:

MONTEREY HARBOR IS ISSUE IN CAMPAIGN
Phillips Answers Question of Constituent
on Waterfront Work
Would Seek Release of Gov't Appropriation to Start Work

The improvement of the harbor of Monterey and the establishment there of an adequate defense against an invading force, two of the main issues in the congressional fight in the Seventh District were answered squarely and unequivocally by W. W. Phillips, Republican candidate for Congress in that district, yesterday in an answer directed by him to A. M. Cranor, local real estate broker, who demanded from the candidate an expression of his policy in the event of election, with regard to these important questions. Phillips declared that if elected he would do all in his power to bring about the commencement of work at Monterey through the release of the government appropriation for the work. Adequate preparation for defense would also be part of his program in Washington, he declared. Cranor's letter and Phillips' reply follows:

Honorable W. W. Phillips.
Candidate for Congress, 7th District, Fresno, California.
Dear Sir

Believing as I do that cheaper transportation, for freight commodities would be of a greater benefit to the people of the San Joaquin Valley than any other work which our representative in Congress could hope to accomplish, and as it is a matter of record by no less authority than the War and Engineering Department of the United States that one-fifth of California's productive area is nearer tidewater connections at Monterey than any other part of California, and that that district so affected, although containing no large cities, constitutes one-tenth of California's total population, and that approximately the same proportion of California's total assessed valuation lies therein, and furthermore, as it is a matter of record that the Pacific Slope Congress, the civic organizations of fifty-two counties of California, in convention assembled, the Chambers of Commerce of San Francisco, Fresno County, Coalinga, Stockton, Napa, San Jose, Visalia and many other civic bodies of the state, have recommended to the state and government the immediate construction of breakwater improvements at Monterey Bay in order to furnish an outlet to sea from the several districts affected and I have information from no less authority than Governor Johnson of this state that the state of California and the federal government have made joint appropriations for breakwater improvements at Monterey, but have as-yet made no beginning of the construction of same, and, as it is generally understood that a cross country rail connection between the San Joaquin Valley and the port of Monterey is delayed pending the actual construction of said breakwater. I am writing to you, to inquire, in the event that you are elected to represent this district in Congress if you will consider it of the first importance to your constituents to work unceasingly and untiringly to bring about the immediate improvement of Central California's harbor at Monterey.

Further I have been advised on good authority that there is absolutely no means of defense or offense on Monterey Bay, to repel in the event of an attack by any hostile nation, and that whereas the harbor of Monterey is but sixty miles from the San Joaquin Valley in the event of any such unhappy event, the San Joaquin Valley and all of Central California would he left absolutely at the mercy of any attacking force. I would be glad if you would first investigate and find if this condition exists and then advise me what your attitude would be looking to the immediate correction of such condition.

Yours very truly.

A. C. CRANOR.

Mr. A. C. Cranor, Fresno, Calif.

Dear Sir:

Your letter of October 9, in which you ask an expression of my stand with reference to harbor improvement work at Monterey and its attendant influence on transportation facilities for this valley, is before me.

As you suggest in your letter, Monterey is the closest future port for this vast agricultural section of California. Doubtless, it will some day be improved, and two or more transcontinental lines will build lines to link it with the valley, but the question of interest is: Will it be done in our own day and generation, so that we may enjoy the resultant benefits?

Knowing that the state of California already has appropriated $200,000 to be expended jointly with the federal government in harbor improvement work in Monterey, and that the federal government has appropriated $600,000 for this work, all that appears to be needed is to get this fund released and the work started. But the work will not be begun as long as there is a string on the federal appropriation delaying the start until steps have been begun for the building of a railroad. The harbor improvement work must first be started. The railroad will follow in time.

My service as president of the Fresno County Chamber of Commerce makes this subject one of special interest to me, and I take this occasion, in replying to your letter, to assure you emphatically that, if elected to Congress, it will be a part of my program of betterments for this valley to cooperate with Congressman Hayes, Republican, who has served the eighth district so many years, in bringing about the commencement of the work at Monterey through the release of the government appropriation for the work.

Of course, the need of fortifications for defense at Monterey is equally imperative. San Francisco and Los Angeles, the entire San Joaquin Valley, indeed would be at the mercy of an invading force as long as Monterey continues to furnish one of the best harbors on the Pacific coast and yet remains defenseless. It is little more than sixty miles through the coast range into this valley from Monterey, and once landed there, a large attacking army might easily invade this valley and approach our large cities from the rear. Adequate preparation for defense is as much a part of my program as harbor improvement and the betterment of transportation facilities.

Very truly yours,
W. W. PHILLIPS.

The same day, *The Fresno Morning Republican* also reported:

REPUBLICANS PLAN MONSTER MEETING
Rally to Be Held October 18 With Johnson and Phillips Speakers
HANFORD, Oct. 11 - Republicans in Kings county will arrange for a monster rally in this city Wednesday, October 18, word having been received today by the county central committee

from Alexander McCabe that Governor Hiram W. Johnson will be here on that date to make an address. W. W. Phillips, Republican candidate for Congress from this district, will be present and will speak at the same time.

The committee is now busy making arrangements for the reception of Governor Johnson, and the meeting that will be held during the evening. The meeting will take place at the opera house. Johnson's candidacy was unanimously endorsed by the Republican county central committee at a meeting held a few days ago.

On October 14, 1916, *The Fresno Morning Republican* reported:

PHILLIPS IS CHOWCHILLA'S BIRTHDAY GUEST
Phillips Will Speak at 4th Anniversary of Colony;
Friends Go Along

W. W. Phillips, Republican candidate for Congress in the Seventh District, will be one of the principal speakers in Chowchilla today on the occasion of the celebration of the fourth anniversary of that colony. Phillips is scheduled to make a non-political speech.

Friends of the candidate, however, are planning to make Phillips' appearance at the Chowchilla celebration one big demonstration, and when the nominee motors from the Republican headquarters here this morning he will be followed by a long string of machines filled with friends. A brass band will accompany the caravan and the drive to Chowchilla will be one long cheer for the Republican candidate.

Phillips will be met at Chowchilla by Arthur M. Free, Santa Clara county district attorney, whose services will be loaned to the support of the congressional nominee during the next six days. Free, a noted speaker, has been assigned to the Phillips forces by Congressman Julius Kahn, Pacific Coast representative of the National Republican Congressional Committee.

Free will make his first speech in furtherance of Phillips' candidacy tonight at a monster meeting in the Lincoln Grammar School Auditorium at Madera. In addition to the several noted speakers who will participate in the meeting, a program of music has been arranged.

On October 19, 1916, *The Fresno Morning Republican* reported:

TARIFF AND DAIRY PHILLIPS' TALK
Republican Candidate for Congress Touring West Side

PATTERSON, Oct. 18. - To the dairymen of the west side of Stanislaus county, W. W. Phillips tonight spoke on the tariff. "When the first shipload of Australian butter reached San Francisco in the spring of 1913, under Democratic free trade, what happened?" Phillips asked his audiences today. "Every dairy rancher in this house can answer that question. Why, it sent the price of butter tumbling 5 cents a pound. Your cream sold for correspondingly less. The value of every dairy herd went down, not up.

"The Underwood Tariff Bill reduced the duty on cheese from 20 cents a pound to 6 ½ cents. It cut importations of butter from 20 cents to 6 cents. What happened? Did it make the rancher or the man in town happier? No. It meant that his business suffered: his income was cut because Australia sent shipload after shipload of butter and cheese into San Francisco. It meant that every family dependent upon the returns from a dairy in this valley was injured. There was less money to buy with. That was free trade as it affected this section of the Seventh Congressional District. Now, you know whether you desire Democratic representation, which stands for and believes in such a policy, or whether you want Hughes and a Republican policy of adequate protection, and representatives in Congress in support of such a policy."

An interesting feature of last night's meeting at Newman was the number of vice-presidents who sat on the stage. The meeting was called to order by W. W. Giddings, cashier of the Bank of Newman. He introduced Prof. E. F. Halley, principal of the high school, who in turn presented Phillips and Arthur M. Free of San Jose, district attorney of Santa Clara County. On the stage were the following vice presidents of the meeting: E. A. Gregory, Mrs. J. L. Kinnear, L. Dobrzensky, Mrs. John Brauer. Mrs. J. A. St. Clair, Mrs. Jose Alves, Walter Kneibes, William Weidemann, Frank P. Gomes, L. H. Parker, William Bunker, J. H. Kaufman.

"It is a paradox in the history of this nation that we must come back in this campaign to an issue that was settled in Washington's time," declared Free. "That is the principle of Americanism. But a Democratic administration with its vacillating policy has forced that issue. And the Republican Party platform this year embodies its eighteen great planks the enunciation that it stands for fullest protection of American lives on land and sea."

Free is frequently interrupted by applause. He declares that California's interest for protection, preparedness and development will best be served by the election of Hughes, Johnson and Phillips.

Wednesday's schedule took Phillips to Denair at 10 a.m., Hughson at 11 a.m., Ceres at noon, Crows Landing at 3 p.m. The night meeting was held at Patterson.

A political cartoon from *The Fresno Morning Republican*
President Wilson is shocked that Republicans would protect local industries
Cartoon accompanied the previous article "Tariff And Dairy Phillips' Talk"

On October 20, 1916, *The Fresno Morning Republican*
reported:

PHILLIPS GREETS LARGE AUDIENCES
Scores Democrats for Abolishing Free Use of Panama Canal

MERCED, Oct. 19. - W. W. Phillips, Republican nominee for
Congress, resumed his swing through Stanislaus and Merced
counties today, making five speeches, four during the day and
concluding the busy schedule with a rally held tonight at Le Grand.
The party, including A. M. Free, district attorney of Santa Clara
county, who is campaigning for Phillips in behalf of the National
Republican Congressional Committee, took the road early this
morning after spending the night at Modesto.

The first stop of the day was at Livingston at 10 o'clock where
the crowd gathered in the street, surrounding the automobile. The
coming of Phillips and Free had been generally heralded in
advance and at each of the following stops of the day: at Cressey at
11 a.m., Winton at noon and Atwater at 2 p.m., a large audience of
town people and ranchers were waiting and listening eagerly.

"I never saw as much genuine interest in any campaign as is
being displayed in the success of the Republican nominees this
fall," declared Frank A. Cressey of Modesto, chairman of the
Republican Central Committee of Stanislaus County.   "The
registration is greater than ever before and a large vote will be
polled. It is a forecast of realization that a crisis in national affairs
exists."

At Patterson last night Phillips and Free spoke to a crowd of
300. The meeting held in the grammar school auditorium was
preceded by a huge bonfire that lighted up the whole town. The
fire bell sounded and the hose cart dashed through the streets. The
whole town turned out and followed to the scene of the rally and
stayed for the speaking. C. J. Carlsen, cashier of the Bank of
Patterson, presided. The meeting was under the auspices of the
Patterson Club. Motor cars and buggies in the streets brought in
many from surrounding ranches.

Phillips scored the Democratic Congress for its repudiation of
free use of the Panama Canal by American coastwise steamers.
California and the San Joaquin Valley had suffered in being denied
an outlet by an all-water route for fruit products and alfalfa hay to
the Atlantic seaboard, he declared. He again called attention to the
need of a tariff policy based upon Republican principles of
protection for the ranch and fruit products of this valley.

"A Democratic tariff commission will furnish data to a Democratic Congress unless there is a change of administration and the tariff schedules will be predicated on a Democratic free-trade theory inimical to this valley's interests," he asserted. "Meanwhile, in normal times, business languishes, and the high cost of living makes new high altitude records. The people are demanding a return to the spirit of real Americanism. Everywhere in this valley is a growing demand for Hughes, unanimity for Johnson, and a demand for a Republican Congress to back up the forward-looking policies of our national standard-bearer."

Phillips and Free will talk at Merced Falls at 8 o'clock Friday night, at Merced at 2 o'clock Saturday afternoon, and Turlock at 8 o'clock Saturday night.

On October 21, 1916, *The Fresno Morning Republican* reported:

PHIILIPS TO SPEAK AT TURLOCK TONIGHT
Republicans Arrange Rally at High School Assembly
TURLOCK, Oct. 20 - W. W. Phillips of Fresno, Republican nominee for congressman from the Seventh District, will address the people of Turlock at the high school assembly hall tomorrow evening at 8 o'clock. H. W. Dockham, editor of the *Turlock Tribune*, will preside at the meeting, and the following will act as vice presidents: J. E. Weaver, Wellington Brown, George S. Keith, Charles Klein, A. J. Eddy, T. B. Whipple, H. S. Crane, Roy Weaver, J. V. Baker, A. V. Hoffmann, A. P. Ferguson, H. W. Rickenbacker, D. J. Walton, C. V. Limdahl, S. T. Webber, E. H. Claypool, W. E. Hester and E. J. Cadwallader. The same men will also serve as a reception committee, meeting Mr. Phillips at the Carolyn Hotel before the meeting.

The same day's paper also reported:

REPUBLICANS TO RALLY IN MERCED
W. W. Phillips and Dr. H. Kylberg Candidate for Assembly, to Hold Street Meeting
MERCED, Oct. 21. - Republicans of Merced are planning a political meeting here for tomorrow afternoon at 2 o'clock, when W. W. Phillips, Republican candidate for the House of Representatives, is to be the speaker. The meeting is under the

auspices of the county Republican central committee and will be held in front of the Hotel El Capitan. Dr. H. Kylberg, Republican nominee for the state legislature, will also make a brief address.

The Fresno Morning Republican reported on October 22, 1916 about a Republican rally held in Turlock the previous day.

W. W. Phillips and A. M. Free
Attack Tariff Law And Mexican Policy

TURLOCK, Oct 21. - This city and the district surrounding it participated in the largest Republican rally of the campaign tonight. The occasion was the address of W. W. Phillips, Republican candidate for Congress, and Arthur M. Free, district attorney of Santa Clara County. The meeting was held in the high school assembly hall at 8 o'clock. H. W. Dockham, editor of the *Turlock Tribune*, presided.

On the stage acting as vice presidents were George S. Keith, Charles Klein, E. J. Cadwallader, W. K. Hester, E. H. Claypool, S. T. Webber, C. V. Lundahl, D. J. Walton, H. W. Rickenbacker, A. P. Ferguson, A. V. Hoffmann, J. V. Baker, Roy Weaver, H. S. Crane. The band furnished music during the meeting.

Phillips pointed out the intimate relation between the needs of the Turlock Irrigation District and the tariff on fruit products from European Countries. The Underwood tariff law enacted by the Democratic Congress struck a direct blow at the industries in which the prosperity of this section is founded, he said. The making of this tariff law was participated in by his opponent, and voted for by him, Phillips declared, notwithstanding the protests raised by commercial bodies here and elsewhere.

Free scored the Mexican policy of Wilson and showed the administration's vacillation in dealing with foreign problems. The reversal of the pledge of the Democratic Party to exempt American coastwise ships from payment of tolls through the Panama Canal at the behest of Great Britain was, in itself, a great commercial blow to this valley, said Free. Phillips' opponent voted against the bread and butter interests of this valley in putting the tolls on such ships, he declared.

The afternoon meeting at Merced at 2 o'clock was novel. A platform was erected on the lawn of the Hotel El Capitan. There the speakers were listened to with close attention. They were introduced by Mr. W. V. Thomas of Merced, chairman of the

Republican County Central Committee. The band was out, and a large Saturday afternoon crowd gathered for the speaking.

Phillips and party returned last night from Merced Falls, where the big lumber mills are located. Workmen cheered the showing up of the free trade policy which closed every lumber mill on the Pacific Coast and rendered thousands idle.

After resting over Sunday at Modesto, the party will visit Oakdale and Riverbank Monday and a big night meeting will be held in Modesto.

On October 27, 1916, *The Fresno Morning Republican* reported:

PHILLIPS TO MAKE WHIRLWIND FINISH
Will Speak in Auditorium Night Before Election;
List of Speeches

The campaign of the Republican candidate throughout this district will be brought to a close Monday night, November 7, at a meeting in the Fresno auditorium. W. W. Phillips, Republican candidate for congress, John Fairweather and A. W. Carlson, candidates for the assembly, will also make speeches. The meeting is the last Republican rally here before the election.

Phillips will speak October 30 in Fowler, October 31 in Coalinga, November 1 in Reedley, November 2 in Selma, November 3 at Hanford, November 4 in Bakersfield and the following Monday night in this city.

In the same day's paper, William was reported to be planning a short speech at a rally that evening at the Fresno auditorium.

On October 31, 1916, *The Fresno Morning Republican* reported that Republican rallies would end the following Monday evening with William making the main speech. The paper reported:

About one hundred friends and supporters of Phillips have arranged for a banquet Monday night at the Hughes Hotel. Arthur M. Free, district attorney from Santa Clara County, will be the speaker at the banquet. This meeting will precede the Republican rally at the auditorium. After the banquet an automobile parade will be formed in front of the Hughes Hotel and Phillips will be escorted to the auditorium for the meeting. L. T. Lockhart will be grand marshal of the parade. The procession will go down I street to Merced, thence to J, thence to Tulare, thence to L and to the auditorium.

Phillips will speak tonight in Coalinga; Wednesday in Reedley; Thursday in Selma; Friday afternoon in Hanford, Friday night in Lemoore; and Saturday in Bakersfield.

Sadly, William lost the election on November 8, 1916 to the incumbent Denver S. Church with the following outcome:

J. F. Butler	Prohibition	5.32%
Denver S. Church	Democratic	51.04%
Harry M. McKee	Socialist	7.23%
W. W. Phillips	Republican	36.42%

William picked up 27,676 votes out of a total of 75,997 votes cast. With 11,112 more votes, William would have become a Congressman. Two years later, a Republican, Henry E. Barbour, won the seat and stayed in office until 1933, many times running unopposed. Democratic Congressman George Miller currently holds this seat which he has held since 1975. The Seventh District today includes portions of Contra Costa and Solano counties, including Richmond, Concord, Martinez, Pittsburg, Vallejo, Benicia and Vacaville.

Denver S. Church did not run again in 1918. Instead, he returned to his Fresno legal practice in 1919 and served as a superior court judge of Fresno County from 1924 to 1930. In 1932, he was again elected to Congress, and returned to serve from 1933 to 1935.

Following the death of his wife Elizabeth, William decided to settle down once again. After being a widower for two years, William married Mrs. Theresa M. Hunt on July 13, 1918, about five months before his son John married my grandmother Ruth. "Hunt" was apparently her married name, and unfortunately we don't know her maiden name, which may or may not have started with the letter "M."

William settled with his new wife Theresa in San Francisco, which allowed my grandfather to start his new family at the River Ranch. While living in San Francisco, William became a member of Trinity Episcopal Church on Gough Street, serving on its Vestry.

Around this time, William bought an apartment building at 1824 Jackson Street in San Francisco, where Edward Dixon Heise's parents eventually lived. Dixon lived there himself in his parents' apartment until he inherited his aunt and uncle's beautiful apartment at Pacific and Webster. Dixon was one of the few people I've known who remembered William. He was a young boy at the time and he remembers William coming to see his parents, perhaps when they lived in Los Angeles[60]. He recalls that William was not a tall man, and he particularly remembered the velvet collar of his overcoat.

Meanwhile, back in Fresno, the raisin growers did form a cooperative and the world's largest raisin plant. Sun-Maid Raisins Plant Number 4 was a major center for raisin packing in Fresno for nearly fifty years. The plant was constructed between 1918 and 1920 on Hamilton and East Avenues. By 1918 more than 85% of California's raisin growers were members of the Sun-Maid cooperative. Raisins were processed and packed there until the 1960s when the cooperative modernized and moved to its current location in Kingsburg, just south of Fresno.

By the time of his second marriage, William was essentially all but retired. In a column of *The Oakland Tribune* on March 1, 1921, they wrote, "In March Mr. and Mrs. William Walker Phillips, for whom there has been a great deal of entertaining, leave for an extended tour of the continent."

On October 18, 1923, *The Fresno Bee* reported that "Mr. and Mrs. W. W. Phillips of Berkeley are visiting the former's son John P. Phillips and family for a few days." While in Fresno, William visited his 3 ½ year-old granddaughter Martha, and his 2 ½ year-old grandson John. Aunt Mary would be born a month later.

On October 22, 1923, *The Fresno Bee* reported, "After a visit with Mr. and Mrs. John P. Phillips, Mr. and Mrs. W. W. Phillips have returned to their home in Berkeley."

On December 13, 1924, *The Oakland Tribune* reported, "Mr. and Mrs. W. W. Phillips, who are leaving New York for Europe in January, have sold their home in Belrose Place and taken an apartment at the Hotel Claremont. They leave for the east on January 15."

Belrose Avenue is just south of the U. C. Berkeley – Clark Kerr campus. The Hotel Claremont was built in 1906, designed by Charles W. Dickey, and contained a fourteen-acre landscaped garden. The area of Berkeley was known as Claremont and I do recall my aunt Martha mentioning that William had built a home there. I had also heard that he lived in a hotel for some five years. I was under the impression that it was The Fairmont Hotel in San Francisco, but it may have been The Hotel Claremont. Unfortunately, The Hotel Claremont does not have any records from this era. Years ago I inquired at The Fairmont Hotel and was told the same thing.

The old Security Pacific Bank building in Fresno is located on the Fulton Mall at Mariposa Street, one block east of where the Farmers Bank was located. In 1912 the four story Hutchinson Building was located there but the property was sold in 1916 to the Bank and Trust Company of Central California[61]. On May 6, 1920, the Bank and Trust Company of Central California merged[62] with the Farmers National Bank of Fresno. The building and merged bank was then called the Fidelity Trust and Savings Bank. Fidelity merged with Los Angeles Trust and Savings Bank on May 29, 1920 and the building and bank consequently became known as the Fidelity Branch of the Los Angeles Trust and Savings Bank, although it soon changed its name to the Pacific Southwest Trust and Savings Bank. In March 1923, the original Hutchinson Building was torn down and the present day building was completed in 1925. The bank then became known as Security First National Bank, and later Security Pacific National Bank which merged in 1992 with Bank of America, formerly known as The Bank of Italy.

Meanwhile, the 1889 building of the Farmers Bank of Fresno, which later became known as the Farmers National Bank of Fresno was torn down after 1925 to make way for a brand new gas station. Today, the location of Mariposa Street and Broadway Plaza has the address 1900 Mariposa Mall, home of the Fresno County Economic Opportunities Commission and other organizations.

Then and Now, A Composite Photo
Showing Mariposa Street in the 1890s superimposed with today
Combining photos courtesy of the California Genealogy and History Room of
the Fresno Public Library and Deborah Ostrander Russell

Perhaps because of the times, Kutner's ceased operations in 1929. By this point, Kutner's was a $2 million per year business.

Thinking of his grandchildren on January 1, 1932, William sat down to write a narrative for them. He wrote: "success attends those who work hard enough to attain it." To his grandsons, which of course included my father, he wrote, "I hope that you will profit by my hard experience in getting a job and my earnest efforts to keep it when I got it." He signed the narrative "your affectionate and loving grandfather."

The following year, William's younger brother Dixon L. Phillips passed away at the age of 75. Probably named in honor of his uncle R. L. Dixon, who was a guardian for two of his uncles, and lawyer for his grandfather's estate, his obituary was published in *The Fresno Bee* on June 16, 1933:

HANFORD (Kings Co.), June 16. - The death of Dixon Phillips, 75, at his home in Oakland yesterday removes one of the earlier superior court judges of Kings County. He was the second to occupy the bench, succeeding the late Justin Jacobs in 1898. He preceded M. L. Short, who died last year and had also served as district attorney of Tulare County before Kings County was separated from it. Judge Phillips was born in Mississippi, the son of a captain[63] in the Confederate Army and came with his family to California, in 1872, settling at Centerville, Fresno County, where he assisted his mother by teaching school at the age of 15. He and his brother planted the first cotton in Tulare County in 1873. Later he taught school in Fresno and, on being admitted to the bar in 1879, became deputy district attorney under W. D. Grady. He came to Hanford in 1881 and married Miss Florence C. Miller, the daughter of Theodore Miller, a prominent California lawyer. Judge Phillips is survived by his widow and four children. Mrs. Clinton C. Conrad, Mrs. George C. Haun, Miss Esther Phillips and Laurence M. Phillips of Oakland; sister, Mrs. Frank McClain[64] of Hanford, and a brother, W. W. Phillips of San Francisco. Funeral services will be held in Oakland tomorrow morning.

Judge Dixon L. Phillips (1858-1933)
Photo courtesy of Nancy Eldred Williams

William's second wife Theresa passed away less than a year later on January 31, 1934, leaving him a widower for a second time.   I have been unsuccessful in finding any information about her.

Just a year later, on January 20, 1935, William Walker Phillips passed away at the age of 83.   After Theresa Hunt passed away, William was living at the Union League Club in San Francisco.   Nearly seventeen years after leaving Fresno, he returned home for a final time.   His funeral was held at St. James Episcopal Cathedral in Fresno with Dean Arthur W. Farlander presiding.   William was buried on January 23, 1935 at the Mountain View Cemetery in Fresno.   His first wife Elizabeth B. Pressley, who was born on December 6, 1854, passed away on March 16, 1916, and is also buried at the Mountain View Cemetery.

The boy from Yazoo City, Mississippi, whose father died
when he was nine, had come a long, long way. The 19-year-old
boy with less than five dollars in his pocket when he reached the
Fresno Plains on January 1, 1871 from Madisonville, Mississippi
(and a $250 debt owed to his cousin) did rather well for himself
indeed. As the eldest living son, he no doubt helped to bring his
mother and the rest of her children out to California from
Mississippi.

Several times, the one-time store clerk and bank manager
campaigned to become an elected official. Nevertheless, William
deserves to be remembered for his contributions and efforts to
organize and protect the raisin and fruit growers of Fresno
County. On their behalf he captured the ear of Grover Cleveland
in 1892, attempted to organize fruit growers as the President of
the Fresno County Horticultural Society in 1896, and defended
their interests as the President of the Fresno County Chamber of
Commerce from 1912-1915. Similar efforts in 1898 by M. Theo
Kearney to form an association of raisin growers also failed
because of grower self-interest. Eventually, the raisin growers
did form a successful cooperative organization known today as
"Sun-Maid Raisins."

The California Bankers Association, which he helped form in
March 1891, is still operating to this day with trillions of dollars
in member assets. And the little bank in Fresno which he helped
start is now a part of Bank of America, ranked the largest bank in
the United States in terms of consolidated assets as of December
31, 2005[65].

David Pressley Anderson (1868-1949)
Photo courtesy of the Phillips Family Collection

DAVID PRESSLEY ANDERSON

My other paternal great-grandfather was David Pressley Anderson, my grandmother's father, who was born on his maternal grandfather Col. David D. Wilson's plantation in Williamsburg County, South Carolina on July 15, 1868. My father and his brother and sisters affectionately called him "Grand Daddy."

His father George Pressly[66] Anderson came to California in 1869, and a year later David, who was about two, and his mother followed. After living in Solano County from 1870-1877, the family moved to San Jose where they lived for two years and in 1879, the family moved to Santa Rosa. David graduated from high school in Santa Rosa in 1886.

Among his six other classmates were three girls, and three boys, including a theologian named George Lowell. Another was Frederic Augustus Juilliard whose uncle, Augustus D. Juilliard, with a $5 million bequest, helped to establish the Juilliard School of Music in New York. Fred's father was Charles Frederick Juilliard, Augustus' brother. Fred went to live with his uncle and worked for his uncle's textile company, the Augustus D. Juilliard Company. As the Juilliards did not have any children, they treated Fred as their own son. The future Governor Clement Calhoun Young, with whom David enjoyed a life-long intimate friendship, was David's third male classmate.

While David's father had been Superintendent of the Baptist Church, his mother, Margaret Gotea Wilson Anderson, known as "Mamo," was Presbyterian. David, along with C. C. Young, joined the Santa Rosa Presbyterian Church together in April 1886.

Clement Calhoun Young (April 28, 1869 - December 24, 1947) was the Governor of California from 1927 until 1931. He also served as a member of the California State Assembly for Alameda County from 1909 to 1919 and as Lieutenant Governor of California from 1919 to 1927. He was a Republican, though during his career in the State Assembly, he also won endorsements from the Progressive and Democratic Parties. He died in 1947 in Berkeley, California.

While still in high school, David went to work for a dentist named Dr. C. W. Savage as an "office boy." He also worked for the surgeon next door named Dr. William Finlaw, who had a medical library. David oftentimes read and studied the doctor's medical textbooks in the library, and since the doctor did not have a nurse, David sometimes assisted with minor operations.

The experience of working in a dental office while in high school motivated him to form the intention of attending the U. C. College of Dentistry which, at that time, consisted of two rooms in a building on Market Street in San Francisco. However, he first wanted to attend the local Southern Methodist College to study some subjects not offered in his high school. By the late fall of 1886, his father became gravely ill. When his father died in February 1887, leaving only a small amount of life insurance, the family lost their means of support. Besides David, who was the oldest, there were four other children under the age of ten. Two children, Emma Anderson and William George Anderson, died in 1877.

David was proud to be able to help raise his younger siblings, including Archibald Barron Anderson, who married Mary Catherine Dozier; Frank Anderson, who also became a dentist; George Pressley Anderson, known in the family as "Buss," who married Adele May McKay and who became prominent in business in the region; and his sister Mary Eleanor Anderson, who married Exum Morris Cox, the principal of Santa Rosa High School.

E. Morris Cox, Jr. (1903-2003)
David Pressley Anderson's nephew, founder of Dodge & Cox
Photo courtesy of his son Tom Cox

Their son, E. Morris Cox, Jr., my grandmother's first cousin, started the investment firm Dodge & Cox during the height of the Depression in 1930. As of March 2006, they manage $104 billion in separate accounts and mutual funds. Morrie was born in Santa Rosa, and attended U. C. Berkeley in the class of 1924, and Harvard Business School in the class of 1928. He was a member of the Pacific-Union Club, the Bohemian Club and the Anglers Club of New York. He served as chairman of the board of trustees or president of the California Academy of Sciences, the San Francisco Museum of Modern Art, and the Berkeley Foundation of the University of California. He also established the E. Morris Cox Chair of Economics at U. C. Berkeley.

Although we never had the occasion to meet, I did speak once or twice on the telephone with him in 1992. Morrie told me how he started his career, following Harvard Business School, with Scudder Investments which is today a part of the Deutsche Bank Group.

Dutifully staying at home to help support the family, David abandoned his plans to attend the U. C. College of Dentistry and instead became an apprentice to Dr. Savage. At the time, the family owned a two-acre wheat field on Sonoma Avenue in Santa Rosa. David took the life insurance his father had left, hired a carpenter and, working with him, built a six-room house on the Sonoma Avenue property. The family moved in on David's nineteenth birthday, on July 15, 1887.

David Pressley Anderson
As a young man circa 1885 in Santa Rosa, California
Photo courtesy of Janyce Anderson

In October 1887, he began to work in the evenings doing the bookkeeping for Luther Burbank, which he continued to do for three years.   Afterwards, David served Luther Burbank in a professional capacity and an intimate friendship formed between them which continued throughout the rest of Luther Burbank's life.

Luther Burbank (1849-1926)
Shaw Photography, Sean Bressie Collection, August 5, 1902

A year later, in October 1888, he passed the examination of the Dental Board of California with a high average. David then bought a one-half interest in Dr. Savage's practice and "Savage and Anderson" was formed. The dental partnership lasted until 1909 when Dr. Savage became ill and moved to Berkeley where he died in June 1928.

On October 1, 1891, David married Mattie L. Reid, my grandmother's mother, who was the daughter of Joseph B. Reid and Louisa J. W. Range. They first lived on Davis Street, which later became a part of Howarth Park, and then moved to Sonoma Avenue. Together they had four children including David Pressley Anderson, Jr. who was born in 1892 and died in 1894; Weston R. Anderson who was born in 1894 and became a dentist; Clarendon Witherspoon Anderson who was born in 1895 and became a lawyer; and my grandmother, Ruth Anderson who was born in 1897.

I never met "Wes," who, I understand, played a great stride piano and died before I was born, but I distinctly remember visiting with Clarendon, whom we called "Judge," at the 80th birthday party Aunt Martha held at her San Francisco apartment for my grandmother. I made a special effort to take a picture of Judge and my grandmother together, although today I am unsure what has become of that photograph. Judge was a World War I naval aviator and was very lucky. He was in New York awaiting transport to France when the war ended. In those days, the life expectancy of a naval aviator was measured in weeks.

Mattie L. Reid
As a young woman in Santa Rosa, California
Photo courtesy of Janyce Anderson

Dr. David Pressley Anderson and Mattie L. Reid Anderson
Photo courtesy of the Phillips Family Collection

Savage and Anderson was the only dental practice in Sonoma
County at the time which offered nitrous oxide and, as a result,
many extractions were performed in their office; local anesthetics
were not yet available. It was also a time before sterilization and
yet David never saw any serious cases of infection amongst his
patients.

In 1894 he became interested in the Santa Rosa Building and
Loan Association, serving initially as a director and then for

many years as its president. Under his leadership, the bank grew from an initial $100,000 to $4 million by 1919. At the start of the Depression, the bank was still worth $1 million and met every obligation. Eventually the bank became known as Santa Rosa Savings which was acquired by Great Western Financial in 1968, which was in turn acquired by Washington Mutual in 1997. Around 1898, he also became interested in and was a director of the Santa Rosa National Bank, resigning about ten years later in 1918.

The Sonoma Democrat from Santa Rosa, California reported on June 15, 1895:

> There was a pleasant social given in the parlor of the Presbyterian church Friday night by members of Y.P.S.C.E. A short program of vocal and instrumental music was rendered by the following: Misses Daisy Bethel, Cora and Grace Burch, Mr. W. Falconer, Miss Katie Chase and the Messrs. G. H. Slater, A. B. Anderson, and Oscar Reeve. After this some games were indulged in. Dr. D. P. Anderson gave an interesting talk on the work of the State conventions at Sacramento where he represented the society as a delegate. Refreshments were served at the close. The social committee, Messrs. E. E. Barnes, chairman, Misses Annie Dayton, Lena Barham and Miss Pearce and Messrs. F. Anderson and R. Nagle are to be congratulated.

Around this time, he was also elected a Trustee of the Santa Rosa Free Library. David began as a director of the library when it was only one small room in the city hall with one librarian.

By 1900 David was also taking an interest in ranching, just as William Walker Phillips had done about six years earlier. David planted the first combination prune and walnut orchard in Sonoma County. This combination is still grown in the area today.

In that same year he and A. T. Crane bought the Sonoma County Abstract Bureau which they co-owned until 1915. During this time, they laid out the "Crane and Anderson" subdivision in Santa Rosa.

Clarendon Witherspoon Anderson (1895-1980)
Photo courtesy of the Phillips Family Collection

A few years later in 1903, he and a partner bought a 1,000 acre grain and sheep ranch in present-day Fairfield.

When Andrew Carnegie gave $20,000 to Santa Rosa in 1903 to build a library, David himself raised the $5,000 needed for a lot upon which to build it.

In 1905 Crane and Anderson also organized a company to manufacture cement block, sewer tile, and other similar development-related products.

In 1906 David became Superintendent of the Sunday School program at the Santa Rosa Presbyterian Church where he was the librarian and taught Sunday School. At various times, he served as a Commissioner to the Presbyterian General Assembly in the county.

The earthquake on April 18, 1906 claimed the lives of two of my grandmother's aunts: Mattie's sister Lottie J. W. (Reid) Moke, wife of Henry H. Moke who was born on December 1, 1873; and her sister, Miss Willie Florence Reid, who was a teacher and who was born on October 20, 1875.

The earthquake also badly damaged the library and leveled the whole town of Santa Rosa from K Street to the Northwestern Pacific Depot. As a consequence, David obtained the necessary funds from Andrew Carnegie to repair the library.

In 1915 David's son Weston R. Anderson joined him as a dentist in the practice, and together they were the only dental office offering orthodontics in the area.

Dr. Weston R. Anderson (1894-1960)
Photo courtesy of the Phillips Family Collection

A year later, in 1916, David attended Columbia University in New York for a post-graduate course in the latest dental practices.

David was elected a director of the Santa Rosa Chamber of Commerce in 1920 where he served for many years, just as my great-grandfather William Walker Phillips had done. William had also served as the President of the Fresno County Chamber of Commerce from 1912-1915.

In 1923 David went to Philadelphia to study local and nerve-blocking anesthesia.

At the urging of his close friend, Governor C. C. Young, he was enticed to run in 1924 for the California State Assembly for the Thirteenth District. He served from 1925-1927 in what he considered to be a costly but valuable experience.

David was also a trustee of the San Francisco Theological Seminary in San Anselmo.

By 1938 David had been in practice for fifty years and was in excellent health, rarely missing a day of work.

On May 15, 1941, *The Oakland Tribune*, in an article entitled "Oakland Chamber Group Guests of Santa Rosa," reported:

> At the luncheon, held in the Occidental Hotel, Dr. D. P. Anderson, representing the Santa Rosa Rotary Club and the Chamber of Commerce, officially welcomed the Oakland delegation. He stated that Santa Rosa and Oakland have many common problems that can be solved by "meetings such as this."
>
> "We are partners in the building of this great empire of ours," Dr. Anderson said, "and we here in Santa Rosa look to Oakland for aid and assistance in meeting many of the problems that we have to face."

On October 1, 1941, *The Fresno Bee* reported:

> D. P. Andersons Are Hosts At Anniversary Tea
> Dr. and Mrs. D. P. Anderson of Santa Rosa, who often visit their son-in-law and daughter, Mr. and Mrs. John P. Phillips, here, were hosts at a reception Saturday afternoon when they received the congratulations of their guests on their golden wedding anniversary. The setting for the affair was the Saturday Afternoon Clubhouse in Santa Rosa.

The clubhouse was decorated with arrangements of Fall flowers and foliage.

Mr. and Mrs. Phillips and Misses Martha Phillips and Mary Phillips and John Phillips, Jr., and David Phillips attended the affair. A number of Fresnans went to Santa Rosa and remained for a weekend visit.

After the reception, Dr. and Mrs. Anderson entertained the friends who assisted at the reception and the members of the family at dinner in the club.

The guest list included friends from all parts of the state.

David Pressley Anderson died on Jan 3, 1949 in Santa Rosa, California when he was 80 years of age.

Mattie L. Reid Anderson eventually came to live with my grandmother in Fresno, and died in her home at 410 Van Ness on November 30, 1958 at the age of 89.

Mattie's parents, my grandmother's maternal grandparents, were Joseph B. Reid and Louisa J. W. Range, daughter of Charles Range and Elizabeth Klipper. Joseph was born on November 4, 1835 in Alabama and married Louisa on March 22, 1864 in Santa Rosa, California. Joseph died on December 1, 1918 in Santa Rosa, California at the age of 83, and Louisa, who was born on December 6, 1841, died on October 5, 1929 in Santa Rosa, California at the age of 87.

Louisa's parents were Charles Range, who was born on June 30, 1819 in Washington County, Tennessee, and Elizabeth Klipper. They married on September 7, 1840 in Washington County, Tennessee. She was listed as "E. Klipper" in the recording, although the name can also be spelled "Clipper" or "Klepper" as a "Sarah Klepper" also married in Washington County in that year.

Ruth Anderson Phillips
"Hoo Hoo" wearing her customary white gloves
Photographed in the mountains by my father circa mid-1980s
Photo courtesy of the Phillips Family Collection

Ruth Anderson Phillips and Phebe B. McClatchy Conley
Best friends at a party in the mid-1980s
Photo courtesy of the Phillips Family Collection

Mary Walker Phillips
January 3, 2003
Photo courtesy of Patricia Abrahamian

Mary Walker Phillips, circa 1950s
Before Mary published best selling books on creative knitting
and macramé, she was a well-known weaver
Photo courtesy of Patricia Abrahamian

Hon. and Mrs. Gilbert H. Jertberg
Photo courtesy of the Russell Family Collection

E. Morris Cox, Jr. (1903-2003)
Co-founder of Dodge & Cox
Photo courtesy of Dodge & Cox

Fresno home of Mr. and Mrs. John P. Phillips (1931-1970)
410 Van Ness, Fresno, California
Now located at 310 N. Fulton, Fresno, California
Photo courtesy of James Newton Russell

John Pressley Phillips
Egypt, 1910
Photo courtesy of the Phillips Family Collection

William Walker Phillips
Egypt, 1910
Photo courtesy of the Phillips Family Collection

A Stagecoach on the way to Shaver Lake, May 2, 1910
Photo courtesy of the Shaver Lake Fishing Club

William Walker Phillips, 1911
(third from the left) Shaver Lake Fishing Club
Photo courtesy of the Shaver Lake Fishing Club

General M. W. Muller, Founder of the Shaver Lake Fishing Club
Photo courtesy of the Shaver Lake Fishing Club

Fresno County Chamber of Commerce, circa 1913
Photo courtesy of the California Genealogy and History Room of the
Fresno Public Library

The Farmers Bank of Fresno
Built in 1889 by English-born San Francisco architect W. H. Armitage
Photo courtesy of the California Genealogy and History Room of the
Fresno Public Library

View from the Courthouse down Mariposa Street
Photo courtesy of the Fresno Historical Society Archives

Judge Dixon L. Phillips
Brother of William Walker Phillips
Photo courtesy of Nancy Eldred Williams

Mary Louise Phillips (1884-circa 1935)
Photo from 1906
Daughter of Judge Dixon L. Phillips and Florence Miller
Photo courtesy of Nancy Eldred Williams

Esther Bernadine Phillips, born in 1888
Photo from 1905
Daughter of Judge Dixon L. Phillips and Florence Miller
Photo courtesy of Nancy Eldred Williams

Florence ("Sid"), Mary Louise and Esther Bernadine Phillips
Daughters of Judge Dixon L. Phillips and Florence C. Miller at Santa Cruz
Photo courtesy of Nancy Eldred Williams

Florence and Mary Theodora ("Mollie") Miller, circa 1860s
The future Mrs. Dixon L. Phillips and Mrs. Seaborn M. Phillips, Jr.
Photo courtesy of Nancy Eldred Williams

Kutner-Goldstein & Co., circa 1875
Photo courtesy of the California Genealogy and History Room of the
Fresno Public Library

Mariposa and "I" Streets looking towards the Courthouse
The Farmers Bank is at the corner on the right.
Streetcar wires, a bicyclist and a horse and buggy are visible.
Photo courtesy of the California Genealogy and History Room of the
Fresno Public Library

The same intersection as viewed on July 8, 2007

The Security Bank Building, one block ahead is visible behind the trees.
Photo courtesy of Deborah Ostrander Russell

Kutner's on Mariposa and 'H' Street circa 1920s
Kutner's is located under the large sign on the left side. With the courthouse
in the background, the Farmers Bank is at the end of the block on the right
Photo courtesy of the California Genealogy and History Room of the
Fresno Public Library

Mariposa Street looking towards the Courthouse
The Security Pacific Bank Building was completed in 1925.
The Farmers Bank Building is still standing, but not for much longer.
Photo courtesy of the Fresno Historical Society Archives

The Lodge at Huntington Lake
An early photo circa 1930s.
Photo courtesy of the California Genealogy and History Room of the
Fresno Public Library

David Pressley Anderson
Photo courtesy of Janyce Anderson

Sarah Grier Britton Britton Wilson (1806-1884)
Mother of Margaret Gotea Wilson Anderson
Photo courtesy of Janyce Anderson

Margaret Gotea Wilson (1847-1934)
David Pressley Anderson's mother as a young girl
Photo courtesy of Janyce Anderson

Ann Esther Pressly (1809-1878)
Mother of George P. Anderson
Photo courtesy of Janyce Anderson

River Ranch Home of William Walker Phillips
Today known as the
Coke Hallowell Center for River Studies
11605 Old Friant Road, Fresno, California
Photo courtesy of the San Joaquin River Parkway and Conservation Trust

Col. Seaborn Moses Collins Phillips (1822-1861)
Photo courtesy of the Phillips Family Collection

V. PHILLIPS, PRESSLEY, ANDERSON AND WILSON

SEABORN MOSES COLLINS PHILLIPS

William Walker Phillips' father was Seaborn Moses Collins Phillips[67], born on August 3, 1822 in Hinds County, Mississippi.

In 1846 when the Mexican-American War broke out, Yazoo County residents responded. Company A of Jefferson Davis' 1st Mississippi Regiment of Infantry was composed of volunteers and Seaborn was Davis' second lieutenant.

Seaborn's brother, Sgt. William Washington Phillips, served in the Battle of Buena Vista as a member of Lt. Fletcher's Co. E., a part of Jefferson Davis' Mississippi Regiment. News of his death during the Mexican-American War was published in the *Gibson Correspondent* on April 3, 1847. Lee Paul Sturdivant discovered the following account of Major Ben McCollouch (1811-1862) who was Major General Zachary Taylor's chief scout:

> It was February 1847, just prior to the bloody Battle of Buena Vista, that General Taylor dispatched Ben McCollouch and one of his men, William Phillips, to locate Santa Anna and fix the Mexican general's position. The two Rangers found the opposing army sixty miles south of Encarnacion. They quietly slipped past Santa Anna's guards, and under cover of darkness, slipped into the enemy camp and stationed themselves on a small hummock, where they quickly, methodically, estimated the enemy troop strength at

20,000 men. Determining Santa Anna's probable direction of march, they returned to General Taylor with their information.

Ben McCulloch and his Rangers fought in the Battle of Buena Vista, and [this battle] was a narrow victory for the United States. It did, however, open the way for General Taylor to advance to Mexico City.

Colonel Jefferson Davis leading the First Mississippi
The Battle of Buena Vista
Painting by Alexandra Alaux
Used with permission, courtesy of the
Mississippi Department of Archives and History

Sam Olden is a former president of the Mississippi Historical Society and a current member of its board of directors. In a column he wrote entitled "Mississippi and the U.S. - Mexican War, 1846-1848" in August, 2005, a portion of which is reprinted here, Mr. Olden wrote:

Hardly had a part of his army left when Taylor learned that a new Mexican Army of some 15,000 men, including 4,000 excellent cavalry and lancers, was marching north to take back Saltillo and Monterrey under command of the same General Antonio Lopez de Santa Anna who had fought the Texans at the Alamo when Texas first rebelled. General Santa Anna had vowed to push the Americans back across the Rio Grande.

With only 4,650 men left, General Taylor moved them to a narrow pass in the mountains south of Saltillo where the Mexicans could be more easily blocked. There the Battle of Buena Vista raged for two days, February 22 and 23, 1847, with Taylor always keeping the Mississippians in readiness beside him. On the second day when a dangerous break in one key line occurred, he ordered them in to save it. The legend is that he did so, saying, "Steady, boys, steady for the glory of Ole Mississippi!" Colonel Davis placed his ranks into a "V" formation which was much praised after the battle. The Mississippi Rifles not only held fast but turned the enemy back. Night soon fell and the Mexican Army retreated. General Zachary Taylor would become a national hero and in 1849, [he became] the President of the United States.

During the same months General Taylor was campaigning, another small force led by Colonel Stephen Watts Kearny, composed of regular Army dragoons, Missouri volunteers, and a battalion of Mormons sent by Brigham Young, made the difficult 895-mile march from Kansas to Santa Fe, taking New Mexico without firing a shot. Continuing the grueling march to Los Angeles, where he learned the U. S. Navy was already holding Monterey and San Francisco, Kearny took formal control of all California for the United States.

Major General Zachary Taylor (1784-1850)
His daughter Sarah Knox Taylor married Jefferson Davis
Courtesy of the Library of Congress

March to Mexico City

Less than two weeks after Buena Vista, General Scott led the first amphibious landing in U.S. history onto a beach south of Veracruz. Bombarding that port city into submission, this second army began its march to take Mexico City. General Santa Anna now seized the presidency and again attempted to stop the

Americans. New volunteer units arrived bringing General Scott's strength up to 10,738. General Santa Anna retreated to the valley surrounding Mexico City awaiting the Americans with another army of 30,000.

Santa Anna and his men put up strong resistance at several towns outside the capital, but the Americans pushed them back into the city. On the final assault against its several gates, Brigadier General Quitman at its west gate, on foot and at the head of his men, won heroic distinction. After Mexico City was captured September 14, 1847, General Scott publicly honored John A. Quitman by naming him the military governor of Mexico City.

A new Mexican government some months later signed the Treaty of Guadalupe Hidalgo with the United States. Its principal terms: (1) the United States paid Mexico $15 million and agreed to settle the many debts owed American citizens by former Mexican governments; (2) Mexico gave up her claims to Texas, New Mexico, and California; (3) all future disputes between the two neighbors would be arbitrated peacefully.

(Reprinted with permission from *Mississippi History Now*, the online publication of the Mississippi Historical Society).

Jefferson Davis, President of the Confederate States
Photo from before 1861
Photo courtesy of the U.S. National Archives and Records Administration

On June 27, 1849, Seaborn married Emily Cushman Walker from Madison County, who was born in Savannah, Georgia on April 26, 1822. They were married by the Rev. J. B. Walker.

Seaborn was a lawyer and during the early 1850s was once the editor of the newspaper *The American Citizen* published in

Canton, Mississippi. From 1853 to 1857, he was a circuit clerk in Yazoo County.

On September 10, 1853, *The American Citizen* published the obituary of his daughter Julia Laurentina Phillips, William Walker Phillips' older sister:

> Died in Marion county on the 2nd of September, at the residence of Major William F. Walker, Julia Laurentina, daughter of S. M. and Emily C. Phillips, aged three years and four months.
>
> The bud of promise has withered; the sunlight and life has faded away, and left the once bright and beautiful form in the night and dews of death. Those blue, deep, earnest eyes, the smile wrapped the cherub face, the rounded form, the dimpled mouth, are cold and sealed in death. Her span was like the azure sky, pure and bright. It was not hers to feel the sorrows that corrode life's amassing years, or to steel the heart against the baffled dreams of hope and bliss. Translated by her God, she passed, as it were, on smiles from earth to heaven. Crushed are a father's fondest hopes; the idol of his dream has fled. No more shall greet the fond mother's ear, the infant prattle or her merry laugh. No more those little arms will circle round her neck, or that rosy lip imprint the good-night kiss. That vacant chair, the neglected toys, the empty couch, in silence tells that in memory is little Julia only there.
>
> Fond parents, there is no balm for a wound like this. Time alone brings healing on its wing. Nerve thy spirits for that unshrinking walk o'er life's stormy path, nor let earth's lone defilements stay thy course, and when a few fleet years have passed, meet thy angel child at heaven's gate, and she will lead thee on through the vistaed joys of heaven's eternal years.

The Yazoo Democrat reported on March 17, 1860:

> The Yazoo Rifles have organized and elected their officers, and will undoubtedly form a company of which the State may be proud. That prince of clever fellows, Mose Phillips, was unanimously honored with the Captaincy. As a gentleman, he is eminently worthy of it. Let the members bear in mind that there will be a meeting today.

According to the 1860 census, Seaborn was 37 years of age and married to Emily Cushman Walker who was then 38.

Seaborn's daughter Julia Laurentina Phillips was born around May 1850 but died in September 1853. Remaining at home in Yazoo City in 1860 were William, my great-grandfather who was 9, Laurentina ("Laura") who was 6, James Jackson who was 4, Burris who was 3 and Dixon L. who was 2. Seaborn Jr. was born in 1860 after the census was taken. Seaborn declared that he had $1,200 in real estate and $10,000 of personal property[68] in the census of that year.

Seaborn's son William remembered how his father "drilled his company" every evening. Young William used to go with his father Seaborn and march at the head of the company beside the drummer boy named John Agnew. William was enthused with the martial spirit and pleaded with his father to let him go to the war with him.

In early April 1861, Seaborn and his company boarded the river steamer The Yazoo City bound for Vicksburg, and from there they took a special train to Pensacola, Florida.

As Peter B. Miazza explains:

> Captain Phillips and his Company K, Yazoo Minute Rifles, probably took a steamer up at Yazoo City and sailed down the Yazoo River to Vicksburg. There, as your great-grandfather said, they boarded a train of the Southern Railroad of Mississippi to Jackson. There they may have picked up other companies, which would comprise the 10th, and rode on to Meridian. There they would have boarded the Mobile and Great Northern Railroad down to Mobile.
>
> The Mobile and Great Northern Railroad from Tensas to Pollard was not finished until the first of November in 1861 and the Alabama and Florida Railroad of Florida from Pensacola to Pollard was not opened until January of 1862. That agrees with page 97 of John Rietti's book where he said that they took a steamer from Mobile to Hall's Landing which was probably near where the Alabama River empties into Mobile Bay. They then marched overland to Pensacola. Doubtless, Captain Phillips and Company K took the same route. I think that he put his company up in a hotel[69] in Pensacola after their march from Mobile.

Confederates in the newly occupied Pensacola forts, 1861
Photo courtesy of the State Archives of Florida
Used with permission

There was a large turnout at the steamboat to bid the company farewell. Relatives of the one hundred volunteers who comprised the company knew they might never see their loved ones again. Young William, then nine years old, was probably too young to appreciate that this would be the last he would ever see of his father again.

After arriving in Pensacola, Seaborn was elected Colonel of the 10th Mississippi Infantry on April 11, 1861, having been Captain of the Yazoo County company which was officially organized on March 2, 1861. Seaborn was sworn in by Richard Griffith who was then the state adjutant general. Richard Griffith later became a brigadier general and was killed during the seven day battle around Richmond. Brigadier General Richard Griffith is buried in Greenwood Cemetery in Jackson, Mississippi.

While at Camp Davis near Warrington, Seaborn wrote to his sister Julia on April 17, 1861:

Columbiad guns of the Confederate water battery
at the entrance to Pensacola Bay, Warrington, Florida
(Photo by J. D. Edwards)
Photo courtesy of the State Archives of Florida
Used with permission

Head Quarters 10th Regiment Mississippi Volunteers
Camp Davis near Warrington, Florida
April 17, 1861
Dear Sister
   I have been anxious to write to you ever since I left home but the truth is I have been so busy that I could not, but having a leisure moment I will devote it to giving you the history of our Campaign up to date. I suppose you are aware of the fact that I commanded a company in Yazoo which I tendered to the Confederate States. On reaching this point Regiments were

organized without any solicitation on my part though two companies from Lowndes (the Captain of one of which was an old comrade in Mexico) and the Company from Itawamba put my name forward for the position of Colonel.

I received every vote in those three companies except four, all of the Port Gibson Rifles except two, just half of the Hill City Cadets and the unanimous vote of my own Company and was elected on the first ballot by a majority of 88 votes over the combined votes of both of my competitors, Gene R. Griffith and Capt. Joe Davis of Madison, a nephew of Jeff Davis. This was a compliment I did not expect and one that I highly appreciate and although a position of high responsibility I shall endeavor to acquaint myself to the satisfaction of my friends and if one have an engagement which we are hourly expecting. I shall remember the glories that cluster around the name of Mississippi and shall not permit them to be disurned in my hands but I shall endeavor to add luster to them.

I said we are hourly expecting a battle. There are six men-of-war standing out of the harbor and they have been for the last two or three days throwing troops and all kinds of munitions of war into Fort Pickens, in full view of us, with the aid of spy-glasses, but beyond the reach of our guns. I was at the headquarters of General Bragg this evening, he is fully satisfied that the enemy will make an attack upon us as soon as they can get ready. We are actively engaged in throwing up sand batteries along the coast and making other defensive preparations. We have a chain of batteries standing from the Navy Yard to Fort McRee a distance of two miles. We have daily about five hundred men at work upon them and would have more but the Corps of Engineers are not sufficient in number to superintend a stronger working force. The works are progressing as rapidly as could be expected under the circumstances and if the enemy do not attack us in the course of a few days we will be in a complete state of defense. There are about five thousand troops here now and we have new arrivals every day or two. My command keep generally healthy. The men are all in high spirits at the prospect of a battle. I was aroused this morning at the announcement that a steamer was entering the harbor. I immediately ordered cartridges to be issued to the whole Regiment and many of them seemed to be disappointed when we ascertained that it was not a man of war but a British merchant vessel. Four companies of my Regiment are in Fort McRee under the command of Sr. Col. Davis and they will very probably have the honor of firing the first gun upon the enemy. They are working like Trojans in the Fort and will soon be ready to deliver a very heavy fire upon the ships that may attempt to enter the channel. The Fort is just 1.4 miles from Fort Pickens, the guns of which will play upon McRee as soon as the ball opens.

The men are exercising night and day in the artillery drill and will be able to do good service. General Bragg is "clearing the deck" for actions. He had ordered all the citizens and merchants and in fact everyone not connected with the army to leave Warrington, a town that surrounded the Navy Yard.

I believe I have given you a full report of matters and things here. Let me know where Harry[70] is, I would like to write to him. My love to all. Tell Mr. D[71]. to write to me.
Yours affectionately,
S. M. Phillips

While in Pensacola waiting for the fighting to start[72], Seaborn passed away on May 21, 1861. Based on a reading of the account of his death, he may have died of the measles.

Rebel battery, Pensacola, Florida
Photo courtesy of the State Archives of Florida
Used with permission

On May 28, 1861, a Mr. McFarland wrote a letter to Judge Burrus of Yazoo County, which was passed to Julia Rebecca Phillips Dixon by Seaborn's wife Emily Cushman Walker Phillips. Harry St. John Dixon was Emily's nephew, whom he called "Aunt Emma," and he made "a true and literal copy" of the letter on July 15, 1861:

New Orleans
May 28, 1861
Hon. J. R. Burrus
My Dear Sir
　　Your esteemed favours of the 11th & 20th just came to hand during my absence and the parts relating to business were only attended to.
　　Our mutual friend Phillips is no more. I visited him the three last days of his life at his quarters – he was greatly cheered up by my presence on the first day, conversed cheerfully on all subjects and was hopeful of recovery. On the next day seeing a change for the worse I suggested calling in of Dr. Femes to the attending Physician Dr. Lipscomb to which he assented and on the next day Dr. Femes accompanied me. We found him the next day much weaker and his death inevitable. Femes prescribed various remedies but the system was too much prostrated by disease to cause a reaction and the remedies were of no avail. Col. White & Hob Rowell were with him constantly, the former made known to him his condition and approaching end. He heard the death warrant pronounced with no trepidation and no fear, but with a dignity and grandeur and bravery unequalled, he gave directions about his affairs without the changing of a muscle of his countenance. He said he regrets not being in the field although he died in the service of his country, spoke of his family, expressed tenderly and affectionately, to whom various messages were sent. He calmly pulled a ring from his finger given him by his wife on the day he left and handed it to Col. White and said "Give that ring to my wife and say to her that I "have never disgraced it and I know that she never will." Then turning to me he said "Give my best respects to Judge Burrus and family, that I could wished to have seen him before I died; tell him to give some attention to my family and if in no wise interfering with his own affairs would like him to see as much as possible to the education of my children."

The Doctor told him the day before that mustard must be applied outwardly in the way of rubbing where he had been blistered and that the operation would be painful. "Apply the remedy," said he "for I could wish the abolitionists present to see that no contention of my countenance was visible."

I asked him if he was afraid to die and if he desired a clergyman. He replied, "I am not afraid to die, although like all humanity and because of the ties of relationships and friendships I could desire to cling to life. But death is the fate of all and there is no use in 'picking against the pricks."

"I have no objections to the presence of a minister, yet I have my own religious view and whilst many of them would differ no doubt many would correspond with his and I have not the physical ability to discuss points with him."

Lieut. Powell noted down all his requests which he will doubtless communicate to you.

It was the most remarkable death I ever witnessed – his mind was clear as when you saw him in days of health and he expressed his desires calmly and without any faltering of account or tremulousness of lips and in choice and dignified language. He was truly a brave man and with his many friends I could have wished that he would have been spared by providence, to assist his struggling country in the great cause in which we are now engaged, and to exhibit those high traits of character his position in the army gave him an opportunity of doing –

"By many a death-bed I have been"

"And many a sinners parting scene"

"But never aught it like this –"

Dr. Femes said it was the grandest and most sublime death he ever witnessed.

Col. White who is by this time at home and who met Mrs. Phillips at Mobile and brought her back, will be able to give you every particular – He certainly acted the part of the Good Samaritan.

I have written to Judge Gibbs an account of Col. Phillips' death and requested him to publish it in the *Democrat* - No doubt there are other friends who will do his character full justice, but I could not withhold an expression of my sentiments to the memory of my brave friend.

Give my kind remembrance to Mrs. Phillips and say to her that her husband although far away from her had all proper attention

bestowed on him by his friends – With kind regards to yourself, Mrs. Burrus and children, I am
Your Friend,
McFarland

According to William, his many friends believed that had he lived another year when the fighting was in full swing, he would have soon become a major general.

On May 31, 1861, *The Daily Evening Citizen*, published in Vicksburg, Mississippi announced the news of his death:

> The news of the death of this brave and beloved Mississippian, which occurred at Pensacola, on the 22nd has cast a feeling of gloom and sorrow not only over his own personal friends but over the whole country wherever his reputation had extended. He was buried on the 23rd – the Mississippi Regiment turned out to do the funeral honors to the deceased, for he was esteemed and beloved by all who surrounded him.
>
> Col. Phillips left his home at Yazoo City as Captain of the Yazoo Minute Rifles, and was elected to the Colonelcy of the Regiment of which his company formed a part, after it arrived at Pensacola.
>
> He was about 35 years of age, and therefore had arrived at that period of life when his capacity for usefulness was highest. By profession a lawyer, and by taste and natural inclination a soldier, he was led into military life, while yet quite in his youth. He was a Lieutenant in the Mexican-American War, and in the iron storm of Buena Vista, revealed those heroic qualities which have culminated in the new and higher sphere of usefulness which had been assigned him in the present war. Appreciating these qualities President Davis, unsolicited, at the commencement of hostilities, appointed him to an honorable post in the regular Army, but he preferred to remain with his immediate associates until the close of the war. All with whom he came in contact in the discharge of his duties, speak in terms of the highest commendation of his zeal in the cause – mingling kindness with discipline, never forgetting in the stern duties of the soldier the tender obligations of humanity. He was frank, openhearted, generous and brave. He leaves behind him a wife and a family of small children. May the Merciful God "who tempers the wind to the shorn lamb" take them in His keeping. He left them but a few weeks ago in the full bloom of

health and the vigor of glorious manhood. "What shadows are we, what shadows we pursue!"

My great-grandfather William remembered:

> My father on his death-bed asked Col. Sharpe to have engraved on his rifle he fought with at the Battle of Buena Vista in Mexico, "Presented to my son, William W. Phillips, by his father." When the Yankees took possession of the city they searched every home for weapons, and found my rifle in Col. Sharpe's home and took it so he was unable to fulfill my father's request. Whenever I met the Colonel he would greet me cordially and say, "Well, Willie, the damn Yankees stole your gun."

Seaborn Moses Collins Phillips is buried in the Phillips plot in Greenwood Cemetery in Jackson, Mississippi. He was just 38 years old. His memorial is inscribed just above the name Phillips: "Erected by his children."

His wife Emily Cushman Walker Phillips, who was born on April 6, 1832 in Savannah, Georgia, died in Los Angeles at the home of her daughter Laurentina ("Laura") Phillips Graves on May 20, 1907. She is buried at the Mountain View Cemetery in Fresno, California.

Grave and Monument of Col. Seaborn Moses Collins Phillips
"Erected by his children," Greenwood Cemetery, Jackson, Mississippi
Photo by the author

Judge John Gotea Pressley (1833-1895)
Photo courtesy of Janyce Anderson

JOHN GOTEA PRESSLEY

My other paternal great-great grandfather was Judge John Gotea Pressley, William Walker Phillips' father-in-law. John was born in Williamsburg County, South Carolina on May 24, 1833.

In 1851 he graduated fourth out of a class of twenty-six from the South Carolina Military Academy, otherwise known as "The Citadel" in Charleston. At the Fifth Annual Commencement held on November 20, 1851, Cadet John G. Pressley, then eighteen years of age, read a speech entitled "Essay On Education."

In the mighty Universe taken as a grand whole, or in any of its departments, can be seen the overruling providence of its Great Original. Man may acquire knowledge, and become wise in his own conceit, but without a due sense of his obligations to his Maker, he is obliged to exclaim with vocation of spirit "all is vanity." He may devote his life to finding out nature; he may investigate cause and effect, but before the chain of sequences is completed, it must be attached to a great First Cause; existing from all eternity independently of and without a cause. But let him not yet be puffed up, "his ways are not as our ways." No man by searching can find them out. No ingenuity or untiring perseverance, can find out the relation which man sustains to his great Author. In this he must humble himself and be taught. In the beginning of his new course of study, let him look for confirmation to the state of nature surrounding him. Let him read the curse imposed upon man that "by the sweat of his brow he shall eat his bread." Then see how carrying out the conditions of this curse, man has worked out for himself all the excellence he possesses; and let him behold the condition of the poor imbecile who refuses to obey this mandate. He can no longer doubt.

It is a law of Industrial Economy that no capital is productive without the application of labour. Were it not for the labour of the husband-man, thorns and weeds would spring up where rich harvests are reaped. Were it not for the ship-builder the monarch of the forest would find none to dispute his right to remain in inactive majesty. He would never plough the briny deep to minister to the comforts and luxuries of man. Were it not for the sculptor how many exquisitely beautiful statues would remain forever hidden in the rugged rock. What labour is to capital what tillage is to the earth, what the fashioning hand of the carpenter is to the rough oak, "what sculpture is to a bleak marble," education is to the human mind.

In education, as in the different departments of industry, that intellectual capital freely bestowed on man, without labour, must remain forever unproductive of good to its possessor. The intellect however rich in resources, without careful cultivation, brings forth only uneasiness and disquiet, where a rich harvest of intellectual enjoyment was expected.

The industry and ingenuity of man has the same material manufactured many different articles, all of different degrees of utility. Of the best material the most precious articles are made, nothing need be lost. So in mind none need be a waste. By judicious management every one may be so improved as to become a useful member of society. Every individual has a part to perform.

> "All are the architects of fate,
> Working in these walls of time,
> Some with massive deeds and great,
> Some with ornaments of rhyme."

By proper tillage the most unproductive soil is not infrequently made the most fertile. And indeed that which is most sterile is generally most susceptible of improvement. So with the mind of man thought some may be at first altogether barren and unproductive, they say in the end be made to yield the richest crops of living ideas.

The cultivator, who would improve his conditions, is careful to exclude all intruders, who take away his produce without leaving anything useful in return.   And on the other hand by proper irrigation he is sure to retain rich sediments the waste of the more fertile. So he who would improve his intellectual condition should be careful to exclude from his attention every subject in which something useful cannot be found. This is opposed to the plan pursued by many who flood their minds with light reading, and while they amuse themselves with the gilded objects of imagination that which should have been the soil in which reason germinates, and grows to maturity is swept away.

In order that labour may be productively expanded, few essential prerequisites are necessary, material and time.   In performing the work of education, the first of these is possessed by man in a most eminent degree. But how often are the material with which, and from which we may learn, entirely overlooked. Nature teams with useful suggestions.   From everything animate or inanimate in earth, air, and water, something may be learnt. Divinity for man's instruction has spoken. The physical world is his first volume, man's intellectual nature is his second.   His revealed will his third. None is so unenlightened that none of these he may not read and gather stores of knowledge. Wise and happy is he who reaps from all three of these fields a harvest.

Time is benevolently allotted us by our Creator. And towards its improvement all intellectual labour should tend. A veil has been kindly and happily for us drawn over the future.

"Heaven from all creatures hides the beak of fate,
All but the page prescribed their present state,
From brutes, what men, from men, what angels know,
Or who could suffer bring here below."

It not only becomes one's duty to be always ready to leave his scene of toil, but to live in anticipation of our threescore and ten years. Though

"This life can little more supply,
Than just to look about us and to die."

Time for all things we have, if Nature's first law is observed. Much in our day may be accomplished. Accustom ourselves to order, and our habits become fixed and regular. We can then tread with an exulting step in the ways of virtue, and deride the folly of those who would entice us to turn aside into the avenue of vice. Those who have not taken the necessary precautions throng those byways man's life passeth as doth the shadow of a flying cloud, overshadowing him but for a moment. Time is almost no more, and Eternity broken forth, before the careless and unreflecting appreciate these precious moments which have been thoughtlessly frittered away. It may with truth be said of the sluggard "he has not lived out half his days, since so little good has been accomplished. Each moment should be spent in such manner, as to make us satisfied with ourselves, if it were our last. But instead of doing this how often are we found murmuring and grieving for what is unavoidable. We should be doing what our hands find, and what our head tells us is right, with all our heart. We thereby make reparation for past errors, and learn from them to shape our course differently for the future. Sympathy is one of the strongest bonds of society. We should feel for another's distress, and be moved to compassion and benevolence. We "should weep with them that weep, and rejoice with them that rejoice." But when we feel sorely the rod of affliction it is both unchristianlike, and unphilosophical to despair. The Christian bows himself in submission to the will of Heaven. He is content to wait that final adjustment in "his Father's mansion." The philosopher takes the past as a lamp to guide his feet through the untrodden paths of the future, and sets about rearing for himself a monument upon which the "destroyer" time, cannot lay his demolishing hand.

> "Genius like Egypt's monarch timely wise,
> Erects its own memorial, ere it dies."

Tried precepts and noble deeds carry the name of the good and great to posterity. "Curses and imprecations are the monuments" of the wicked and slothful. How many see their locks whitened by the frosts of many winters, without accomplishing anything to which they can look with pride; because they allow themselves to become depressed by the follies of youth. Nature admonishes us to action. The decline, death and decay of everything around us, tell us to be up and doing, and not remain the whole day idle.

When we take a review of the creation wonder after wonder presents itself to our gaze. And of all things strange the most wonderful is man. A worm of the dust, and yet a little lower than the angels. He is the best and the noblest work of God. The only one which he has honored by fashioning after his own image.

> "For him kind nature works her genial power;
> Suckles each herb, and spreads out every flower;
> Annual for him the grape, the rose renew;
> The juice nectarous, and the balmy dew;
> For him the mind a thousand treasures brings,
> For him health gushes from a thousand springs,
> Seas roll to waft him, suns to light him rise;

His footsteps earth, his canopy the skies."

But that which enables him always to maintain his supremacy, high above the rest of the creation is mind.

"That which in itself contains the fountain of all that's beauteous or sublime."

Why the Creator should have made a distinction among his creatures, it is not the province of reason to inquire. And though this apparent partiality, when we reflect, there is nothing in the creation derogatory to the Divine character. Mind and thought belong not to the brute, and of "his doings God takes no account." But for the use which man makes of his high prerogatives he is held accountable.

I move in that sphere in which his Greater intended that he should, man must be educated. His body, his head, and his heart were never intended to remain as he found them. It would be contrary to the order of nature. Each has its function to perform, and with a view to these functions should they be trained. Educate and expand the mind, without imparting strength to the body, and live like a sword that cutteth through its scabbard, it destroys its possessor. Educate his head and not his heart, and you ___ for him a cup in which is the gall of bitterness. Educate his head and heart and not his body, and the oil is consumed in the lamp of life ere the night is half gone.

John studied law with Judge Benjamin Chaplin Pressley, a Baptist who influenced John to become a Baptist at the Second Church of Charleston, in 1854.

In February, 1854, John married Julia Caroline Burckmyer who was born in South Carolina on December 2, 1833. Together they had numerous children: Elizabeth B. ("Bettie") Pressley, who married my great-grandfather William Walker Phillips, born in 1854; Margaret Jane Pressley, born in 1856 who died in 1877 in California; Mary Adams Pressley, born on January 14, 1858 who died on May 4, 1859; John B. Pressley, who was born around 1860; Mary C. Pressley, who was born around 1860; Cornelius Pressley, who was born around 1862; Benjamin Chaplin Pressley, who was born around 1868 and who died in California in 1934; Hugh Gotea Pressley, who was born around 1870 and who died in California in 1876; Lawrence A. Pressley, who was born around 1872 and who died in California in 1923;

Anna Levina Pressley, who was born around 1873 and who died in California in 1877; and William B. Pressley, who was born around 1875.

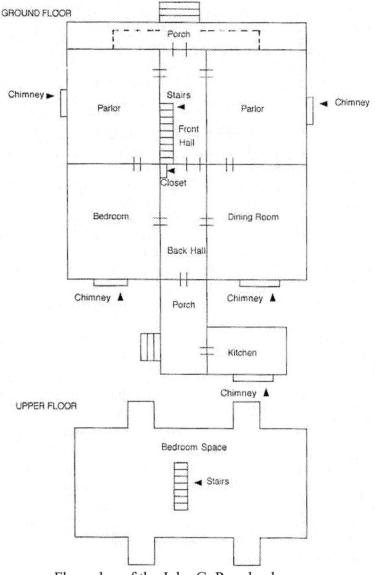

Floor plan of the John G. Pressley home
Kingstree, South Carolina, 1855-1869

The house in which they lived in Kingstree, South Carolina had two levels. The top of the floor plan represents the front of the house. On the ground floor, there were two adjacent parlors and a dining room, leaving room for only one bedroom downstairs. A second bedroom area occupied the entire second floor.

In September 2004 I visited the house. Today the right parlor has been converted into a second bedroom downstairs, and a bathroom was added in the back hall. The home has also been extended in the back to bring the kitchen indoors and to make room for a family room and an additional downstairs bathroom. The upstairs bedroom area now comprises two bedrooms and a small third bathroom.

The Col. John G. Pressley home, located at 216 North Academy Street in Kingstree, was named to the National Register of Historic Places on June 10, 1997 as building 97000534.

Kingstree, South Carolina home of John Gotea Pressley
Matilda Frances Elizabeth Phillips, age 3, on the steps
216 North Academy Street, Kingstree, South Carolina
September 2004, photo by the author

In June 1854 John was admitted to the bar before he was of age by special dispensation of Presiding Judge J. B. O'Neall. He settled in Kingstree and helped to make the Bethlehem Baptist Church respected and influential. He was ordained a deacon in 1856 and started a law practice.

In 1858 he became a member of the South Carolina State Legislature.   On December 20, 1860, following the recent Presidential election of Abraham Lincoln, John became the youngest signer of the Ordinance of Secession for the State of South Carolina.

With this document, which he signed at the age of 27, lay the Civil War.

South Carolina Ordinance of Secession
Signed and Ratified at Charleston, South Carolina
AN ORDINANCE to dissolve the union between the State of South Carolina and other States united with her under the compact entitled "The Constitution of the United States of America."

We, the people of the State of South Carolina, in convention assembled, do declare and ordain, and it is hereby declared and ordained, That the ordinance adopted by us in convention on the twenty-third day of May, in the year of our Lord one thousand seven hundred and eighty-eight, whereby the Constitution of the United States of America was ratified, and also all acts and parts of acts of the General Assembly of this State ratifying amendments of the said Constitution, are hereby repealed; and that the union now subsisting between South Carolina and other States, under the name of the "United States of America," is hereby dissolved.

Done at Charleston the twentieth day of December, in the year of our Lord one thousand eight hundred and sixty.

Declaration of the Immediate Causes
Which Induce and Justify the Secession
of South Carolina from the Federal Union
The people of the State of South Carolina, in Convention assembled, on the 26th day of April, A.D., 1852, declared that the frequent violations of the Constitution of the United States, by the Federal Government, and its encroachments upon the reserved rights of the States, fully justified this State in then

withdrawing from the Federal Union; but in deference to the opinions and wishes of the other slaveholding States, she forbore at that time to exercise this right. Since that time, these encroachments have continued to increase, and further forbearance ceases to be a virtue.

And now the State of South Carolina having resumed her separate and equal place among nations, deems it due to herself, to the remaining United States of America, and to the nations of the world, that she should declare the immediate causes which have led to this act.

In the year 1765, that portion of the British Empire embracing Great Britain, undertook to make laws for the government of that portion composed of the thirteen American Colonies. A struggle for the right of self-government ensued, which resulted, on the 4th of July, 1776, in a Declaration, by the Colonies, "that they are, and of right ought to be, FREE AND INDEPENDENT STATES; and that, as free and independent States, they have full power to levy war, conclude peace, contract alliances, establish commerce, and to do all other acts and things which independent States may of right do."

They further solemnly declared that whenever any "form of government becomes destructive of the ends for which it was established, it is the right of the people to alter or abolish it, and to institute a new government." Deeming the Government of Great Britain to have become destructive of these ends, they declared that the Colonies "are absolved from all allegiance to the British Crown, and that all political connection between them and the State of Great Britain is, and ought to be, totally dissolved."

In pursuance of this Declaration of Independence, each of the thirteen States proceeded to exercise its separate sovereignty; adopted for itself a Constitution, and appointed officers for the administration of government in all its departments-- Legislative, Executive and Judicial. For purposes of defense, they united their arms and their counsels; and, in 1778, they entered into a League known as the Articles of Confederation, whereby they agreed to entrust the administration of their external relations to a common agent, known as the Congress of the United States, expressly declaring, in the first Article "that each State retains its sovereignty, freedom and independence, and every power, jurisdiction and right which is not, by this Confederation, expressly delegated to the United States in Congress assembled."

Under this Confederation the war of the Revolution was carried on, and on the 3rd of September, 1783, the contest ended, and a definite Treaty was signed by Great Britain, in which she acknowledged the independence of the Colonies in the following terms: "ARTICLE 1-- His Britannic Majesty acknowledges the said United States, viz: New Hampshire, Massachusetts Bay, Rhode Island and Providence Plantations, Connecticut, New York, New Jersey, Pennsylvania, Delaware, Maryland, Virginia, North Carolina, South Carolina and Georgia, to be FREE, SOVEREIGN AND INDEPENDENT STATES; that he treats with them as such; and for himself, his heirs and successors, relinquishes all claims to the government, propriety and territorial rights of the same and every part thereof."

Thus were established the two great principles asserted by the Colonies, namely: the right of a State to govern itself; and the right of a people to abolish a Government when it becomes destructive of the ends for which it was instituted. And concurrent with the establishment of these principles, was the fact, that each Colony became and was recognized by the mother Country a FREE, SOVEREIGN AND INDEPENDENT STATE.

In 1787, Deputies were appointed by the States to revise the Articles of Confederation, and on 17th September, 1787, these Deputies recommended for the adoption of the States, the Articles of Union, known as the Constitution of the United States.

The parties to whom this Constitution was submitted, were the several sovereign States; they were to agree or disagree, and when nine of them agreed the compact was to take effect among those concurring; and the General Government, as the common agent, was then invested with their authority.

If only nine of the thirteen States had concurred, the other four would have remained as they then were-- separate, sovereign States, independent of any of the provisions of the Constitution. In fact, two of the States did not accede to the Constitution until long after it had gone into operation among the other eleven; and during that interval, they each exercised the functions of an independent nation.

By this Constitution, certain duties were imposed upon the several States, and the exercise of certain of their powers was restrained, which necessarily implied their continued existence as sovereign States. But to remove all doubt, an amendment was added, which declared that the powers not delegated to the United States by the Constitution, nor prohibited by it to the States, are reserved to the States, respectively, or to the people.

On the 23d May, 1788, South Carolina, by a Convention of her People, passed an Ordinance assenting to this Constitution, and afterwards altered her own Constitution, to conform herself to the obligations she had undertaken.

Thus was established, by compact between the States, a Government with definite objects and powers, limited to the express words of the grant. This limitation left the whole remaining mass of power subject to the clause reserving it to the States or to the people, and rendered unnecessary any specification of reserved rights.

We hold that the Government thus established is subject to the two great principles asserted in the Declaration of Independence; and we hold further, that the mode of its formation subjects it to a third fundamental principle, namely: the law of compact. We maintain that in every compact between two or more parties, the obligation is mutual; that the failure of one of the contracting parties to perform a material part of the agreement, entirely releases the obligation of the other; and that where no arbiter is provided, each party is remitted to his own judgment to determine the fact of failure, with all its consequences.

In the present case, that fact is established with certainty. We assert that fourteen of the States have deliberately refused, for years past, to fulfill their constitutional obligations, and we refer to their own Statutes for the proof.

The Constitution of the United States, in its fourth Article, provides as follows: "No person held to service or labor in one State, under the laws thereof, escaping into another, shall, in consequence of any law or regulation therein, be discharged from such service or labor, but shall be delivered up, on claim of the party to whom such service or labor may be due."

This stipulation was so material to the compact, that without it that compact would not have been made. The greater number of the contracting parties held slaves, and they had previously evinced their estimate of the value of such a stipulation by making it a condition in the Ordinance for the government of the territory ceded by Virginia, which now composes the States north of the Ohio River.

The same article of the Constitution stipulates also for rendition by the several States of fugitives from justice from the other States.

The General Government, as the common agent, passed laws to carry into effect these stipulations of the States. For many years these laws were executed. But an increasing hostility on the part of the non-slaveholding States to the institution of slavery, has led to a disregard of their obligations, and the laws of the General Government have ceased to effect the objects of the Constitution. The States of Maine, New Hampshire, Vermont, Massachusetts, Connecticut, Rhode Island, New York, Pennsylvania, Illinois, Indiana, Michigan, Wisconsin and Iowa, have enacted laws which either nullify the Acts of Congress or render useless any attempt to execute them. In many of these States the fugitive is discharged from service or labor claimed, and in none of them has the State Government complied with the stipulation made in the Constitution. The State of New Jersey, at an early day, passed a law in conformity with her constitutional obligation; but the current of anti-slavery feeling has led her more recently to enact laws which render inoperative the remedies provided by her own law and by the laws of Congress. In the State of New York even the right of transit for a slave has been denied by her tribunals; and the States of Ohio and Iowa have refused to surrender to justice fugitives charged with murder, and with inciting servile insurrection in the State of Virginia. Thus the constituted compact has been deliberately broken and disregarded by the non-slaveholding States, and the consequence follows that South Carolina is released from her obligation.

The ends for which the Constitution was framed are declared by itself to be "to form a more perfect union, establish justice, insure domestic tranquility, provide for the common defence, promote the general welfare, and secure the blessings of liberty to ourselves and our posterity."

These ends it endeavored to accomplish by a Federal Government, in which each State was recognized as an equal, and had separate control over its own institutions. The right of property in slaves was recognized by giving to free persons distinct political rights, by giving them the right to represent, and burdening them with direct taxes for three-fifths of their slaves; by authorizing the importation of slaves for twenty years; and by stipulating for the rendition of fugitives from labor.

We affirm that these ends for which this Government was instituted have been defeated, and the Government itself has been made destructive of them by the action of the non-slaveholding States. Those States have assumed the right of deciding upon the propriety of our domestic institutions; and have denied the rights of property established in fifteen of the States and recognized by the Constitution; they have denounced as sinful the institution of slavery; they have permitted open establishment among them of societies, whose avowed object is to disturb the peace and to eloign (take away) the property of the citizens of other States. They have encouraged and assisted thousands of our slaves to leave their homes; and those who remain, have been incited by emissaries, books and pictures to servile insurrection.

For twenty-five years this agitation has been steadily increasing, until it has now secured to its aid the power of the common Government. Observing the forms of the Constitution, a sectional party has found within that Article establishing the Executive Department, the means of subverting the Constitution itself. A geographical line has been drawn across the Union, and all the States north of that line have united in the election of a man to the high office of President of the United States, whose opinions and purposes are hostile to slavery. He is to be entrusted with the administration of the common Government, because he has declared that that "Government cannot endure permanently half slave, half free," and that the public mind must rest in the belief that slavery is in the course of ultimate extinction.

This sectional combination for the submersion of the Constitution, has been aided in some of the States by elevating to citizenship, persons who, by the supreme law of the land, are incapable of becoming citizens; and their votes have been used to inaugurate a new policy, hostile to the South, and destructive of its beliefs and safety.

On the 4th day of March next, this party will take possession of the Government. It has announced that the South shall be excluded from the common territory, that the judicial tribunals shall be made sectional, and that a war must be waged against slavery until it shall cease throughout the United States.

The guaranties of the Constitution will then no longer exist; the equal rights of the States will be lost. The slaveholding States will no longer have the power of self-government, or self-protection, and the Federal Government will have become their enemy.

Sectional interest and animosity will deepen the irritation, and all hope of remedy is rendered vain, by the fact that public opinion at the North has invested a great political error with the sanction of more erroneous religious belief.

We, therefore, the People of South Carolina, by our delegates in Convention assembled, appealing to the Supreme Judge of the world for the rectitude of our intentions, have solemnly declared that the Union heretofore existing between this State and the other States of North America, is dissolved, and that the State of South Carolina has resumed her position among the nations of the world, as a separate and independent State; with full power to levy war, conclude peace, contract alliances, establish commerce, and to do all other acts and things which independent States may of right do.

— Adopted December 24, 1860 —

Delegates from WILLIAMSBURG:
Anthony White Dozier, Sr.
Richard C. Logan
John Gotea Pressley

Lt. Col. John Gotea Pressley
Photo courtesy of the Williamsburgh Historical Museum
Kingstree, South Carolina

At the beginning of the war in 1861, John Gotea Pressley joined the Confederate Army. On letterhead of the "Confederate States of America" War Department, Richmond, dated September 12, 1862, John was informed that "the President has appointed you Lieutenant Colonel of the Twenty-fifth South Carolina Regiment." Earlier in the year he was referred to as "Major."

John would have fought in the following battles:

- James Island, South Carolina (May 31, 1863)
- Grimball's Landing, James Island South Carolina (July 30, 1863)
- Charleston Harbor[73], South Carolina (August - September 1863)
- Mouth of Vincent's Creek, South Carolina (August 4, 1863)
- Port Walthall Junction, Virginia (May 6, 1864)

On May 6, 1864, while in battle at Port Walthall Junction, Virginia, he nearly lost an arm. As a result of new medical procedures at the time, his arm was saved, but it was useless to him for the rest of his life.

After his injury, his regiment would have continued to fight in the following battles:

- Swift Creek, Virginia (May 9, 1864)
- Drewry's Bluff, Virginia (May 12, 1864)
- Drewry's Bluff, Virginia (May 16, 1864)
- Cold Harbor, Virginia (June 1-3, 1864)
- Petersburg Siege, Virginia (June 1864 - April 1865)
- Weldon Railroad, Virginia (August 21, 1864)
- 2nd Fort Harrison, Virginia (September 30, 1864)
- 2nd Fort Fisher, North Carolina (January 13-15, 1865)
- Bentonville, North Carolina (March 19-21, 1865)
- Carolinas Campaign, South Carolina (February - April 1865)

- Bentonville (March 19-21, 1865)

John often prayed with his men around the camp-fire, and was a brave soldier. There is a copy of his diary while serving in the Civil War which was published in *The Southern Historical Society Papers* published in the late 1880s and early 1900s, which comprises 52 volumes. A portion of this diary from September 1863 is reprinted here:

1st September.   Ordered to Wagner... Embarked from Fort Johnson all of the regiment except Company A, in a light draft steamer. Company A went in a rowboat. The steamer stopped near Sumter; harbor very rough. I got in the only boat the steamer had for debarking us, with about fifty officers and men. When we had got half way from the steamer to Cummings Point, a bombardment of Sumter by monitors commenced and the steamer returned to Fort Johnson with the balance of the regiment. At Cummings Point I found Company A, making with the men I brought, eighty or ninety men of my command, and no prospect of getting the others till next night. Reported to General Colquitt, in command, and was ordered to the sand hills in rear of Wagner. So we spent the balance of the night in what the soldiers called "private bomb-proofs" - holes in the sand. Not finding these comfortable, I myself spread my blanket between two sand hillocks. Fort Wagner and the enemy exchanged shots slowly all night.

2nd September.   Went into Wagner at daylight. Found the enemy's sap within about 120 yards of the salient; enemy working industriously. Garrison busy repairing damages and keeping up a slow fire. My command detailed as a working party for Battery Gregg.   Enemy shelling Wagner, Gregg and Sumter all day. Transferred to Wagner at night, and by 11 p.m. the balance of my regiment arrived and reported to me. My companies, as they arrived, were stationed around the parapet, relieving the North Carolina regiment.

We occupied from the extreme left along the sea face around the left salient and part of the land force; the Twenty-fifth Georgia the rest. These two regiments, with the artillerists, occupied the fort; another regiment, the Twenty-seventh Georgia, was in the sand hills in the rear. Enemy fired very little tonight. I was up most of the night posting and visiting my men; towards morning I took a nap in the left salient, resting my head against the parapet.

3rd September. One or two of our guns and one mortar keep up fire against the enemy's approaching sap.

My command in high spirits, a great many building loopholes with sand bags for sharpshooting. This has become very dangerous work; as soon as a hole is darkened on either side, a shot from the opposite sharpshooter follows, and with frequent success. Not much artillery fire by or at Wagner, but the enemy are hard at work and approaching. Our James Island batteries are firing briskly on the enemy's trenches. During the day from one-third to one-fourth the garrison are kept at the parapet, the rest in the bomb-proof - at night all are turned out. The Yankees are so near they can hear when we turn out, and quicken their fire. The garrison is heavily worked repairing damages.

Colonel Keitt, Twentieth South Carolina, relieved General Colquitt last night in command of Morris Island. I was up nearly all night, slept a little before day in the same salient as last night.

4th September. Quite a lively bombardment from the enemy today, number of the sand bag covers for sharpshooters knocked away. Sharpshooting still very brisk, however... Batteries on James Island do good shooting, particularly Battery Simkins. Major Warley, chief of artillery, wounded; Captain Hugenin replaces him. Our parties very hard at work repairing damages. A corporal of Company A and several men wounded in my regiment. Several killed and a good many wounded in the balance of garrison. The enemy's fire slacked after dark. They display a calcium light tonight upon Vincent's creek. Towards day I tried to get a little sleep in my old place in the left salient. The shells from Fort Moultrie were passing immediately over it. A fragment from one of our own mortar shells came back into the fort and nearly struck me. This has been happening for some time, the enemy were so close...

5th September. The fleet early this morning opened upon the fort, the land batteries also cannonading with great fury - 200 and 100-pound Parrotts, 8 and 10-inch mortar shells and 15-nch shell from the navy pouring into us. The shells are exploding so fast they cannot be counted. All our guns are silenced. Working them under such a fire is out of the question. The men are being wounded and killed in every direction. I have been around amongst my men a good many times and am covered with sand when I return. The three-fourths of the garrison are still kept in the bomb-proofs. The suffering of these from the heat and want of water is intolerable. The supply of water brought from the city is very inadequate; that from the shallow wells dug in the sand in and adjacent to the fort is horrible. Famishing thirst alone enables the men to drink it. ... I have seen some horrible sights - men mangled in almost every manner. I saw a sharpshooter knocked from the parapet to the middle of the parade, some forty or fifty feet, and going fully twenty feet in the air. This was Rawlinson, of Company G, and the brave fellow clutched his rifle to the last. Of course, he lived but a short time. Lieutenant Montgomery, of Company C, was killed this morning - his head taken off by a shell.

An attack upon Battery Gregg is expected tonight; a detachment of my regiment, under Captain Sellars, and of the Twenty-eighth Georgia, under Captain Hayne, are to be sent to re-enforce it. As they march out Captain Hayne enquires of Lieutenant Blum for Captain Sellars; a shell kills both. ... It is apparent that our force manning the parapet tonight must be as small as possible. ... In making our arrangements for the night there are many casualties in our detachment, commanded by Lieutenant Ramsey, Company Twenty-fifth. In a short time after it was posted every man but one was killed or wounded. The fleet has withdrawn and the land batteries slacked their fire, save the mortars, which are as active as ever. I have seen four shells start from the same battery at the same time.

There was an alarm of an assault tonight. It was felt to be a relief - the prospect of changing this passive endurance of artillery into the hot blood of an infantry fight. The enemy's calcium light illuminated the whole fort, and the sharpshooters, contrary to custom, were at work all night. The enemy attacked Gregg and were repulsed... Wells dug in the bomb-proofs give some relief in better water, but not enough.

John was a trustee of Furman University, a frequent member of Baptist State Conventions, and in 1868 was a member of the Southern Baptist Convention in Baltimore. This convention following the war initiated growing relations between the Southern and Northern Baptists.

In 1869 John and his family moved to California with members of the Anderson and Dozier families, first settling in Suisun City, and entered into a lucrative legal practice.

John helped to organize the College of California, and was a trustee and secretary of the college board until he moved to Santa Rosa in 1873. The College of California later became the

University of California, and in the year that John moved to Santa Rosa, the University of California moved from Oakland to its present day location in Berkeley, California.

In Santa Rosa he joined the Baptist Church and was chosen as their deacon and Sunday school superintendent.

In 1875 he was elected county judge. *The Sacramento Daily Union* reported on March 20, 1876: "Ramon Sanchez, under $3,000 bonds to keep the peace on complaint of W. D. Jones, of Russian River township, was taken before Judge Pressley on a writ of habeas corpus and discharged, the prosecuting witness having consented to withdraw the charge on condition that Sanchez leave the neighborhood."

In 1879 he was nominated by the Democrats and endorsed by Republican, Workingmen and the Temperance parties for superior court judge, and was elected.

The Sonoma Democrat reported on November 5, 1887: "The proceedings in the Muther case were dismissed by Judge Pressley yesterday. An order was issued to have the children visit their mother at the Grand Hotel, on Tuesday and Saturdays, between 2 and 6 p.m."

In 1889 Lewis Publishing Company published *An Illustrated History of Sonoma County, California*. They devoted two pages to John Gotea Pressley:

> Hon. John Gotea Pressley, who is one of the judges of the Superior Court of Sonoma County was born in Williamsburg district (now county), South Carolina, on the 24th of May, 1833. His parents were John B. and Sarah (Gotea) Pressley, both "natives and to the manor born," and of ancestry identified for generations with the history of South Carolina.
>
> His father was a successful planter of Williamsburg district and a man of great personal worth and social influence. The son enjoyed the advantages of early moral and religious training, and, after a preparatory course in the country schools of the neighborhood, received an appointment in January, 1848, to the State Military Academy at Charleston - an institution whose system and course of instruction was very similar to that of West Point. He graduated in November, 1851.
>
> While a cadet he was, in the year 1850, detailed to act as assistant professor of mathematics, and at his graduation, in 1851,

he ranked fourth in a class of twenty-six, and held the command of one of the companies of the Cadet Corps.

From the military academy he entered as a student of law the office of his kinsman, B.C. Pressley, Esq., then one of the leading members of the bar of Charleston, and now an honored circuit judge of the State, where, under the guidance of this relative and friend, he pursued his studies until February, 1854. By a special dispensation of the Court of Appeals of South Carolina he was accorded an examination in May, 1854, while still under age, and received his commission as attorney upon attaining his majority a few weeks afterward.

He immediately opened a law office at Kingstree, the county seat of Williamsburg district, and entered upon the practice of his profession, which he pursued with diligence and success in the districts of Williamsburg, Marion, Darlington, Georgetown and Clarendon until January, 1861, when the war destroyed his lucrative and growing business and literally closed the doors of his office for five years. In those early years of his professional life, he represented his district in the Legislature of the State during the sessions of 1858 and 1859, being the youngest member except one in the Lower House, and assistant cashier of that body.

Then came the war. He entered the military service in January, 1861, as captain of infantry, and rose to the rank of Lieutenant-Colonel of the Twenty-fifth Regiment, South Carolina Volunteers, and commanded that regiment almost continuously and with marked ability and gallantry until the end of the war. His regiment experienced hard and dangerous service and was engaged in some of the most desperate and destructive conflicts of the war, in one of which, near Petersburg, in 1864, he himself received a dangerous wound from the effects of which he still carries a partially disabled arm.

In January, 1866, he reopened his law office at Kingstree and resumed the practice of his profession. At the annual session of the Legislature for that year (under the reconstruction plan of President Johnson) he was elected district judge of Williamsburg district, but on account of the inadequacy of the salary, declined to qualify. He maintained the struggle against the adverse influences of the "reconstruction" period until weary of the unequal strife, discouraged concerning the future outlook, and having regard for the interest of his family, he sought a haven and a home for them on the Pacific coast. He arrived in California on the 24th of April, 1869[74], via the Isthmus of Panama, and took up his residence first in Suisun, Solano County, and opened his law office there and afterward at Fairfield, the county seat.

He became the city attorney of Suisun and held this position three years and until his removal to Santa Rosa. In January, 1873, he moved to Sonoma County, and took up his residence in Santa Rosa, where he formed a partnership with Judge A. Thomas, an old and respected citizen and able lawyer.

In the fall of 1873 he became the city attorney of Santa Rosa, and at the judicial election in 1875, he was elected county judge of Sonoma County. From this time until January, 1880, he continued upon the bench of the county court, and at the same time practiced at the bar of the district court.

The constitution of 1879 reorganized the judicial system of the State, abolishing the district and county courts and substituting for them a Superior Court for each county. At the first election in Sonoma County under the new system, John G. Pressley and Jackson Temple were elected judges of the new court and took their seats on the 1st of January, 1880.

Both of these judges were re-elected in 1884. Judge Temple has since been removed to the bench of the Supreme Court of this State while Judge Pressley still adorns the Superior Court bench.

His decisions have rarely been reversed by the Supreme Court. In religion, Judge Pressley is and has for many years been an earnest and zealous Baptist, but not a narrow sectarian.

In February, 1854, Judge Pressley married Miss Julia C. Burckmyer, daughter of Cornelius Burckmyer, a prominent merchant of Charleston, South Carolina. To them have been born ten children, six of whom survive and are residents of California.

An alternate and more brief biography was also published in the same year under the title *A History of Sonoma County*:

In 1851 he graduated State Military Academy at Charleston, "The Citadel." In May 1854 a few weeks before his 21st birthday, he was the only law student ever accorded an examination under the age of 21.

He immediately opened a law office at Kingstree, the county seat of Williamsburg district, and entered upon the practice of his profession, which he pursued with diligence and success in the districts of Williamsburg, Marion, Darlington, Georgetown and Clarendon until January 1861, when the war destroyed his lucrative and growing business and literally closed the doors of his office for five years.

In those early years of his professional life, he represented his district in the Legislature of the State during the sessions of 1858 and 1859, being the youngest member except one in the Lower House, and assistant cashier of that body. (He was the youngest to sign the Articles of SC Secession at end of 1860).

Of his participation in the great strife, no sketch of his life would be complete without some mention. From the commencement until its disastrous end, he gave himself up unselfishly and wholly to the cause of the South and rendered it loyal and efficient service. His regiment experienced hard and dangerous service and was engaged in some of the most desperate and destructive conflicts of the war.

The war over, he honestly and with patient submission accepted in good faith the situation. In January, 1866, he reopened his law office at Kingstree and resumed the practice of his profession. At the annual session of the Legislature for that year (under the reconstruction plan of President Johnson) he was elected district judge of Williamsburg district, but on account of the inadequacy of the salary, declined to qualify. He maintained the struggle against the adverse influences of the "reconstruction" period until weary of the unequal strife, discouraged concerning the future outlook, and having regard for the interest of his family, he sought a haven and a home for them on the Pacific coast.

He arrived in California on the 24th of April, 1869, via the Isthmus of Panama, and took up his residence first in Suisun, Solano County, and opened his law office there and afterward at Fairfield, the county seat. In January 1873 he moved to Sonoma County, and took up his residence in Santa Rosa, where in three short years he was elected County Judge, and in Jan 1880 was selected for the Superior Court earning the reputation as the best Superior Court in the State.

Judge Pressley is emphatically a popular man. He is always and under all circumstances courteous, genial, considerate and kind, a warm friend and a charming companion. Upon the bench he presides with grace and dignity, without severity. He is always an attentive and willing listener. He is as prompt and positive in his rulings as is consistent with due deliberation and prudent care. When the occasion calls for it, he is patient and laborious. In every walk of life his Christian faith, generous, genial temper, and courteous manner, adorn a character marked by purity of mind, truthfulness and sincerity of purpose, fidelity to principle and love and charity for men.

Col. James Fowler Pressley (1835-1876)
Courtesy of the Williamsburgh Historical Museum

John Gotea Pressley's brother, James Fowler Pressley, my third great-granduncle, was a medical doctor who served as

Colonel of the 10th South Carolina Volunteer Infantry, of which George Pressly Anderson served initially as a sergeant.

A brief sketch of James' life includes:

- S.C. Military Academy (The Citadel), 1852-1856
- Graduated Charleston Medical College (today known as Medical University of South Carolina), 1858
- Married Emma Wilson on April 15, 1858, the sister of Margaret Gotea Wilson Anderson
- Settled on the West side of Black Mingo Swamp, Williamsburg County, South Carolina
- Practiced medicine until early 1861
- Organized Company E, Black Mingo Rifle Guards, 10th South Carolina Volunteer Infantry on May 31, 1861
- Elected Captain of Company E, May 31, 1861
- Commander, 10th & 19th Infantry Regiments, January 1862 to April 1864
- Acting Brigadier General, Battle of Chickamauga, September 20, 1863, under Lieutenant General James Longstreet
- Wounded, Battle of Atlanta, during advance featured in the Atlanta Cyclorama on July 22, 1864
- Elected to South Carolina Legislature in 1864
- Recommended for promotion to Brigadier General on December 16, 1864
- Commanded State Militia during Potter's Raid, saving Williamsburg County and slowing the advance toward Sumter and Camden, South Carolina, April 1865
- Set up a medical practice in Cynthiana, Kentucky in partnership with Dr. A. J. Beale, his Surgeon in the 10th Regiment around 1867
- Moved with his extended family to Suisun City, CA, by ship via the Isthmus of Panama in 1869
- Established a medical practice in Suisun City in 1870
- Moved to San Jose, California in 1874 or 1875
- Died in San Francisco, California on February 13, 1876

- Buried in Fairfield Cemetery, Solano County, California

James Fowler Pressley and Emma Wilson Pressley
Photo courtesy of Janyce Anderson

On February 14, 1876, the *Weekly Solano Reporter* printed the obituary of Col. James Fowler Pressley, M.D.:

> Deceased was a victim of that scourge, [tuberculosis]. Notwithstanding he was a man with a delicate organism, he was so devoted to his profession, so scrupulously conscientious in the discharge of his duties, prompted by enlarged sympathies, that he did not hesitate to expose himself to our bleak winds, which gradually wore away his vigor, and finally contracted the loathsome disease of which he died.
>
> He was a victim of a noble pride for his profession and sympathy for suffering humanity. After the repeated solicitation of his friends, he was persuaded to retire from his extensive and lucrative practice in Suisun

In November, 1876, he sold his interests here and gave up his practice and went to San Jose, there to live in quietude and receive all the benefits of that gentle climate. His death will be generally and sincerely mourned by his community. He was a faithful member of the Odd Fellows Lodge of this place, by which order he will be buried tomorrow. He leaves a wife and two children, besides other relatives in the county to mourn his death.

In 2003, Bruce Tognazzini, Col. James Fowler Pressley's great-grandson and my third cousin once removed, wrote:

For the past year, I have followed the footsteps of Col. Pressley, my great grandfather, across the South he loved. James F. Pressley was a man of contradictions. He was a professional soldier, dedicated to the taking of life. He was at the same time a doctor, dedicated to the saving of life.

In his heart burned the fierce fire of freedom. He and his countrymen threw off the yoke of Northern oppression when it threatened their most precious right—the freedom to own slaves. These were the same slaves--or "servants," as he called them--he treated with care, respect, and even friendship, ministering to their ills with the same care as he gave his own family, a paradox to those of us born in the North, but familiar to those from the South.

He was also a man of constant honor. He was brave beyond all modern measure, both in war and beyond. The experiences of all the warriors of that great civil conflict are beyond the imagination of those of us in the modern world, where major wars are fought and won with the loss of 100 to 200 American lives. In just one battle[75] on one single day of the Civil War, [over 12,000] brave Americans met their death, and the rest went on to continue the fight.

John Gotea Pressley
Published in *The Sonoma Democrat* obituary, July 13, 1895

The Sonoma Democrat reported on April 20, 1889:

The army of bachelors is one less! Clem Kessing, a pioneer merchant, was made happy in matrimonial alliance with Mrs. Catharine Hornbeck yesterday. Judge Pressley pronounced the sentence that made them one forever, at the residence of Mrs. Johnson, on Second St. Mr. Kessing and his bride went to San Francisco by the afternoon train. We, with many other friends unite in wishing the bride and groom all the bliss that attains to the wedded state and admonish the other old bachelors to follow Clem's example.

The Sonoma Democrat reported on July 1, 1889, "A decree of divorce has been issued by Judge Pressley in the case of Elizabeth McReynolds (nee Gardner) vs. R. E. L. McReynolds."

On April 12, 1890, *The Sonoma Democrat* reported:

> M. F. Von Gelden was denied a divorce from her husband, Joseph Von Gelden, by Judge Pressley, Tuesday. The action was based on willful neglect and the complaint charged a failure to provide the necessaries of life, the defendant having the ability to do so. The court held that this means a failure by the husband who has property, and the evidence not showing that the defendant had any means, and profligacy, idleness or dissipation not being charged, the divorce was denied.

The same year, on July 1, 1890, John wrote a long private memorandum (some of which I cannot decipher) to his wife to be read after he died. The first few pages are transcribed here for the first time:

> Pray without ceasing. And whatever ye shall ask in my name that will I do, that the father may be glorified in the Lord.
>
> If ye shall ask anything in my name I will do it.
>
> I have tested the truth of this scripture. I regret now that I had not commenced long ago to keep something like a diary and noted therein all of the answers to prayer that I have had. It would I hope be encouraging to my children after "I am gathered to my fathers." I have been praying since my childhood. The infantile prayer taught me by my mother (dear Mother) soon ceased to satisfy me. I learned the Lord's Prayer. That was not specific enough to satisfy my longings, and at a very early age, I can say now when I began to tell God what I wanted. I have no doubt that I prayed without much discretion, and asked for many things that I ought not to have. Sometimes I prayed the Lord to withhold an answer if it was better for me that my prayers should not be answered. Sometimes I prayed that an answer be withheld if it were better for

the people, for right and for justice. I early in life debated with myself whether I ought to ask my Heavenly Father for mere temporal gifts.   I came to the conclusion that if my Heavenly Father loved me like my dear father in the flesh (and I he did) I could take everything to Him. I am firm in the belief that I ought not to do anything that I can not ask God to help me in, nor should I desire anything that I can not ask Him to give me. I have long been in the habit of going to Him in the name of Jesus for anything that I want. I am not aware that I ever undertake anything of any consequence without asking His assistance. I have also been for a long time in the habit of praying for my enemies. When I am injured the first thing I do is to take the party injuring me to God and beseech my God to change his heart, and make him see his error. I have often [asked] God to let my enemies and those who wrong me see just how I think and feel towards them.

I cannot remember a tenth part of the answers that I have had to my prayers, but I will record just a few.

When I set out in life, I felt great distrust of my abilities. I saw many lawyers who had failed at attaining even a moderate degree of success that I esteemed as my equals in point of capacity. I trembled for my future. I went to my God, and asked him to give me success at least so far as to be able to earn a competency for such family as He might send me. In answer to this, my life has not been a failure.

I asked my God to spare my life through the war. Answer. After many escapes which were Providential, I am now alive.

I remember two occasions, once my daughter Bet[76] was sick, once my son John was sick. This was at Kingstree.

Later I asked my God to spare their lives. They are alive[77]. As they were then under the age of ___ sensibility their conduct will prove ____. These answers were blessings to them and to me or the contrary. I now pray God in the name of Jesus that the sparing of their lives may be a blessing to me and to both of them. I have one child now an angel with God, I will soon see this dear child. I love all my children. I would rather my Heavenly Father take them to himself in infancy than to have them grow up and forget God. It is infinitely better for them to die early than to live spared and forget God. I desire for them that which is best for them.

At the close of the war I found myself a citizen of a grieved and bankrupt country. I had well grounded fears that my family would come to want. In answer to prayer God sent me plenty for us all.

For some wise and inscrutable purpose from which God was not to be moved by the prayers of his people, He allowed my poor country to be greatly afflicted and ruined. Peace was greatly desired by me for myself and my family, I determined to move to California. I had much anxiety of mind, I prayed night and day. My hopes rose in the day, my heart sank at night. Although I concluded to put all my trust in God, and make the [best of it]. I am in California, my wife and children have not wanted. God has been with me. Bless his holy name!

I got practice in Suisun where I settled. I could not now enumerate the efforts of the bar which God [helped] me in. I know I made speeches that were beyond my ability, I know that my Heavenly Father put the ideas and words into my mind and mouth. I remember some with great gratitude and thankfulness how I rose above myself in the case of the People vs. Autoria Manuel charged with the murder of Chas. Fer____. It was such a desperate case. The proof was very sparse. The people said it was a cold blooded murder. The court thought it was murder, no one expected to see my _____. His own nephew tried to get me to offer to plead guilty to manslaughter, the District Attorney said he would not have consented to the plea if I had offered. I refused. I put my trust in God, prayed to Him. He answered my prayers, gave me a great victory, my client went free, and my reputation as a criminal lawyer was established in Solano County…

In that year, *The Sonoma Democrat* reported on December 6, 1890, "J. A. Banks and Miss Mamie Wescott were married in the parlors of the Grand Hotel, Tuesday, by Judge Pressley."

Judge John Gotea Pressley died on July 5, 1895 while camping at "Camp Pressley" near Santa Rosa, California at the age of 62.

His wife Julia Caroline Burckmyer died in Santa Rosa on December 30, 1907 at the age of 74.

*   *   *

George Pressly[78] Anderson, the father of David Pressley Anderson, was born on June 8, 1838 in Georgia.

He attended Furman University in Greenville, South Carolina, from 1856-1859. George enlisted in the 10th South Carolina Volunteer Infantry, Company E as a sergeant on July 19, 1861 at Whiles Bridge under Captain James F. Carraway's Co. at the age of 23. The company was known as the "Black Mingo Rifle Guards."

He was then promoted to second lieutenant, then first lieutenant, and was made captain on July 8, 1862.

George was severely wounded, at Kinston, North Carolina in March of 1865[79]. His name appears on the Register of the Pettigrew General Hospital No. 12, in Raleigh, North Carolina from March 11-19, 1865, when he was transferred to Greenville County, South Carolina.

The "Chronology of Battles and Skirmishes of the South Carolina Tenth Regiment[80]" shows this regiment, in Mississippi, Kentucky and Tennessee through July 1863. This Tenth Regiment was commanded by John Gotea Pressley's brother Colonel James Fowler Pressley.

In August 1863 the Black Mingo Rifle Guards, as they were known, started the Georgia Campaign, with battles in Alabama and Tennessee, lasting until January of 1865 when they started the Campaign of the Carolinas.

There are two major battles mentioned at the time Captain George Pressly Anderson was wounded. One was The Battle of Aversborough (Taylor's Hole Creek) in North Carolina, and the other was the Battle of Bentonville in North Carolina.

This regiment surrendered at Bennett's House, Durham Station, North Carolina on April 26, 1865 about one month after he was wounded.

After his marriage on June 19 1867, to Margaret Gotea Wilson (the daughter of David D. Wilson and Sarah Grier Britton Britton), George established his home in South Carolina and taught school until 1869. Later that year, he went to California with the Pressley and Dozier families.

George's wife, Margaret, and son, David Pressley Anderson, followed to California in 1870. There George taught school in Suisun, Solano County, California.

In 1876 George and the family moved to San Jose where he taught for two years. In 1878 he and the family then moved to Santa Rosa where John Gotea Pressley had moved five years previously. In Santa Rosa, George taught and was made principal of the old Davis Street School (later known as the Lincoln School).

On Saturday, February 26, 1887, the weekly paper, *The Sonoma Democrat* published his obituary.

> Professor George P. Anderson, who has been ill for some weeks past with dropsy of the heart, died at his home in this city Wednesday morning at 10 o'clock. His protracted sufferings were borne with a bravery and calmness of spirit which has ever characterized him.
>
> He served as Captain in the Confederate army during the late war. Soon after the close of the war he moved to this State and took up his residence in Solano county where he taught school for several years. Some years later he moved to this city and served as Vice-Principal of the High School until elected Principal of the Davis Street School, the duties of which position he faithfully and satisfactorily discharged until his recent and fatal illness. He was a member of the Santa Rosa Lodge, the I.O.O.F., and also of the Knights of Honor.
>
> The deceased leaves a widow and five children to mourn his loss besides many friends and relatives, among whom may be mentioned his cousin Judge J. G. Pressley.
>
> The deceased was a native of Georgia, aged 48 years, 8 months and 15 days. The funeral will take place from Old Fellows Hall, today, at 1 P.M.
>
> In memory of the deceased the teachers of the city assembled Wednesday afternoon and passed the following:
>
> We, the teachers of the public schools of Santa Rosa, In convention assembled, do pass the following resolutions namely:
>
> Resolved, That in the death of our colleague, Mr. George P. Anderson, we recognize the will of the Most High, that has seen fit to remove him in the prime of manhood from a life of happiness and usefulness.

Resolved, That in him we lose a warm and generous-hearted friend, and that while we bow to the decree of the All Wise, we grieve to know that his ringing voice and merry laugh will never fall pleasantly upon our ears again; that in our friendly gatherings his familiar face will be no more seen, in our councils his voice will never more be heard.

Resolved, That we do tender to his bereaved family our hearty sympathy in this, their great bereavement, and do trust that the hand which has dealt the blow will kindly soften it to their hearts, and tenderly care for them through the difficulties of life.

Resolved, That a copy of these proceedings be furnished to the press of our town; and to the family of the deceased.

M. Dabney, Secretary.

George Pressly Anderson passed away on February 23, 1887 in Santa Rosa, California at the age of 48.

Forty-seven years after George died, his widow Margaret Gotea Wilson Anderson, my grandmother's grandmother, passed away in Santa Rosa on November 6, 1934 at the age of 87. She was born on February 28, 1847 in Kingstree, Williamsburg County, South Carolina.

Margaret Gotea Wilson Anderson (1847-1934)
Affectionately known as "Mamo"
Photo courtesy of the Phillips Family Collection

On November 7, 1934, *The Santa Rosa Democrat* published her obituary:

With a smile, the life book of Mrs. Margaret Wilson Anderson closed peacefully yesterday morning. The much respected woman died at the home of her son, Dr. David P. Anderson, in Sonoma Avenue. That home had been hers for close to half a century following the death of her husband, Captain George P. Anderson, pioneer Santa Rosa educator.

Up to within a few weeks of her passing, Mrs. Anderson had maintained a close contact with the world about her. She had been interested in everything, particularly in the welfare of those who by birth had been closely connected by family ties. For more than half a century she had resided in Santa Rosa. She died happy in the belief that death meant only transition to a more perfect life in a brighter and better world. She was essentially a Christian. She was a lifelong member of the Presbyterian Church, and throughout her long life she steadfastly adhered to her belief in Christianity. Mrs. Anderson, a native of South Carolina, came to California as a young woman. She was born of distinguished parentage and was schooled in the kindly characteristics constituting preparation for a useful life.

Her father[81] was a large plantation owner in Williamsburg County, South Carolina, operating a plantation that had been in the southern family since 1732. Her grandfather was an officer in the Revolutionary War[82]. After the close of the Civil War, Margaret Wilson was wed to the late Captain G. P. Anderson, an officer in the Confederate Army, at a ceremony in the old Wilson family plantation home. It was there that Dr. David P. Anderson of Santa Rosa, former state assemblyman from this county, was born. In 1870, the Anderson family moved to California, residing first at Suisun and then later at San Jose. Captain Anderson taught school in both communities, coming to Santa Rosa in 1879. Mrs. Anderson had resided here ever since.

The late Captain Anderson was principal of the old Davis Street School, now known as the Lincoln School. He died in 1887. Since his death, Mrs. Anderson made her home with her son, Dr. David P. Anderson. He and his wife manifested toward her the sincerest filial relationship and ministered to her every need. Mrs. Anderson was the mother of seven children, two of whom died as children. The others are Dr. David P. Anderson, Santa Rosa, dentist and former assemblyman; George P. Anderson, former mayor of Ukiah; Mrs. E. Morris Cox, widow of a former superintendent of schools of this city; and the late Archie B. Anderson, former president of the San Francisco State Teachers College, and the late Dr. Frank Anderson of Petaluma. Nine grandchildren, including Dr. Weston Anderson and Clarendon Witherspoon Anderson, local attorney, and four great-grandchildren also survive. The family connections are extensive throughout the state.   Mrs. Anderson always maintained a developing interest in the progressive changes which were unfolded as the years progressed.   She was a woman of a quiet unostentatious disposition.   She loved her home, and when her husband died, leaving her with a family of children, she undertook the responsibility which developed into their training for useful careers.   Up to the closing days of her long life she maintained a kindly interest in them and in the world about her.   Private funeral rites will be held Thursday afternoon from the Anderson home in Sonoma Avenue, with the Rev. E. E. Ingram, D.D. pastor of the First Presbyterian Church, officiating.

Internment will be in the Odd Fellows cemetery.

VI. PHILLIPS, PRESSLEY, ANDERSON AND WILSON

JUDGE JAMES PHILLIPS, JR.

The father of Seaborn Moses Collins Phillips was Judge James Phillips, Jr He was born in South Carolina on August 5, 1789 and moved to Mississippi before February 15, 1812[83] when the present day state of Mississippi was part of the larger Mississippi Territory.

He was a captain of a company in the 13th Regiment of the Mississippi Militia in Marion County under the command of Lt. Colonel George Henry Nixon during the War of 1812. Another captain in the same Regiment was Moses Collins.

On May 30, 1816, James married Sarah Collins (Hatcher), who was born on October 9, 1787 in Winton County, South Carolina, the daughter of Moses Collins, Sr. (who was born about 1753, possibly in Pennsylvania, and who died on January 29, 1816 in Alabama) and Hannah Willis (who was born on December 10, 1754 in New Kent County, Virginia, and who died on January 15, 1833 in Hinds County, Mississippi).

South Carolina Records indicate Moses Collins and his wife, Hannah (Willis) Collins of Richmond County, Georgia sold 710 acres on The Three Runs in Winton County to Needham Coward on Sept. 23, 1775.

It was a first marriage for James Phillips, but a second marriage for Sarah Collins. She was previously married to Rhesa Hatcher, Sr. and together they had a son named Rhesa Jr., born in

1810, whom William Walker Phillips referred to as his "step uncle." Step uncle Rhesa Hatcher became the mayor of Jackson, Mississippi temporarily in 1869 and again from 1871-1872. Rhesa Hatcher, Sr. was murdered before 1816.

Together James and Sarah had numerous children, not necessarily in this order:

- William Washington Phillips, a sergeant in the Battle of Buena Vista who was reported killed on April 3, 1847 in *The Gibson Correspondent*. William married Rebecca Gallman and together they had three children: William, Louisa Jane and John[84] Bunyan Phillips;

- James Jackson ("Jack") Phillips, whose guardian was Judge R. L. Dixon after Sarah died, was of age by 1848; Sarah's will refers to him as "James A. J. Phillips" although Seaborn, an executor wrote "James J. Phillips." In her diary[85], Louise Dixon Mordecai wrote, "I sure wish Jack Phillips were here, he loves to hunt");

- Americus and Columbus Phillips, twins not mentioned as heirs in the 1838 probate;

- Andrew Phillips who was mentioned in James' will but not mentioned in Sarah's will;

- Julia Rebecca Phillips who was born on November 11, 1818 in Marion, Mississippi and married Judge Richard Lawrence Dixon on April 11, 1837[86] in Hinds, Mississippi;

- Louisa Maria Phillips and Lucinda Phillips, twins born about 1820 in Marion County, Mississippi (Lucinda married the Rev. William Young on November 7, 1833 in Hinds, Mississippi and Louisa married H. R. Hall on February 27, 1834 in Marion, Mississippi);

- Seaborn Moses Collins Phillips, my great-great-grandfather, born in Hinds County, Mississippi in 1822;

- Hadley Brandon Phillips who was born about 1831 in Hinds County, Mississippi (when his mother Sarah died in 1843, Judge R. L. Dixon became his guardian);

- Quintus and Cincinnatus Phillips, twins born in 1834 and not mentioned as heirs in the 1838 probate.

James became the presiding justice of Marion County by 1822. During this time, there were many deeds recorded that he witnessed. There are also references to James Phillips "County Surveyor." James Phillips Sr., died circa 1828, but both father and son were at various times lawyers, judges and surveyors.

The following are miscellaneous deeds from Marion County, Mississippi[87]:

September 15, 1818. Witness; James Phillips Jr. & Benjamin Lee[88]. James Phillips appeared before Wm. Lott Judge of Quorium & attested to deed.

Christiana Robertson gives to granddaughters for natural love & affection: Beloved granddaughters Susannah Haines and Sary Ann Haines (Christiana Robertson moving) a Negro boy named William. Dated September 15, 1818. Witness; James Phillips Jr. & Benjamin Lee.

William Lott Sr. for natural love and affection to son William Lott Jr., a minor & infant, a certain Negro women named Sal and her child named Lancaster. Dated July 24, 1820. Witness; James Phillips Jr. & Sarah Phillips.

Moses Collins for love & affection to daughter Ailcy Woodruff one Negro girl named Betsy on condition that she is not under the control of her present or any other husband, July 24, 1815. Witness; Moses Collins Jr and Sarah Hatcher.

John Townsend of St. Tammany Parish, State of Louisiana, for love and affection which I bear towards my two sons John Henry

Townsend and William Raily Townsend (both minors) a certain Negro girl about 12 or 13 years of age named Betsy. Dated March 7, 1821. Witness; James Phillips Jr. & Elias Phillips.

James Phillips on plea of trespass from Samuel Perkins in amount of $100 due from instrument of writing dated February 15, 1812. Bond of James Phillips, countersigned by James Mikell. Charges of Samuel Perkins against Phillips. Plaintiff Phillips was charged twenty five dollars & costs of County.

Survey made by James Phillips for David Ford on Feb 19, 1818. Contains 360 acres one quarter & eighteen poles, Henry Mitchell & Asa Lee sworn as chain bearers.

Survey by James Phillips for Fleet Magee on May 27, 1819 for nineteen acres two quarters and two poles. John Magee & Fleet Magee chain bearers.

Survey made by James Phillips County Surveyor for (???) December 3, 1818. Contains 249 60/100 acres, John Ervin & Thomas Ford chain bearers.

Indenture between James Phillips Jr., & Luther Preston for sale of a town lot to Preston. Dated July 11, 1822.

Gronow Floyd and Elizabeth Floyd, for love & affection towards our beloved nieces & relatives Mahaley Morgan, Thursy Morgan, Elizabeth Morgan, minors and children of Batson Morgan of Amite County a certain Negro girl slave Molly. Dated March 27, 1821. Witness; Sarah Phillips and Hannah Collins.

Gronow Floyd & Elizabeth Floyd to niece Elizabeth Morgan, daughter of Batson Morgan of Amite County 3 cows & calves. Dated March 27, 1831 Witness; James Phillips, Sarah Phillips, Hannah Collins

James Phillips certifies to the plat of a certain town survey laid off into lots by me on the east side of Pearl River Formerly known and distinguished by the name of Lott's Bluff, which town was laid off as aforesaid at the request of the Gen. Assembly of the State to fix on the permanent seat of Justice for Marion County, passed the thirteenth day of January, 1818

Cornelius Burt, County of Tatnel, State of Georgia, to Robert Stacy and William Phillips for $300 land in the State of Georgia, Habersham County, in the original survey the number 156 District, number 10, tract or lot of land being drawn in the late Land Lottery. Dated July 16, 1821. Witness; Jas. Phillips & John Mixon

John Ford sells to Thomas Griffin for $600 a Negro girl named Emily. Dated December 31, 1821. Witness; James Phillips, Jr

Bond: Gilbert Stovall, Charles Stovall, & Reuben Wright are bound to Walter Leeke, Esq., Governor of the state of Mississippi, for $5,000. Gilbert Stovall is appointed clerk of the County Court of Marion County. Dated August 23, 1822. James Phillips certifies bond of Gilbert Stovall, August 23, 1822

Henry Henninger, John Lott Sr., & Hiram G. Runnels, commissioners of Marion County, sell to James Phillips Jr., a town lot in Columbia. Certification of above deed by Gilbert Stovall, Justice of the Peace. Dated November 13, 1822.

October 18, 1822 Lewis Haguewood & Josephus Simmons sell to Wm. Graham a tract of land for $1,465. Certification of above deed of conveyance to William Graham. Delpha Haguewood relinquishes her right to the conveyed property of the deed, October 18, 1822. James Phillips, Justice of Marion County, certifies that Delpha Haguewood signed the above document voluntarily.

James Phillips, presiding justice, approved Thomas C. Patterson and Charles Stovall, securities to foregoing bond.

Samuel Harper and Charles Stovall and Josiah Newsome are bound unto Walter Leake for $300, dated September 8, 1823. Samuel Harper elected and commissioned coroner, Marion County. Approval of C. Stovall and Josiah Newsome as securities to the above office bond. James Phillips, Presiding Justice, September 8, 1823. Certification of Samuel Harper as coroner, oath administered by James Phillips. Recorded by Gilbert Stovall, September 11, 1823.

Ezekiel White, Charles Stovall, and Hugh McGowen are bound to Walter Leake for $700. Ezekiel White appointed constable, void if he does not serve. Oath taken by Ezekiel White, administered by James Phillips, presiding justice. Recorded by Gilbert Stovall.

Anna Strong willed to son John Strong a Negro wench, Peg, a girl 13; a girl named Lillan, 10; boy Dave, 4 years old; and their increase. Dated February 9, 1815. Witness; Thomas G. Strong, David Sumerall. David Sumerall verifies he saw foregoing deed signed voluntarily. Sworn to before James Phillips, presiding Justice, Marion County. Deed recorded May 26, 1824 by Gilbert Stovall

Amos Granberry and Thomas Rogers and Samuel Rawling are bound to Walter Leake for $500, dated July 20, 1824. Amos Granberry will be constable. Recorded September 12, 1824. Amos Granberry sworn to faithfully discharge duties before James Phillips. Recorded September 14, 1824.

William Jenkins, John Kellar, and Christopher Bert are bound to Walter Leake for $500, dated October 4, 1824. William Jenkins shall become constable. Securities approved October 5, 1824, James Phillips.

Oath of office taken by William Jenkins, October 4, 1824, before James Phillips. Recorded December 15, 1824, by Gilbert Stovall.

Henry G. Rogers takes oath of office before James Phillips. Recorded December 15, 1824

Barbara W. Moore to Luther Preston for $500 a tract of land on east side of Pearl River containing 320 acres. Dated October 4, 1824. Signed before James Phillips, Justice.

Simeon Duke, Charles Stovall, and Samuel Harper are bound to Walter Leake for $4,000, dated March 9, 1825. Simeon Duke appointed and commissioned as assessor and collector of taxes for Marion County.   Securities approved for foregoing bond before James Phillips. Simeon Duke is sworn into office. Office bond filed March 29, 1825; recorded June 4, 1825 by Gilbert Stovall.

William Millon, C. Stovall, and Hugh McGowan are bound to James Phillips for $5,000, dated April 15, 1825. William Millon on

April 5, 1825, commissioned treasurer of Marion County for 2 years. Securities approved by James Phillips, April 15, 1825.

Thomas Cox and William Cox are bound to Walter Leake for $700, dated June 4, 1825. Thomas Cox appointed constable. Oath of office taken by Thomas Cox before James Phillips.

Alfred C. Moore, Benjamin Lee and Charles Stovall are bound to Walter Leake for $6,000, dated August 15, 1825. Alfred C. Moore duly elected sheriff. Securities approved August 5, 1825, by James Phillips.

Henry Askew said that a certain promissory note given by James Phillips for $38.75, dated January 24, 1825, is lost, destroyed, mislaid, cannot be produced. Sworn April 16, 1825.

James Philips, Jr., to John Cooper for $600 for land, 160 acres, dated February 14, 1825, before James Phillips. Sarah Philip, wife of James Philip, Jr., was questioned if she was giving voluntary relinquishment of dower on land in foregoing deed. Recorded December 10, 1825, Gilbert Stovall.

October 11, 1825 Samuel Lard to Marcus E. Carter for $300 two tracts of land, east half of northwest quarter of section No. 23. Signed before James Phillips. Recorded January 5, 1826.

October 3, 1826 Indenture between William Owens and James Phillips. William Owens has two promissory notes bearing dates October 3, 1826, and another payable on 1 January 1829, each for the sum of $550. Wm. Owens in consideration of debt of $1,100 owing to said James Phillips, Jr, gives tract of land in east fractional section number 7, as guarantee of payment. If not paid, Phillips will take possession. Above mortgage filed in office on October 3, 1826, recorded in Book B, October 6, 1826, James Phillips, Dept. Clerk.

James Phillips, Sr., for $75 to Joshua Lott a farm or piece of land on Phillips now resides. February 7, 1828. Witness; Henry and John Kellar Recorded April 9, 1828.

James Phillips Sr. for love to daughter Sarah Lee a Negro woman slave 39 years old by name of Hager. She will remain in the possession of James Phillips and Nancy Phillips but at their decease go to Sarah. Dated June 27, 1828. Witness; Joshua Lott and Sarah Phillips. Testimony of Joshua Lott to above deed before John Kellar, June 29, 1828. Recorded August 14, 1828.

John Lott Sr. to John Rogers for $100 a tract of land lying next to the town of Columbia, which commences at Roger Lotts corner etc. (this was a town lot) Dated November 2, 1820. Witness; James Phillips, Jr, William Purvis.

John Lott Sr. Innkeeper, for $1,000 to Stephen Nobles, lots in the town of Columbia number 17, 18, 19, 20 & 25. Dated May 12, 1821. Nobles also right title interest to ferry landing on Pearl River binding these lots. Witness; James Phillips & Sarah Phillips.

John Lott Sr. and Joseph Pierce for $500 a certain lot on the east side of Pearl River, north of the town boundary of Columbia, it being the lot or parcel of land whereon the house of the said Pierce now stands. Dated July 10, 1821. Witness; James Phillips & S. Duke

September 24, 1825 Nathan Lott to John Lott, Jr., for $200 a tract of land, east half of southwest quarter of section 3, township 3, range 17, 80 acres and 40/100 acre more or less. Signed, sealed, and delivered before James Phillips. Sarah, wife of Nathan Lott, hereby relinquishes all claim on land. Dated September 24, 1825.

James Clark, James Rawls, and William Yarborough are bound to James Phillips for $1,500, dated June 28, 1824. James Clark is guardian to Emeline Melinda Hagan in account with the Orphans County as directed by law. If he does not fulfill duties, his guardianship shall cease. Signed and acknowledged in open County. Recorded September 13, 1824 by Gilbert Stovall.

Emeline Malinda Hagan, minor, to be placed under guardianship of James Clark. He was required to make inventory of all property and report to authorities. Witness; James Phillips, Esqr. Dated June 28, 1824. Recorded September 14, 1824, Gilbert Stovall.

Simeon Duke, Lewis Hegewood and James Phillips Jr. are indebted to George Poindexter, Governor of MS., in the amount of $6,000. Dated April 24, 1821. Simeon Duke is to be Tax Collector & Assessor.

Indenture: November 6, 1823 between Jeptha Duke and James Thigpen for $500 paid to Duke by Thigpen for tract of land located in Section 15, Township 3, 160 acres. Filed January 10, 1824 by Gilbert Stovall.

From 1828-1835 and from January until he died on August 11, 1838, Judge James Phillips served as the treasurer of the State of Mississippi.

He was originally appointed by Governor Scott in 1828, resigning in January 1835, saying of himself in his annual report, "Twenty-two mark my residence in Mississippi, twenty years of which have in some station or other been devoted to public life."

On July 4, 1836, a Fourth of July dinner and ball was held in one of the local Jackson hotels.

One of the gentlemen present described the dinner as a "display of all the luxuries of the season, all the delicacies which our country could afford." The tables were loaded with representations of "the vegetable and animal kingdom in all its variety of fish, flesh, fowl, and a hundred other good things." He continued his description: "After the din and bustle of changing plates, the clashing and rattling of knives and forks had ceased, the happy faces of the company indicated that in the way of eating, they had indulged to satiety. The cloth was removed, the conflict with Port, Claret, Madeira and Champagne was about to commence, and the battles of '76 to be 'fought o'er again.'" Judge James Phillips, assisted by Alexander Montgomery and C. C. Mayson, presided during the toasts, and martyrs of Texas were the theme of the day. "The dinner company broke up in good order and at an early hour, nothing having occurred to interrupt the harmony of the day, nothing interposed to prevent its enjoyment in perfection and without alloy." After dinner, the gentleman who described the dinner dressed for the ball. He recounted: "Our 'Long tail'd blue' was called into requisition, and after a fine brushing, received a luster worthy of its younger and better days."

He put on his silk hose, satin stocks, white kid gloves, took his walking cane, and away he went to the ball.[89]

In 1837 James was a representative of Hinds County in the state legislature, and was then elected again for State Treasurer on November 6, 1837. At that time, Charles Lynch[90], a South Carolina native, was governor of Mississippi.

Alexander G. McNutt became Mississippi governor in January 1838, a time when Mississippi was entering a period of severe economic depression. Until the Panic of 1837, there had been a period of great economic prosperity in Mississippi. Former Governor Hiram Runnels promoted the charter of the Union Bank through the legislature. Runnels then became the bank's president at a salary of $10,000. Of the $5 million derived from the bonds sold and invested in the bank, over $2 million was loaned out without any collateral. Most of the balance was loaned out, with a bale of cotton valued at $60, as collateral. At this point in time, cotton sold in England at $30 a bale, meaning that the collateral on the loans was insufficient[91].

In 1837 McNutt was elected president of the Mississippi state senate and, as president, signed the bill that established the Union Bank of Mississippi. McNutt's 1837 campaign for governor, however, was on an anti-bank platform.

As governor, McNutt signed bonds that were sold by the Union Bank of Mississippi to raise capital. Nevertheless, the Union Bank failed in 1839 after Judge James Phillips had died, causing the collapse of a number of Mississippi banks. When Governor McNutt refused to allow another issue of bonds to be sold, hostility developed between him and Hiram G. Runnels, the governor of Mississippi from 1833-1835, who served as state auditor until 1830[92].

In 1841 the state decided not to repay the bonds due to the high interest rates, which led to nearly a century and a half of dispute with investors and their heirs that continues to the present day[93].

Mississippi Union Bank Bond, 1838
Signed by James Phillips in the lower left corner
and Gov. Alexander McNutt in the lower right corner.

The decision to repudiate the bonds issued during these years was ratified by the state legislature, and remained a political issue until 1890 when the Mississippi state constitution prohibited the state from ever redeeming the bonds. While treasurer, Judge James Phillips signed these bonds. One example, which I recently purchased[94], has his signature in the lower left corner with Governor McNutt's signature in the lower right corner.

Recently, on December 19, 1996, the Supreme Court of Mississippi ruled on a statute of limitations case related to this bond, in case number 94-CA-00032-SCT. The Supreme Court of Mississippi stated the facts of the case:

The origin of this case is in the mid-nineteenth century when in 1830 the Mississippi Legislature chartered the commercial banking establishment called the Planters Bank. The unusual feature of the bank was its financing. It was to be practically a state-owned bank, for $2,000,000 of its $3,000,000 of capital would be subscribed by the state government.

The Planters Bank bonds were issued in 1831 and in 1833. The Legislature in response to a demand for more banking institutions chartered the Union Bank in 1838 with bonds issued that same year. In 1841, there was a default in interest on both the Planters and Union Bank bonds. The Union Bank bonds were repudiated by the Governor of Mississippi in 1842, and the Planters Bank bonds were repudiated under a referendum vote of the people in 1853. The Union Bank bonds matured as to the principal in 1850 and 1858. The Planters Bank bonds matured as to principal in 1861 and 1866.

A statute of limitations was enacted in 1873 that dealt with actions to collect debt owing on bonds. Chapter 26, Mississippi Laws of 1873, effective April 19, 1873, provided in pertinent part that "all actions of debt... founded upon any bond, obligation, or contract, under seal... shall be commenced within seven years after the cause of said action, and not after." Section 2685, Code of 1880 (now codified as 15-1-3), provided that the completion of the limitations period "shall defeat and extinguish the right as well as the remedy."

These suits were filed in the Chancery Court in July of 1993, which was 152 years after the default in interest, 141 years after the vote by the people to repudiate the Planters Bank bonds, and 126 years after the last bonds reached maturity. This was also 120 years after a 7-year statute of limitations went into effect which would have extinguished any possible right on the bonds in 1880 at the latest.

Section 258 of the Mississippi Constitution of 1890, which provided that the State should not "assume, redeem, secure or pay any indebtedness or pretended indebtedness" on the bonds, was approved as an amendment of the previous Constitution by the people in November 1875, to go into effect in January of 1876. The default on the bonds had in reality occurred nearly thirty years earlier, and this action was brought in the Chancery Court 117 years after the Constitution was ratified.

However, the Appellants claim that prior to 1873, Mississippi enacted a "savings statute" in 1857 providing that the statute of limitations does not run during the period when a person is prohibited by law from commencing or prosecuting an action or remedy. Miss. Code Ann. 15-1-57. Relying on this "savings statute," the Appellants argue that they were prohibited from bringing suit against the State to enforce payment on the bonds because of Section 258 of the Mississippi Constitution of 1890. Hence, the statute of limitations had not run, and they were not time barred from bringing suit.

The State filed a Motion for Summary Judgment and for a Judgment on the Pleadings in lieu of filing an answer to the complaint. The State asserted the present claims were barred as res judicata as a result of the disposition in the earlier federal suit of Barry v. Fordice, supra, that was dismissed because of the Eleventh Amendment bar to suits against a State. Further, the State claimed that all possible statute of limitations had run and/or in the alternative, that the Appellants were barred from now bringing suit by the doctrine of laches.

The chancellor ruled that the acts of repudiation, including the vote by the people to deny payment and the amendment by the Legislature that was later incorporated into the Mississippi Constitution of 1890, were violative of the United States Constitution with regards to impairments of contracts. He then found the statute of limitations had run in favor of the State during the period in which the acts of repudiation had taken place. Thus, any suit was indeed time barred.

From that decision the Appellants have appealed to this Court contending that the ruling of the court below violates the statutory tolling law of this State, established principles of estoppel, fundamental due process protections of the United States Constitution, and the 1794 "Jay Treaty" between Great Britain and the United States, and triggers the running of the statute of limitations against the American bondholders when a condition precedent to the running of the limitations period had not occurred.

The court ruled: "These claims were brought over one hundred years after the right to demand payment had accrued. The bondholders mistakenly read Section 258 to preclude suit to seek payment on the bonds, when in reality the section only prohibited payment. The seven-year statute of limitations began to run in 1873 and expired in 1880. No demand was made until 1993 when the suit was filed in Chancery Court. The chancellor correctly held that the statute of limitations had run and the bondholders were barred from pursuing their claim. The determination that Section

258 of the Mississippi Constitution is unconstitutional was error because the running of the statute of limitations was dispositive in granting the State's Motion for Summary Judgment."

The Mississippi State Capitol at Jackson

Mississippi State Capitol, Jackson, Mississippi, 1875
Sketch by J. Wells Champney

Judge James Phillips, Mississippi State Treasurer, died on August 11, 1838 at the age of 49. His parting advice was: "that by extending legislative patronage, not to any particular, local or sectional interest, but to the increasing and enterprising industry of the great body of people throughout the State, thereby stimulating them to put in requisition the whole of their moral and physical energies, the time will ere long arrive when the onerous system of direct taxes may with perfect safety be stricken from the pages of our statute book."

Grave of Judge James Phillips (1789-1838)
Greenwood Cemetery, Jackson, Mississippi
The broken piece was recently discovered by Peter B. Miazza
Photo by the author

Many years after his death, the Report of the Secretary of State in Mississippi recorded the following in 1899:

> James Phillips who had been State Treasurer from 1828 to 1835 and since January 1838 died in August of that year. As stated by Governor McNutt in his message of January 1839 the auditor John H. Malloy was a defaulter to the amount of $54,079 "nearly all on account of town lots and three percent seminary and sinking fund." The Treasurer, James Phillips had been authorized to receive from the United States Treasury the State's quota of the surplus. No authority was given to him to receive of the government of the United States anything but gold and silver or the notes of specific paying banks, yet in defiance of law[95], he received payment of the treasury drafts in such depreciated paper as Agriculture Bank chose to give him, about $200,000 of this was deposited in the Planters Bank at Jackson, and that branch has ever since the suspension refused to pay out anything to the public creditors except Brandon money.

Richard L. Dixon, who married Julia Rebecca Phillips, was the son-in-law of James and Sarah Phillips, and the executor of

James' estate. Sarah had made Richard the guardian of her young sons Hadley Brandon Phillips, who was born in 1831, and James Jackson Phillips[96].

No doubt McNutt's words about James Phillips, made posthumously in his January 1839 message, enraged Richard L. Dixon. As a Madera teacher and local historian, Bill Coate wrote in his March 15, 2005 article entitled "Richard Lawrence Dixon suffered a grave injustice" and republished on August 15, 2006 as "Dixon gave no insult and took none," by *The Madera Tribune*:

> It didn't take Richard Dixon long to earn the enmity of Mississippi Gov. Alexander McNutt by referring to him in denigrating terms. On one such occasion, Dixon told a group of cronies that he had "spit on the damned rascal (McNutt)" and that he intended to insult him whenever he should meet him.
>
> When a friend of the governor's repeated these words in the local paper and impugned Dixon's veracity, the latter issued a challenge to the former, and when satisfaction was denied him, he went to the Statehouse and caned his detractor out of the building. Such was the temper of the man and his times.
>
> © 2007 The Madera Tribune and William S. Coate.

A more full account is found in *The Story of Jackson, A History of the Capitol of Mississippi 1821-1951*, Volume 1, by William D. McCain, published by J. F. Hyer Publishing Company[97], Jackson, Mississippi in 1953:

> Another episode in Jackson threatened to embroil prominent Jacksonians in a shooting affair. On the evening of April 25, 1839, several gentlemen were sitting on the front gallery of the Union Hall on Capitol Street when Governor Alexander G. McNutt walked by on his way to the Capitol. After the governor had passed, R. L. Dixon turned to the group, which included George Finucane, James H. Clark, John P. Oldham and H. Hobbs, and "remarked ... that he had spit on the damned rascal, and that he intended to insult him whenever he should meet him." A. J. Paxton, one of the governor's friends, took the matter up as soon as he heard of it and secured signed statements from those present that Dixon did not offer any indignity to Governor McNutt. He

published these statements in *The Mississippian* on May 3 [1839] and added a few of his own opinions of Dixon, as follows:

> From all the circumstances it is manifest that Dixon has manufactured a gross falsehood for the purpose of gratifying a most paltry revenge and heralding forth his own infamy. It is extraordinary, that an affair of this kind could have occurred without being observed, either by the gentlemen present or Gov. McNutt. The whole story carries a falsehood on its face.
>
> A more sickly attempt to get up a reputation for courage was never perpetrated, especially when it is known to all citizens of Jackson that this same ferocious Mr. Dixon was, not long since, publicly caned in his own office, and had not the courage to resent it, but like a whipped Spaniel tamely submitted.
>
> This fellow's enmity to Governor McNutt grew out of the fact that the Governor had reasons to believe that he (Dixon) was misusing certain funds belonging to the State, left in the hands of the late Treasurer, James Phillips, at the time of his decease[98], and promptly communicated his just suspicions to the Legislature at their last session.
>
> In addition, it is only necessary to remark, that if Dixon has told this story, without the indignity having been offered, as is manifest, he is an infamous liar and puppy. If he did, in fact, perpetrate this disgusting obscenity, he is a filthy blackguard and cowardly poltroon. ... I am informed that Dixon has not been seen on the streets since the above occurrence, and that he left shortly afterwards for Oxford... and it is not known when he will return.

His wife Sarah Collins (Hatcher) Phillips, who died on November 30, 1843, and whose will was probated on November 27, 1844, listed the following children in her will: Reice Hatcher[99], S. M. Phillips, William W. Phillips[100], James A. J. Phillips and Hadley B. Phillips. Her will called for half of her estate to be left in equal parts to Reice Hatcher, Seaborn Moses Collins Phillips and William W. Phillips, and the other half equally to James A. J. Phillips and Hadley B. Phillips because they would require more to raise and educate them. Her daughter Julia, who was not named, was by then married to Richard

Lawrence Dixon. Her son Andrew, named in James' will, was not mentioned in Sarah's will.

While writing this book, Sarah's grave was discovered next to her husband's. The grave was revealed on Memorial Day, May 28, 2007.

Grave of Sarah Collins Hatcher Phillips (1787-1843)
Discovered by Peter B. Miazza on May 28, 2007
Greenwood Cemetery, Jackson, Mississippi
Photo courtesy of Peter B. Miazza

Peter B. Miazza, my fourth cousin, once removed, is a descendant of Sarah's sister Susannah Collins. On June 3, 2007, he wrote:

In 1841, one of her slaves stole a fifty dollar note and she had to make it good and pay court costs. At that time she was living in Jackson and died just two years later. So she just had to have been buried there at Greenwood Cemetery. However, the ground was so hard (we are in the middle of a drought) that I had difficulty making just a hole for the little flag. So I knew that I would be unable to probe deep enough to determine other graves in the

Phillips' lot so just made a few perfunctory stabs with a metal rod and luckily hit the marker. I was able to scrape away enough of the overgrowth to determine that it was a marker. I then went home and got some tools and uncovered the fragments. There may be a few more fragments still covered. The cemetery records have been burned twice, once during one of the Union occupations of Jackson and again in the 1930s. Transcriptions have been made three times since then of the existing monuments. The oldest one was done in 1940. In none of these was Sarah's monument noted so it has been covered for many years.

After examining the fragments from Sarah's monument, I think they were made by the same marble cutter as was James'. Also, his brick tomb is not original but of course the marble slab on top is original. That has been done in the last fifty or sixty years or maybe more. I have no idea who built it. I think that his slab was also on the ground. Sarah's grave probably subsided and her monument broken and covered over. Then someone came along and erected James' brick tomb. It could have been because he was the state treasurer at one time. Right now we are working with the Mississippi Department of Archives and History to survey all of the monuments in the cemetery of people who held state office to determine their condition and the cost of restoring them and hopefully getting some money through the Legislature."

On June 21, 2007, Peter wrote, "We poured a slab and assembled the fragments of Sarah's monument. As it turned out, one of the fragments was a corner from James' monument."

Monument of Sarah Collins (Hatcher) Phillips (1787-1843)
Discovered and reconstructed in June 2007 by Peter B. Miazza
Greenwood Cemetery, Jackson, Mississippi
Photo courtesy of Peter B. Miazza

Peter was right. One of the fragments he found buried under the grass was the missing broken portion of James' marble slab. Today, the marble looks weathered and grey. However, the newly discovered missing pieces of Sarah's monument are a beautiful shade of light brown, the result of discoloration from the dirt. Hopefully, the marble monuments of both James and Sarah will one day be cleaned to reveal the white marble beneath years of being exposed to the elements.

*   *   *

Major William F. Walker was Seaborn's wife Emily Cushman Walker's father. Her mother was Emily T. Branch Walker, with Walker being her married name. William F. Walker had a plantation in Madisonville, Mississippi. William Walker Phillips wrote about his grandmother Emily T. Branch Walker and his grandfather William F. Walker:

> Soon after [my father died] my grandfather sent a four-mule team from his plantation in Madison County to move us over to a place near his home. I became the messenger boy for my grandmother and used to ride to Canton, eight miles away, to bring the mail. I well remember when the news came of President Lincoln's assassination. I was approaching the home. My grandmother, who by the way was a radical Southerner and secessionist, called to me what the War news was, expecting no doubt to hear of some big battle and its results. I answered her that Lincoln had been assassinated. Her reply was, "Thank God for that." Owing to the intense hatred of the Southern people against Mr. Lincoln, this expression of her feeling was not to [be] wondered at.

Major William F. Walker was described as a "Major" in the obituary of Seaborn's daughter Julia Laurentina Phillips. However, my efforts to discover what war he may have fought in and from which state have so far not revealed any information.

His wife Emily's obituary was published by *The American Citizen* in Canton, Mississippi in 1878:

> Died on April 6, 1878, in Phillips County, Arkansas, at the residence of her son-in-law, H. C. Bosworth, Mrs. Emily T. Walker, relict of the late Wm. F. Walker, for many years a resident

of Madisonville, in this county. The deceased was a native of Greene County, Ga., and her maiden name was Branch.

William F. Walker married Emily T. Branch on January 26, 1826, in Morgan County, Georgia.

The 1850 census of Madison County, Mississippi reveals that William F. Walker was a planter with assets of $25,000, and that his wife Emily T. Walker was 40 years of age, having been born in North Carolina.

H. C. Bosworth was the publisher of *The American Citizen* in Canton, Mississippi, the newspaper of which Seaborn Moses Collins Phillips was a one-time editor. H. C. Bosworth was Seaborn's brother-in-law.

William was also referred to as "Col. W. F. Walker" in his daughter's wedding announcement in the *Vicksburg Daily Whig*:

> Married by the Rev. C. K. Marshall on the 14th inst. at the residence of Col. W. F. Walker of Madison County, Miss., Viola A., his youngest daughter, to Mr. James C. Harris of Warren County, Miss.

There was a Supreme Court decision from 1850 which dismissed a case from the Circuit Court of the United States for the Southern District of Mississippi. Madison County is located within this district[101]. The case, which was one of the early Supreme Court decisions establishing federal immunity, involves a promissory note that William F. Walker and his associates claim was paid before being endorsed to the United States. They appealed to a Court of Equity and won despite the United States claim of "sovereign immunity," meaning that the government can only be sued if it gives its consent. The Supreme Court of 1850 reversed the lower court, finding that the Court of Equity lacked jurisdiction and dismissed the case.

Today the federal government still has sovereign immunity and may not be sued unless it has waived its immunity or consented to suit. The United States has waived sovereign immunity only to a limited extent.

U.S. Supreme Court

HILL v. UNITED STATES, 50 U.S. 386 (1850)

50 U.S. 386 (How.)

WILLIAM J. HILL, DAVID M. PORTER, AND
WILLIAM F. WALKER,

v.

THE UNITED STATES ET AL.

January Term, 1850

The bill must therefore be dismissed.

THIS case came up from the Circuit Court of the United States for
the Southern District of Mississippi, upon a certificate of division
in opinion between the judges thereof.

It was a bill filed on the equity side of the court, by Hill and the
other complainants, against the United States, the Mississippi and
Alabama Railroad Company, William M. Gwin, and William H.
Shelton, to enjoin a judgment obtained against the complainants by
the United States.

The circumstances were these.

In 1835, the receiver of public moneys for the Choctaw district in
the State of Mississippi was found to be in debt to the government.

On the 26th of September, 1835, the Solicitor of the Treasury
issued a distress warrant, under the act of May, 1820, for the
purpose of collecting the debt, and inclosed it to William M. Gwin,
then Marshal of the United States for the State of Mississippi.

The history of the transaction between 1835 and 1839 need not be
stated.

In 1839, the marshal, by direction of the Solicitor and Secretary of
the Treasury, received from the representative of the debtor (who

was then dead) the sum of $30,000 in the notes of the Mississippi and Alabama Railroad Company, as collateral security for the debt, for the collection of which he had a distress warrant. The Railroad Company, in order to avoid a suit upon its notes, transferred to the District Attorney upwards of $78,000 of bills receivable of the bank. Amongst these bills receivable was a promissory note for four thousand dollars, dated on the 12th of April, 1838, payable six months after date to the Mississippi and Alabama Railroad Company, negotiable and payable at their banking-house in Brandon, and signed by William J. Hill, J. S. Rowland, D. M. Porter, and W. F. Walker. The note was joint and several; Hill was the principal, and the others sureties.

Page 50 U.S. 386, 387

On the 15th of June, 1839, the District Attorney brought suit upon the note, in the name of the United States, against all the parties, and at November term obtained judgment.

In January, 1840, a fi. fa. was issued, and in May, 1840, Hill, Porter, and Walker filed a bill on the equity side of the court against the United States, the Mississippi and Alabama Railroad Company, William M. Gwin, and William H. Shelton, setting up certain equities, which need not be here particularly stated, and praying for an injunction, which was granted.

All the parties answered, the District Attorney answering on behalf of the United States.

In May, 1846, the cause was set down for hearing upon the bill, answers, and exhibits.

In November, 1846, the following proceedings took place.

The United States, by attorney, made the following motion, to wit:-

'Motion by R. M. Gaines, U. S. Attorney, to dissolve the injunction and dismiss the bill, as to the United States, for want of jurisdiction as to them, and also on the merits.

'R. M. GAINES, U. S. Att'y.

'And afterwards, to wit, at the May term, A. D. 1847, of said court, to wit, on the 20th day of May, in the year of our Lord 1847, this cause came on to be heard before the Honorable Peter V. Daniel and Samuel J. Gholson, upon the motion of the United States of America to dismiss this suit as to them, and dissolve the injunction, for want of jurisdiction, and was argued by counsel. And the court having taken time to consider, and not being able to agree in opinion what decree should be made in the cause on said motion, one of the judges being of opinion that the said motion should be sustained, and the said bill dismissed and injunction dissolved, and the other being of opinion that the said motion should be overruled, it is therefore ordered, at the request of the counsel for both complainants and defendants, that said difference of opinion be certified to the Supreme Court of the United States for their decision, whether the said motion should be sustained or overruled.

'P. V. DANIEL. S. J. GHOLSON.' Upon this certificate the case accordingly came up.

It was argued by Mr. Johnson (Attorney-General), for the United States, no counsel appearing upon the other side. He contended that, the United States not being liable to be sued

Page 50 U.S. 386, 388

except with its own consent given by law, and there being no law giving such consent in this case, jurisdiction did not exist, and cited the case of United States v. McLemore, 4 Howard, 286.

Mr. Justice DANIEL delivered the opinion of the court.

This case comes before us from the Circuit Court for the Southern District of Mississippi, upon a certificate of division in opinion between the judges on the following facts and questions certified from that court.

The United States, as the endorsees of the Mississippi and Alabama Railroad Company, instituted an action of assumpsit in the court above mentioned, on a promissory note given by William J. Hill, J.

S. Rowland, D. M. Porter, and W. F. Walker to the said railroad company, for the sum of four thousand dollars. At the November term of the court in 1839, the United States, upon a trial at law upon issues joined, first, upon the plea of non-assumpsit, and secondly, upon the plea of payment of the note before its endorsement and delivery to the plaintiffs, obtained a verdict and judgment in damages for the sum of $4,353.32. Upon the suing out of an execution on this judgment, the defendants filed a bill on the equity side of the Circuit Court, and obtained from the District Judge an injunction, upon grounds which perhaps might, under the pleadings in the cause, have been as regularly insisted upon at law, between the proper parties, as they could be in equity; but whether forming a well-founded defence at law, or not, is immaterial in the inquiry now presented. In the bill filed by Hill and others, the United States are made directly parties defendants; process is prayed immediately against them; they are called upon to answer the several allegations in the bill, and a perpetual injunction is prayed for to the judgment obtained by them. To the bill of the complainants the attorney for the United States filed in their behalf an answer in extenso, but afterwards moved the court to dissolve the injunction and dismiss the bill as to the United States, for want of jurisdiction as to them, upon which motion the order and certificate now before this court were made in the following terms:-'And afterwards, to wit, at the May term of said court, viz. on the 20th day of May, A. D. 1847, this cause came on to be heard before the Hon. Peter V. Daniel and Samuel J. Gholson, upon the motion of the United States of America to dismiss this suit as to them, and dissolve the injunction for want of jurisdiction, and was argued by counsel. And the court having taken time to consider, and not being able to agree in opinion what decree

Page 50 U.S. 386, 389

should be made in the cause on said motion, one of the judges being of opinion that the said motion should be sustained, and the said bill dismissed and injunction dissolved, and the other being of opinion that the said motion should be overruled, it is therefore ordered, at the request of the counsel for both complainants and defendants, that said difference of opinion be certified to the Supreme Court of the United States for their decision, whether the said motion should be sustained or overruled.'

The question here propounded, without any necessity for recurrence to particular examples, would seem to meet its solution in the regular and best-settled principles of public law. No maxim is thought to be better established, or more universally assented to, than that which ordains that a sovereign, or a government representing the sovereign, cannot ex delicto be amenable to its own creatures or agents employed under its own authority for the fulfilment merely of its own legitimate ends. A departure from this maxim can be sustained only upon the ground of permission on the part of the sovereign or the government expressly declared, and an attempt to overrule or to impair it on a foundation independently of such permission must involve an inconsistency and confusion, both in theory and practice, subversive of regulated order or power. Upon the principle here stated it has been, that, in cases of private grievance proceeding from the crown, the petition of right in England has been the nearest approach to an adversary position to the government that has been tolerated; and upon the same principle it is that, in our own country, in instances of imperfect land titles, special legislation has been adopted to permit the jurisdiction of the courts upon the rights of the government. Without dilating upon the propriety or necessity of the principle here stated, or seeking to multiply examples of its enforcement, we content ourselves with referring to a single and recent case in this court, which appears to cover the one now before us in all its features. We allude to the case of the United States v. McLemore, in 4 Howard, 286, where it is broadly laid down as the law, that a Circuit Court cannot entertain a bill on the equity side of the court, praying that the United States may be perpetually enjoined from proceeding upon a judgment obtained by them, as the government is not liable to be sued, except by its own consent given by law. We therefore direct it to be certified to the Circuit Court for the Southern District of Mississippi, that the motion on behalf of the United States in this cause should have been sustained, and that the bill as to

Page 50 U.S. 386, 390

the United States should be dismissed, as having been improvidently allowed.

Order.

This cause came on to be heard on the transcript of the record from the Circuit Court of the United States for the Southern District of Mississippi, and on the point or question on which the judges of the said Circuit Court were opposed in opinion, and which was certified to this court for its opinion, agreeably to the act of Congress in such case made and provided, and was argued by counsel. On consideration whereof, it is the opinion of this court, that the motion in behalf of the United States in this cause should have been sustained, and that the bill as to the United States should be dismissed, as having been improvidently allowed. Whereupon it is now here ordered and decreed by this court, that it be so certified to the said Circuit Court.

*   *   *

Sarah Collins' mother Hannah Willis (1754-1833) was the daughter of William Willis III (circa 1725-1760) and Susannah Toney who were married in 1746.

Susannah Toney's mother was Elizabeth Gulliam. She was born in 1699 in New Kent, Virginia. Susannah's father was Edmund Toney. Edmund's parents were most likely William Toney, who was born around 1634 in Bristol, England, and died around 1675 in New Kent, Virginia, and Anne Bishop, who was born around 1638 in James City, Virginia.

According to Joyce Zachman who descends from Benjamin Youngblood (whose wife was Susannah Collins (1775-1866), the daughter of Moses Collins Sr. and Hannah Willis), the Willis ancestry is known to my 15th generation, beginning with the father of Hannah Willis:

8.   William III born circa 1725 and died in 1760

9.   William Willis Jr., born after 1709 and Hannah Burnham.

10.   William Willis (circa 1675-1717) and Sarah Willis, cousins who were married in 1709.

11.   John Willis (circa 1648-1715) and Matilda Thornton.

12.   William Willis, born circa 1632.

13.   Rev. John Willis, born circa 1587.

14.   Rev. Francis Willis (circa 1540 – 1596).

15.   Francis Willis, born circa 1515.

*   *   *

John Gotea Pressley's parents were John Brockinton Pressley (son of John Pressley and Mary Barr Brockinton), born on February 18, 1810 in Williamsburg County, South Carolina, and Sarah Gotea (daughter of John Gotea and Elizabeth Scott), born on April 24, 1812 also in Williamsburg County. His parents were married on January 5, 1830 in Williamsburg County.

John Brockinton Pressley died on May 7, 1863 in Williamsburg County at the age of 53. Sarah Gotea Pressley died on April 4, 1874 in Suisun, Fairfield County, California at the age of 61.

Monument of John Brockinton Pressley (1810-1863)
Pressley Family Cemetery,
Williamsburg County, South Carolina
Photo courtesy of Bruce Tognazzini

Headstone:

IN

MEMORY OF

JOHN B. PRESSLEY.

BORN 18TH FEBRUARY 1810.

DIED 7TH MAY 1863.

"MARK THE PERFECT MAN AND BEHOLD

THE UPRIGHT, FOR THE END OF

THAT MAN IS PEACE."

John Brockinton's epitaph is from Psalms 37, verse 37. Sarah Gotea's grave is not located within the Pressley Family Cemetery because she went to California in 1869 and died in Fairfield, California in 1874.

Their son John Gotea Pressley wrote:

> I have now brought these sketches down to my own parents.
>
> John Brockinton Pressley (son of John and Mary B. Pressley) married Sarah Gotea (daughter of John and Elizabeth [Scott] Gotea) on the 5th day of January A.D. 1830. To write sketches of their lives that would give my children an adequate idea of the respect, love and affection, which is in my heart for them would furnish me with employment to the exclusion of other occupation for a much longer time than I have a right to take from the public, and I shall therefore not attempt it. I hope my children will talk to me about them, I will tell them all that I know about them if they would like to hear. Bless God: there is nothing that they have ever

done that is a family stain or discredit. Let my children who may read this be assured by me that they may feel an honest pride in knowing that they have descended from respectable, intelligent, upright, Christian grandparents on both sides.

My father when a young man was a sufferer with dyspepsia. It never entirely left him during his life, but he grew better as he grew older, and looked healthier and very little older in 1863 the hour he died than when I first knew him. My father took up residence in the house of his mother-in-law upon his marriage. He and my mother lived there, and father managed the plantation for the benefit of the whole family until 1839, when he moved to Turkey Creek and settled on the place at which his family were reared, and to which I have so often referred. He left my grandmother Gotea and Aunt Maggie on the Cold Water Run (Gotea Plantation) but still had a general supervision over their business till the marriage of my Aunt Margaret. Four of my father and mother's children were born in the old Gotea house, Sister Mary, I, my brother James, and sister Martha Fowler.

My father had very little school education, but by his study and reading acquired more than an average store of learning. A good many years of his boyhood and early manhood were spent in the employ of Black Mingo.

This Cleland Belin is a descendant of one of my Brockinton ancestors.

My father was much given to politics, but never for himself. He was a "power" for his friends in local elections.

He had a passion for hunting and fishing, the favorite sports of the Southern gentleman.

As slavery is a thing of the past it might interest those who come after me to hear how a Southern planter spent his time. My father's means did not in his judgement justify his hiring an over-seer, and he personally managed his plantation. After a moderately early breakfast he went to his fields and inspected the work of the day before. Then he visited the different gangs of hands (Negro laborers) and saw that they were all at work and doing tasks assigned them for the day. After this the planter returned to his house and the balance of the day was spent with his family, or reading, visiting, entertaining company, or such other amusements as accorded with his taste and fancy. Just before or after supper the "head man" of the Negroes reported on the work of the day and for orders for the next day. The most trusted man among the Negroes and one who could command the respect of his fellow servants, was selected as "head man" sometimes called "driver." My father never used on his plantation this latter term to designate the leader of his black people. On the larger plantations the head man did not work that to look after the others. Where the number of hands were not sufficient to require all of his time he worked as the others, but not so much was required of him. Both the Master and Mistress of the plantation looked after the sick. An old woman, under the eye of the mistress, had supervision of the children, who had reached the age to be left at home by their mothers. Every mother with an infant had a nurse assigned her, one of her older children, and if she had none the child of some other woman that could be spared. When the babies were old enough for the mother to work these nurses accompanied the mothers to the field and took care of the babies in a house built for that purpose, or under the shade of a tree where the cries of the baby would be in the reach of the mother's ear who could attend to its wants without loss of much time. Deductions were made in her work when necessary. The clothing of the Negroes was made by the mistress, or by seamstresses under eye. The special duty of the boys of the family was to superintend the feeding and generally of the livestock. They were the first of the white family out of bed.

Negroes were by law accounted "chattels," but my experience is that very few slave owners regard them as such, or in any other light than as a part of the household, standing in the estimation of the master and mistress next below the children. A sale of one was generally looked upon as a great calamity. They were very seldom over worked, indeed it often happened that the (mistaken) affection of the master led him to require less work of the Negro than he should have been required to do. On many plantations one Saturday every fortnight was "Negro Saturday" on which no one was required to work. When the character of the work was such as to permit the assignment of tasks an industrious active Negro could frequently gain a day out of the week, which added to his "Negro Saturday" gave him more leisure than white laborers whose families are dependent on their daily wages. Sometimes the masters paid them for extra work. My father's Negroes showed the effects of kind treatment. They were all devotedly attached to the family, and proud of "we white people" as they called their master and his family.

My father was very liberal to his children. Three of us had left the paternal roof before his death, and when we set up for ourselves he made a liberal division of his Negroes with us.

When the war commenced father wished to volunteer, but his boys would not consent. He had two sons in the service from the beginning and five before the end came. We thought he was giving enough, and that he could serve his country best at home, making provisions for the soldiers at the front.

John Brockinton Pressley, died on the 7th of May, 1863, of a fever and disorder which brought on hemorrhage of the bowels. I was with him in his last illness. We laid him to rest with his forefathers in our private graveyard at "Boyd's Old Field."

My mother survived him and in 1869 she and her whole family left S. C. and came to California. We sailed from Charleston on the 27th of March of that year, for New York on the Steamer *Champion*, and from New York on the 1st day of April in the steamer *Arizona* for Aspinwall. From Aspinwall we crossed the Isthmus of Darien on the railroad, and from Panama we sailed in the *Montana* for San Francisco. The last named steamers belong to the Pacific Mail Steam Company's line.

USS Champion, 1864
Lithograph by Middleton, Strobridge & Company, Cincinnati, Ohio, 1864,
after a drawing by Chas. A. Fisher.
Courtesy of President Franklin D. Roosevelt, 1936.
Photo courtesy of the U.S. Naval Historical Center

The Montana, San Francisco, December 5, 1868
Photo courtesy of The Society of California Pioneers, San Francisco
Used With Permission

We arrived in San Francisco on the 24th day of April, 1869, remained in San Francisco till June, and early in that month went up to Suisun, Solano County. My mother remained in Suisun City till after crops were harvested, and then settled with her sons William Burrows Pressley, Harvey Wilson Pressley, her daughter Jennette D. Pressley, and her son-in-law Daniel Dwight Barr, and his children Nettie, Margaret, John Pressley, and George, in Suisun Valley on a ranch purchased from William Ledgerwood. Here they went to farming and remained till the summer of 1873 when they sold out, and mother went to live with her daughter Jennette D. Dozier, who while the family lived in Suisun Valley, married Edward C. Dozier, (son of Anthony W. Dozier) who with his whole family has come to California from Williamsburg County.

Sarah Pressley, nee Gotea, my mother died in Suisun City at the house of my brother Dr. James F. Pressley, on the 4th day of April, 1874. She is buried in the cemetery near Fairfield in a lot purchased by my brother James F. Pressley.

John Gotea Pressley's wife Julia Caroline Burckmyer Pressley was born on December 2, 1833 in Charleston, South Carolina and died on December 30, 1907 in Santa Rosa at the age of 74. Her parents were Cornelius D. Burckmyer, and Elizabeth Sarah Adams who was born in Charleston, South Carolina.

Cornelius was born on October 10, 1800 in Charleston, South Carolina and was, at the time he died, a deacon of the Wentworth Street Baptist Church. He died of congestion of the liver on July 1, 1848, at the age of 47 years 9 months and 21 days, and is buried at the First Baptist Church in Charleston. He married Elizabeth Sarah Adams on December 4, 1821 in Charleston, at the St. John Lutheran Church in Charleston, South Carolina.

*   *   *

George Anderson and his wife Ann Esther Pressly Anderson, the parents of George Pressly Anderson, were in charge of a Dekalb County, Georgia teaching academy. For the last eight years of his life, he was a classical instructor in different schools in the state of Georgia.

George was born in 1803 and studied for the ministry of the Presbyterian Church. Although his health was failing, he taught, and was suddenly ill while en route from Athens, Georgia to Yorkville, South Carolina, and died at the residence of Mr. Briant, in Anderson District, South Carolina. A short time before he died, he had been elected to take charge of Bethel Academy, in York District, South Carolina.

George Anderson died on February 23, 1843 at the age of 40, leaving a wife and small children, including David C. Anderson who was 14 and born in Georgia; George P. Anderson who was 12 and born in Georgia; Mary E. Anderson who was 9 and born in Georgia; and William Henry Anderson who was 7 and born in York District, South Carolina.

George's wife, Ann Esther Pressly Anderson, died at Fort Mill, South Carolina on May 25, 1878 at the age of 70.   Her obituary from the June 20, 1878 issue of *The Baptist Courier* said, "She lived with Christ and died the death of the righteous, and her last end was like His. But a short while before her death she sang, with a weak, faltering voice, 'Jesus, lover of my soul, Let me to thy bosom fly.'"

                    *   *   *

David D. Wilson and Sarah Grier Britton Britton were the parents of Margaret Gotea Wilson, affectionately known as "Mamo," the wife of George Pressly Anderson, David Pressley Anderson's father.

David was born in 1790 in Indiantown, Williamsburg District, South Carolina. He was elected in 1824 and 1826 to the state House of Representatives in Williamsburg County, South Carolina.

Indiantown Presbyterian Church, which was founded in 1757, was burned by the British Lieutenant-Colonel Banastre Tarleton during the American Revolution, an act which increased the loyalty of the area people to his primary opponent, American General Francis Marion[102].

He was elected in 1827 to the Session of the Indiantown Presbyterian Church, "the supreme court of all that section." During his tenure, the Session fought against dancing and other "sins," as well as "obstinacy," when the dancers refused to stop dancing.

David and Sam McGill, Sr., placed the successful $1,700 bid to build the new church building in Indiantown. The whole session resigned in 1834 after their victory over, ironically, the same Sam McGill, who insisted on his right to hold dances at his house.

David then became a state senator in 1834, on a pro-Union platform against the Nullifiers during the first movement to secede from The Union. He served as a senator until 1842.

During the years 1835 to 1842, David also served as Senate Justice of Peace and Justice of Quorum. He was commissioner to the superintendent in the opening of navigation on Black Mingo Creek. Additionally, he was the commissioner of free schools and a colonel of the Pee Dee militia which served in the Mexican-American War[103]. He became vice president of the Education Society formed at Indiantown Presbyterian Church in 1836, and was a ruling elder from 1827-34 and from 1836-61.

In Georgetown, South Carolina, he married Mary Wilson in 1815, the daughter of John Wilson and Ann Matthews. In 1827 he donated the land for the Union Methodist Church.

On April 23, 1840, he then married Sarah Grier Britton Britton, our ancestor, the wife of Benjamin Britton who had died. Her maiden name was also Britton.

He educated all of his children and stepchildren at the Indiantown Academy under, among others, Dr. Samuel Davis McGill, Jr. David had been the one to influence Dr. Sam's father to send Sam to receive a "classical education." Sam, as well as David's son, Ned, attended Bethany Academy in Iredell County, North Carolina.

Col. David D. Wilson died in 1868 and was buried in the Indiantown Presbyterian Churchyard. His headstone reads, "He being dead, yet speaketh."

Sarah Grier Britton Britton, his wife, was born on February 13, 1806 at Horry, South Carolina. She married Benjamin F. Britton in April 1827 at Horry, South Carolina. Benjamin shared her last name and perhaps they were cousins. She then married David on April 23, 1840. Sarah Grier Britton Britton Wilson died on September 17, 1884 in Williamsburg County, South Carolina, at the age of 78.

The parents of Sarah Grier Britton Britton Wilson, wife of David D. Wilson, were Thomas Goddard Britton, who was born circa 1784 in Horry, South Carolina, and Ann Durant, who was born circa 1781 the daughter of Bethel Durant. They married circa 1803 in Horry, South Carolina.

PART II

At this point in my family history, we have the last known member of my Phillips family, James Phillips Sr. Nearly everyone else, with the exception of our Willis and Collins ancestors lived in Williamsburg County, South Carolina.

In the wonderful book *History of Williamsburg* written by William Willis Boddie[104] published in 1923, my ancestors are prevalent through much of the pre-Civil War chapters. In Chapter 16, on page 210, this single paragraph provides an excellent example:

> In 1813, a new road was laid out five hundred eight yards from the junction formed by the Indiantown road and the post road from Witherspoon's Ferry on Lynch's Creek, and the road leading by Loveless Gasque's plantation in the most direct way from the said State road to the Black Mingo bridge where the old ferry was established. This road was laid out at the expense of Thomas Williams, Sr., of Williamsburg. In 1813, James M. Grier, Nathan Gasque, Loveless Gasque, John Dozier, Benjamin Britton, and David Wilson Jr. were appointed commissioners for the purpose of erecting and building a bridge over Black Mingo Creek.

With the exception of Gasque and Williams, the names mentioned in this one paragraph are all family names, including Witherspoon, Lynch, Grier, Britton, Dozier and Wilson. These family names will predominate much of the rest of this book.

While I don't have any record of a direct Dozier ancestor, the Pressley, Anderson and Dozier families traveled together to California from South Carolina.   Anthony White Dozier, like John Gotea Pressley, signed the Ordinance of Secession of South Carolina on December 20, 1860.   *The Oakland Tribune*, for example, reported on August 31, 1906 that "Mr. and Mrs. W. W. Phillips of Fresno are the guests of Mrs. E. C. Dozier at her home on Telegraph Avenue."   My grandmother's aunt was Mary Catherine Dozier who married her father's brother Archibald Barron Anderson.   There were Pressley family members as well who married into the Dozier family.

VII. PHILLIPS, PRESSLEY AND WILSON

James Phillips, Sr., father of Judge James Phillips, was probably born around 1750-1755 since we know he had a son William who was born around 1775. We don't know where James was born[105] or who his parents are.

After the birth of his children in South Carolina, the family moved to Mississippi presumably before February 15, 1812[106]. He is listed as a Mississippi property owner as early as 1813.

Mississippi is named for the Mississippi River which forms its western boundary and empties into the Gulf of Mexico. The name, roughly translated from Native American folklore, means "Father of Waters." The translation comes from the Chippewa words "mici zibi" meaning "great river" or "gathering in of all the waters" and the Algonquin word "Messipi.[107]"

In 1798, Congress organized the Mississippi Territory, and Natchez was the Capitol. The 31st parallel bounded the south side, the Mississippi River bounded the west, and a line bound the north east from the mouth of the Yazoo River, and on the east by the Chattahoochee River. In 1803 the Mississippi River was made part of the United States by the Louisiana Purchase. The river made development of the area much easier, because ships could sail to the Gulf of Mexico.

Congress extended the Mississippi Territory north to the border of Tennessee in 1804, and in 1812, more land was added. In 1812 the land lying east of the Pearl River, which was known as the West Florida Republic, was added to the Mississippi Territory.

During the War of 1812, the Choctaw Indians under Chief Pushmataha remained friendly. They joined the Mississippi Militia (of which Judge James Phillips and Moses Collins Jr., his future brother-in-law, were company captains) and aided General Andrew Jackson in putting down the uprisings of the Creek Indians and defeating the British Army in the Battle of New Orleans.

In 1817 Congress divided the Mississippi Territory into the state of Mississippi and Alabama Territory. On December 10, 1817, Mississippi was admitted to the union as the 20th state. During the Civil War, Mississippi was the second state to secede, and was then called The Republic of Mississippi[108].

James Sr. was also at varying times a lawyer, a judge and a Marion County property surveyor mentioned in the various deeds of Marion County. This was in the days before any bar exam; anyone wishing to hold themselves out as a lawyer could do so. He appears to have died around 1828, although we don't know for sure when he died.

There are numerous reasons why we've reached an impasse in our Phillips line, including various early wars and fires which destroyed early records, poor recordkeeping, and ignorance on our parts in knowing where to look. Families moved around frequently and we lack the information to know when or where they moved. Additionally, since most people could not read, write or spell properly back then, looking for the correct records becomes even more difficult. Some names may have been spelled five or more different ways and therefore they are not always recognizable as the family we are searching for. Additionally, the old documents are frequently very difficult to read because of poor script, and many are also very faded.

In his will, which is very difficult to read today, James made reference to his wife Nancy, but her maiden name is not mentioned. While she is most likely the mother of all of his children, even this is not known with certainty.

James had ten children, not necessarily in this order:

- Charles, who married a woman whose name is not known;

- William, who was born in 1775 and died on January 19, 1832 in Hinds, Mississippi (who was married to Rebecca[109] whose maiden name is not known);

- Martha[110], who married Robert Stacy on May 7, 1819 in Marion County, Mississippi;

- Nancy, who married a man by the last name of Broom;

- Lucy, who was born in about 1787 and died in September 1849 in Hinds, Mississippi, who married Charnel Brent in about 1804 (who was born in about 1782 and died on August 23, 1833 in Hinds, Mississippi);

- James, the judge and Mississippi state treasurer, my great-great-great-grandfather, who was born on August 5, 1789 in South Carolina, died on August 11, 1838 in Jackson, Mississippi and is buried at Greenwood Cemetery; he married Sarah Collins (Hatcher) on June 2, 1816 in Marion County, Mississippi; she was born on October 9, 1787 in Winton County, South Carolina, and died on November 30, 1843 in Hinds County, Mississippi;

- Elias, who was born before 1790 and died on February 4, 1843 in Paulding (Jasper County) Mississippi and who married Mary (whose maiden name is not known) on June 12, 1824 in Marion County, Mississippi, who died on February 5, 1843 in Paulding, Mississippi;

- Joseph Thompson, who was born on January 2, 1798 in South Carolina and died in 1835 in Hinds County, Mississippi, who married Lydia Seale on January 1, 1818 in Marion County, Mississippi; she was born on October 21, 1800 in South Carolina and died about 1874 in Tallassee, Alabama (east of Montgomery);

- Susannah, who was born on September 13, 1799 in South Carolina and who died on September 12, 1840 in Hinds County, Mississippi; she married Lewis Perry Seale on February 5, 1818 in Marion County, Mississippi (he was born on December 29, 1798 in South Carolina and died on February 5, 1878 in Jasper County, Texas); and

- Sarah Lee[111] ("Sallie"), born about 1812 who on February 15, 1831 married Daniel Boone Seale in Hinds County (who was born on July 14, 1807 in Mecklenburg, North Carolina and died around 1864 in Bastrop County, Texas). They are buried at Hogeye Baptist Church Cemetery, Bastrop County, Texas.

His will must have been written after February 5, 1818 because that is the date that his daughter Susannah married Louis P. Seale and she is shown as a Seale in the will. The will must also have been written before May 7, 1819 since this is the date that Martha Thigpen Phillips married Robert Stacy.

It appears that James Phillips Sr. and Nancy were alive on June 27, 1828 according to a deed of the slave Hager to his daughter Sarah Lee. This deed[112] was recorded August 14, 1828 which stated:

> James Phillips Sr. for love to daughter Sarah Lee a Negro woman slave 39 years old by name of Hager. She will remain in the possession of James Phillips and Nancy Phillips but at their decease go to Sarah. Dated June 27, 1828. Witness; Joshua Lott and Sarah Phillips. Testimony of Joshua Lott to above deed before John Kellar, June 29, 1828. Recorded August 14, 1828.

His will left his land by deed of gift to his son "Thompson" with the balance to be divided amongst the remaining children listed in the following order: Sarah Lee, Charles Phillips, William Phillips, Elias Phillips, Martha Thigpen, Lucy Brent, James Phillips, Jr., Nancy Broom, and Susannah Seale. The executors were James Phillips, Jr. and Elias Phillips. The will was witnessed by David Ford, Jesse Lee and James Jones.

The Will of James Phillips, Sr., circa 1818-1819
A slightly sharper image of a portion of the first page.
Courtesy of Peter B. Miazza

The Will of James Phillips, Sr.

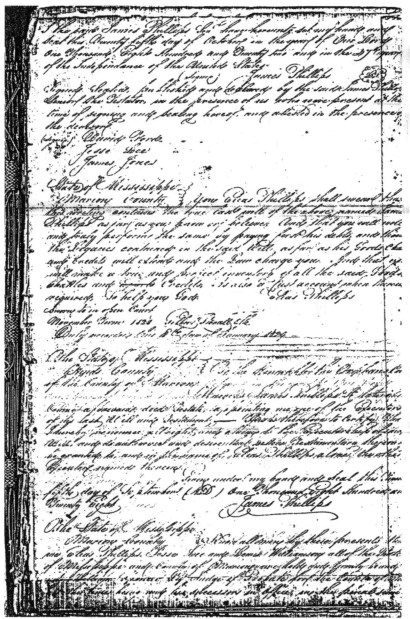

The Will of James Phillips, Sr.

Other deeds can be found in Book 2 of the *Orphan Court Record 1825-1832*:

Pg 114   Elias PHILLIPS swears that the will of James PHILIPS, Sr. was true and correct. Dated: OCT 25, 1822.

Pg 115   BOND: Elias PHILIPS, Jesse LEE, & William WILLIAMSON   are bound to William SPENCER for $1500. Dated: NOV 24, 1828. Elias PHILIPS is executor of the Will of James PHILIPS, dec'd.

Pg 234 - 236   Petition of James PHILIPS for the title to the land of James PHILIPS, Sr., dec'd. Elias PHILIPS aggress to the petition

                BOND: James PHILLIPS is bound to Elias PHILLIPS for $400. Dated: MAY 24 1813. After April 1, 1816, James PHILLIPS would receive title to the land. Wit: James LEE, Simon E. DUKE, Robert DUKE.

Pg. 249   Inventory of the estate of James PHILLIPS, Dec'd. Dated: NOV 26, 1828

Pg. 250   James BARNES, Henry KELLAR, & Joshua LOTT are authorized to appraise the estate of James PHILLIPS

                Account of the sale of personal estate of James PHILLIPS (Sr.) dec'd.

Pg 251   Elias PHILLIPS certifies as executor of the estate of James PHILLIPS (Sr.) that the account presented is true & correct.

Pg 252   Account of the estate of James PHILLIPS, Sr. dec'd. by Elias PHILLIPS, executor. Dated: JUN 07, 1831

His name has been spelled both "Phillips" and "Philips." There is further confusion in the following entries where the last name is spelled "Phillip."

1813 Property Census – Lawrence County, Mississippi

FLOYD	0
PHILLIP, James	160 acres, 5th class, 2nd quality, 32¢ Pearl River, 1 pole, 3 slaves $2.16 2/3
COLLINS	0

Additionally, the Orphan Court Records published in the *Abstracts of Wills and Estates*, Marion County, Mississippi October 1812 to March 1859 list:

1813 Tax List

James LEE	123 acres, 5th class, 1st quality; 123 acres, 5th class, 2nd quality; 52¢ Pearl River, 1 pole, 5 slaves $3.16 2/3
James PHILLIP	160 acres, 5th class, 2nd quality; 32¢ Pearl River, 1 pole, 3 slaves $2.16 2/3
David MORGAN	160 acres, 5th class, 2nd quality 32¢ Bogochitto River, 1 pole, 6 slaves $3.66 2/3
John COOPER	259 ½ acres, 4th class, 1st quality, 259 ½ acres 4th class, 3rd quality, 77¢ Pearl River, 1 pole 66 2/3 ¢
William BRACEY	422 acres, 5th class, 2nd quality $2.37 ½; 380 acres, 5th class, 1st quality, $3.37 ½ Pearl River, 2 slaves $1.00

While we don't know his wife Nancy's maiden name, there is a possibility that it was "Thompson," "Thigpen" or "Lee." There is a James Lee in the 1813 tax list next to "James Phillip." This could potentially be Nancy's brother or father[113]. The evidence is the daughter's name "Sarah Lee." Nancy's maiden name could equally be "Thigpen" if daughter Martha was not married to a Thigpen, or even "Thompson" since their son Joseph's middle name was Thompson[114]. All of these appear to be family names; Thigpen and Lee might provide a clue as to Nancy's family while Thompson equally could provide a clue to the family of James Phillips Sr.

The final word on our Phillips[115] line might rest with my father's DNA. As of this writing, his DNA matches fairly closely with other Phillips families who originally settled in Maryland. Statistics suggest that there is a 90% chance we are related to these families within 20 generations (which equates to approximately 500 years). One member of this project has DNA which differs from my father's on 5 markers out of 64. That member traces his family back to James Phillips who was born in 1540 in Gwinear, Cornwall, England. We are certainly related to this James but unsure whether he is a common ancestor or the descendant of a more distant common ancestor.

The DAR Patriot Index, Volume III, published by the National Society of Daughters of the American Revolution, 2003, does not list any Revolutionary War soldier named James Phillips as having died in Mississippi.

As I close this chapter on our line of Phillips ancestors, I must point out that my father and I are the last known men with the surname Phillips from this line. To date, I have not met a single man with the surname Phillips who I can, with certainty, call a relative.

*   *   *

The parents of Sarah Collins (Hatcher) Phillips were Moses Collins Sr. who was born circa 1753 and Hannah Willis, who was born on December 10, 1754 in New Kent County, Virginia. Moses and Hannah were married on August 6, 1774. He and his family lived in Jackson County, Mississippi when his sons fought in the War of 1812. Moses died on January 29, 1816 in Alabama. Hannah died in 1833.

Moses was a Revolutionary War[116] soldier from South Carolina and applied for a war pension while living in Georgia. He and his son Moses Jr. voted in the May 25, 1813 elections in Jackson County. He and his family moved to Pike County, Mississippi circa 1814-1815. Moses Sr. died while visiting his son Joseph in Alabama.

*   *   *

John Gotea Pressley's father was John Brockinton Pressley. His parents were John Pressley (the son of William Pressley[117] who died circa 1790 and Eleanor Orr) and Mary Barr Brockinton, who was the daughter of John Brockinton and Martha Screven Fowler.

John Gotea Pressley wrote:

> I do not know from what part of Europe the family came, John Pressley the father of my father: John B. Pressley, died when his children were quite young, and they got from him very little of the family history.

John Pressley was born on August 19, 1780 in Williamsburg District, South Carolina and married Mary Barr Brockinton on April 12, 1804. He died on May 14, 1821 at the age of 40. His wife Mary was born on January 15, 1783 and died on August 10, 1849 at the age of 66.

Their marriage notice in the *Charleston Courier* read:

> Married on the 10th instant, by the Rev. Mr. Botsford, John Pressley, Esq. of Black Mingo, to the amiable and accomplished Miss Mary Brockinton, daughter of the late Capt. John Brockinton, all of that place.

Monument of John Pressley (1780-1821)
Pressley Family Cemetery, Williamsburg County, South Carolina
Photo courtesy of Bruce Tognazzini

Headstone:

IN
memory of
JOHN PRESSLEY
who departed this life
on the 14th day of
May A. D. 1821
aged 40 years 3 months
and 25 days.

He maintained a character
throughout life of sterling
worth and integrity,
living esteemed
and respected by all
who knew him,
and died in the hope and
faith of the Gospel.

Footstone:

J.P. 1821

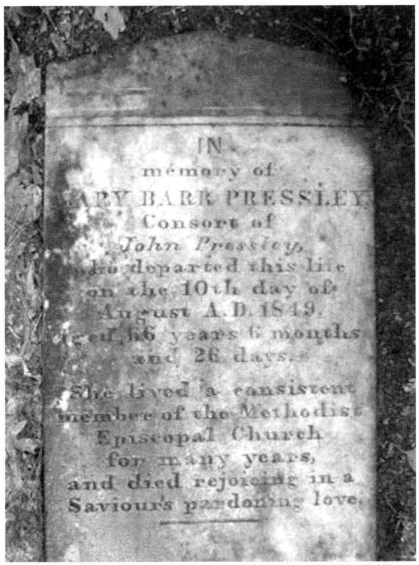

Monument of Mary Barr Brockinton Pressley (1783-1849)
Pressley Family Cemetery,
Williamsburg County, South Carolina
Photo courtesy of Bruce Tognazzini

Headstone:

IN
memory of
MARY BARR PRESSLEY
Consort of
John Pressley,
who departed this life
on the 10th day of
August A. D. 1849,
aged 66 years 6 months
and 26 days.

She lived a constant
member of the Methodist
Episcopal Church
for many years,
and died rejoicing in a
Saviour's pardoning love.

Footstone:

M.B.P. 1849

John Gotea Pressley wrote:

I now come nearer to my own family, and take up for a few observations my own grandmother, Mary Barr Brockinton (1783-1849). Why she was given that name of "Barr," I do not know. There was a family of that name in Williamsburg, but they were in no way related to the Brockintons. She married John Pressley. Neither of them at the date of their marriage owned much property, indeed so little, that when my grandfather John Pressley died leaving a widow and five small children, it required close economy and prudent management on the part of my grandmother to maintain her family. She was not able to give her boys and girls much education. They had to content themselves with such knowledge of books as could be got in the schools taught in the neighborhood, and according to my father's account of them, they were not of a high character. The two of the children were possessed of intellectual capabilities that made up for a lack of opportunity, and enabled them to acquire for themselves an education above that of the ordinary farmer. My grandmother and her husband settled on Turkey Creek. The house which they first lived in was gone before my day, and the place where it had stood was known as the "Old House Field" and was marked by a large mulberry tree of the white variety. The house which I remember so well, and in which I spent so many happy days, and some very unhappy nights[118], was then built of a better class than most of their neighbors. My grandmother's slaves increased, being well treated and taken care of, so that at my earliest recollection, she was considered as being what people called "well off." She was in very easy circumstances.

In writing about his Pressley side, John Gotea Pressley wrote:

The ancestors of the family emigrated from Scotland to Ireland. The tradition in the family is that the name was Priestly[119] when they were in Scotland, and that Dr. Joseph Priestly of Fuldhead near Luds belonged to the same family. The doctor was a very distinguished theologian. His religious views did not suit the rest of the Priestly family. He never was an infidel but "had the courage of his convictions" and followed them wherever they led.

He passed through all changes from Calvinism to Unitarianism. Some of the family who were Calvinists were very much offended by his course, and to distinguish themselves from him, changed their name from Priestly to Pressley There has been some controversy as to how the name was spelled. Some of the families spell it Pressley and others Pressly. Both sides claim to be right. Relationship is claimed with the Pennsylvania family of which John S. Pressley, D.D. was the most distinguished member. They claim relationship with the S. C. branch while they were Northern Prisoners during the great Civil War. These Pressleys sprang from a brother of the Williamsburg brothers who settled first on the James River in VA. And then went west. Two brothers William Pressley and David Pressley appear in the records of that church. David Pressley left Williamsburg[120] and settled in the northern part of the state in what is now York County. From him descended the Pressleys of the upper part of S.C. many of whom and their descendants have moved west, and the name can now be found in every southern state from S. C. to TX.

William Pressley mentioned above married Eleanor Orr. I have heard nothing of her ancestry. They lived on the western side of Black River above what, in my time was known as the Lower Bridge, and had that name long before I was born. He died and is buried in a private grave yard on Hawthorn Swamp. After the death of William Pressley, his widow moved to Heitly's Creek west of Black River, and settled near where there is an old dam across the creek. The waters from one end of the pond run into and down Heitly's Creek and from the other end in a westerly direction down Long Branch by my father's homestead (now Brockinton's house) into Turkey Creek. I may be wrong about the direction in which this water runs. I remember that there is a continuous stream from the pond to Turkey Creek, but the waters may divide, and after reflection, I believe they do divide at a point on the stream westwardly from the pond. So many years have elapsed since I have been over the woods there, that while I remember places well, I have forgotten some of the details. Eleanor the widow after her removal, married one Boyd. I do not know where he came from, or anything of [the] history. William Pressley and Eleanor (Orr) had children born to them: John Pressley and Margaret Pressley.

As wife of Boyd there was born to Eleanor a daughter Sarah Boyd. I do not know whether she survived Boyd or not, but she left her three children living. Before her death she selected what was then a beautiful spot under some large oak trees, (long since gone) as a burial ground. She is buried there and her grave is covered by brick work, very much dilapidated now. This was the family burial ground till I left S. C. There repose till the resurrection day, besides Eleanor, my grandfather and grandmother Pressley, and all their children and grandchildren bearing the name in S. C.

In writing about his grandmother, Mary Barr Brockinton Pressley, John Gotea Pressley wrote:

In 1839 my father settled on the same plantation on the east side of Turkey Creek, and took charge of my grandmother's business. They united forces and farmed together dividing the crop in proportion to their slaves cultivating it. Their cattle which were also numerous were kept together, and the proceeds of the stock divided. It became my special business to look after this stock as soon as I was old enough, and many a day have I spent in the saddle, as the western men would call a "cowboy." I was very proud of it when the weather was not too hot, and water too scarce; then I suffered a great deal from the sun and thirst. I was very fond of visiting my grandmother in the day and time, and managed to dine there at least once a week. I have a feeling recollection even at this day of the nice chicken and toothsome bread which I was acquainted to eat at her house. I have in my mind as ineffaceable picture of the old lady sitting in her great arm chair, on her piazza in summer and by her fireside in the winter giving directions to Hester, the cook or Amy, the house servant. As fond as I was of my old grandmother and as much as I liked to visit her in the day, I never stayed in her house at night if I could help it, unless I had other boys for company. Amy, the house girl, who was a great favorite with children, would fill our minds with ghost stories. My grandmother was in the habit of retiring almost as soon as the chickens, and when she sent me to bed, Amy's ghost stories could come so vividly to my mind, that I could almost see the goblins which she had painted, in such horrible colors. I invariably covered my head for fear I would see them. Upon Amy's authority I was afraid of seeing John Cooper's ghost any night. He was one of my cousins who died in my grandmother's company room. Grandma was very fond of her grandchildren and they of her. We enjoyed meeting at her house and spending a day (or a night when two or three of us could sleep together and have Amy for a protector to exorcise the spirits which we almost believed she could call up). The children were too polite, and loved the old lady too much, to remind her that she was getting in the habit of telling the same story two or three times, we would affect intense interest in her story just as much as if we had never heard it, and when she came to the end, would exclaim, "Why, Grandma," and laughed heartily if the story was intended to amuse. I believe that, after Mary and John Cooper whom she took charge of when they were almost infants, I was her favorite grandchild. She provided for my education entirely. She first offered to do so if I would study for the ministry. I entertained so high a respect for that calling that I felt my unfitness. Perhaps I may have to some extent been influenced by the thought that I would have to give up some worldly pleasures. At any rate, I declined to accept of her bounty on the proposed conditions, and asked her to send me to the S. C. Military Academy. After some hesitation and delay the good old lady acceded to my wishes, and I went to the institution at her expense on the 15th day of January 1848. My grandmother died before I completed my course of study, but charged the property devised to my father and Aunt Martha Mouzon with the expense of my education.

*   *   *

The parents of Sarah Gotea, wife of John Brockinton Pressley (and John Gotea Pressley's mother) were John Gotea (son of John Gotea and Elizabeth Barnes) and Elizabeth Scott, the daughter of William Scott and Mary Baxter. John and Elizabeth were married on March 15, 1807. John Gotea died on January 3, 1826 at the age of 44. Elizabeth died on October 27, 1851 at the age of 61.

John Gotea Pressley wrote:

The maiden name of my grandmother on my mother's side was Elizabeth Scott born the 6th day of May 1790. I do not know of her mother's maiden nor given surname, nor do I know her father's given name. He died and his widow my great grandmother married a Mr. McConnell [James] whose name I regret my inability to state. My grandmother married John Gotea who was my grandfather on my mother's side. My grandmother was left a widow with two children, Sarah my mother, and Margaret Jane, my aunt. Grandma lived on the road leading from Kingstree via Black Mingo to Georgetown on a small stream called Cold Water Run. Her plantation lay on both sides of this stream, and extended to Black Mingo Swamp. It was of considerable extent and very fine land. She owned a few Negroes, and some livestock. Her property sufficed my good management to keep her and her children in comfort. Upon her husband's death his estate was partitioned between the widow and her two daughters, but was kept together on the plantation. Upon my father's marriage on the 5th day of January 1830, he took up his residence with his mother-in-law, and with his Negroes and those of my grandmother and her two daughters, carried on the farm for their joint benefits till the summer of 1839, when he moved to Turkey Creek and joined forces with his own mother.

After the death of my grandfather (and perhaps before) my grandmother opened her house as a way-side inn. Being about half way between Georgetown and Kingstree, and being an excellent house-keeper it became a very popular stopping place, and her income was considerably increased. She was a fine looking proud old lady, very popular with her friends, and much loved by her grandchildren. My brother James seemed to be her favorite, and remained with her for a considerable time after the removal of my father and family to Turkey Creek. After the death of her daughter, Margaret Jane (1823-1845) who married Robert Harvey Wilson[121], she took up her residence in my father's house, where she lived from June 1846, till she died on the 27th day of October 1851. Her life was terminated by an accident. She was on a visit to her half-sister the wife of Hugh McCutchen (Mary McConnell) and fell in an attack of vertigo from the piazza (about five feet) to the ground.

Several of her ribs were broken and probably the head of the femur. It was some time before she could be brought home, and then in a bed suspended from the sides of a wagon body. The bones refused to knit. She was never on her feet again, and died after weeks of suffering. She was a consistent member if the Indiantown Church (Presbyterian).   The mother of Elizabeth Scott married James McConnell.

In discussing his Gotea family, John Gotea Pressley wrote:

I will now return to my mother's side of the house. The last of her line mentioned was her mother Elizabeth Gotea (nee Scott).

The Gautiers were Huguenots, and after the Revocation of the Edict of the Nantes in Oct. 1685[122], which gave toleration to Protestants, came to Carolina and settled in Williamsburg. I have been told that the ancestor of the family in France was a nobleman. My ancestor, whose name I do not know, came to America in company with the Laurence family. I am not able to say whether he was my great-grandfather or one generation further off, but from the time my grandfather was born I would say the latter.   One of my ancestors in America changed the name to Gotea.

John Gotea Senior (will dated March 24, 1818) married Elizabeth Barnes.

I know nothing about my great grandmother, not even her given name. Nor do I know anything about my great grandfather. They had ____ children. My grandfather had a brother whose name I do not know. He was the father of George Gotea who married Jennie Heddleston, and Jane Gotea who was the wife of Thomas McCants. I am certain that there was also a sister who was the mother of the McCants family.

John Gotea Junior, and Elizabeth Scott were married on the 5th day of March, 1807. They lived on Cold Water Run as I have already said in the sketch of grandmother Gotea.

John Gotea was Clerk of the Court of Common Pleas and General Sessions of Williamsburg District, and made an excellent officer. He wrote a plain bold hand, and with neatness. My grandmother gave me very few incidents of his life. He died while the incumbent of the Clerk's Court, in Kingstree on the 3rd day of January 1826. His death was very sudden, none of his family were with him. Death came without any warning. My mother said the disease was quinsy. He was a Lieutenant in that portion of the Army of the United States in the War of 1812 assigned to the defense of the Southern Coast, and with his company was stationed on Cat Island near the entrance of Winyah Bay below Georgetown. A land warrant was issued to his widow in 1851 as a reward for his services. It came after her death. My mother was then acquiring my legal education and starting in life.

John Gotea and his wife Elizabeth, nee Scott, had children born to them.

John Gotea Pressley then listed the children of John Gotea and Elizabeth Scott, all of whom died in infancy or childhood except his mother Sarah Gotea and his Aunt Margaret Jane Gotea who was born on March 26, 1825. Of her, he said:

Margaret Jane Gotea was the only one of my grandfather and grandmother Gotea's children that I remember. She was of a very lovable disposition, and above the average in good looks. My brother James and I called her "big sister," our sister Mary we designated as "little sister." She married Robert Harvey Wilson, a half brother of Emma Pressley nee Wilson, the widow of my brother James F. Pressley, and died on the 19th of June 1845, leaving her surviving husband but no children.

*   *   *

The parents of Cornelius D. Burckmyer (the father of John Gotea Pressley's wife Julia Caroline Burckmyer) were John Burckmyer (son of Daniel John Burckmyer and Margaret Anna Lebert) and Ann Mary Cobia.

John Burckmyer died on May 27, 1812 in Charleston, South Carolina at the age of 48 after a long illness. *The South Carolina Historical and Genealogical Magazine* reprinted his obituary:

> Mr. John Burckmyer, a native of this place.... He has left a wife and five children to bemoan the loss of an affectionate husband and tender parent. His remains were interred in the burial ground of the German Lutheran Church. The German Fusileers of this city, under Capt. Strobel, of which he has been a member, attended and performed military honors on the occasion.

His funeral was held on June 4, 1812 at 76 Wentworth Street in Charleston, South Carolina. His wife Ann Mary Cobia was born on November 6, 1774 in Charleston, South Carolina and died on October 6, 1829 at the age of 54.

*   *   *

The parents of Ann Esther Pressly (the wife of George Anderson) were William Pressly (son of David Pressly and Esther whose maiden name is not known) and Eliza Eleanor Adams, the daughter of David Adams and Ann Chaplin.

William was born in 1778 in South Carolina. He was known as a "factor," a merchant who bought and sold on commission. He married Eliza on December 13, 1804 and was buried on April 6, 1820 at the Second Presbyterian Church in Charleston, South Carolina.

Eliza, who was born on January 18, 1784 at St. Helena Parish, South Carolina, died on July 24, 1818 in Charleston at the age of 34, and is said to be buried at Bethel Church.

*   *   *

The parents of David D. Wilson, the father of Margaret Gotea Wilson (affectionately known as "Mamo" who married George Pressly Anderson) were David Wilson and Jane Morrow.

David Wilson, the son of David Wilson and Mary Witherspoon, is considered a patriot[123] since he provided material aid by sending supply provisions and forage for Continental Army and militia use in 1781 and 1782.

David Wilson was born on April 11, 1742 in Indiantown, Williamsburg County, South Carolina. He married a woman whose name is not known in 1762 in South Carolina. He later married Jane Morrow in 1772 in Indiantown. He died on June 8, 1812 in Indiantown at the age of 70.

His wife Jane Morrow Wilson, our ancestor, was born in 1755 in Williamsburg Township, South Carolina. She died on April 14, 1831 in Indiantown and is buried at the Presbyterian Cemetery, Williamsburg County, South Carolina.

David's mother Mary Witherspoon, the daughter of first cousins John and Janet Witherspoon, was the sister of James Witherspoon who built Thorntree house and plantation in Kingstree, South Carolina. James Witherspoon is my 5th great-granduncle. The South Carolina Department of Archives and History describes the house as follows[124]:

> The oldest known residence in the Pee Dee area, Thorntree is an excellent example of the earliest plantation houses constructed entirely of native materials. Built by James Witherspoon in 1749, the house possesses a progressive rural domestic design. The house was located in the wilderness and adapted to the New World, but with refinements recalling the good life of the Old World. The two-story frame "I-House" type house has a hall and parlor plan with exterior end chimneys, and full-length piazzas on the front and rear elevations. Its brick piers support hand-hewn heart pine beams. All twenty-four windows have pine paneled shutters fastened with hand-forged strap hinges. The entire interior is pine: the floors, walls, ceilings, cornices, mantels and all overmantels (except two that are plastered).

As a restoration project of the Williamsburg County Historical Society[125], the house was moved from an inaccessible rural site for preservation. The original site was unavailable for purchase, and unprotected against fire and vandalism.

As Andrew Chandler from the South Carolina Department of Archives and History writes[126]:

> Thorntree House was built on the south side of Black River about a mile south of the intersection of US 521 and SC 377, just east of SC 377's intersection with old Lenud's Ferry Road. Just to the east of the house site is Stoney Run, a tributary of Black River. Approximately two and a half miles to the west is Thorntree Swamp. The Witherspoons owned a considerable amount of land that probably extended to and included areas on one or both sides of Thorntree Swamp because I believe either James or Robert Witherspoon make reference to their "Thorntree Plantation."

The present site is within the city of Kingstree on land donated as a memorial park. The South Carolina Department of Archives and History also describe the house: "Victorian trim, south piazza, and shed rooms added circa 1800 have been removed. The house now stands as it was in the eighteenth century."

The house was listed in the National Register of Historic Places on October 28, 1970 as building 70000606.

Thorntree, the plantation home of
James Witherspoon (1700-1768)
Kingstree, South Carolina
Photo courtesy of the South Carolina Department of Archives and History

After the death of James Witherspoon, Thorntree became the home of Gavin Witherspoon, the son of James and Elizabeth Witherspoon. During the Revolution, the hated British officer Banastre Tarleton with one hundred British dragoons, and a large number of Tories under Col. Elias Ball, encamped at the plantation of Gavin Witherspoon, south of the lower bridge, on Black River, early in August 1780.

Thorntree, the plantation home of
James Witherspoon (1700-1768)
Kingstree, South Carolina
Courtesy of the South Carolina Department of Archives and History

Thorntree, the plantation home of
James Witherspoon (1700-1768)
Main upstairs bedroom
Kingstree, South Carolina
Courtesy of the South Carolina Department of Archives and History

Also in Kingstree, South Carolina is the "Brockinton-Scott" House, listed with the National Register of Historic Places as building 80003712. This was the home of Elizabeth Burgess Scott Brockinton (1835-1893) and John Fowler Brockinton (1822-1881). John Fowler Brockinton is my first cousin five times removed.

VIII. COLLINS, PRESSLEY, BROCKINTON, SCOTT, PRESSLY, ADAMS AND WILSON

The father of Moses Collins, Sr. was John Collins III who was born circa 1700 in New Kent, Virginia. He married Elizabeth Odom, the daughter of William Odom of New Kent County. They moved southward, settling for a time in Barnwell County, South Carolina and had at least eight children, all sons. Despite being a large landowner with thousands of acres, he moved location often. John Collins III died in Barnwell County, South Carolina in 1790.

*   *   *

Williamsburg County, located in the southern tip of the Pee Dee, was named Williamsburg in honor of the Protestant King, William of Orange, otherwise known as William III of England.

William Willis Boddie wrote *History of Williamsburg* published in 1923 and William Gilmore Simms (1806-1870) wrote the book *The Life of Francis Marion* in 1844. From these two sources, a brief history of Williamsburg County and the Kings Tree (later Kingstree) emerges[127]:

> Williamsburg was one of eleven townships that were ordered by King George II in 1730 for colonial Governor Robert Johnson to develop. This was considered the "back country" of the

Carolina Province. The townships were to consist of 20,000 acres and to front a river, which in this case was the Black River.

In partial compliance, eight townships were laid out, including Williamsburg. This particular spot on the river had a white pine tree, which stood straighter and taller than the other local pine trees. It was marked by an unknown early surveyor with the King's Arrow to claim it for the king, and to identify it as a potential mast for a ship.

It was never claimed nor cut, but became the center of the new township, referred to as "The King's Tree." Kingstree eventually became the chief town of Williamsburg township. The township was a part of Craven County, one of the original four counties that encompassed present day South Carolina. Williamsburg Township then included most of the present Pee Dee region. It was later divided and became a number of separate counties, including present day Williamsburg County at the center.

The township was named after William of Orange. In 1732 a colony of forty Scotch-Irish led by Roger Gordon came up the river by boat and settled in the vicinity of the King's Tree. They were poor Protestants, having escaped persecution by previous moves until they came to America.

It was an exceedingly difficult and primitive life for the early settlers and the life expectancy for those who did not die in infancy was around 50 years. The settlers were surrounded by Indians of the Wee Nee, the Wee Tee, the Chickasaw, the Creek, the Waccamaw, and the Pee Dee tribes, but had few conflicts with them.

A hazard for the settlers was poisonous snakes and wolves which were very common in the early years.

Though the entire colony was Anglican, and no churches or schools could be established without the consent of the Lord Bishop or his agent, these people had suffered persecution from the Church of England. The colony quickly established a religious society which was actually Presbyterian, though the name was not applied until later. In 1736 they called The Rev. John Willison from Scotland to be their minister. They built a meeting house that became Williamsburg Presbyterian Church. Soon new daughter churches were established at Indiantown and Black Mingo

In 1780 John Witherspoon, grandson of one of the early settlers, who were all deceased by then, wrote: "...they were servers of God, were well acquainted with the Scriptures, were much engaged in prayer, were strict observers of the Sabbath, in a word, they were a stock of people that studied outward piety as well as inward purity of life."

They also prospered. The wilderness abounded in deer, wild turkeys, fish and muscadine grapes. As the colony grew, they established plantations. Wheat from Europe grew poorly, but corn produced abundantly. Flax was grown for cloth, later it was gradually replaced by cotton. Cattle and hogs that they brought with them reproduced and found abundant forage, running wild in the swamps and forests, with only the owner's mark to identify them. In about 1750, the crop indigo was introduced, and many of the plantation owners became wealthy from it. Rice was grown along the river. Eventually a large naval store industry developed and this was followed by timbering which has continued into modern times.

In 1759 during the French and Indian War, the French enlisted the large Cherokee tribe as allies. Though they lived to the northwest of Williamsburg, they threatened the entire state, and two companies of volunteer militia were organized to fight for King George II (and for self-defense). Together with other companies from the rest of coastal Carolina, a regiment was formed, which mustered and drilled at Kingstree. They also built a stockade for the residents in case of Indian attack.

When the American Revolution broke out some of the young men joined the army and were sent for the defense of Charleston. After Charleston surrendered to the British in early 1780, the soldiers were paroled and returned home, expecting to remain neutral from then on.

The British quickly established garrisons throughout South Carolina, including a fort at nearby Georgetown on the coast. In the upstate were a larger number of Tories, who joined the British forces, but the Williamsburg Presbyterians were not fond of King George III, and were inclined to sit out the war, until the British made a tactical error. An order was proclaimed that all who had taken parole must now take up arms for the King. This was considered by the people to be a unilateral violation of the terms of their parole. They sent a local militia officer as representative, Captain John James, to the fort at Georgetown for clarification, where he was treated abusively by the commander, Captain Ardesoif. Fleeing from Georgetown, he quickly raised a militia of four companies, which were put under the command of Francis Marion.

Marion was one of the most effective military officers of the Revolution, and he had the fervent loyalty of this militia, who served with no pay and no promise of pay, who provided their own weapons and horses, or secured them whenever they defeated the British.

The only area of South Carolina that was not occupied by the British was the Williamsburg area. The British tried to establish a garrison at Willtown, but Marion's men defeated them and drove them off in the Battle of Mingo Creek. Marion not only won tactical victories against superior forces with small cost, but also won a moral victory which turned the tide in the Revolution in South Carolina. He did this in two ways, first by holding a section of the colony that the British could not penetrate, which raised morale of Patriot forces elsewhere. And secondly he gave receipts for horses, boats, weapons and food supplies that were commandeered, or were destroyed to keep from falling into the hands of the British. This was in stark contrast to the British officers Banastre Tarleton and James Wemyss who burned and looted Williamsburg early in the war. Especially angering the public was the British burning of the Williamsburg and Indiantown Presbyterian Churches, which the British called "hotbeds of sedition." Many of Marion's receipts were presented to the new state government after the war, and the state paid the claims.

Proof of Marion's moral victory was the speed at which he gained information about British movements. Meanwhile, British officers collected very little as they repeatedly tried to neutralize him. Both relied on spies among the populace, but Williamsburg was loyal to Marion. Tarleton, cursing Marion, when he could not catch him, gave him his epithet, "The Swamp Fox." The Williamsburg Militia served as needed, coming quickly when called, but remaining at home to plant and harvest crops and other duties whenever possible. Toward the end of the war, Marion could quickly call up a couple thousand men. Marion's men held their territory alone until General Nathanael Greene arrived later in the war. They then helped Greene's forces evict the British from their upstate garrisons and drive them back to Charleston, from whence they eventually surrendered and left by ship.

*   *   *

William Pressley, who died circa 1790, married Eleanor Orr, who married John Boyd after William died. Eleanor was born circa 1765 and died circa 1803. Unfortunately, we don't know when they were married. Eleanor Orr is the mother of John Pressley, father of John Brockinton Pressley.   Eleanor is presumed to be buried in The Pressley Family Cemetery, Williamsburg County, South Carolina in an unmarked grave where her son John and other family members are buried.

What will follow later in this book is the matter of precisely which "William Pressley" married Eleanor Orr[128].

*   *   *

Captain John Brockinton, son of John Brockinton Sr. and Mary Barr, married Martha Screven Fowler who was born in 1756 or 1757, the daughter of James Fowler and Elizabeth Screven. They married on April 21, 1773. John was born in 1754 and fought on the side of the Loyalists (England) in the Revolutionary War.   He died on November 16, 1801 in Willtown, Black Mingo, Williamsburg County, South Carolina. Martha died in 1825.

John Gotea Pressley writes:

John Brockinton Jr. (1754-1801), the father of my grandmother, Mary Barr B. Pressley (1783-1849), died leaving his children minors of tender years. The same maybe said of John Gotea, my grandfather on my mother's side. These facts will account for the paucity as to incidents, names, etc. in the history which I am about to write.

From the position which the Brockinton, Screven, and Fowler families held in South Carolina before and during the Revolutionary War, I think it would be safe to say that they came from England and belonged to the better class of people of that country.

Tory John Brockinton Jr. married (as it appears from that instrument referred to) 1773 Martha Fowler. He was a very intelligent man, of splendid physique, and wealthy for the times. At the beginning of the Revolutionary struggle he espoused the cause of the King, as did a majority of the wealthy planters of Carolina, and became a Captain in the British service. He gave General Francis Marion and his command much trouble. Unfortunately for family tradition, owing to the youth of his children when he died, very few of his adventures as a solider have been handed down to his posterity.

The old Town of Black Mingo in which he lived was situated on a large navigable Creek of the same name, one of the principle tributaries of Black River.   On one occasion he pursued Marion from Williamsburg (or Craven County as it was then called) up into North Carolina, but failed to catch him or make him fight. After Marion's escape, the British forces returned, and went into camp near Black Mingo. Feeling perfectly secure the commanding officer was not as vigilant as soldiers ought to always be. The Creek was crossed by means of a bridge was not picketed as it should have been. Then Marion had eluded his pursuers, presuming on their feeling of security induced by their pursuit and his long retreat, he turned back on their tracks. When he reached the bridge he directed the blankets of his men spread and thus deadened the sound of their horses' feet. The bridge was crossed and with this command he charged the British camp, and completely surprised his late victorious pursuers. The Red Coats were routed, and many who escaped were driven in to the neighboring swamp. I have no means of ascertaining the number killed or wounded. The family tradition is that Capt. John Brockinton's children were all so young at the time I would sooner rely on the statement of the biographer than on their memory. As the affair was not well managed we will let Col. Ball have all the credit.

Capt. Brockinton was a brave man, and gallant soldier, and his descendants may rest assured that he did his duty with his usual courage in the engagement.

I have never heard from my grandmother or any of his grandchildren, or old men of the neighborhood who were boys during that war, that Capt. Brockinton conducted military operations other than in accordance with the laws of civilized warfare. The great confidence shown in him by his neighbors after the war is the best proof that he was a brave soldier and conscientious man. There was, during the Revolutionary struggle, bitter animosity between the Loyalists and Whigs, and no doubt, as the case is in every civil war, there were acts of violence and lawlessness on both sides. None can be established as having been practiced by authority of Captain Brockinton, I believe.

The Captain had the courage of his convictions, and never surrendered, as did many of the Loyalists. After the war when the legislature of South Carolina passed confiscation acts his name was included in the list of the unrepentant. (See Vol. 7 Statues at large of South Carolina).

He lost much of his property in moving it from place to place to keep it out of reach of the officers charged with the execution of the confiscation laws. The repeal of these laws left him or his estate with considerable land, but of no great value. In fact, its [lack] of value is the only reason I can think of for its not being confiscated. It must in some way have escaped the notice of the officers of the law, or it may have been, and I think probably it was, that his neighbors through sympathy for him and his family would not bid on his land when exposed for sale.

I find among the papers left by him a (copy of a) petition in behalf of his wife and children addressed to the legislature of South Carolina by seventy-three of his fellow citizens. On this list of petitioners I recognize the names of some of the most respectable people of Williamsburg. This petition represents his family as being "reduced from easy circumstances, to poverty and distress," his estate confiscated and "he on the banishment list." This petition is without date, but was probably sent to the Legislature when Capt. Brockinton was in hiding with his Negroes with him. How much of his property escaped confiscation, I have no means of ascertaining, but he had some left, and his family after the repeal of the confiscation acts were not so destitute as they appear by the petition to have been previously.

Some of the lands were sold by his heirs, after I came to the bar, with my assistance. (See case of Sarah Jacks vs. Carraway & Perkins, Court of Equity, Williamsburg District, South Carolina.) My father gave up his claim to the poorer heirs.   Capt. Brockinton's house was standing within my recollection (but in ruins) on the right hand side of the main street as one enters the Town of Black Mingo from the land side. It had for the times been a fine structure. Its owner had much of the spirit of the British Cavalier.

Capt. John Brockinton was urged by his fellow citizens after the war to consent to serve them in the Legislature, but he declined, feeling, probably that those who had gained their independence against his opposition should govern themselves without the assistance of their former enemies. I have heard of but one manifestation of bad spirit after the war was over on the part of

Capt. Brockinton. That was directed against two ex-Captains of Marion's command I believe their names were White and Simons. When these two soldiers came into town he would dress his two young sons in British uniform and have them show themselves to the two old Whigs that he might enjoy their anger. He was a man of so much courage and strength that they never ventured to vent their rage on him, which it was probably his purpose to have them do.

When an uprising of the people succeeds it is a glorious revolution, when it fails it is a rebellion. The participants in the former case are "patriots," in the latter "rebels." Had the cause of the Colonies failed Capt. Brockinton's name would have gone into history as a distinguished patriot and soldier. How unjust to the conscientious man that righteousness of his cause, and with the narrow minded, his honesty and patriotism must be proved by success; risking fortune, family and life in maintaining political opinions and principles is the highest proof a man can give of his honesty and patriotism.

After the death of her husband, Martha Brockinton left Black Mingo, and settled near Dickey's Bay, waters of Turkey Creek, Williamsburg District. There she lived the remainder of her life. Her son, William Brockinton, lived with her and managed her small plantation; at the same time taking care of the large estate of William Burrows (his brother-in-law) of which he was the executor, and Guardian of his nephew, the son and only child of his brother-in-law and his sister.

The place where Mrs. Brockinton lived was known within my recollection as Brockinton's Old Field. The houses were all gone before my day. The title to the land passed by conveyance after Mrs. Brockinton's death to the Gamble family, and is still in them.

Martha Screven Fowler's father, James Fowler, the son of Richard Fowler and Sarah (whose maiden name is not known) married Elizabeth Screven, daughter of Rev. Elisha Screven and Hannah (whose last name was either Johnson or Commander). He was a planter and a merchant, born circa 1730. He died in 1772. Elizabeth was a Baptist, born in 1738 and died after 1772.

Richard Fowler was born and probably died in England. He and his wife Sarah (whose maiden name is not known) were there at the time of their son James's death in 1772.

*   *   *

John Gotea, son of John Gotea and Eleanor (Elender or Elander) McCutchen, married Elizabeth Barnes.

*   *   *

William Scott, Elizabeth Scott's father, was a soldier born in 1760. He married Mary Baxter, daughter of Thomas Baxter in 1778. He died in 1806. His wife Mary was first married to James McConnell and died on November 13, 1823 at the age of 61.

Thomas Baxter, the father of Mary Baxter, was born in 1739 and died in 1765.

Thomas' first cousin Thomas Lynch, Jr. (Thomas Lynch III) was the youngest signer of The Declaration of Independence from South Carolina.

Thomas Baxter's father, the Rev. John Baxter was a minister and a merchant who was born circa 1699-1700. He was Presbyterian and is credited with starting at least eight churches in South Carolina.

He began preaching as a young man as early as 1729 when he baptized John Nelson at Black Mingo Church. In 1733 he moved to Berkeley County and began preaching; he was the regular minister at Cainhoy Presbyterian Church. About this time, in 1733 he married Sarah Lynch (daughter of Thomas Lynch and Sabina Van Der Horst) who was from one of the wealthiest families in South Carolina.

It is known and documented that Rev. John Baxter was a great writer and orator. One of his most famous sermons was titled "Tryals to the Presbytery." Regrettably, all of the records were burned by General Sherman in the Civil War.

Near Black Mingo Presbyterian Church there was a Belin Baptist Church where Rev. Charles Woodmason was pastor. John and Charles were apparently friends and business partners, but trusted the wrong people. Relatives from the Lynch family had to come to John's rescue to keep him from losing all he owned due to a failed business venture.

By 1770, Rev. John was reported as feeble and died before July 18, 1789, the date a letter was written from Adam Marshall to his mother, Janet Gregg Marshall in Ireland, stating "Uncle John Baxter is dead." He had immigrated to South Carolina before August 18, 1740.

Rev. John's wife Sarah Lynch was born circa 1715-1720 and died in 1787.

*   *   *

Daniel John Burckmyer married Margaret Anna Lebert on April 8, 1766 at St. John's Lutheran in Charleston, South Carolina. He died on July 7, 1774 in Charleston at the age of 42. In his will, he left 400 acres of land on Turkey Creek to his son George Henry Burckmyer. His wife Margaret died on July 30, 1781 in Charleston.

*   *   *

David Pressly, the father of William Pressly who married Eliza Eleanor Adams, is the immigrant ancestor of David Pressley Anderson. He was formerly of Long Cane, but at the date of his will in 1785, he was in Charleston. He left his distributive share of the land on Hard Labor Creek, which was divided between his brother William and himself, to his son David. The will mentions his sons Samuel, David, John and William, as well as daughters Agnes (wife of Henry Wylie), Mary Ann and Esther.

William Laurens Pressley described the three Pressly brothers who originally settled in Kingstree. He wrote:

> It is known that there were three Pressly brothers: David, John and William, born in Scotland, who moved to Ireland and migrated from Ireland to America.
>
> It is not known the year in which they moved to Ireland. They came from Scotland to Ireland, perhaps with the Witherspoon family, for the Witherspoon family and the Pressly family were inter-married and probably their movements occurred about the

same time. It is known that the Witherspoon family migrated from Scotland to Ireland in 1695 and settled in County Down, Ireland.

On September 14, 1734, David, John and William Pressly and the John Witherspoon family boarded the ship named The Good Intent and sailed for America.

They were delayed off the coast of Ireland for two weeks due to contrary winds, but they reached Charleston, South Carolina around December 1, 1734 and they were warmly received.

After Christmas, the immigrants sailed up the Carolina coast to Winyah Bay. They made the passage in the depth of winter and were exposed to inclement weather day and night. The patron and his boatmen, as a result, made a blasphemous expression which greatly disturbed them.

From Winyah Bay they pushed up the Black River to Potato Ferry and lay for sometime in a barn, while the men pushed on further toward Kingstree to build shelters for their families.

During the winters of 1749 and 1750, and the winter of 1751, a terrible plague broke out in the community, possibly small pox. About eighty of the leading citizens of the community died as a result.

David and John decided to migrate and went to the northwest corner of the State into the 96 District.

William remained in Kingstree, and died of this plague in 1751. His family remained in Kingstree, however, until the end of the Confederate War.

This William, the immigrant, is the great-grandfather of Judge John Gotea Pressley and his brother James Fowler Pressley who migrated to California with the Anderson and Dozier families.

Later, David and his family pushed further on and settled in the southwestern corner of what is now Anderson County.

Judge Benjamin Chaplin Pressley, who helped John Gotea Pressley become a lawyer, wrote a letter in 1882 which provides some additional background about the Pressley family. However, in 1988, the *Presley/Preslar/Pressly Newsletter* found some errors. Apparently Judge Benjamin thought that he was related to John Gotea Pressley through the same set of immigrant brothers who came to Charleston in 1734. The editor points out below that Judge Benjamin's grandfather, David Pressly, immigrated in 1767, and that his grandfather was from a different set of brothers than the ones W. L. Pressley writes about.

However, it should be pointed out that Judge Benjamin Chaplin
Pressley was the brother of Ann Esther Pressly who married
George Anderson, the grandparents of David Pressley Anderson.
Our "David Pressley Anderson" line to the original Pressly
immigrant is therefore the same as Benjamin's.

Summerville, S.C.
January 30th, 1882.
J.N. Miller, Esq.:
Dear Sir:
   Your aunt, Mrs. Torbit, supposes that I know very much of the
Pressley family (or Pressly) but in reality, my inquiries in that
direction are very fragmentary, because of lost records in this State.
The family was of the ancient Briton stock, formerly living near
London, but were driven northward with the other original
inhabitants, by the Danish and Saxon invasions of England. The
family crest was a cockatrice, thus showing that it is not the name
of Priestly[129], which some suppose. The Priestly crest was a demi-
lion. Our family having passed over into Scotland, not far from
Glasgow were, for many generations known as lowland Scotch.
Thence immigrating to the county of Dawes in north of Ireland,
they became Scotch-Irish.   In 1733, some of them came to this
State and united with others in settling Kingstree in Williamsburg
County. Many of them were cut off by a fatal sickness which swept
over that county in 1749-50-51. Of those left, two, David and John
removed to Abbeville, Calhoun settlement. David was my
grandfather[130], and John was your great-great-grandfather. His sons
were David, William, John and Joseph. His son David married Jane
Patterson and by her he had five sons. Samuel, (your grandfather)
John T., Dr. George W., Dr. James P. and William. They are all
dead except William who is living in Illinois or Ohio. Your
grandfather married Elizabeth Hearst, and three of her sisters
married three of the other brothers, to-wit: John T., George W., and
James P. They have not left many descendants. John T's most
distinguished son, Joseph, died four years ago at Erie,
Pennsylvania. He was a D.D. and bid fair to excel his father as an
eloquent preacher. His sister Malinda survives him and resides at
Alleghany, Pennsylvania - now absent in Europe. Your granduncle,
Dr. George, left one son, Joseph, now an eminent physician at the
old Cedar Spring settlement. Dr. James P. left several sons, of
whom Frank and David are ministers of the gospel and are said to

be very promising. The other branches of the family you probably do not feel interested in. I will, however, add, that the distinguished preacher Dr. Ebenezer Pressly was the son of William, your great-grandfather's brother, Dr. John E. Pressly, of Coddle Creek, N.C., was a nephew of Ebenezer, being a son of his brother William. Dr. Samuel Patterson Pressly, who died at Athens, Georgia in 1835, being then Prof, of Belles-letters in the State University was the son of John, another brother of your great-grandfather.

The remnant of the family which remained at Kingstree, the old first settlement in this State, all died out except a few who removed to California 13 years ago. One of them, John G. Pressly, who studied law with me at Charleston, is now one of the Judges of the Supreme Court at Santa Rosa, California. He was in command of the 25th S. C. Regiment all through the late war, and the people of California seem to admire him because he has always openly avowed in his past actions and opinions.

My branch of the family, descendants of David, brother to your great-great-grandfather has representatives in several States. My oldest brother was a lawyer, but died young. My other two brothers were physicians, one of them Dr. William died at Charlotte, N. C. The other is Dr. Samuel, now practicing at Society Hill, Darlington County, S. C. W.B. Pressly, D.D. of Statesville, N.C. is son of my cousin Richard. The rest are in Georgia, Tennessee, Louisiana and Texas, and I seldom hear from them. Mrs. Barron, wife of Dr. Barron of Yorkville, S. C. is my only living sister. She has a son named after me. B. Pressly Barron[131] who is quite a promising, or I may say, already eminent lawyer at Manning, Clarendon County, S. C.

You will see that I spell my name Pressley. It was so on my father's tombstone, but I think it was a mistake of his Executors.
Yours Very Truly,
B.C. Pressley

The Editor of *The Presley/Preslar/Pressly Newsletter*, Vol. 3, No. 4, page 46, (an Association which is apparently no longer in existence) made the following observations about this letter in 1988:

Ed. Note: The above letter contains useful documentation, as well as several errors. Judge Benjamin Chaplin Pressley (see Mar. 1988 Newsletter, p. 44) repeated 106 years ago the apparent misinformation that his grandfather had first come to Williamsburg

Co., S. C., in 1733 before moving to Abbeville Co. As we have previously indicated, David Pressley[132], his grandfather, was the immigrant who arrived in S. C. in 1767 (Sept. 1986 Newsletter, p. 11) and died in Charleston in 1785 (Mar. 1988 Newsletter, p. 42-3), thirty years before the Judge was born.

How could Benjamin Pressley have been mistaken about his grandfather's coming to Abbeville County? One might speculate as to how the story could have begun. When Benjamin C. Pressley of Abbeville Co. and John G. Pressly of Williamsburg Co. studied law together in Charleston, they might have discussed the possibility of their being related. Benjamin, no doubt, knew that his grandfather, David, had come from Ireland in the 1700s, and possibly that he had a brother, John, who also came to Abbeville Co. His friend, John G. Pressly, had probably heard stories of his family's arrival in S. C. Perhaps there were three brothers named William, David, and John, and his great-grandfather being William, he may have known nothing of what became of David and John, and did not realize that a David Presley wrote his will in 1749 and a John Pressly wrote his will in 1750. The two friends might have assumed that John and David Pressley, the Abbeville immigrants were the same as John and David Pressley, the Williamsburg immigrants, and the story was thus passed along. This is pure speculation, both as to the origin of the story and as to the actual family relationships, but it is a plausible explanation as to how such a story could have begun.

Judge Benjamin Chaplin Pressley and John Gotea Pressley were to become related through the Adams family by virtue of John's marriage to Julia. David Adams, the patriot and his wife Ann Chaplin were the parents of Eliza Eleanor Adams, the mother of Judge Benjamin Chaplin Pressley. They were also the parents of Elizabeth Sarah Adams, the mother of John Gotea Pressley's wife Julia Caroline Burckmyer. John and Julia were married in February 1854, the year John finished studying the law with Judge Benjamin Chaplin Pressley.

The Rev. John S. Pressly, a relative, started to write a narrative about the Pressly family but the work was finished by William A. Pressly, D. D. S. of Rock Hill, South Carolina. I interject throughout this letter to make necessary points.

A Brief Memoir of
The Pressly Family in The United States
By the Rev. John S. Pressly

A desire to know something of our Ancestry, those from whom we have directly descended, would seem to be natural to man, to have some knowledge of our antecedents, of those who have preceded us in Genealogical descent, to those to whom under providence we are indebted for our natures and lives, our names, in some sort for our reputations in society, our education, it may be in whole or in part, our earthly substance, our civil and religious liberty; to know something of these things, I say, is not only natural, but even commendable.

Prompted by such considerations have I been influenced in undertaking to prepare a brief memoir of the Pressly family in the United States.

From an examination of some of the old records found in Williamsburg district, we learn something of the original settlement of our family.

It would seem that the Witherspoons and the Presslys came together. They hailed from County Down, Ireland, and settled on Black River in Williamsburg in the year 1733 or 34. From an examination of the records in Charleston, in the Ordinary's Office, we derive the following facts:

First, An inventory of the estate of David Pressly of St. James, Santee, planter, dated March 1748, his widow was Sarah Pressly (he married Sarah Witherspoon on the voyage over) his residence was just on the margin of Williamsburg. The conclusion seems to be supported by probability that he had left the original settlement and moved in a southerly direction across the Santee River.

I will interject here to point out that Sarah Witherspoon was the sister of John and Janet Witherspoon who came to Charleston on the ship The Good Intent in 1734. So, according to Rev. John S. Pressly, the David Pressly above would have immigrated in 1734.

Second. In the same document I found the will of John Pressly of Williamsburg Township, date 1750. This will names his widow, Margaret, one son, William, and four daughters; Jane McCalla, Eleanor Thompson, Sarah and Susannah. His brother William and his son William are named as executors of the will.

I will interject again to point out that this is an example of a Pressly from Williamsburg with a son named William. This son, William, is the one who Bruce Tognazzini calls "William The Younger" and who, Bruce posits, was the William Pressly who married Eleanor Orr.

> Third. Again there is found in the same record, an inventory of the estate of William Pressly, Senior by his administrator, William Pressly, Junior, both of Williamsburg, date 1751.

If William and John are both from Williamsburg and their entries are from the same record, this is highly suggestive that John and William are the brothers who arrived in 1734. Together with the David Pressly above, it would seem that these are the three original Williamsburg brothers who emigrated from Scotland via Ireland to Charleston in 1734. Additionally, the original brother, William, is said to have died in Williamsburg of the plague in 1751, and this is the year of the inventory.

> Fourth, There is also found the will of John Pressly of Ninety Six District. The testator deceased in 1778. His executors were David Pressly and John Livingstone. This will names his widow, Elizabeth, and four sons, David, William, John and Joseph, and two daughters, Mary Patterson and Martha. It bequeathed land on Rocky Creek to his daughter, Mary Patterson (when a boy I have frequently heard Uncle David Pressly say that formerly in land conveyances the water course, which we now known as Rocky River, was known by the name of Great Rocky Creek.) and a tract of three hundred acres (300) to be equally divided between his sons David and William. This last named tract was probably situated on or near Hard Labor Creek.
>
> Fifth. There is also recorded the will of David Pressly, formerly of Long Cane, but then, at date of will, 1785, of Charleston. It bequeaths his distributive share of the land on Hard Labor Creek, divided between his brother William and himself, to his son David. The will mentions the sons of the testator as Samuel, David, John and William and three daughters; Agnes, (wife of Henry Wylie) Mary Ann and Esther.

The writer, Rev. John S. Pressly, confirms below (in the section about David Pressly of Charleston, formerly of Long Cane) that William, this David's fourth son, is the father of Benjamin Chaplin Pressley. This confirms what the *Newsletter* said, that this David was not one of the original three brothers who immigrated to Charleston in 1734. It also confirms that there were two Davids, one who had a widow named Sarah Witherspoon Pressly, and the other who died in 1785 who had seven children. The former is the original Williamsburg brother while the latter is the Pressly ancestor of David Pressley Anderson.

Sixth. There is also found in this same office a record of John Pressly of John's Parish, lying between Williamsburg and Charleston, who died about 1790. His widow, Catherine, makes reference to him in her will dated 1792. His descendants were Margaret, Catherine and John. They all died without issue. Their father, John Pressly, although there is no positive proof of it, probably removed from Williamsburg to Charleston. Thus we have endeavored to trace our line from its earliest settlement in this country. From the data, foregoing, we reach the conclusion that their earliest settlement was in Williamsburg near the "King's Tree" in the year 1734. (Howe's *History of the Presbyterian Church in the Carolinas* gives the date of the coming of this colony to "King's Tree" on Black River as 1741.) It will, I think, be impracticable to trace a connected chain of lineal descent from father to son up to that David Pressly whose will is dated 1748 and John Pressly, whose will bears date of 1750. We are therefore driven to the alternative of endeavoring to bridge chasm by conjecture or permit the chain to remain thus broken and the same remark is true in relation to the collateral kindred mentioned in this connection.

But while involved in some doubt and uncertainty in relation to this matter, we will direct attention to that part of our history which comes within my own personal knowledge.

It will be seen that there was a John Pressly, of Ninety Six District, who died in 1778 and whose will mentions his children as David, William, John, Joseph, Mary Patterson, and Martha. With all these children, except Mary Patterson, the writer was personally acquainted.

David was the father of Rev. John Taylor Pressly, D. D., and William, of Rev. E. E. Pressly, D. D., and John, of Rev. Samuel P. Pressly, D. D., and Joseph of Rev. John N. Pressly. Mary Patterson, who married Robert Martin, of Rocky River near Vernon's ford. Martha lived alternatively with her brother William and her sister, Mrs. Robert Martin.

In the record we see the will of David Pressly of Charleston, formerly of Long Cane, Abbeville Dist. He had four sons and three daughters, viz.: Samuel, David, John and William; Agnes, wife of Henry Wylie, Mary Ann and Esther. Samuel, the eldest, was the father of the writer, David, the second son, in part raised the writer. John, the third son, was the father of Richard M. Pressly, of York District. William, the fourth son, was the father of Benjamin C. Pressly, Esq. of Charleston. Agnes married Henry Wylie, of Reedy Branch in the lower part of Abbeville Dist.; Mary Ann married Stephen Thomas of Charleston and Esther did not marry.

After listing the children of the first three sons of David Pressly of Charleston, formerly of Long Cane, Abbeville District, Rev. John's manuscript abruptly ended. Rev. John died on June 1, 1863.

William A. Pressley of Rock Hill, South Carolina received this unfinished manuscript as a portion of papers of his uncle Judge Benjamin Chaplin Pressley. William then discussed the family of William Pressly, the fourth son of David of Long Cane and Charleston:

William Pressly, the fourth son of David of Long Cane, was married in Charleston, December 13th, 1804, to Eliza Eleanor Adams, daughter of David Adams and Ann (Chaplin) Adams. Issue:

Ann Chaplin, Born Feb. 15th, 1806 (in Charleston) died June 17th, 1807. Buried under the First Baptist Church.

David Adams, Esq. Born April 10th, 1807 (in Charleston) died at the summer home - Hicklin Place- York Dist, 1841. Educated at Yale College and a Scotch University.

Ann Esther. Born Jan, 16th, 1809 (in Charleston) Died at Fort Mill, in May 1878. Married Professor George Anderson, of Athens, Ga., who studied for the ministry of the Presbyterian Church. Health failing, he taught. Was taken

suddenly ill while en route from Athens, Ga. to Yorkville, S.
C. and died at Abbeville.

I will interject to point out that William A. Pressley confirms
what Rev. John didn't finish writing: namely, that William
Pressley, who married Eliza Eleanor Adams, was the son of
David Pressly of Charleston, formerly of Long Cane.

> Elizabeth Adams. Born Nov. 14th, 1810 (in Charleston).
> Died Mar. 8th, 1812. Buried under First Baptist Church.
> Mary Adams. Born May 10th, 1812. Died Dec. 21, 1884.
> Married Archibald Ingram Barron, M.D. of Yorkville, Feb. 23,
> 1830.
> William Adams, M.D. Born Aug 26th, 1826 (at Summer
> Home) Died Dec. 25th, 1874 (at Charlotte N. C.). Married
> Lavinia Elizabeth Steele, 1849.
> Benjamin Chaplin, Esq. Born Feb. 14th, 1815 (at Hicklin
> Place) died Sept. 5th, 1894. 1st married Louise Wheeler. 2nd
> Mary Burckmeyer.
> Samuel Henry, M. D. Born March, 1817 (in Charleston)
> Died Feb. 18th, 1885 at Society Hill, 1st married Jane
> Edwards. 2nd Sarah McIvor. No issue.

My conclusion from reading all of this is that the ancestor of
David Pressley Anderson is David Pressly of Charleston,
formerly of Long Cane, who is distinct from the other David
Pressly, one of the three original brothers who arrived in 1734
and settled in Williamsburg. According to *The
Presley/Preslar/Pressly Newsletter*, David Pressley Anderson's
immigrant ancestor David Pressly, formerly of Long Cane,
immigrated to Charleston, South Carolina in 1767.

On the other side of the family, it seems clear that the Pressly
ancestor of John Gotea Pressley was one of the three brothers.
Traditionally, it has been thought that brother William's son
William Jr. married Eleanor Orr. However, as we see above, the
other brother John, who married Margaret, also had a son named
William. Bruce Tognazzini points out that we don't know which
of these two William Presslys married Eleanor Orr. Bruce also
points out that the more likely of the two was the younger
William, the son of brother John.

The result of this analysis is that we cannot say with any certainty whether my grandparents are related in the Pressley/Pressly branch of the family. If they are, then the common ancestor must have lived during an earlier time in England or Scotland, a time when as John Gotea Pressley points out, one family name may have been Priestly. Equally, perhaps they were not related at all if, as Judge Benjamin Chaplin Pressley points out, that the name (at least on his side) was not Priestly.

The other implication is that while we know William Pressly married Eleanor Orr, we don't know whether his father was brother John or brother William. Nevertheless, the ancestry would converge within the Pressly family in the previous generation.

*   *   *

David Adams Jr., (the father of William Pressly's wife Eliza Eleanor Adams and the son of David Adams and Catherine Grimball) was born on November 8, 1753 in Edisto Island, South Carolina.

He married Ann Chaplin (daughter of Benjamin Chaplin and Eleanor [Elinor] Reynolds) who was born on July 29, 1758. She died before 1791. In July 1791 he remarried Mary Lawrence. David died on August 24, 1828 in Charleston, South Carolina at the age of 74. He was buried at First Baptist Church in Charleston, South Carolina.

David Adams Jr. served in the Revolutionary War[133] in the Old Militia Company of Edisto Island, known as the "Edisto Island Company." His name will be found on the roll of that company. He was a planter and a "factor" (one who buys and sells on commission), and was also a Baptist deacon. He and his wife ("Phoebe") Ann were second cousins once removed: His great-grandparents and her great-great-grandparents were Richard Capers and Mary Barnet(t)[134].

According to Walter Barron of Camden, South Carolina:

David Adams fought in the battle of Sullivan's Island, Charleston, in June 1776. In this battle a rag time army repulsed the British navy, marines, and army, and the British returned to New York City. This was one of the most important battles and victories of the American Revolution as it prevented the capture of South Carolina, the South, and the entrapment of General Washington in the mid-Atlantic area. The British did not return to the South until 1779 when Savannah fell, and in 1780 Charleston and the entire Continental Army in the South was taken by the British.

The *News and Courier* was published many years ago in Charleston, South Carolina by Alexander Samuel, Jr., born in 1871. He discovered an old Company roll among several others belonging to the Edisto Island Old Militia Co.

This is a letter from Col. Glover addressed to the Hon. Henry Laurens, Esq., President of the Council of Safety, Charles Town. The letter is endorsed on the back by Col. Joseph Glover, and was presented to the Council of the Third Commissions, signed the October 2, 1775:

Sir:

Several men whose names are subscribed to the within association in Edisto Island to form themselves into a Volunteer Company agreeable to a resolution of the Provincial Congress have made applications to me to procure commissions to the following gentlemen to command them, viz:

Joseph Jenkins to be their Captain, Archibald Whaley, First Lieutenant, Joseph Fickling, Jr., Second Lieutenant and Jeremiah Easton, Third Lieutenant or Ensign. I have applied to the Governor some time ago for those very commissions, with some others which he refused to grant. I, therefore, now pray the Council of Safety will direct commissions to be made out for the above gentlemen. If approved by them I believe it will be necessary for me to return the enclosed paper to the officers when the Council of Safety have done with it.

I am, Sir, with regard your very humble servant,

Joseph Glover.

N.B. Please procure an Ensigns Commission for the Edisto Island Old Militia Company. They have choose Mr. John Adams to be Ensign for the Company. (Captain Joseph Jenkins Company)

We the subscribers, do agree to form ourselves into a volunteer Company under the command of the following officers: Mr. Joseph Jenkins, Capt., Mr. Archibald Whaley, First Lieutenant, Mr. Joseph Fickling, Jr., Second Lieutenant. The uniforms to be blue coats with white cuffs and lapel with Jackettes and Breeches of white with a fantail hat, to meet at least once a week, to go through the exercises. We further agree to the orders of the above officers till such time as commission is granted.

Nathaniel Adams, Benjamin Jenkins, Richard Jenkins, John Adams, William Stanyarne and David Adams, Jr. ...

The above represent some of the many names of those who signed.

The inscription on the tomb of David Adams, Jr. at the First Baptist Church Yard in Charleston, South Carolina reads:

Sacred to the memory of David Adams, Jr. who was born November 8, 1753 and died August 24, 1828. He was an officer in the Revolutionary Army, commanded one of the guns at Fort Moultrie. He was a consistent member of the Baptist Church and died triumphant in the faith.

*   *   *

David Wilson was born in 1700 in Ireland. David married Mary Witherspoon (the daughter of first cousins John Witherspoon and Janet Witherspoon) in 1724 in Drumbo, Down, Ireland. He died in 1750 in Williamsburg County, South Carolina. Mary's previous marriage was to James Bradley in 1722. After David died in 1750, she married Archibald McKee in 1751 in South Carolina. Mary was born in 1707, died in 1765 in Williamsburg County, South Carolina and was buried in Williamsburg Township.

Mary Witherspoon was the first cousin of Rev. John Witherspoon who signed The Declaration of Independence.

William Wilson, David Wilson's father, was born the son of James Wilson in 1672 in Scotland. He married Jane Witherspoon, the daughter of James Alexander Witherspoon and Helen (whose maiden name is not known) in 1698 at

Knockbracken, Down, Ireland. He died in 1750 in Williamsburg County, (then Craven County) South Carolina. Jane Witherspoon died in 1731 in Northern Ireland.

IX. COLLINS, BROCKINTON, SCOTT, ADAMS,
WITHERSPOON AND PRESSLY

The father of John Collins III was John Collins Jr., who was born circa 1660 in King and Queen County, Virginia. He married a woman whose name is not known and had at least two children, Edmund and John, although there must be more. John Collins Jr. died in New Kent County or Nansemond County, Virginia.

*   *   *

John Brockinton Sr. (the father of Loyalist Captain John Brockinton) was born on September 16, 1727 in Ireland. He married Mary Barr, daughter of Gavin Barr and Mary (whose maiden name is not known) in 1751. He died in 1795. Mary Barr was born in 1732 and is presumed to have also died circa 1795.

William Brockinton, father of John Brockinton Sr., was born in 1688 at County Down, Ireland. He married Sarah Griffin on July 5, 1715 in St. Thomas, St. Denis Parish, South Carolina. He died on April 21, 1742 in Black Mingo, South Carolina. Sarah was born circa 1698 and died on March 31, 1760.

Gavin Barr, the father of Mary Barr, died at sea. He married Mary (whose maiden name is not known). His wife Mary was also married to Nathaniel Drew. She died in 1762.

John Gotea Pressley wrote:

John Brockinton Sr. (1722-1795), is the first of whom I can give any account. I have as old agreement for a marriage settlement made on the twenty-first day of April A.D. 1773 by and between John Brockinton Sr. and Benjamin Screven, as Trustees, and John Brockinton Jr. and Martha Fowler, who were about to be married. Screven did not sign, however. (Martha Screven Fowler [1757-1825] daughter of James Fowler and Elizabeth Screven).

I am unable to say how the Brockintons derive their descent from the Screvens, but I know descent from that family has always been claimed by them. The name has been perpetuated in the family as a given name, I think that the wife of John Brockinton Sr. was a Screven, and this Benjamin Screven the trustee was probably her brother, and possibly her grandfather on her mother's side.

Benjamin Screven was the brother of Elizabeth Screven who married James Fowler, parents of Martha. John Gotea Pressley continues:

John Brockinton Sr. and his wife had a son, John Brockinton Jr. who is one of the parties to the marriage articles. They may have had other children, but I have no means now of ascertaining, and do not remember of having heard of any others. I am not able to give any of details of the life of John Brockinton Sr. nor the date of his death. He lived on Black River or near that stream, and not far from the old town of Black Mingo in Craven County, Colony of South Carolina, afterwards known as Williamsburgh District, State of South Carolina. The Screvens and Brockintons lived in the bend of Black River below what is now known as Whitmans or Potato Ferry, and above the ferry known as Browns Upper or Rope Ferry. That section of country was then in Prince Fredricks Parish. Benjamin Screven and Martha Fowler, when the marriage articles were signed, were described as "of Black River in Prince Fredricks Parish, South Carolina." John Brockinton Jr. as "of Black Mingo" in the same parish.

*   *   *

John Gotea Jr., son of John Gotea Sr. (born circa 1720 and died on November 21, 1807) and Elizabeth McConnell (born circa 1730), married Eleanor (Elender or Elander) McCutchen, daughter of Hugh McCutchen and Isabella Cooper. He was previously married to Margaret McConnell before he married Eleanor McCutchen. He was born circa 1750 and died before 1807. Eleanor, our ancestor, died in July 1848.

John Gotea Sr., father of John Gotea Jr. who married Eleanor McCutchen, married Elizabeth McConnell, who was born circa 1730. He was born circa 1720 and died around November 21, 1807.

Hugh McCutchen, father of Eleanor McCutchen, was the first known McCutchen in South Carolina. He married Isabella Cooper, who was born in 1730, and the daughter of William Cooper and a wife whose name is not known. Hugh died before 1760. Isabella died in 1769.

William Cooper, Isabella's father, married a woman whose name is not known. He also married Jane James. He was born circa 1700. We descend from the wife whose name is not known.

*   *   *

William Scott's father Thomas Scott, the son of John Scott, immigrated to South Carolina before 1742. He married Jannet Watson, daughter of John Watson. Thomas was born before 1721 in Ireland and died circa 1766 in Williamsburg, Old Craven County, South Carolina. Jannet was born in 1730 and died around March 29, 1772 in Williamsburg, Old Craven County, South Carolina.

John Scott, Thomas Scott's father, was the original Scott settler in the area, according to a letter to W. M. Scott, dated July 28, 1927.

John Watson, Jannet's father, left £200 to the Williamsburg Presbyterian Church and the remainder of his estate to be equally divided among the daughters of Thomas Scott, of Williamsburg, deceased. These daughters of Thomas Scott were John Watson's granddaughters. John was born circa 1700 in Prince Frederick's Parish, Old Williamsburg District, South Carolina. He died on September 12, 1766 in the Old Williamsburg District, South Carolina.

*   *   *

David Adams was born in 1718 in Wadmalaw Island, South Carolina. He married Ann Jenkins, daughter of John Jenkins, on December 6, 1739.   He then married Catherine Grimball, daughter of Paul Grimball and Mary Stone, on February 1, 1753. He died in 1786. Catherine was born on September 10, 1733 and died in 1772. We descend from Catherine Grimball.

The following is a transcript of David Adams' will, recorded in Will Book A page 612 (1783-1796) and Vol. 21, book B, Charleston County page 798, Historical Commission, Columbia, South Carolina:

In The Name of God Amen; I David Adams of Wadmalaw Island in the province aforesaid, being weak in body but of perfect and sound memory, Thanks be to God for it and considering the Uncertainty of this present Life & knowing that it is appointed to all Men once to die, I do make and ordain this and no other to be my last Will and Testament that is to say that First of all I recommend my Soul unto God who gave it in Hopes of a glorious Resurrection unto eternal Life and my Body I recommend to the Earth from whence it was taken to be buried after a decent and Christian Manner at the Discretion of my Executors herein mentioned. And as touching such Worldly Estate wherewith it has pleased God to bless me with, I give and bequeath in Manner and Form the following; Item. My Will and Desire is that all my just Debts and funeral charges be first paid. Item. I give and Bequeath unto my Son Barnard Adams the Tract of Land I now live on and the Tract of Land I bought from Mr. Daniel Townsend to him and his Heirs forever. Item. I give and bequeath unto my Son Will Adams that Tract of Land laying between my Brother Benjamin Jenkins and the Place I now live on to him and his Heirs forever. Item. I give and bequeath unto my son Barnard Adams, Jack, Rose, Flora, Will; they and their increase forever. I give and bequeath unto my son William Adams, Syrus, Will, Isaac, Jamy, Nan, Island Rose, Prince and their increase forever. Item. I give all my wearing apparel, Household & kitchen Furniture to be equally divided between my three Sons Nathaniel, David, and Barnard Adams. Item. It is my Will and Desire that my three Sons Nathaniel, David, and Barnard Adams shall build my son William Adams a house and Kitchen upon any Part of the Land he thinks proper with good

Materials & a Brick Chimney to the Dwelling House and Kitchen, to be the same dimensions of the House and Kitchen I now live in and a Corn and Pea House. Item. I leave the island on Muskeeto Creek and the House and land in Charles Town to be sold at Vandue and all the moneys arising therefrom to be equally divided between my four Sons Nathaniel, David, Barnard and William Adams and their Heirs forever. Item. It is my Will that my two Sons Barnard and William Adams shall have six Cows and six Calfs and one Bull apiece with their Increase to them & their Heirs forever. Item. It is my Will that all the rest of my personal and moveable Estate shall be appraised & my four Sons Nathaniel, David, Barnard, and William Adams shall have and equal share by the Appraisement. Item. It is my Will that the Moneys of the Crop after Paying for the Buildings of my son William shall go to pay a Bond due to Daniel Townsend of my Son David Adams; if there be as much left; if not to pay as far as it will go. Lastly I constitute ordain and appoint my beloved Sons Nathaniel, David, Barnard, and William Adams to be my Executors of this my last Will and Testament. In Witness whereof I have here unto set my Hand and Seal this twenty seventh day of November one thousand seven hundred & eighty one.
-- David Adams (L.S.)

Signed Sealed and Declared in the presence of John Paterson, William Paterson, Mary Paterson. Proved (by virtue of a Dedimus from Charles Lining Esquire OCTD) before Richard Moncreef, Esquire. January 30, 1786. At same time qualified Barnard Adams Executor.

*   *   *

Ann Chaplin's father Benjamin Chaplin was a planter who was born in 1723 in Port Royal Island, South Carolina. He married Sarah Ladson on October 1, 1751 in St. Helena Parish, South Carolina. He then married Eleanor (Elinor) Reynolds on January 29, 1756. He died in 1768 in Port Royal Island, South Carolina. Eleanor, our ancestor, was born on December 17, 1738 and died on September 13, 1771 at the age of 32.

*   *   *

John Witherspoon, son of David Witherspoon, was born in 1670 in Begardie, Glasgow, Scotland.   He married Janet Witherspoon, the daughter of David's brother James Alexander Witherspoon and Helen (whose maiden name is not known), in 1695 in Scotland.   John died in 1737 in Boggy Swamp, Williamsburg County, South Carolina.

Janet was the first cousin of her husband John. He, Janet and their children sailed from Ireland to Charleston, South Carolina in 1734 on the ship The Good Intent.   My sixth great-grandmother, Janet Witherspoon, died on this voyage.

Their grandson Robert Witherspoon, my first cousin six times removed and the son of James Witherspoon, described the voyage and arrival in South Carolina in a few letters written in 1780.   The following comes from *History of Williamsburg*, by William Willis Boddie, pages 10-20:

John Witherspoon and Janet Witherspoon were born in Scotland about the year 1670. They lived in their younger years in Glasgow, at a place called Begardie, and were married in 1693. In 1695, they left Scotland and settled at Knockbracken, in the Parish of Drumbo, County of Down, Ireland, where they lived in comfortable circumstances and good credit until the year 1734. He then removed with his family to South Carolina.

We went on board the ship called The Good Intent on the 14th of September, and were detained by headwinds fourteen days in the Lough at Belfast. On the second day after we set sail, my grandmother, Janet, died and was interred in the boisterous ocean, which was an affecting sight to her offspring.

We were sorely tossed at sea with storms, which caused our ship to spring a leak; our pumps were kept incessantly at work day and night for many days together and our mariners seemed many times at their wits' end. But it pleased God to bring us all safe to land, except my grandmother, about the first of December.

But to return, my grandfather and grandmother had seven children. Their names were as follows, viz.: Janet (or Jennet), David, James, Elizabeth, Robert, Mary, and Gavin. Their daughter Janet was born in Scotland and was married to John Fleming in Ireland. They had a large family of children born in Ireland and brought seven of them to this place, Williamsburg, viz.: Isabella, John, Elizabeth, James, Janet, Penelope, and William. My uncle, John Fleming, died in 1750, in a good old age; my aunt Janet died in 1761 in the sixty-sixth year of her age. My uncle David was born in 1697, married to Ann Pressley and brought with him to this place two children, viz.: Sarah and Janet. He died in the year 1772 in the sixty-seventh year of his age.

My aunt Elizabeth was married to William James and they brought with them to this place four children, viz. Mary, Janet, John, and William. They both died in the year 1750, he forty-nine and she forty-seven years of age.

My uncle Robert was married to Mary Stuart and by her had two children, Mary and John; his first wife, Mary, died in Ireland. He married his second wife, Hester Jane Scott a short time before he left Ireland and brought his two children with him to this place. His wife, Hester Jane, died in 1756, aged forty years; he died in 1758, aged fifty-three years.

My aunt Mary was married to David Wilson in Ireland, and brought to this place two children, William and John. My uncle David died in 1750, aged fifty years, and she died in 1765, in the fifty-eighth year of her age.

My uncle Gavin, the youngest son of my grandparents, was born in 1712, and was unmarried when he left Ireland.

It is to be remembered that we did not all come over in one ship, nor in the same year, for my uncles, William James and David Wilson, and their families, with uncle Gavin, left Belfast in 1732[135], and uncle Robert followed in 1736. As I said, we landed in Charleston three weeks before Christmas in 1734. We found the inhabitants very kind. We remained in that place until after Christmas were put on board an open boat, with tools, one year's provisions, and one steel mill for each family. Our provisions consisted of Indian corn, rice, wheat flour, beef, pork, some rum, and salt; and, for each hand over sixteen years of age, one axe, one broad and one narrow hoe.

We were much distressed in our passage, as it was in the depth of winter and we were exposed to the inclemency of the weather by day and by night; and that which added to the grief of all persons on board were the profane and blasphemous oaths and expressions of the patron and his boatmen. They brought us up as far as Potato Ferry on Black River, about twenty miles from Georgetown, where they put us on shore.

We lay for some time in Samuel Commander's barn, while the boat made her way up to the King's Tree, with the goods and provisions on board, and was probably the first boat that had ever ascended the River to that place. While the women were left at Commander's the men went up to build dirt houses, or rather potato houses, to take their families to. They also brought up a few horses and what help they could get from the few inhabitants, in order to carry their families, children, and other necessary articles up; as the woods were full of water, and the weather very cold, it made it go very hard with the women and children.

We set out in the morning the last of January, a part reached Mr. McDonald's, others as far as Mr. Plowden's, and Mr. James Armstrong's, and a part to my uncle, William James'. Their little cabins were as full that night as they could hold and the next day every one made the best he could to his own place. This was on the first of February, 1735, when we came to the place called the Bluff, three miles below the King's Tree. My mother and we children were still in expectations of coming to an agreeable place, but when we arrived and saw nothing but a wilderness, and instead of a comfortable house, no other than one of dirt, our spirits sank; and what added to our trouble was that the pilot who came with us from uncle William James' left us as soon as he came in sight of the place. My father gave us all the comfort he could by telling us that we would soon get all the trees cut down and in a short time there would be plenty of inhabitants and that we would be able to see from house to house.

While we were here, the fire went out that we brought from Boggy Swamp. My father had heard that up the river swamp was the King's Tree. Although there was no path nor did he know the distance, he followed up the meanderings of the swamp until he came to the branch and by that means he found Roger Gordon's place. We watched him as far as the trees would let us see and returned to our dolorous hut, expecting never to see him or any human being more. But after some time, he returned with fire and we were somewhat comforted, but evening coming on the wolves began to howl on all sides. We then feared being devoured by wild beasts, as we had neither gun nor dog, nor even a door to our house, howbeit we set to and gathered fuel and made a good fire and so we passed the first night.

The next morning being clear and moderate, we began to stir about, and about midday there arose a cloud at Southwest, attended with high wind, lightning, and thunder. The rain quickly penetrated through the poles of the hut and brought down the sand with which it was covered and which seemed for a while to cover us alive. The lightening and claps were very awful and lasted for a good space of time. I do not remember to have seen a much severer gust than that was. I believe we all sincerely wished to be again at Belfast. But the fright was soon over and the evening cleared up comfortable and warm.

The boat that brought up the goods arrived safe at King's Tree. People were much oppressed in bringing away the articles, for as there were no houses near, they were obliged to toil hard and carry them on their backs, consisting of clothing, beds, chests, provisions, tools, pots, bowls; and, as at that time there were but few roads or paths, every family had to travel the best way it could, which was near double distance to some, for they had to follow swamps and branches as their guides at first and after some time, some men got such a knowledge of the woods as to be able to blaze paths, so that the people soon found out to follow blazes from place to place.

As the winter season was far advanced, the time to prepare land for planting was very short, yet the people were generally healthy and strong. All that could do anything wrought diligently and continued clearing and planting as long as the season would admit. So they made provisions for that year. As they had but few beasts to feed, a little served them; and as the range was good, there was no need of feeding creatures for several years.

I remember that the first thing my father brought from the boat was his gun, which was one of Queen Anne's muskets. He had her loaded with swan shot, and one morning while we were at breakfast there was a traveling 'possum passing by the door, my mother screamed out, "There is a great bear!" Mother and we children hid ourselves behind some barrels and a chest at the far end of the hut, while father got his gun and steadied her past the fork that held up the other end of our house and shot him about the hinder parts, which caused him to grin in a frightful manner. Father was in haste to give him another bout, but the shot, being mislaid in the hurry, could not be found, and we were penned up for some time. Father at last ventured out and killed him with a pole. Another circumstance which gave us much alarm was the Indians when they came to hunt in the spring. They came in great numbers like the Egyptian locusts, but were not hurtful.

We had a great deal of trouble and hardships in our first settling, but the few inhabitants were favored with health and strength. We were also much oppressed with fear on divers other accounts, especially of being massacred by the Indians, or bit by snakes, or torn by wild beasts, or of being lost and perishing in the woods, of whom there were three persons who were never found.

My uncle Robert, with his second wife and two children, Mary and John, arrived here near the last of August, 1736. He came on the fine ship The New-built which was a ship of great burthen and brought a great many passengers, who chiefly came and settled here and had to travel by land from Georgetown, and instead of being furnished with provisions, etc., as we were, they had money given them by the public. When they arrived, our second crop had been planted and was coming forward, but the season being warm and they much fatigued, many were taken sick with ague and fever, some died and some became dropsical and also died.

About this time, August or September, 1736, the people began to form into a religious society, built a church and sent to Ireland for a minister. One came whose name was Robert Herron, who stayed only three years and returned to Ireland. The first call was made out for Reverend John Willison of Scotland, author of the *Mother's Catechism*, *A Practical Treatise on the Lord's Supper* and of the *Discourses on the Atonement*.

The following anecdote is handed down by tradition of Mr. Gavin Witherspoon; meeting a neighbor one day, this conversation is reported to have taken place.

"Wull, we must have a minister.'

'Wull, Mister Witherspoon, wha wull ye git to be your minister?'

'Wull, wha but Mister Willison o' Dundee? But the minister must have a muckle sight o' money for his living,'

'And that we must gie him,' says Mr. Witherspoon.

'An' how much, Mr. Witherspoon, wull ye gie?'

'Ten pounds', was the ready reply.

'But, Mr. Witherspoon whar'll ye git the ten pounds?'

'Why if wus comes to wus, I ien can sell my cow,' says he.

Mr. Willison, of Dundee, was accordingly sent for to preach the Gospel in the wilds of America.

In the fall of the year 1737, my grandfather, John Witherspoon, took a disease called Rose-in-the-leg, which occasioned a fever from which he died.   He was the first person buried at the Williamsburg Meeting House, which he had assisted to erect. About the same time, 1737, my father had a daughter, Elizabeth, that died, aged three years, born at the place called the Bluff, where we lived.

My grandfather was a man of middling or common stature, of a fine, healthy constitution, of fair complexion, and somewhat bow-legged.   He was well acquainted with the Scriptures, had volubility in prayer, and was a zealous adherent to the principles of what was called in his day the Reformed Protestant Church of Scotland. He had also a great aversion to Episcopacy, and whoever will impartially read the history of the times of his younger years in Scotland will see that his prejudices were not without cause. It was his lot to live in a time of great distress to the persecuted Church, during the reign of James the Seventh of Scotland and Second of England.   Being one who followed field-meetings, he and some others of his kindred were much harassed by the Papists. Yet, notwithstanding, if his younger years were attended with some trouble, he still enjoyed great peace and tranquility in his after life and had the comfort and happiness of living to see his seven children all creditably married and settled for themselves; and, except the death of my grandmother, his beloved wife, he never knew what it was to part by death with one of his own immediate family, a blessing which few persons have granted to them, especially at his advanced age.

My father's name was James, the third child and second son of my grandparents. He was born at the beginning of the present century, lived with his parents at Drumbo, County of Down, until he was twenty-five years old, when he married my mother, whose name was Elizabeth McQuoid, in the twentieth year of her age.

My grandfather, Robert McQuoid, married Sarah Campbell. They both died in Ireland, he in 1728, aged eighty-six, and she aged about eighty. My father and mother settled in the Parish of Graba, near the Canningburn Mills, where they lived about nine years and sold their possessions to embark for America. My father brought the family to my grandparents at Knockbracken about the 1st of May, 1734, and left us there until the 1st of September. In the meantime, he wrought at the reed-making business.   He brought four children on board of the ship, viz.: David, Robert, John, and Sarah. Sarah died in Charleston shortly after their arrival, and was the first person buried in the Scotch Meeting House Yard.

In May, 1743, the Reverend Mr. John Ray arrived here from Scotland. He came upon a call which his congregation had sometime before sent to the Reverend Mr. John Willison, of Dundee. Mr. Ray continued a faithful, zealous, and laborious worker in the congregation until 1761. He being abroad on a visit up Black River was taken sick with the pleurisy and died. The remains of this eminently pious man were brought down from Salem, where he died, and buried at the church where he had for eighteen years successfully labored, being about forty-six years of age. 'Blessed are the dead that die in the Lord from henceforth: Yea, saith the spirit, that they may rest from their labors, and their works do follow them.'

I was born in Ireland on the 20th day of August, 1728, was my father's second son; in my youth he taught me to weave, as he also taught my elder brother, David, to make reeds. The family lived together at the Bluff until March, 1749. My father then moved to Thorntree, a place situated between the Lower Bridge on Black River and Murray's Ferry on the Santee. I there went out and wrought at the weaving business with my uncle, Gavin Witherspoon, who lived at a place called Megart's (McGirts) Swamp, until the September following. I went next to overseeing for a Mr. Fleming, near Black River Church, twenty-five miles below King's Tree, where I remained until January, 1752, and then returned to my father's.

The reason of my return was that it had pleased God – in that last awful epidemic that prevailed in Williamsburg in the year 1749 and 1750, usually called the 'Great Mortality', and which had carried off near eighty persons, many of them head of families – to remove by death my elder brother, David, and my sister, Jane, both in the year 1750. My father being then in a very feeble and infirm state of health and unable to attend to his own business, I left my own to take care of his. 1 remained with my parents until 1758, when, on the 2nd of March, I married Elizabeth Heathly, a young lady then in the eighteenth year of her age, and settled for myself four miles below King's Tree and near the River.

I afterwards removed and settled one mile higher up the River nearer King's Tree, in 1761, and immediately on the public road leading from that place to the Lower Bridge on Black River. Here

I had a more comfortable and healthy residence, and here also, I expect to spend the remainder of my days.

Our first son, James, was born on the 20th of March, 1759; our second son, Thomas, was born on the 22nd of March, 1761, and died on the 8th of September, 1765, aged four years and six months; our first daughter, Ann, was born January 4, 1763; our third son, John, was born January 20, 1765, and died on the 24th of July, 1767, aged two years and six months; our fourth son, Robert, was born January 29, 1767; our second daughter, Mary, was born March 20, 1769; our third daughter, Elizabeth, was born July 25, 1771; our fifth son, John, was born March 17, 1774; our sixth son, Thomas, was born July 23, 1776.

My honored mother departed this life on the 22nd day of January, 1777, in the seventy-second year of her age, I was the last surviving branch of the old stock of our family. As I have had an intimate personal knowledge of their lives and deaths, I bear them testimony that they were servers of God, were well acquainted with the Scriptures, were much engaged in prayer, were strict observers of the Sabbath, in a word, they were a stock of people that studied outward piety as well as inward purity of life.

Indeed God blessed this settlement at first with a number of eminently pious and devoted men, out of whom I chose to set down some of their names, viz.: William Wilson, David Allen, William Hamilton, John Porter, William James, David Wilson, John James, James McCleland, Robert Wilson, Robert Paisley, James Bradley, John Turner, William Frierson, to whom I add my Own father and my three uncles, David, Robert, and Gavin. These were men of great piety in their day, indeed they were men of renown. May the glorious King and Head of the Church for His own glory still maintain and keep up men of piety and holiness as a blessing to this place and congregation to the latest posterity is the heart request of the unworthy scribe.

X. COLLINS, SCREVEN, ADAMS, GRIMBALL, CHAPLIN AND WITHERSPOON

The father of John Collins Jr. was John Collins, who was born in King and Queen County, Virginia. He married Mary Wyatt, the daughter of Mrs. Amy Wyatt, and had at least five children and possibly others. They were planters in Orange County. John Collins died on March 5, 1748 in Orange County, Virginia.

*   *   *

Rev. Elisha Screven, son of Rev. William Screven and Bridget Cutts, was the founder of Georgetown, South Carolina. He was born on September 1, 1698. He married Hannah (whose last name was either Johnson or Commander), the daughter of Joseph Johnson and Elizabeth (whose maiden name is not known), circa 1724

Rev. Elisha died on December 3, 1757 at the age of 59. Some suggest his wife Hannah was Hannah Commander while others suggest she was Hannah Johnson. As Bruce Tognazzini explains:

> Some would have Elisha Screven Sr. marrying both (then show them as having identical dates of death). The Screven Family Bible indicates a single Hannah, and a note in the bible further claims that Hannah was the daughter of Joe Johnson. This is not

definitive, since we don't know whether the note making Hannah the daughter of Joe was added at the time or later on. Perhaps an examination of the original bible may be required.

It should be noted that a Joe Johnson married a Brockinton, and Elisha, Jr., also married a Brockinton, so the families at some point knew each other. Joseph Johnson's wife was Sarah Jane Brockinton who was too young to be Hannah's mother. Hannah Johnson's mother could have been, among at least three possibilities, the first wife of Joe Johnson, the wife of Joseph Johnson, Jr., or the wife of an unrelated Joseph Johnson. Johnson is, after all, the second-most frequent last name in America.

On the other hand, Hannah Commander's father was an original member of William Screven's community, so there is no question that Elisha and Hannah Commander knew each other as well. Additional research is needed.

Joseph Johnson, the putative father of the wife of Rev. Elisha Screven, married Elizabeth (her maiden name is not known). Elizabeth, however, was also married to Samuel Commander, son of Thomas Commander.

*   *   *

David Adams, the son of Nathaniel Adams and Hannah Wilmot, is the son-in-law of John Jenkins, father of David's first wife, Ann Jenkins. He was born on November 19, 1682 in Charlestown, Massachusetts. He was christened on March 6, 1687 or 1688. He married Elizabeth Capers (daughter of Richard Capers and Mary Barnet(t)) in 1710 at Charleston, South Carolina. He was lost at sea in 1720. William Barnet(t), Mary Barnet(t)'s father, was born in Jamaica.

Elizabeth Capers, the widow of David Adams, outlived her second husband John Jenkins for many years. She married John Jenkins on April 12, 1727. She was born circa 1690 in St. Helena Island, South Carolina, and died after 1741 in South Carolina. Her father Richard Capers married Mary Barnet(t), daughter of William Barnet(t).

*　　*　　*

Paul Grimball was a planter in Edisto Island who married several times. Mary Stone appears to be his second wife. John Jenkins was an executor of his will. He was born in 1703. He married Mary Stone on November 29, 1738 and died in 1750 in Edisto Island, Colleton County, South Carolina.

*　　*　　*

John Chaplin, son of John Chaplin and Ann Skinner, was born in July 1682 in James Island, South Carolina and married Phoebe Ladson, born on June 27, 1691, daughter of John Ladson and Mary Stanyarne in 1715. He died on February 3, 1752 in St Helena Island, South Carolina at the age of 69.

*　　*　　*

James Alexander Witherspoon, son of James Alexander Witherspoon and Lucy Welch, married Helen (whose maiden name is not known) who was born in 1644. (He did not marry Helen Welch who was married to David Witherspoon). He was born in 1640 in Brighouse, Scotland. He died and was buried after 1690 in Scotland.

James Alexander Witherspoon was also known as Rev. James Witherspoon, Jr. Some of his children with Helen include:

- Janet, who married her first cousin John and together had a daughter named Mary Witherspoon

- Jane, who married William Wilson; their son David Wilson married his first cousin Mary Witherspoon

- James Witherspoon III, who married Ann Walker; their son Rev. John Witherspoon was a signer of The Declaration of Independence.

Rev. John Witherspoon (1723-1794)
A signer of the Declaration of Independence

Some signatures on the Declaration of Independence
Signature of Rev. John Witherspoon highlighted on the right
Signature of Thomas Lynch, Jr. highlighted on the left
The space below Edward Rutledge was reserved for Thomas Lynch, Sr.

The Rev. John Witherspoon is my first cousin seven times removed.   He served as the president of The College of New

Jersey from 1768 until 1794 (later called Princeton University in 1896). In John Trumbull's famous painting of the signing of The Declaration of Independence, Rev. John Witherspoon is the second seated figure from the viewer's right, among those shown in the background facing the large table.

His signature can be found in the fifth column, fourth signature from the bottom.

*   *   *

David Witherspoon, the other son of James Alexander Witherspoon and Lucy Welch, married Helen Welch. He was born in 1642 in Scotland and was buried after 1675 in Scotland.

I am unsure how Lucy Welch may be blood-related to Helen Welch. This is not the same "Helen" whose last name is unknown and who married James Alexander Witherspoon, the son of James Alexander Witherspoon and Lucy Welch.

XI. COLLINS, SCREVEN, LYNCH, ADAMS, GRIMBALL, CHAPLIN AND WITHERSPOON

The father of John Collins was William Collins who was born in 1612 in Maidstone, Kent, England. He married Ann Wilds, the widow of Thomas Wilds. William came to Virginia Colony at the age of 23 in 1635 on The Plain Joan. William died in 1705 in King and Queen County, Virginia.

*　　*　　*

Rev. William Screven, a Baptist, was born in 1629 in Somerton, Somersetshire, England. He married Bridget Cutts, (born circa 1660 in Kittery, Maine, daughter of Robert Cutts and Mary Hoel) on July 23, 1674 in Kittery, York County, Maine. The people of Kittery and York County, within the province of Maine, had submitted an oath of allegiance to Massachusetts in 1652.

He got in trouble "for not frequenting the public meetings on the Lord's day." Fortunately, he was not found guilty[136]. He became Constable in 1676 and was licensed to preach as of January 11, 1682 in Boston. He was put in prison later that same year for his views, expressed publicly, on infant baptism. Persecution drove him to leave Kittery, Maine for South Carolina.

He died on October 10, 1713 in Georgetown, South Carolina. Bridget died in 1717 in Georgetown, South Carolina.

Bridget's parents were Robert Cutts, who was born circa 1640, and Mary Hoel, who was born circa 1643. She was previously married to Francis Champernowne who, like Robert, was an early Kittery pioneer. Robert Cutts' house in Kittery, Maine, is open to visitors under the name, "Whipple House." Whipple House was added to the National Register of Historic Places in 1979 and is identified as building 79003910, located at 88 Whipple Road, Kittery, York County, Maine.

Another daughter of Robert Cutts married William Whipple, the father of William Whipple, Jr., a chosen aide to General George Washington. General William Whipple commanded contingents of New Hampshire troops at Saratoga and he participated in General Sullivan's expedition to Rhode Island in 1778. He was elected a delegate from New Hampshire to the Continental Congress and signed The Declaration of Independence[137]. General William Whipple is my first cousin nine times removed.

Signature of William Whipple
The Declaration of Independence
Sixth column, second signature from the top

All of the signatures on the Declaration of Independence

General William Whipple (1730-1785)
A signer of The Declaration of Independence

*   *   *

Thomas Lynch, the father of Sarah Lynch who married Rev. John Baxter, was the son of Jonah (previously called Jonack) Lynch and Margaret Johnson. He married Sabina Van Der Horst, our ancestor who was the daughter of John Van Der Horst. He also married Mary Fenwick. Thomas Lynch emigrated from Scotland in 1677. He was born circa 1675 and died in 1752[138].

Thomas and Sabina's grandson was Thomas Lynch, Jr. (Thomas Lynch III), my first cousin, eight times removed, who was the fifty-second signer of The Declaration of Independence on August 2, 1776. There are six columns of signatures in The Declaration. His can be found as the second name from the bottom in the second column, just to the left and above Thomas Jefferson.

Thomas Lynch, Jr. (1749-1779)
A signer of the Declaration of Independence

His father Thomas Sr., my seventh great-granduncle, pushed Thomas Jr. into signing The Declaration of Independence. Both were members of the Continental Congress and a delegation from South Carolina. Unfortunately, he suffered a stroke before the signing ceremony. In his honor, the South Carolina delegation left a space between the signatures of Edward Rutledge and

Thomas Heywood, Jr., just above where Thomas Jr. signed. That space represents the signature of Thomas Sr.

Thomas Jr. was born in Winyah, Prince George's County, South Carolina, the son of Thomas Lynch II. He attended the Indigo Society School in Georgetown before being sent to England, where he studied at Eton College and at Gonville & Caius College, Cambridge. He studied law in London, and returned to America in 1772. He became a company commander in the 1st South Carolina Regiment in 1775 and was elected to the Continental Congress. He became ill in late 1776 and with his wife, Elizabeth Shubrick, sailed for the West Indies. Their ship disappeared at sea with everyone on board. He was just 27 years old.

Thomas Jr. was born at the family estate built by his father at Hopswee Plantation. Located 12 miles south of Georgetown, South Carolina, it is open today to the public.

*　　　*　　　*

Nathaniel Adams, son of Nathaniel Adams and Mary Portmort, was born on September 10, 1653 in Boston, Massachusetts. He made block and tackle for ships and was the blockmaker to Joseph Lord of Boston. He married Hannah Wilmot (born on February 10, 1660 in Boston, Massachusetts) circa 1679.

In a town riot in 1687, he was stabbed by Unton Dearing of The Rose Frigate man of war[139]. Hannah, our ancestor, died on January 24, 1699 in Charlestown at the age of 38. Nathaniel then married Anna Coolidge in 1700 in Charlestown, Massachusetts. He was christened on March 13, 1709 and died on March 18, 1710 in Charlestown, Middlesex County, Massachusetts at the age of 56.

His will mentioned his son David by his first wife. David received five shillings despite "not being able to do any more for them because I have done so much for them formerly."

Will of Nathaniel Adams of Charlestown, Blockmaker:

1. To wife Anna, house and all estate to sell to bring up two children Mary and Anna which I had by my wife Anna; wife Anna to be sole executrix, and to get seat in meeting house;

2. "I give unto my five children which I hand (sic) by a former wife, viz Nathaniell, David, Mary, Ann, Willmut, each of them five shillings not being able to do any more for them because I have done so much for them formerly." Witnesses: Nicholas Hopkins, Joseph Health, Abigail Watkins. Dated Jan 27, 1709/1710, Sworn and exhibited: April 4, 1710

Includes following two items: Mary my eldest child was 6 when her father died and she died in her 13th year. Ann was 1 when her father died and charges for 6 years and 7 months at £9 per annum are £59/05/00 - disallowed. Middlesex County MA

Deeds:

Liber 14, folio 239 Charles Chambers of Charlestown, Marriner to Nathaniel Adams of same, blockmaker. For £120 current money of New England, three parcels in Charlestown which Chambers had bought of Nathaniel Adams the previous September 6th; Adams had originally bought the first parcel from the estate of Edward Carrington dec'd. and the other two from Fownel Everton. Signed by Charles Chambers and Rebecca Chambers his wife. Dated March 14, 1706/1707, Sworn March 21, 1706/1707, Recorded March 21, 1706/1707. Witnesses: Joseph Lord and Samuel Phipps.

Liber 14, folio 240 Nathaniel Adams of Charlestown, Blockmaker to Joseph Lord of Boston, Marriner For £240 silver money of New England (at 8 shillings to the ounce), the same three parcels as in 14:239. Signed by Nathaniel Adams and Anna Adams his wife. Dated March 15, 1706/1707, Sworn March 21, 1706/1707, Recorded March 22, 1706/1707, Receipted in full: March 26, 1707 Witnesses: Samuell Phipps and Charles Chambers.

*   *   *

Thomas Grimball, son of Paul Grimball and Mary Stoney, was born in 1675 in England. He married Elizabeth Adams before 1707.   She is our ancestor and daughter of William Adams.   He then married Sarah Pert on August 8, 1722.   He died in Edisto Island, Colleton County, South Carolina.   Elizabeth died on August 5, 1715 in Edisto Island.

In Thomas' will, he left his wife Sarah the use of his plantation where he lived, and his personal estate in three equal parts: one-third to his wife for life, then to all his sons.   The two thirds he left to his four sons Paul, Thomas, Joshua and Isaac.   The younger sons were to receive their shares at age 21; the eldest son Paul was to receive his share immediately.   He asked that "all possible endeavors be used to give each of my children a competent measure of learning and education, at least that they may be taught to read perfect English, write a legible hand fit for public business or office, and arithmetic through the rule of Fellowship."   After the death of his wife Sarah, his son Paul was to receive the 1,000 acre plantation where he lived.

*   *   *

John Chaplin (the father of John Chaplin who married Phoebe Ladson) was born in England in 1636 and married Ann Skinner in England.

He was an immigrant who arrived in Charleston from England (perhaps via Barbados) in either 1662 or 1672, initially as an indentured servant.   He originally settled in James Island, and then moved to St. Helena in 1720.   He and his wife Ann received a warrant for land in South Carolina on January 25, 1678.

John and Ann testified before the Grand Council that he had been among the Yemassee Indians and that he had personally witnessed arms being delivered by the Spanish to the Indians.   This was prior to the Yemassee uprising of 1715.

*   *   *

James Alexander Witherspoon, the father of James Alexander Witherspoon and David Witherspoon, was born in 1610 in

Brighouse, Scotland. He married Lucy Welch, the daughter of John Welch and Elizabeth Knox, in 1634 in Scotland. He died circa 1649-1650 in Brighouse, Scotland and was buried in Scotland. Lucy was born in 1620 in Glasgow, Scotland. She died and was buried after 1650 in Glasgow.

Alexander Witherspoon, father of James Alexander Witherspoon (who was the son of John Wedderspon and Anne Patterson), was born in 1583 in Brighouse, Scotland. He married a woman whose name is not known and then married Jane Wilson on November 19, 1626. He died in 1649 in Brighouse, Scotland. We descend from the first wife whose name is not known.

John Wedderspon (the father of Alexander Witherspoon and the son of Alexander Wedderspon and Catherine Hamilton) was born in 1540 in Brighouse, Scotland. He married Anne Patterson (who was born in 1561 in Scotland) on May 3, 1582 in Scotland. He was buried in 1604 in Brighouse, Scotland.

XII. COLLINS, LYNCH, ADAMS, GRIMBALL AND WELCH

The father of William Collins was John Collins Jr. who was born in Maidstone, Kent in circa 1590. His first wife, the mother of William, died in England. He followed his son William to Virginia in 1655 after Charles I was executed by supporters of Parliament.

John inherited from his father the life rights as Keeper of the Gael of Maidstone. The right granted to John Collins by Charles I was a position of power and influence. As an adherent to the King, John Jr. sought safety in Virginia, and was known as one of the group called "Cavaliers." The family held positions of importance and were prosperous land owners in Virginia.

John Jr. came to Surry County, and soon after his arrival he married Elizabeth Caufield, the daughter of William and Dorcas Caufield. William Caufield had sponsored John's passage from England. When John Jr. died, his will, recorded in Surry County, listed only one child, William, who had come to Virginia in 1635.

*   *   *

Jonah Lynch, the son of Thomas Lynch and Margaret Quinn, (who changed his first name from Jonack when he arrived in America) married Margaret Johnson, who was born circa 1670 and believed to be the daughter of Sir Nathaniel (Gov.) Johnson.

He immigrated to America, perhaps stopping in the West Indies en route. He was born in 1656 and died circa 1711.

*   *   *

Nathaniel Adams, son of Nathaniel Adams and Sarah (whose maiden name is not known) was born in 1630 in England. He was a blockmaker who came to Weymouth, Massachusetts with his parents. In 1652, he and his parents moved to Boston, Massachusetts where he married Mary Portmort later that year on November 24, 1652.

From the *American Genealogist*, No.118, Vol. 30, No. 2, page 66, April, 1954:

> Nathaniel Adams, a blockmaker (one who makes block and tackle, as for ships) came to Weymouth with his parents and moved with them to Boston in 1652. His only official position was Tythingman in Captain Turill's Company in 1685. He received his house and a share of wharves from his Father's estate.
>
> In his will of March 22, 1690, proved May 8, 1690, (Suffolk Prob. 1726) he names wife Mary executrix, his sons Joseph, Isaac and Nathaniel Jr. (of Charlestown) and his daughters Mary Hipditch, Sarah, Wife of Richard Honywell, and Elizabeth, Wife of Ebenezer Chaffin. Overseers to be Obadiah Gill and Jacob Howan. Witnessed by Daniel Turoll, Samuel Burrill and Eliezer Moody. The inventory, taken 8th of May, 1690 by William Robie, Hezekiah Henchman and Timothy Wadsworth, totaled £236-7-0 of which £120 was for land.
>
> His widow Mary gave to his son Joseph on March 4, 1691/1692 and January 1, 1700/1701. Mary also sold some of the property to her brother-in-law, Jonathan Adams on May 31, 1698. The balance of the property was sold to Thomas Harris by the heirs on February 17, 1707/1708. On August 5, 1707 administration de bonis non was granted to his sons Joseph and Isaac. An inventory taken September 5, 1707 by John Barnard, John Nichols and William Shipreeve, totaled £104-7-6 of which £-70 was for land.

Nathaniel Adams was buried at Copps Hill. Mary Portmort was born in 1630 in Alford, England. She died on June 11, 1707 in Boston.

His parents were Nathaniel Adams and Sarah, whose maiden name is not known.

A chart called "Genealogy of the Adams Family" is in our family collection, which was created by our relative Benjamin Pressly Barron, who lived 1840-1898. His son Walter L. Barron, who was born in 1890, made a copy in 1916 that was passed to my grandmother.

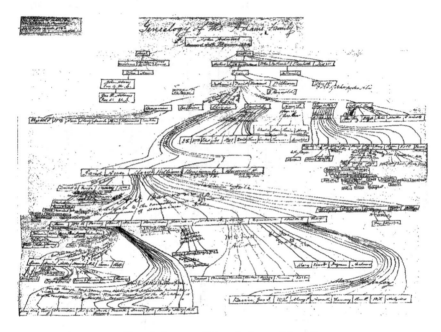

Genealogy of the Adams Family
The entire chart created by Benjamin Pressly Barron,
as copied by his son Walter L. Barron in 1916
From the Phillips Family Collection

This chart shows a John Adams who "arrived with the pilgrims in 1620" and shows a son Hugh below and to the left. Three generations below, President John Adams and his son President John Quincy Adams can be found. Our ancestry on this chart comes from the other son of this original John Adams, and works its way down two branches. However, I have been unable to verify much of this early ancestry.

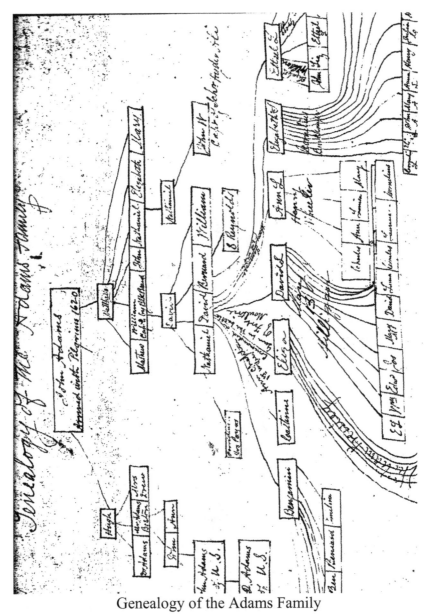

Genealogy of the Adams Family

An excerpt from a large chart created by Benjamin Pressly Barron,
as copied by his son Walter L. Barron in 1916
From the Phillips Family Collection

This chart was given to Walter's mother by his uncle Judge Benjamin Chaplin Pressley. This chart connects[140] our Adams family to the Adams family of President John Adams. David Pressley Anderson wrote, "On my father's side I trace my ancestry to the Mayflower through the Adams family of Massachusetts."

What is known is that President John Adams was the great-great-great grandson of John and Priscilla Alden, Pilgrims who landed at Plymouth Rock in 1620. The Barron chart shows this, although the Plymouth Rock ancestor in the chart is listed as John Adams, not John Alden.

John Alden, who was born circa 1599 and who died on September 12, 1687, was one of the Pilgrim Fathers who came to America on the Mayflower, signed the Mayflower Compact, and founded Plymouth Colony in 1620. Thereafter he held various public offices, including that of deputy governor of Massachusetts (1664-1665, 1667). He married fellow Pilgrim Priscilla Mullins. Their daughter Ruth Alden married John Bass of Braintree, Massachusetts, where they lived and had seven children. Their daughter Hannah Bass married Joseph Adams Jr., the son of Joseph Adams[141]. Hannah and Joseph's son John Adams married Susannah Boylston, the parents of President John Adams.

We can trace our Adams ancestry back as far as Nathaniel Adams who had a land grant in Weymouth, Massachusetts in 1642. The first Adams in the President's family was Joseph Adams Jr. who was born on December 24, 1654 in Braintree, Norfolk County, Massachusetts. It could be that Joseph Adams Jr. is somehow related to our Nathaniel Adams, but so far I have not been able to determine this relationship. Perhaps the chart put together by our Barron relatives may provide a clue as to how our Adams family is related to the family of President John Adams.

The President's Adams family starts with Henry Adams, the father of Joseph Adams Sr. Henry's widow Edith Squire married John Fussell in Weymouth, Massachusetts. They had a daughter named Mary Fussell who married a Nathaniel Adams in 1677 in Weymouth. Our Nathaniel Adams married Mary

Portmort and survived their Nathaniel when he died in 1689, so these two Nathaniels are not one and the same.

Returning to my great-grandfather's words, "On my father's side I trace my ancestry to the Mayflower through the Adams family of Massachusetts," it would appear that what he meant was that we are related to President John Adams who descended from Mayflower ancestors. Our earliest known Adams ancestor is Nathaniel Adams who was born perhaps around 1605 in England. Perhaps the family were related in England.

*　　　*　　　*

Paul Grimball, of Edisto Island was born in 1630 in England and was the first and only one of that name to come to the shores of South Carolina or anywhere else in America as far as is known. He was a wealthy English merchant and married his wife Mary Stoney in England.

In 1663, South Carolina, along with an area that would later comprise 16 states, was given to nine powerful Englishmen, known as the Lords Proprietors, by King Charles II of England, (hence the name "Carolina" which is a feminine form of Charles).

On April 10, 1681, Lord Shaftsbury gave a grant of 3,000 acres of land to Mr. Paul Grimball, Merchant, bound for Ashley River to settle there.

Paul Grimball reached Charleston circa 1682-1683, but did not settle on the Ashley River. Instead, he went to Edisto Island. He lived in the Colony for 14 years before his death and held nearly every governmental position except governor. He must have been an officer in the colonial militia as well.

It is recorded that "In the summer of 1686, the Spanish raided Edisto Island. They came with three galleys, a hundred white men and a force of Negroes and Indians. They sacked the home of Governor Morton and Mr. Grimball, the Secretary of the Province. They carried off money, plate and 13 slaves and murdered the brother of the governor."

Paul Grimball resided in the Province of South Carolina from 1682 to 1696. He was appointed Secretary and Receiver General of South Carolina by the Lords Proprietors on October 10, 1687. He was a Lords Proprietor Deputy and Member of the Grand Council. He died between December 13, 1695 and February 20, 1696 in Edisto Island, South Carolina. His wife Mary Stoney died in 1715 in Edisto Island.

*　　*　　*

William Adams, the father of Elizabeth Adams (who married Thomas Grimball), was a glover (one who made or sold gloves) who was born circa 1650 in Sudbury, Massachusetts and died in 1707 in Charles Towne, South Carolina. In his will, he directed that his daughter Jane live with her sister Eliza, wife of Thomas Grimball, until she should "be brought up to her needle."

The genealogical compilation *The Bells in USA and Allied Families 1650-1977* suggests that there seem to be at least two Adams branches in South Carolina from which we are descended: one founded by William Adams (who was from the Province of Maine, of which Massachusetts was then a part) who lived in Charles Towne, South Carolina in 1698; the other one founded by David Adams, who was born in 1682 and died in 1720 and was a New England mariner.

In Alexander Samuel Salley's book *Natives of Early Carolina 1650-1708*, published in 1911, there is mention of the records of the First Church at Dorchester, which state that on October 20, 1695, Joseph Lord and others were transferred from that church for the "gathering of a church for the south coralina." William Adams of Sudbury is listed as part of this group.

What is interesting about this passage is that Nathaniel Adams was a blockmaker to Joseph Lord. Perhaps William and Nathaniel were related.

*　　*　　*

John Welch, the father of Lucy Welch who married James Alexander Witherspoon, was born in 1558 in Irongray, Ayrshire, Scotland. He was a Presbyterian minister and married Elizabeth Knox who was born in 1569 in Irongray, the daughter of John

Knox and Margaret Stewart.   John Welch died in 1622 in London, England.   Elizabeth Knox died in 1625 at Ayrshire, Scotland.

John Welch is also known as "Rev. John Welsh of Ayr." John was one of seven dissenters to King James VI of Scotland's attempt to unite the Presbyterian Church of Scotland with the Anglican Church of England. As a result he was imprisoned on the orders of King James VI of Scotland, and in 1606 he was exiled to France, where he continued his activities for many years. His grandson was the Covenanters' leader, John Welsh of Irongray.

XIII. COLLINS, JOHNSON, ADAMS AND KNOX

John Collins, Sr., the father of John Collins, Jr. was born in 1569.   He was from Maidstone, Kent, England, and was granted life rights as Keeper of the Gael of Maidstone which he passed on to his son, John Jr., in his will. The right had been granted by King Charles I and was a position of power and influence. He died in 1644.

Maidstone's town status was confirmed when it was incorporated in 1549.   It had originally been governed by a portreeve, 12 brethren and 24 commoners under the direction of the Archbishop of Canterbury.   However, when the people of Maidstone rebelled against the crown in support of Thomas Wyatt in 1551, this charter was revoked, although a new charter was established five years later when Maidstone was created a borough.

*   *   *

Sir Nathaniel (Gov.) Johnson is the putative father of Margaret Johnson who married Jonah (Jonack) Lynch. He was born on April 7, 1644 or 1645 at Kibblesworth, Durham, England.

Sir Nathaniel was a colonel in the English Army and a Member of Parliament.   He left England for America on September 13, 1679 on the sloop The True Friendship. He was knighted on December 28, 1680.

Sir Nathaniel married Anne (Lady) Overton, daughter of Robert (Col.) Overton and Anne Gardiner. He was the Governor of the Leeward Islands (the Islands of Antigua, Montserrat, St. Christopher, and Treves).

Returning to England with his family from the Leeward Islands, they were taken prisoners by the French and kept a year, during which time Anne died.

He was made a Cassique in 1686 and a Landgrave in 1703. He was twice the Governor of the Province of South Carolina (1703-1709), a turbulent period when the French and Spanish were threatening the tiny English colony. In 1706 the Colony was attacked by the French. Johnson was successful in driving them back, killing their commander and some 300 men.

Sir Nathaniel introduced the cultivation of silk worms to the province, thus the name "Silk Hope" for his 5,518 acre plantation (which was later sold to the Manigaults).

Another source lists his departure from England as April 19, 1679 on the ship The Friends Adventure for Antigua. He began his career in the British Army. Sir Nathaniel died in July 1712 or 1713 at the age of 68.

* * *

Nathaniel Adams was a "dishturner" or lathe operator. He was first at Weymouth, Massachusetts where he had a grant of land in 1642 and became a freeman in 1647. His eldest son Nathaniel was probably born in England and the other four sons were probably born in Weymouth, Massachusetts, although only Abraham's birth is recorded there.

In 1649 he was on a committee to lay out a road from Weymouth to Dorchester. In 1652 he moved to Boston, where he served as a surveyor in 1654 and 1655, a Constable in 1657, a Water Bailiff in 1663 and 1664, and a Clerk of the Markets in 1665 and again in 1674.

He joined the Second Church on January 16, 1658 or 1659. After coming to Boston, he gradually acquired several pieces of land and wharves, so that at his death, he left each of his sons a house. These were all in the North End. After his widow's death in 1685, his wharves were divided among his four sons, Nathaniel, David, Abraham and Jonathan. In his will dated July 14, 1675, he named his wife Sarah as executrix, with a life interest in his property; his sons Nathaniel, David, Abraham, Jonathan and Isaac (if alive); David's children, Sarah and David (to have Isaac's share if he was dead); and Mary Timewell. David and Abraham were to be "overseers."

In his widow Sarah's will of October 10, 1684, she named her sons Nathaniel and Abraham executors and left them all of her property as David and Jonathan had previously received £60 each. On July 5, 1685, the four sons reached an agreement on the division of the estate. His children were Nathaniel, who was born about 1630 and died in Boston on March 30, 1690; David, who was born about 1640 and died in Boston July 3, 1705; Abraham, who was born on January 16, 1641 or 1642 and died in Boston on April 6, 1700; and Jonathan, who was born about 1643 and died in Boston on April 7, 1707. Isaac's birth year is unknown; he probably died before 1684 when his mother's will was written. Isaac may have been lost at sea.

Nathaniel Adams died in 1675 in Boston, Massachusetts. We do not know Sarah's maiden name, when she was born, when they married or when she died, presumably in Boston.

*   *   *

John Knox was a Presbyterian minister who first married Marjory Bowes. Many historians consider John Knox the father of the Presbyterian Church. He certainly had the greatest influence on its formation. His influence, however, extended also to the Church of Scotland, now the Reformed Church, as well as the Anglican and Episcopalian Church.

The following is a short chronology of his life:

1505   Born in Gifford, Haddington, Lothian, Scotland.
1536   Graduated from the University Of St. Andrews.
1536   Became a priest, notary, and tutor.
1545   Became a bodyguard of George Wishart, the Scottish Reformer.

1546	Lost his job when George Wishart was burned at the stake. Catholic Cardinal Beaton was killed in retaliation. The good cardinal, under his oath of celibacy, had managed to father 14 children before his untimely demise.
1547	Joins reformers at St. Andrews Castle.
1547	French capture castle, offer Knox a job as a galley slave. Knox accepts.
1549	Knox fired as galley slave after 18 months.
1549	Becomes a pastor in Berwick, then Newcastle, England.
1551	Becomes chaplain to King Edward VI.
1552	Turns down job as Bishop of Rochester.
1553	King Edward VI dies and "Bloody" Mary Tudor, in Knox's words, "that idolatrous Jezebel," ascends the throne. Mary, at one point, states she fears Knox's sermons and prayers more than the English Army.
1554	Knox travels abroad, ministering to ex-patriots in Frankfurt, Germany, meeting with Calvin in Geneva.
1555	Knox returns to Scotland and marries Marjory Bowes.
1556	Moves to Geneva, Switzerland with his wife and mother-in-law.
1558	After two years of living with these women, he publishes *The First Blast Of The Trumpet Against The Monstrous Regiment of Women.*
1558	Elizabeth I crowned queen.
1559	Returns to Scotland, where he preaches publicly, despite threats, working to establish Presbyterianism in Scotland.
1560	Parliament adopts Knox's *Scots Confession Of Faith.*
1561	Mary, Queen of Scots, after returning to Scotland from her exile in France, meets with John Knox.
1562	Knox publishes the *Book of Common Order*, still used in slightly-modified form today in the Reformed
1564	Knox marries Margaret Stewart.
1567	Mary abdicates and her infant son, James, is crowned King James VI of Scotland. Knox is invited to the coronation to preach.

1568   Mary flees to England, where she is promptly imprisoned.

1570   Knox suffers a stroke.

1572   Knox dies.

John Knox (1505-1572)
"The Somerville Picture" published in 1836

Some have gone so far as to credit John Knox with the ideas behind the American Revolution.   Looking at the following passage from *Summary of the Proposed Second Blast of the Trumpet*, one can see why:

1. It is not birth only, nor propinquity of blood, that makes a king lawfully to reign above a people professing Christ Jesus and his eternal verity; but in his election must the ordinance, which God has established in the election of inferior judges, be observed.
2. No manifest idolater, nor notorious transgressor of God's holy precepts, ought to be promoted to any public regiment [government], honour, or dignity, in any realm, province, or city that has subjected itself to his blessed evangel.
3. Neither can oath nor promise bind any such people to obey and maintain tyrants against God and against his truth known.
4. But if either rashly they have promoted any manifestly wicked person, or yet ignorantly have chosen such a one, as after declares himself unworthy of regiment above the people of God (and such be all idolaters and cruel persecutors), most justly may the same men depose and punish him, that unadvisedly before they did nominate, appoint, and elect.

John Knox was born in 1505 at Giffordsgate, Haddington, and married Margaret Stewart, daughter of Andrew Stewart and Agnes Cunningham, in 1564 in Scotland. He died on November 24, 1572 in Edinburgh, Scotland. Margaret, our ancestor, was his second wife, born in 1547 at Carrick, Argyllshire, Scotland.

XIV. LYNCH AND STEWART

The Lynch Family

There exists a 1727 chart of the Lynch Family prepared by Elias Horry, the husband of Margaret Lynch. The chart traces the family line from 12th century Ireland down to 18th century South Carolina and includes those of the name living at the time the chart was made. Listed below are generations 13 through 25 starting with the father of Jonah (Jonack) Lynch:

- 13. Thomas Lynch, the third son of Pierce Lynch and Ellin Martin, was born circa 1630 and married Margaret Quinn who was born circa 1630. These are Jonah (Jonack) Lynch's parents.

- 14. Pierce Lynch, born circa 1610, who married Ellin Martin (born circa 1610) was the third son of Jonah Lynch (born circa 1590) and Eltish Skerritt (born circa 1590). He lived in Galway, Province Of Connaught, Ireland.

- 15. Jonah Lynch, born circa 1590 who married Eltish Skerritt (born circa 1590) was the third son of Stephen Fitzpatrick Lynch (born circa 1570) and Margaret Athy (born circa 1570). He lived in Galway, Province Of Connaught, Ireland.

- 16.   Stephen Fitzpatric Lynch, born circa 1570 who married Margaret Athy (born circa 1570) was the son of Dominick Duff Lynch. He lived in Galway, Province Of Connaught, Ireland. He was an only son and heir who built St. Augustine's Abbey in 1500 in Galway, Ireland.

- 17.   Dominick Duff Lynch was the third son of John Benjamin Lynch.   He "brought the Charter for the Mayor." He lived in Galway, Province Of Connaught, Ireland.

- 18.   John Benjamin Lynch was the third son of Thomas FitzJames Lynch.

- 19.   Thomas FitzJames Lynch was the son of James De Lynch.

- 20.   James De Lynch was the second son of Thomas De Lynch.   James had three sons, two of whom were murdered by the Culloughs in Galway.   The third escaped.   Thomas Lynch FitzJames brought over a foot company from England to reduce the rebels.

- 21.   Thomas De Lynch was a son and heir of William Lynch.

- 22.   William Lynch was a son and heir of Walter Morisall De Lynch.

- 23.   Walter Morisall De Lynch was the eldest son and heir of Thomas De Lynch.

- 24.   Thomas De Lynch seated himself at Galway in the Province of Connaught.   The line is of Austrian origin. From Austria later generations through the centuries gradually moved westward to Germany, France, England and Ireland.

- 25. Thomas de Lynch was the second son of "Lynch" in the County Of Dublin, 12th Century.

As an aside, Patrick Lynch[142] of Lydican Castle near Galway married Agnes Blake. Their second son, Patrick, was born in 1715 and left Ireland in the 1740s settling in Buenos Aires in 1749. He married Rosa de Galaya de la Camera, a wealthy heiress. It was from this marriage that Che Guevara's grandmother, Ana Lynch y Ortiz, was descended and born in 1868. She married Roberto Guevara Castro, and their eldest son was Ernesto Guevara Lynch, who was born in 1900. Ernesto married Celia de la Serna de la Llose in 1927, and their first child, who would be known internationally as "Che," was born in Rosario, Argentina, in 1928. The young "Che" trained as a doctor, but left his homeland in 1953 because of his opposition to the Peron regime. He went to Cuba, where he joined the revolution led by Fidel Castro which overthrew the Batista dictatorship in 1959. He went to the Congo in 1965 to fight against white mercenaries, and later returned to South America where he attempted to lead a peasant uprising in Bolivia. That conflict cost him his life in 1967[143].

Ernesto "Che" Guevara Lynch (1928-1967)
With his mother and father Ernesto Guevara Lynch Sr.

The Stewart Family

Elizabeth Knox was the daughter of John Knox and Margaret Stewart. The following represents the 13th through the 23rd generations within our Stewart family

- 13. Margaret Stewart was born circa 1548. She was the daughter of Andrew Stewart, 2nd Lord Stewart of Ochiltree and Agnes Cunningham. She married John Knox in March 1564. She died sometime after 1612.

- 14. Her father Andrew Stewart, who succeeded his father as 2nd Lord Stewart of Ochiltree in 1549, was born after 1521. He was the son of Andrew Stewart, 1st Lord Stewart of Ochiltree and Margaret Hamilton. He married Agnes Cunningham, daughter of John Cunningham, 5th of Capringtoun, before October 27, 1549. He died on March 21, 1601/2.

- 15. Andrew Stewart, 1st Lord Stewart of Ochiltree was born before 1505. He married Margaret Hamilton, daughter of James Hamilton, 1st Earl of Arran and Beatrix Drummond, before August 22, 1515. He died in 1548. He was created 1st Lord Stewart of Ochiltree on March 15, 1542 when he exchanged his Avandale title with James Hamilton for the Ochiltree title. The exchange was ordained by Parliament in 1542. According to *The Complete Peerage*, Margaret Hamilton's father was James Hamilton, 1st Earl of Arran who was born circa 1475. Her mother was Beatrix Drummond.

- 16. James Hamilton was the son of James Hamilton, 1st Lord Hamilton and Mary Stewart, Princess of Scotland.

- 17. Mary Stewart, Princess of Scotland was born before May 16, 1452. She was the daughter of James II Stewart, King of Scotland and Marie von Geldern. She first married Thomas Boyd, 1st Earl of Arran (son of Robert Boyd, 1st Lord Boyd of Kilmarnock, and Mariot Maxwell) before April 26, 1467. She then married James Hamilton, 1st Lord Hamilton (son of Sir James Hamilton, 5th of Cadzow, and Janet Livingston) between February 1474 and April 1474. Dispensation from the Pope was granted April 25, 1476, thereby legitimizing the two children already born. She died circa May 1488. Mary Stewart, Princess of Scotland gained the title of Princess Mary of Scotland. As a result of her marriage, Mary Stewart, Princess of Scotland was styled as Countess of Arran before April 26, 1467[144]. Mary Stewart, Princess of Scotland's well-documented ancestry is:

- 18. James II Stewart, King of Scotland and Marie von Geldern

- 19. James I Stewart, King of Scotland and Lady Joan Beaufort

- 20. Robert III Stewart, King of Scotland and Annabel Drummond.

- 21. Robert II Stewart, King of Scotland and Elizabeth Mure of Rowallan. Robert was the only son of Walter

Stewart, 6th High Steward of Scotland (who died in 1326) and Marjorie Bruce, daughter of King Robert I of Scotland and his first wife Isabella of Mar.

- 22. Marjorie Bruce, Princess of Scotland and Walter Stewart, the 6th High Steward of Scotland.

- 23. Robert I, King of Scotland, who married Isabella of Mar, was the famous "Robert The Bruce" who secured Scotland's independence from England. His ancestry is also well-documented back for many generations.

As a result of this ancestry, I am Queen Elizabeth II's 16th cousin, with King James II being, to my knowledge, our most recent common ancestor.

On Queen Elizabeth II's side, the descendancy from King James II of Scotland is:

1. James III of Scotland and Margaret of Denmark
2. James IV of Scotland and Margaret of England
3. James V of Scotland and Mary De Guise-Lorriane
4. Mary I of Scotland and Henry of Darnley Stuart
5. James VI of Scotland (James I of England) and Anne of Denmark
6. Elizabeth Stuart and Frederick V of Bohemia
7. Sophia of Hanover and Ernest Augustus
8. George I and Sophie Dorothea Prinzessin von der Pfalz
9. George II and Caroline
10. Frederick Lewis and Augusta
11. George III and Sophie Charlotte Herzogin von Mecklenburg-Strelitz
12. Edward Augustus and Marie Luise Victoire Prinzessin von Sachsen-Coburg-Saalfeld
13. Victoria Alexandrina Hanover and Albert Prinz von Sachsen-Coburg und Gotha
14. Edward VII Saxe-Coburg and Gotha and Alexandra Caroline Marie Charlotte Louise Julia von Schleswig-Holstein-Sonderburg-Glücksburg, Princess of Denmark
15. George V Windsor and Mary Prinzessin von Teck

16. George VI Windsor and Lady Elizabeth Angela Marguerite Bowes-Lyon
17. Elizabeth II

On our side, our descendancy from King James II of Scotland is:

1. James Hamilton and Mary, Princess of Scotland
2. James Hamilton and Beatrix Drummond
3. Andrew Stewart and Margaret Hamilton
4. Andrew Stewart and Agnes Cunningham
5. John Knox and Margaret Stewart
6. John Welch and Elizabeth Knox
7. James Alexander Witherspoon and Lucy Welch
8. James Alexander Witherspoon and Helen (whose maiden name is unknown)
9. William Wilson and Jane Witherspoon
10. David Wilson and Mary Witherspoon
11. David Wilson and Jane Morrow
12. David D. Wilson and Sarah Grier Britton Britton
13. George Pressly Anderson and Margaret Gotea Wilson
14. David Pressley Anderson and Mattie L. Reid
15. John Pressley Phillips and Ruth Anderson
16. William David Phillips and Mary Frances Renning
17. John Renning Phillips

XV. ANCESTRY TO THE 17TH GENERATION

Ancestors of the Author

2 Parents
William David Phillips (b. November 13, 1927, d.   )
Mary Frances Renning (b. November 20, 1935, d. October 2, 1999)

3 Grandparents
John Pressley Phillips (b. July 18, 1891, d. September 10, 1954)
Ruth Anderson (b. May 23, 1897, d. March 28, 1995)

4 Great-Grandparents
William Walker Phillips (b. July 20, 1851, d. January 20, 1935)
Elizabeth B. Pressley (b. 1854, d. March 16, 1916)
Mattie L. Reid (b. March 5, 1869, d. November 30, 1958)
David Pressley Anderson (b. July 15, 1868, d. January 3, 1949)

5 2nd Great-Grandparents
Seaborn Moses Collins Phillips (b. August 3, 1822, d. May 22, 1861)
Emily Cushman Walker (b. April 6, 1832, d. May 20, 1907)
John Gotea Pressley (b. May 24, 1833, d. July 5, 1895)
Julia Caroline Burckmyer (b. December 2, 1833, d. December 30, 1907)
George Pressly Anderson (b. June 8, 1838, d. February 23, 1887)
Margaret Gotea Wilson (b. February 28, 1847, d. November 6, 1934)
Joseph B. Reid (b. November 4, 1835, d. December 1, 1918)
Louisa J. W. Range (b. December 6, 1841, d. October 5, 1929)

6 3rd Great-Grandparents
James Phillips, Jr. (b. August 5, 1789, d. August 11, 1838)
Sarah Collins (Hatcher) (b. October 9, 1787, d. November 30, 1843)
William F. Walker

Emily T. Branch (b. circa 1810, d. April 6, 1878)
John Brockinton Pressley (b. February 18, 1810, d. May 7, 1863)
Sarah Gotea (b. April 24, 1812, d. April 4, 1874)
Cornelius D. Burckmyer (b. October 10, 1800, d. July 1, 1848)
Elizabeth Sarah Adams
George Anderson (b. 1803, d. February 23, 1843)
Ann Esther Pressly (b. January 16, 1809, d. May 1878)
David D. Wilson (b. March 16, 1790, d. April 29, 1868)
Sarah Grier Britton (Britton) (b. February 13, 1806, d. September 17, 1884)
Charles Range (b. June 30, 1819, d.   )
Elizabeth E. Klipper (b. December 31, 1822, d.   )

7 4th Great-Grandparents

James Phillips (b. circa 1750-1755, d. circa 1828)
Nancy (b.   , d. circa 1828)
Moses Collins, Sr. (b. circa 1753, d. January 29, 1816)
Hannah Willis (b. December 10, 1754, d. 1833)
John Pressley (b. August 19, 1780, d. May 14, 1821)
Mary Barr Brockinton (b. January 15, 1783, d. August 10, 1849)
John Gotea (b. February 2, 1781, d. January 3, 1826)
Elizabeth Scott (b. May 6, 1790, d. October 27, 1851)
John Burckmyer (b. April 6, 1764, d. May 27, 1812)
Ann Mary Cobia (b. November 6, 1774, d. October 6, 1829)
William Pressly (b. 1778, d. 1820)
Eliza Eleanor Adams (b. January 18, 1784, d. July 24, 1818)
David Wilson (b. April 11, 1742, d. June 8, 1812)
Jane Morrow (b. 1755, d. April 14, 1831)
Thomas Goddard Britton (b. circa 1784, d.   )
Ann Durant (b. circa 1781, d.   )

8 5th Great-Grandparents

John Collins III (b. circa 1700, d.   )
Elizabeth Odom
William Willis III (b. circa 1725, d. 1760)
Susannah Toney
William Pressley (b.   , d. circa 1790)
Eleanor Orr (b. circa 1765, d. circa 1803)
John Brockinton, Jr. (b. 1754, d. November 16, 1801)
Martha Screven Fowler (b. 1757, d. 1825)
John Gotea (b. circa 1774, d. March 1818)
Elizabeth Barnes
William Scott (b. 1760, d. 1806)
Mary Baxter (b. May 30, 1762, d. November 13, 1823)
Daniel John Burckmyer (b. November 1731, d. July 7, 1774)
Margaret Anna Lebert (b. 1745, d. July 30, 1781)
David Pressly (b. 1731, d. January 15, 1785)

Esther
David Adams (b. November 8, 1753, d. August 24, 1828)
Ann Chaplin (b. July 29, 1758, d. before 1791)
David Wilson (b. 1700, d. 1750)
Mary Witherspoon (b. 1707, d. 1765)
Bethel Durant

9 6th Great-Grandparents
John Collins Jr.
William Odom
William Willis Jr. (b. after 1709, d.   )
Hannah Burnham
Edmund Toney
Elizabeth Gulliam
John Brockinton Sr. (b. September 16, 1727, d. 1795)
Mary Barr (b. 1732, d. circa 1795)
James Fowler (b. circa 1730, d. 1772)
Elizabeth Screven (b. 1738, d. after 1772)
John Gotea (b. circa 1750, d. before 1807)
Eleanor McCutchen (b. circa 1756, d. July 1848)
Thomas Scott (b. before 1721, d. circa 1766)
Jannet Watson (b. circa 1730, d. March 29, 1772)
Thomas Baxter (b. 1739, d. 1765)
David Adams (b. 1718, d. 1786)
Catherine Grimball (b. September 10, 1733, d. 1772)
Benjamin Chaplin (b. 1723, d. 1768)
Eleanor Reynolds (b. December 17, 1738, d. September 13, 1771)
William Wilson (b. 1672, d. 1750)
Jane Witherspoon (b. 1672, d. 1731)
John Witherspoon (b. 1670, d. 1737)
Janet Witherspoon (b. 1670, d. September 1734)

10 7th Great-Grandparents
John Collins (b. circa 1655, d. March 5, 1748)
Mary Wyatt
William Willis (b. circa 1675, d. circa 1717)
Sarah Willis
William Toney (b. circa 1634, d.   )
Anne Bishop (b. circa 1638, d.   )
William Brockinton (b. 1688, d. April 21, 1742)
Sarah Griffin (b. 1698, d. March 31, 1760)
Gavin Barr
Mary (b.   , d. 1762)
Richard Fowler
Sarah
Rev. Elisha Screven (b. September 1, 1698, d. December 3, 1757)

Hannah Johnson or Commander (b. April 10, 1709, d.   )
John Gotea (b. circa 1720, d. circa November 21, 1807)
Elizabeth McConnell (b. circa 1730, d.   )
Hugh McCutchen (b.   , d. before 1760)
Isabella Cooper (b. 1730, d. 1769)
John Scott
John Watson (b. circa 1700, d. September 12, 1766)
John Baxter (b. circa 1699, d. after 1770)
Sarah Lynch (b. circa 1720, d. 1787)
David Adams (b. November 19, 1682, d. 1720)
Elizabeth Capers (b. circa 1690, d. after 1741)
Paul Grimball (b. 1703, d. 1750)
Mary Stone
John Chaplin (b. July 1682, d. February 3, 1752)
Phoebe Ladson (b. June 27, 1691, d. January 12, 1764)
James Wilson
James Alexander Witherspoon (b. 1640, d. after 1690)
Helen (b. 1644, d.   )
David Witherspoon (b. 1642, d. after 1675)
Helen Welch

11 8th Great-Grandparents
William Collins (b. 1612, d. 1705)
Ann
John Willis (b. circa 1648, d. circa 1715)
Matilda Thornton
Rev. William Screven (b. 1629, d. October 10, 1713)
Bridget Cutts (b. circa 1660, d. 1717)
Joseph Johnson
Elizabeth
William Cooper (b. circa 1700, d.   )
Thomas Lynch (b. circa 1675, d. 1752)
Sabina Van Der Horst
Nathaniel Adams (b. September 10, 1653, d. March 18, 1710)
Hannah Wilmot (b. February 10, 1660, d. January 24, 1699)
Richard Capers
Mary Barnet(t)
Thomas Grimball (b. 1675, d.   )
Elizabeth Adams (b.   , d. August 5, 1715)
John Chaplin (b. 1636, d.   )
Ann Skinner
John Ladson
Mary Stanyarne
James Alexander Witherspoon (b. 1610, d. 1649)
Lucy Welch (b. 1620, d. after 1650)

12 9th Great-Grandparents
John Collins Jr. (b. circa 1590, d. January 1663)
William Willis (b. circa 1632, d.   )
Robert Cutts (b. circa 1640, d.   )
Mary Hoel (b. circa 1643, d.   )
Jonah (Jonack) Lynch (b. 1656, d. circa 1711)
Margaret Johnson (b. circa 1670, d.   )
John Van Der Horst
Nathaniel Adams (b. 1630, d. March 29, 1689)
Mary Portmort (b. 1630, d. June 11, 1707)
William Barnet(t)
Paul A. Grimball (b. 1630, d. February 20, 1695/96)
Mary Stoney (b.   , d. 1715)
William Adams (b. circa 1650, d. 1707)
Alexander Witherspoon (b. 1583, d. 1649)
John Welch (b.1558, d. 1622)
Elizabeth Knox (b 1569, d. 1625)

13 10th Great-Grandparents
John Collins (b. 1569, d.   )
Rev. John Willis (b. circa 1587, d.   )
Richard Cutts
Thomas Lynch (b. circa 1630, d.   )
Margaret Quinn (b. circa 1630, d.   )
Sir Nathaniel (Gov.) Johnson (b. April 7, 1644, d. 1713)
Nathaniel Adams (b.   , d. 1675)
Sarah
John Wedderspon (b. 1540, d. 1604)
Anne Patterson
John Knox (b. 1505, d. November 24, 1572)
Margaret Stewart (b. 1547, d.   )

14 11th Great-Grandparents
Rev. Francis Willis (b. circa 1540, d. circa 1596)
Pierce Lynch (b. circa 1610, d.   )
Ellin Martin (b. circa 1610, d.   )
William Johnson
Margaret Sherwood
Alexander Wedderspon (b. 1515, d. 1569)
Catherine Hamilton (b. circa 1517, d.   )
William Knox
Andrew Stewart (b. after 1521, d. March 21, 1601 or 1602)
Agnes Cunningham

15 12th Great-Grandparents
Francis Willis (b. circa 1515, d.   )
Jonah Lynch (b. circa 1590, d.   )
Eltish Skerritt (b. circa 1590, d.   )
William Hamilton (b. circa 1506, d.   )
Catherine Kennedy (b. circa 1510, d.   )
Andrew Stewart (b. before 1505, d. 1548)
Margaret Hamilton
John Cunningham

16 13th Great-Grandparents
Stephen Fitzdominick Lynch (b. circa 1570, d.   )
Margaret Athy (b. circa 1570, d.   )
Alexander Hamilton (b. circa 1485, d.   )
Marion Cunningham (b. circa 1488, d.   )
Gilbert Kennedy (b. circa 1485, d. August 1527)
Isabel Campbell (b. circa 1491, d. after 1529)
Andrew Stewart
Margaret Kennedy (b.   , d. before May 28, 1542)
James Hamilton (b. 1475, d. 1529)
Beatrix Drummond

17 14th Great-Grandparents
Dominick Duff Lynch
Walter Stuart (b. 1430, d. before 1488)
Elizabeth Arnot
John Kennedy
Elizabeth Seton-Gordon
James Hamilton (b. 1415, d. November 6, 1479)
Mary Stewart (b. before May 16, 1452, d. circa 1488)

XVI. ACKNOWLEDGEMENTS

Much appreciation and gratitude is extended to the following individuals and organizations for their assistance: Janyce Anderson for her assistance with researching the Anderson and Adams families; Robert Boro for his amazing and perhaps only candid photo of the interior of The Farmers National Bank in 1904; the Society of California Pioneers for their 1868 photograph of the ship, The Montana, which carried my Pressley and Anderson ancestors in 1869 from Panama to San Francisco; Andrew Chandler of the South Carolina Department of Archives and History for his assistance in reviewing a rough draft of this book; Charles Christian, a docent at the Rural Cemetery in Santa Rosa who has researched John Gotea Pressley and oversaw the placement of a new grave marker noting his rank of Lt. Col. in the Civil War; William S. Coate for his article on Richard Lawrence Dixon in *The Madera Tribune* and for his project to transcribe the diaries of George Washington Mordecai and Louise Hunter Dixon Mordecai; Roger Conrad for providing a photo of Seaborn Moses Phillips which was corroborated by a photo my father also had; Tom Cox for his photo of his father E. Morris Cox, Jr.; Charles P. Doud, editor of *The Madera Tribune* for his assistance with the article by William S. Coate; Nancy Eldred Williams for the information she has provided about Judge Dixon L. Phillips and his family; Nancy Kiser of the Phillips Worldwide DNA Project for assistance with our continued search for our earliest known Phillips ancestor;   the

Fresno Historical Society and in particular Sharon Hiigel, Curator of Collections and Education Coordinator and Maria Ortiz, Archivist/Librarian for their significant photographic research; Joanna Liston for assistance with research about the Anderson Family; Darryl Lundy of thepeerage.com for his assistance in verifying the lineage from Margaret Stewart to Mary, Princess of Scotland, Princess Mary's ancestry and for all of the proper names of members of the Royal Family, John B. Kent for his years of assistance to me in learning about my Phillips family, and in particular, information about Judge James Phillips, Jr. and his father James Phillips, Sr.; The Mississippi Department of Archives and History and the Mississippi Historical Society for their permission to use Sam Olden's article on the Battle of Buena Vista and the accompanying painting by Alexandra Alaux; Peter B. Miazza for his incredible assistance in gathering numerous information about Sarah Collins (and a huge "thank you" from all of us for discovering her grave which has been covered for more than a century); Sam Olden of Yazoo City, Mississippi for his article on the Battle of Buena Vista; Curtis Paullins at the California Bankers Association for locating the speech William Walker Phillips read in 1891; The State Archives of Florida for their permission to use the photographs taken in 1861 at Pensacola, Florida; Nancy Ramirez, librarian at *The Fresno Bee* for her assistance in locating the obituary of my grandmother and a photograph of her taken in 1965; Dan Riley at UCSF for explaining E. Dixon Heise's generous bequest; James Newton and Deborah Ostrander Russell for the recent photographs of Mariposa and Broadway Plaza and the Phillips home formerly at 410 Van Ness in Fresno; William Secrest, Jr. at The Fresno Public Library for his assistance in providing numerous old photographs from Fresno; Ray Steele, editor of *The Fresno Bee* for his assistance and permission to publish my grandmother's obituary written by Roger Tatarian as well as the words of James McClatchy at my grandmother's memorial service; Lee Paul Sturdivant for locating a memoir about William Washington Phillips' service in the Battle of Buena Vista; The Three Rivers Historical Society in Hemingway, South Carolina for their assistance with the Lynch family; Bruce Tognazzini for his assistance with the family history written by John Gotea Pressley as well as the grave photographs and the gedcom file he created which made much of this book possible; The Williamsburgh Historical Museum and The Williamsburg County Historical Society in Kingstree, South Carolina, and Joanne Brown in particular; and Joyce Zachman for her assistance with the Willis family.

I would also like to especially thank Maria Elena Rodriguez in Los Angeles for her excellence in copy-editing my manuscript. Maria gave me many hours of assistance and I appreciate it.

I also wish to extend my heart-felt gratitude to my friend David Costa, owner of the world-renowned firm of *Wherefore Art?* in London. The design he has created, in my mind, perfectly captures the essence of this book.

As a graphic designer, David is in a class by himself, and his 35-years of work for clients including The Beatles[145], The Rolling Stones, Sir Elton John, Eric Clapton, Cat Stevens, Phil Collins, Genesis, as well as corporate clients such as Virgin Atlantic and Philip Morris to name but a few, speaks for itself. I have been aware of David's work since I was 12 years of age, and I am so very proud to have his help. Bravo!

Finally, I would like to thank my wife, Tuula Annikki Törrönen Phillips, and my daughter, Matilda Frances Elizabeth Phillips, for their patience, love and understanding while I deprived them of many hours of my devotion while putting together this book.

XVII. BIBLIOGRAPHY, SOURCES AND NOTES

Books:

Bell, Getha Gina, *The Bells in USA and Allied Families 1650-1977* (Published originally in 1977. Now available only on CD.)

Boddie, William Willis, *History of Williamsburg: Something About the People of Williamsburg County, South Carolina, from the First Settlement by Europeans About 1705 until 1923* (Columbia, SC: The State Company, 1923.) pp. 10-20; 210.

Bond, Henry, *Genealogies of the Families and Descendants of the Early Settlers of Watertown, Massachusetts* (Boston, MA: Little, Brown & Company, 1855), p. 747.

Brown, Reba Holmes, *American Shoots from the Baskerville Family*. Published in 1975.

Brown, Reba Holmes, *The Youngblood Family*. Published in 1975.

Carr, Ezra Slocum, *The Patrons of Husbandry of the West Coast* (San Francisco, CA: A. L. Bancroft and Company, 1875)

Chaddock, Emory Leroy with Alice Chaddock Yvanovich, *120 degrees in the shade (and no shade): Amusing recollections of a Fresno pioneer* (Fresno, CA: Lifelines, 1989)

Chamberlain, George Walter, "The Early New England Coolidges," *The New England Historical and Genealogical Register* 77:4 (Oct 1923) (Boston, MA: New England Historic Genealogical Society, 1923), p. 275.

Collins, Dr. Mary Landin, *Collins & Travis Families & Their Allies.* Published in 1982. (Available by request at: http://www.rootsweb.com/~mshinds2/publications.htm)

Cross, Ira Brown, *Financing an Empire: History of Banking in California*, (Chicago, IL: S. J. Clarke Publishing Company, 1927)

The DAR Patriot Index, Volume III, published by the National Society of Daughters of the American Revolution, 2003.

Dickinson, Edward B., *Official Proceedings Of The National Democratic Convention, Held in Chicago, Ill. June 21st, 22nd and 23rd, 1892*, (Chicago, IL: Cameron, Amberg & Co., 1892.)

Gamma Phi Beta, *The Crescent of Gamma Phi Beta*, 1919, p. 52.

Hedges, Charles (compiled by), *Speeches of Benjamin Harrison, Twenty-third President of the United States,*(New York, NY: United States Book Company, successor to John W. Lovell Company, 1892), pp. 365-366.

Leavitt, Emily W., "Descendants of George Lawrence," *The New England Historical and Genealogical Register*, 46:2 (Apr 1892) (Boston, MA: New England Historic Genealogical Society, 1892), p. 150.

McCain, William D., *The Story of Jackson, A History of the Capitol of Mississippi 1821-1951*, Volume 1, (Jackson, MS: by J. F. Hyer Publishing Company, 1953)

No Specific Author, *The Bay of San Francisco: The Metropolis of the Pacific Coast and Its Suburban Cities : a istory* (Chicago, IL: Lewis Publishing Company, 1892) Digitized July 2006. Available as .pdf)

No Specific Author, *The Memorial and Biographical History of the County of Fresno, Tulare, and Kern, California*, (Chicago, IL: Lewis Publishing Company, 1892). p. 468.

Salley, Alexander Samuel, *Narratives of Early Carolina 1650-1708*, (New York, NY: C. Scribner's Sons, 1911), p. 191.

Savage, James and John Farmer, and Orrando Perry Dexter, *A Genealogical Dictionary of the First Settlers of New England, showing three generations of those who came before 1692* (Boston, MA: Little, Brown and Company, 1860-62.), 1:14, 1:15, 3:60, 4:581.

Stackpole, Everett Schermerhorn, *Old Kittery and Her Families*, (Lewiston, ME: Press of Lewiston Journal Co., 1903), pp 207-208.

The Southern Historical Society Papers, 1876-1956. 52 Volumes published in CD ROM, includes letters and records of citizens and military officials of the Confederacy. (Dayton, OH: Morningside Press, no date)

Toney, Benjamin C., *Toney - The First Millennium*. Published in 1994, 1996. Electronic version available at: http://www.toneyweb.com/exchange/ben.htm

Torrey, Clarence Almon, *New England Marriages Prior to 1700* (Baltimore, MD: Genealogical Publishing Co., 1985.), p. 5.

Weir, Alison, *Britain's Royal Family: A Complete Genealogy* (London, U.K.: The Bodley Head, 1999), page 233-234.

Williams, E. Russ. *Marion County Mississippi Miscellaneous Records, Containing Orphans Court Records; Wills and Estates, 1812-1859; Deeds, 1812-1840; Territorial and Federal Census Records and Mortality Schedules; Old Road Books; 1813 Lawrence County Tax Lists.* (Greenville, SC: Southern Historical Press, Inc., 1986)

White, Edna McDaniel and Blanche Findley Toole, *Sabine Co. Historical Sketches And Genealogical Records.* (Beaumont, TX: La Belle Printing Co., 1972)

Wyman, Thomas Bellows, *The Genealogies and Estates of Charlestown in the County of Middlesex and Commonwealth of Massachusetts, 1629-1818: In a riot in town, in 1687*, Middlesex Co., MA Probate Case #209 (Somersworth, MA: New England History Press, 1982) p. 9

Newspapers and Periodicals:

The American Citizen, published in Canton, Mississippi.

American Genealogist, No.118, Vol. 30, No. 2, page 66, April, 1954

The Daily Evening Citizen, published in Vicksburg, Mississippi.

The Daily Evening News, published in Modesto, California.

The Fresno Bee.

The Fresno Daily Republican.

The Fresno Morning Republican.

The Fresno Weekly Republican.

The Madera Tribune.

The Mississippian.

The Oakland Tribune.

Presley/Preslar/Pressly Newsletter (published 1985-1995)

The San Francisco Chronicle.

The Santa Rosa Republican.

The Sonoma Democrat.

The Visalia Times.

The Yazoo Democrat. (published in Yazoo City, Mississippi)

Web Publications:

"An Early History of the Shaver Lake Fishing Club," by E. L. Chaddock with Alice Chaddock Yvanovich
http://www.shaverlake.org/history.html

"Biography of John Alden and Priscilla Mullins," Alden Kindred of America, Inc.
http://www.alden.org/our_family/aldenbiography.htm

"Che Guevara: Father of Revolution, Son of Galway,"
http://www.fantompowa.net/Flame/che_guevara_irish_roots.htm

"Chronology of Battles and Skirmishes of the South Carolina Tenth Regiment," Horry County Historical Society, 606 Main Street, Conway, SC 29526-4340 (Published online at http://www.hchsonline.org/military/battles.html)

ColonialHall.com, *"William Whipple (1730-1785)"*
http://www.colonialhall.com/whipple/whipple.php

Evans, Lela, and Helen Arnold, *A Brief History of Mississippi*,
http://www.rootsweb.com/~mstallah/history/mshist.html

Huntington Lake Big Creek Historical Conservancy
http://www.huntingtonhistorical.org/history.html

Kauffman, Bill, *"The Child Labor Amendment Debate of the
1920s"* http://www.mises.org/resources/2665

Mississippi Now, *"Hiram G. Runnels"*
http://mshistory.k12.ms.us/features/feature47/governors/7_hiram
_runnels.htm

South Carolina Department of Archives and History
http://www.nationalregister.sc.gov/williamsburg/S10817745009/
index.html

Wikipedia: *"Alexander G. McNutt"*
http://en.wikipedia.org/wiki/Alexander_G._McNutt

Wikipedia: *"California Republic"*
http://en.wikipedia.org/wiki/California_Republic

Wikipedia: *"Indiantown, South Carolina"*
http://en.wikipedia.org/wiki/Indiantown,_South_Carolina

Wikipedia: *"Mexican-American War"*
http://en.wikipedia.org/wiki/Mexican-American_War

Wikipedia: *"Mississippi"*
http://en.wikipedia.org/wiki/Mississippi

Archival Sources:

1841 State Census, Scott, Mississippi.

1850 Census, Yazoo, Mississippi.

1850 Census, Hinds, Mississippi.

1850 Census, Rankin, Mississippi.

1850 Census, Scott, Mississippi.

1850 Census Police District 2, Pike, Mississippi.

Court Records of Winton and Barnwell Counties, South Carolina, Will Book 1, pp. 77-78.

DAR. LA Genealogical Records Comm. DAR, 1937, p.35-43.

HILL v. UNITED STATES, 50 U.S. 386 (1850).

Holcomb, Brent, *Abstracts from Winton County, South Carolina, Minutes of County Court & Will Book 1785-1791*.

Marion County Territory Tax Roll of 1817. (State of Mississippi)

Marion County Marriage Book A, pages 129, 132, 254, 269. (State of Mississippi)

Marion County Marriage Book B, pages 122, 149, 64. (State of Mississippi)

Proceedings of the California Bankers Association, Held at Los Angeles, March 11, 12 and 13, 1891," published in 1891 by The Times-Mirror Printing and Binding House.

Report of the Bank Commissioners of the State of California, 1886, 1889.

Spotsylvania, Virginia Will Book B, pages 134, 167, 329.

Supreme Court of Mississippi, Case Number 94-CA-00032-SCT.

Privately Held Papers:

Anderson, David Pressley, *Narrative*, circa 1935.

Pressley, John Gotea, *Family History, Containing these names: Pressley, Brockinton, Fowler, Gotea, Scriven, Burrows, Nesmith, and others*, 1889.

Phillips, William Walker, *A Narrative of My Life*, a private memorandum, 1932

Interviews:

Ferguson, Debbie

Kent, John B.

Miazza, Peter B.

Tognazzini, Bruce

Zachman, Joyce Gehring

Genealogical Reference for British Nobility:

Mary Stewart, Princess of Scotland

Cokayne, G.E.; with Vicary Gibbs, H.A. Doubleday, Geoffrey H. White, Duncan Warrand and Lord Howard de Walden, editors, *The Complete Peerage of England, Scotland, Ireland, Great Britain and the United Kingdom, Extant, Extinct or Dormant*, new ed., 13 volumes in 14 (1910-1959; reprint in 6 volumes,

Gloucester, UK: Alan Sutton Publishing, 2000), volume VI, page 256. Hereinafter cited as *The Complete Peerage*.

Cokayne, and others, *The Complete Peerage*, volume I, page 219.

Cokayne, and others, *The Complete Peerage*, volume VI, page 255.

Cokayne, and others, *The Complete Peerage*, volume I, page 220.

Cokayne, and others, *The Complete Peerage*, volume II, page 260.

James Hamilton and Beatrix Drummond

Cokayne, G.E.; with Vicary Gibbs, H.A. Doubleday, Geoffrey H. White, Duncan Warrand and Lord Howard de Walden, editors, *The Complete Peerage of England, Scotland, Ireland, Great Britain and the United Kingdom, Extant, Extinct or Dormant*, new ed., 13 volumes in 14 (1910-1959; reprint in 6 volumes, Gloucester, U.K.: Alan Sutton Publishing, 2000), volume VI, page 256. Hereinafter cited as *The Complete Peerage*.

Cokayne, and others, *The Complete Peerage*, volume I, page 221.

Cokayne, and others, *The Complete Peerage*, volume I, page 220.

Cokayne, and others, *The Complete Peerage*, volume I, page 158.

Cokayne, and others, *The Complete Peerage*, volume I, page 199.

Mosley Charles, editor, *Burke's Peerage and Baronetage*, 106th edition, 2 volumes (Crans, Switzerland: Burke's Peerage (Genealogical Books) Ltd, 1999), volume 1, page 4. Hereinafter cited as *Burke's Peerage and Baronetage*, 106th edition.

Andrew Stewart and Margaret Hamilton

Cokayne, G.E.; with Vicary Gibbs, H.A. Doubleday, Geoffrey H. White, Duncan Warrand and Lord Howard de Walden, editors, *The Complete Peerage of England, Scotland, Ireland, Great Britain and the United Kingdom, Extant, Extinct or Dormant*, new ed., 13 volumes in 14 (1910-1959; reprint in 6 volumes, Gloucester, U.K.: Alan Sutton Publishing, 2000), volume I, page 222. Hereinafter cited as *The Complete Peerage*.

Cokayne, and others, *The Complete Peerage*, volume I, page 221.

Andrew Stewart and Agnes Cunningham

Cokayne, G.E.; with Vicary Gibbs, H.A. Doubleday, Geoffrey H. White, Duncan Warrand and Lord Howard de Walden, editors, *The Complete Peerage of England, Scotland, Ireland, Great Britain and the United Kingdom, Extant, Extinct or Dormant*, new ed., 13 volumes in 14 (1910-1959; reprint in 6 volumes, Gloucester, U.K.: Alan Sutton Publishing, 2000), volume X, page 3. Hereinafter cited as *The Complete Peerage*.

Cokayne, and others, *The Complete Peerage*, volume I, page 222.

Mosley Charles, editor, *Burke's Peerage, Baronetage & Knightage*, 107th edition, 3 volumes (Wilmington, DE: Burke's Peerage (Genealogical Books) Ltd, 2003), volume 1, page 712.

Margaret Stewart and John Knox

Mosley Charles, editor, *Burke's Peerage, Baronetage & Knightage*, 107th edition, 3 volumes (Wilmington, DE: Burke's Peerage (Genealogical Books) Ltd, 2003), volume 1, page 712.

END NOTES

[1] The Pressley family spelled their name "Pressly" in the oldest known wills on both sides of my Pressley family. At various points in time, the family began to spell the name "Pressley."

[2] Just as the name Pressly eventually became spelled Pressley, so too did family members of the Brockinton family change the spelling to Brockington. The change in spelling of this family probably occurred in generations following my Brockinton ancestors.

[3] Bruce Tognazzini is twice my father's third cousin. The common ancestors are John Brockinton Pressley and Sarah Gotea, as well as David D. Wilson and Sarah Grier Britton.

[4] Because Ruth married in 1918, she did not graduate with the class of 1919. In the 1920 edition of *The Crescent of Gamma Phi Beta*, she was listed as belonging to the class of 1920.

[5] See *The Crescent of Gamma Phi Beta*, by Gamma Phi Beta, published in 1919, p. 52.

[6] What my great-grandfather called the River Ranch is today known as the Coke Hallowell Center for River Studies, located at 11605 Old Friant Road, Fresno, California 93720. At various times, it was also referred to as "The Riverview Ranch."

[7] According to press reports from Stanford, the fatal accident followed a day of "brawling" between freshman and upper classmen at Stanford. Witnesses said he was helping his fraternity brothers, who were using a firehose and water bags to disperse the freshmen. He lost his balance and fell headfirst from the third-story window of the Beta Theta Pi house during a freshman raid on Fraternity Row. The John Pressley Phillips, Jr. Memorial (Honors) Scholarship was established at Stanford University in his memory. One memorial printed in the Stanford newspaper wrote, "Everyone who knew Johnny Phillips, and there were few who did not, knew him as a friend who always had a smile to spare."

[8] The Fresno Art Museum was originally known as the Fresno Art Center. As a child I took painting classes there and during high school I spent Saturday mornings studying calligraphy under the direction of Robert Boro.

[9] I don't know what became of this wonderful Mexican restaurant, but I do recall one evening when my grandmother noticed the conductor of the Fresno Philharmonic Orchestra having dinner near our table. I was probably about 11 at the time, and in typical fashion, she encouraged me to wander over and introduce myself, which I did.

[10] Freddy Albert is a painter and an old friend of Mary Walker Phillips.

[11] Edward Dixon Heise, referred to as "E. Dixon Heise" or simply "Dixon Heise.

[12] Dan Riley sent to me this explanation by e-mail on June 9, 2007.

[13] A Guide to Historic Architecture in Fresno, California at http://historicfresno.org/index.htm initially referred to the home which was once located at 410 Van Ness as the Ivan Carter McIndoo Home, built in 1913. Today, the Guide referrs to the house as the "McIndoo-Phillips home." Ivan Carter McIndoo can be found in the 1904 photo of the interior of the Farmers National Bank of Fresno as the third gentleman from the left. This photo is courtesy of Robert Boro.

[14] Joan Jertberg Russell recalls the evening of this tragic event. Her parents were having dinner at my grandparents' home when James McClatchy called to inform them of Uncle John's death. Aunt Mary went to spend the night with the Jertbergs that evening. Joan recalls Uncle John as a "terrific young man, an Eagle Scout, someone everybody thought (he) was one of the finest young men in the world. He was just so friendly, and radiated being such a good person."

[15] See *The Crescent of Gamma Phi Beta*, by Gamma Phi Beta, published in 1919, p. 52.

[16] Aunt Mary Walker Phillips, who currently lives in Fresno, received a Masters in Fine Art from Cranbrook Academy of Art in Bloomfield, Michigan around the time I was born. She elevated knitting to an art form, and published a best-selling book called "Creative Knitting." She followed this with a best-selling book called "Step-by-Step Macramé" in the early 1970s in which she mentions me. She was a good friend of Jack Lenor Larsen and lived in Greenwich Village, New York for many years. In the early 1970s she was interviewed by Barbara Walters for "The Today Show" about one of her books.

[17] See http://en.wikipedia.org/wiki/California_Republic

[18] See http://en.wikipedia.org/wiki/Mexican-American_War

[19] Edward Turner Dixon is the namesake and grandfather of E. Dixon Heise.

[20] This biography of Burris R. Phillips comes from *Memorial and Biographical History of the Counties of Fresno, Tulare and Kern, California*, The Lewis Publishing Company, Chicago, 1892.

[21] Published by A. L. Bancroft and Company in San Francisco. Also listed as a member is "C. E. Phillips." This might be a typo if the reference is to William's mother Emily Cushman (Walker) Phillips.

[22] This would have preceded the Barton Opera House which was built in 1890.

[23] A. M. Drew, with a first name of Arthur, is (according to my friend from Fresno) a relative of his Drew family.

[24] According to "The Bay of San Francisco," Vol. 1, page 639, Lewis Publishing Co., 1892.

[25] The Sherman Silver Purchase Act, enacted in 1890, increased the amount of silver the government was required to purchase every month. The law required the Treasury to buy the silver with notes that could be redeemed for either silver or gold. Investors then exchanged their silver U.S. Treasury notes for gold dollars, thus depleting the government's gold reserves. After the Panic of 1893, President Grover Cleveland oversaw the repeal of the Act in 1893 to prevent the depletion of the nation's gold reserves.

[26] William's first cousin, Harry St. John Dixon, father of Maynard Dixon.

[27] This may be a reference to Cornelius Pressley, born in 1862 the son of Judge John Gotea Pressley and his wife Julia Carolyn Burckmyer.

[28] *Speeches of Benjamin Harrison, Twenty-third President of the United States*, Compiled by Charles Hedges, United States Book Company, successors to John W. Lovell Company, 1892, pp. 365-366.

[29] Edward Turner Dixon, the grandfather of Edward Dixon Heise.

[30] *The Official Proceedings of The National Democratic Convention, Held in Chicago, Ill. June 21st, 22nd and 23rd, 1892*, by Edward B. Dickinson, published in 1892 by Cameron, Amberg & Co.

[31] George Washington Mordecai was twice elected as a Democrat to the California State Legislature in 1890 and 1892.

[32] Actually, it was at least ten years prior.

[33] This was the practice known as "sectionalism."

[34] William R. Clark was the mayor of Stockton, California.

[35] In fact, the railroad offered free drinks at the local tavern for anyone who voted for their candidate William R. Clark.

[36] This is an example of the efforts of William Walker Phillips, as early as 1896, to organize the dried fruit industry, which although did not directly mention raisins, was probably foremost on his mind.

[37] While this article does not make it clear, it appears that this incident transpired in San Francisco. The reference to the Orpheum Theater is interesting, as the present-day Orpheum Theater in San Francisco was not built until 1926. There is also the reference to "W. W. Phillips who knew W. D. Grady in Fresno…"

[38] Rebecca Dixon, daughter of Harry St. John Dixon, was Maynard Dixon's sister.

[39] Bill Gates, see http://www.rowanlea.com/report/2/historyofbgates.html

[40] Ivan Carter McIndoo was the first owner of the Phillips family home at 410 Van Ness.

[41] George Roeding is famous in Fresno for having donated the land which became known as Roeding Park.

[42] General Muller was the founder of the Shaver Lake Fishing Club who served as club president for many years.

[43] This might be John Gotea Pressley's son Cornelius Pressley; many of his children had a middle initial "B" which probably stood for Burckmyer, the maiden name of their mother.

[44] Julia Dixon was the mother of E. Dixon Heise.

[45] Shaver Lake is named after C. B. Shaver. In 1891, C. B. Shaver moved from Michigan to Fresno and with L. P. Swift formed the Fresno Flume and Irrigation Company of which he was president and manager. They hired John Eastwood to design a dam on Stevenson Creek (producing the original small Shaver Lake), and a flume to carry lumber 47 miles from the Shaver Lake mill to Clovis.

[46] The Fulton Mall in Fresno was named after Fulton G. Berry.

[47] The Barton Opera House opened on September 29, 1890, built by vineyardist Robert Barton.

[48] Photo © Mystic Seaport, Rosenfeld Collection, Mystic, CT, #ANN6466, www.rosenfeldcollection.org ~ rosenfeld@mysticseaport.org

[49] These Shaver Lake Fishing Club stories were written by Emory Leroy Chaddock (1873-1959) and were published in 1989 by Alice Chaddock Yvanovich in a book titled *120 degrees in the shade (and no shade): Amusing recollections of a Fresno pioneer.* More information can be found at http://www.shaverlake.org/history.html

[50] Huntington Lake Big Creek Historical Conservancy, see http://www.huntingtonhistorical.org/history.htm

[51] This would have become part of California's Highway 99.

[52] *The Fresno Bee* reported on May 20, 1956 that E. L. "Roy" Chaddock, the last living charter member of the Shaver Lake Fishing Club was the inventor of a raisin seeding machine and that he estimated that his successful patent fight saved growers $1 billion over the 18-year life of the patent.

[53] Leon Levy was the great-grandfather of my friend Robert Boro.

[54] At the time, Teddy Roosevelt had split the Republican Party; some Republicans then joined his "Bull Moose" Progressive Party.

[55] W. W. Phillips was still a Democrat in 1890. He did not become a Republican until sometime after 1898.

[56] This house is gone now, perhaps torn down during the time that Highway 41 was constructed.

[57] John A. Neu announced his retirement and the closing of his piano dealership at 1027-1029 "I" Street in Fresno on November 15, 1907.

[58] "The Child Labor Amendment Debate of the 1920s," by Bill Kauffman http://www.mises.org/resources/2665

[59] The Withdrawal Act of 1909 sought to withhold from the public certain lands for purposes of preservation.

[60] While growing up in Los Angeles, Dixon Heise became close friends with actor Robert Stack, a friendship which continued until the day Mr. Stack died; I called Dixon on the telephone to tell him that I had read in the newspaper that Mr. Stack had passed away.

[61] The Bank of Central California changed its name on October 15, 1915 to the Bank & Trust Company of Central California

[62] According to *Financing an Empire: History of Banking in California*, by Ira Brown Cross, published in 1927 by the S. J. Clarke Publishing Company, the Farmers National Bank of Fresno was "purchased" by the Bank & Trust Company of Central California.

[63] His father Seaborn was elected Colonel of the 10th Mississippi Regiment.

[64] Actually, a step-sister in law. When Theodore Miller died, Mary Louise "Bama" Johnson Miller remarried John Alexander McClain and had two sons, Frank and Alex. This would be the wife of Frank.

[65] According to the Federal Reserve System, National Information Center.

[66] The family name was originally Pressly, although we know that George P. Anderson's son spelled his name "Pressley." George P. Anderson may have assumed the spelling "Pressley" during his lifetime if not before. I have not researched birth or death certificates to see if the spelling was changed before or during his lifetime. For consistency with this side of the Pressly/Pressley family which descends from David Pressly who arrived in Charleston in 1767, I have decided to call him "George Pressly Anderson" but acknowledge that family members have always thought of him as "George Pressley Anderson."

[67] Traditionally, he has been referred to as "Seaborn Moses Phillips" or "S. M. Phillips." However, I have seen references to "Seaborn Moses Collins Phillips" and I am not sure whether this is actually his birth name or not. I have decided to use this alternate name as a way of distinguishing between him and his son Seaborn Moses Phillips, Jr.

[68] Personal property at this time would have included slaves.

[69] Seaborn's service record includes some receipts, one reimbursing him for $840 for clothing for his company; in another, he said that when they arrived in Mobile, his men were hungry and had nowhere to camp, so he had them put up in a hotel - he was reimbursed $128 for that; there was also a standard requisition of food and supplies.

[70] Harry St. John Dixon, Seaborn's nephew

[71] Richard Lawrence Dixon, Seaborn's brother-in-law

[72] April 12, 1861, the Civil War started when the Confederate artillery opened fire on Fort Sumter in Charleston Harbor. Fighting had not yet reached Pensacola, Florida.

[73] A portion of John's diary regarding this battle is printed in *The Southern Historical Society Papers*.

[74] April 24, 1869 is not the earliest known date my ancestors first arrived in California. Mattie L. Reid's father Joseph is said to have married her mother Elizabeth Klipper in Santa Rosa, California on March 22, 1864.

[75] The Battle of Atlanta fought on July 22, 1864.

[76] Elizabeth B. Pressley, wife of William Walker Phillips.

[77] Had his daughter Bettie died at this time, my grandfather John Pressley Phillips would never have been born.

[78] The origin of the Pressly family name in this line starts with David Pressly, formerly of Long Cane, who later moved to Charleston and died in 1785. His son, William Pressly, married Eliza Eleanor Adams and had a daughter, Ann Esther Pressly, who married George Anderson. Their son George Pressly Anderson may have changed his name to "George Pressley Anderson" during his lifetime, for his son's name was spelled "David Pressley Anderson."

[79] Had George P. Anderson died in this battle, his son David Pressley Anderson would never have been born. This is in contrast to William Walker Phillips who, like his wife Elizabeth, were born before the Civil War.

[80] Published online at http://www.hchsonline.org/military/battles.html

[81] Her father was David D. Wilson who was born in 1790.

[82] The Wilson Plantation dates back to David Wilson and Mary Witherspoon. Her grandfather, David Wilson, the son of David and Mary, was considered a patriot as he rendered material aid, sending supply provisions and forage for Continental and militia use in 1781 and 1782, see DAR record 299975.

[83] This is the date of a deed of trespass recorded in Marion County, Mississippi.

[84] This is the first known "John" in my Phillips family. My first name comes from John Gotea Pressley.

[85] On March 8, 1891, Louise Hunter Dixon Mordecai wrote from Refuge, "I have just received a letter from Mr. Mordecai [her husband] today. He is in Sacramento serving in the legislature. He is trying to get his bill passed concerning these pesky coyotes and wolves. They are everywhere. It is so frightening to go outside after dark. If the bill passes, there will be a bounty of $3.00 for the hides. Now if only Jack Phillips were here. He loves to hunt. He could make a lot of money. In the meantime, I will just keep putting the lanterns out to scare them away." Earlier on February 15, 1874, she wrote: "Today I woke up and ate the breakfast that our cook had made. Father [Richard L. Dixon] is writing a family history. As Father writes the history, Harry will copy it. The writing will include a great deal of information about Grandfather and Grandmother Dixon, as well as the Phillips family.

[86] The Wissler family believe that their wedding date was April 20, 1837.

[87] These deeds can be found in the book *Marion County Mississippi Miscellaneous Records, Containing Orphans Court Records; Wills and Estates, 1812-1859; Deeds, 1812-1840; Territorial and Federal Census Records and Mortality Schedules; Old Road Books; 1813 Lawrence County Tax Lists*, by E. Russ Williams, published in 1986 by Southern Historical Press, Inc.

[88] Lee may also be a family name. Judge James Phillips' sister Sarah Lee "Sallie" Phillips has the name "Lee" as a family name. This Benjamin Lee could be related if his mother Nancy's maiden name was Lee.

[89] Unfortunately, having secured only a photocopy of a page from a book, I am unsure which book this quote came from.

[90] Possibly a relative of our Lynch family from South Carolina.

[91] Background of the causes of the failure of the Union Bank provided by Peter B. Miazza.

[92] See Mississippi History Now at http://mshistory.k12.ms.us/features/feature47/governors/7_hiram_runnels.htm

[93] See http://en.wikipedia.org/wiki/Alexander_G._McNutt

[94] This bond, which I purchased in 2005 for $350.00 carries over $17,000 in unpaid interest at 5%, however the State of Mississippi has already decided that the statute of limitations has long since run on any claim.

[95] I am not surprised that Richard Lawrence Dixon was angry with Governor McNutt. This appears to me to be an attempt to place the state's financial woes with James Phillips who was not alive to defend himself, or upon Dixon himself: McNutt insinuated that Dixon, being the executor of Judge James Phillips' estate, was responsible for the missing funds. Only the Governor claims that James was told not to accept anything but "gold and silver or notes of specific paying banks." More research may be required, but I suspect that no such requirement existed. Rules and regulations were very relaxed when it came to finances in those days.

[96] Sarah referred to him in her will as "James A. J. Phillips." Louise Hunter Dixon Phillips referred to him as "Jack Phillips." James might be the father of the young man photographed at The Farmers National Bank in 1904.

[97] I have been unsuccessful in locating this publisher in Jackson, Mississippi or the author William D. McCain to request permission to reproduce this passage. I trust that they will not mind.

[98] The assumption was that because Richard L. Dixon was the executor of the estate of Judge James Phillips, Jr., he was misappropriating funds left with James when he died. No wonder Richard L. Dixon despised Gov. McNutt.

[99] I am not sure why Rhesa Hatcher, Jr.'s name was spelled "Reice" in her will.

[100] The location of William Washington Phillips' name in this listing of her heirs suggests that William was younger than Seaborn.

[101] See also WALKER v. ROBBINS, 55 U.S. 584 (1852).

[102] See http://en.wikipedia.org/wiki/Indiantown,_South_Carolina

[103] Like William Washington Phillips and his brother, my great-great-grandfather Seaborn Moses Collins Phillips, David D. Wilson served in the Mexican-American War.

[104] William Willis Boddie must descend from William Willis, hence he is clearly a relative through Sarah Collins who married James Phillips, Jr.

[105] Some, including John B. Kent of Baton Rouge, Louisiana, speculate that James Phillips Sr. was from Massachusetts. They point to James Sr.'s son Joseph Thompson, who he called simply "Thompson" in his will. Thompson is a family name, and there were examples of Phillips families in Massachusetts and the surrounding area with sons named James and

Thompson. However, our efforts to connect to any of these families have so far been without success.

[106] There exists a deed of trespass which suggests that James Phillips was in Mississippi as early as February 15, 1812.

[107] From Wikipedia's entry for "Mississippi" found at http://en.wikipedia.org/wiki/Mississippi

[108] The preceeding four paragraphs are attributed to Lela Evans and Helen Arnold who have published a brief history of Mississippi at http://www.rootsweb.com/~mstallah/history/mshist.html.

[109] Not Rebecca Gallman who married William Washington Phillips.

[110] Martha is named as "Martha Thigpen" in her father's will. If divorce was uncommon in those days, then Thigpen should also be a family name.

[111] If Sarah Lee ("Sallie") was Nancy's child, and Nancy was the mother of all of the children, then she must have been at least 54 when Sarah Lee was born since William was born in 1775. Some think that "Lee" was Sarah's married name. Her name is listed before Charles and William in James Sr.'s will, suggesting that she was older than both Charles and William. However, one possible explanation is that Nancy was the mother of Sarah Lee, who was listed first, and that the other children were a by previous marriage by James Sr. If this were the case, it is a shame that James Sr. did not reference his former wife, if any. The conclusion I draw, despite the suggestion that Sarah may have been married, is that she was not married and that "Lee" is a family name.

[112] The 1820 census of Hinds County, Mississippi purports to show that Nancy was no longer alive by this time. She was also not named in her husband's will which was written between 1818-1819. Yet, this 1828 deed states that Hager should remain with "James Phillips and Nancy Phillips," suggesting that she was still alive in 1828.

[113] Benjamin Lee also witnessed deeds with James Phillips, Jr. in 1818.

[114] There have been instances of Phillips families in, for example, Massachusetts who had sons by the name of James Phillips and Thompson Phillips. To date, we have been unsuccessful in making a definite connection to any of these families.

[115] Even more curious, according to John B. Kent of Baton Rouge, Louisiana, the 1816 Marion County, Mississippi census shows a James Phillips, Jun (meaning "junior") with two adult males, one adult female, one male under twenty-one, and two females under twenty-one. This should be the family of James and Nancy. The two females under 21 should be Susannah and Sarah Lee. The census also further demonstrates that Sarah Lee was under 21. Thompson would appear to be the male under 21 and James, the future judge and treasurer, appears to be the other male over 21. We must conclude that for this census to list James as a Jun, then he too must be the son of a James. James, who became the judge and then the treasurer, would be at least the third James if this is true. We might also conclude that his father was alive at the time of the 1816 census. By the time of the 1820 census he is listed as Sr.

and Judge James Phillips is listed as Jr. However crucial to this argument that James Phillips Sr. was the son of a James depends upon whether the pen marking after his last name is really "Jun." Peter B. Miazza argues that it is really "Sr." He sent to me examples of the "Sr." marking for comparison and, to the untrained eye, it is very difficult to discern. The only implication is whether, in the previous generation, we should be looking for a James Phillips. In the final analysis, perhaps not. In any event, more research may be needed to determine whether the marking is really "Jun" or not.

[116] Rev. War Accts., voucher issued January 18, 1785 for 187 ½ acres in Franklin County, Georgia.

[117] As will be shown later in this book, William Pressley, who married Eleanor Orr, was the son of either William or John Pressly, two of the three Pressly brothers who immigrated to South Carolina in 1734 on the ship The Good Intent with the Witherspoon family. Traditionally he has been said to be the son of William. However, Bruce Tognazzini points out that John's son William would have been closer in age to Eleanor Orr. At some point during this time, the family name Pressly in this line became known as "Pressley."

[118] The "unhappy nights" were the result of "ghost stories" told to him as a boy by Amy, the house girl.

[119] Judge Benjamin Chaplin Pressley disagrees with the suggestion that the Pressleys were originally known in Scotland as "Priestly." However, these two men were descended from possibly two distinct Pressly families which may account for this distinction.

[120] Here I think John Gotea Pressley makes a slight error that he was not aware of. It appears that the David Pressley to whom he refers was actually David Pressly who immigrated to South Carolina in 1767, and was not one of the original three Pressly brothers who settled in the Williamsburg district.

[121] Robert Harvey Wilson was the half-brother of Emma Wilson, who married James Fowler Pressley, and Margaret Gotea Wilson, who married George Pressly Anderson.

[122] See http://history.hanover.edu/texts/nonantes.html

[123] See DAR record 299975.

[124] This description can be found on the South Carolina Department of Archives and History website at http://www.nationalregister.sc.gov/williamsburg/S10817745009/index.htm

[125] The Williamsburg County Historical Society is today known as the Williamsburgh Historical Society, located in the Williamsburgh Historical Museum in Kingstree, South Carolina.

[126] E-mail from Andrew Chandler to the author dated July 9, 2007.

[127] See Wikipedia's entry for "Early history of Williamsburg, South Carolina" which draws upon these two sources: http://en.wikipedia.org/wiki/Early_history_of_Williamsburg%2C_South_Carolina

[128] Bruce Tognazzini refers to "William The Elder" (e.g., William Pressly Jr., son of William Pressly who immigrated to South Carolina on The Good Intent

in 1734) and "William The Younger" (e.g., William, son of John Pressly who with his brother William immigrated to South Carolina on The Good Intent in 1734). Bruce points out that we don't really know which of these two William Presslys married Eleanor Orr, but Bruce speculates that the more likely of the two was the younger William, despite the traditional understanding. Regardless of which brother was the father of William, the genealogy converges with the parents of brothers William and John.

[129] Here, Judge Benjamin Chaplin Pressley disagrees with John Gotea Pressley about the name Pressly having originally been Priestly in Scotland.

[130] This is the mistake. Benjamin Chaplin Pressley presumed that his grandfather David Pressly was one of the original three Pressly brothers who sailed on The Good Intent and arrived in Charleston in 1734. This is not the case.

[131] Benjamin Pressly Barron created the original version of the "Genealogy of the Adams Family" chart, which was later copied by his son Walter L. Barron in 1916.

[132] Even more confusing, this Newsletter refers to him as "David Pressley" when in fact the Rev. John S. Pressly reviewed the will of the same "David Pressly." Worse, they continually refer to "John G. Pressly" even if "Pressly" is the correct original family name.

[133] See DAR record 749739, as well as DAR papers National No. 108, 405, National No. 44, 731 and DAR paper National No. 171, 153.

[134] The family name has been spelled both Barnet and Barnett.

[135] Mary Witherspoon and her husband David Wilson left Belfast, Ireland in 1732. Others arrived on The Good Intent in 1734. Mary and David's son David was born in 1742, about ten years after their arrival in South Carolina.

[136] *Old Kittery and Her Families*, by Everett Schermerhorn Stackpole, Press of Lewiston journal Co., Lewiston, Maine, 1903, pp 207-208.

[137] See http://www.colonialhall.com/whipple/whipple.php

[138] According to T. Whit Athey, the Lynches were one of the "14 Tribes of Galway." 14 Families joined together in the 14th century to build a wall around Galway. (Lynch & Athy were 2 of the 14). These families held power until the upheavals of the 1600s.

[139] *The Genealogies and Estates of Charlestown in the County of Middlesex and Commonwealth of Massachusetts*, 1629-1818, by Thomas Bellows Wyman: In a riot in town, in 1687, he was stabbed by Union Dearing of The Rose Frigate, man of war ship. Middlesex Co., MA Probate Case #209.

[140] The claim is made that we are related to the family of President John Adams (and to The Mayflower). However, there are problems with this chart and I am unable, so far, to show the family connection, assuming one exists.

[141] See http://www.alden.org/our_family/aldenbiography.htm

[142] I am not sure how this Patrick Lynch is related to our Lynch family, but having been born in the same area, he must be related. It is important to note that Thomas Lynch Jr., who signed The Declaration of Independence, died without children, ending his Lynch line. However, he stipulated in his will

that his heirs must adopt the Lynch surname if they chose to live on the family estate. Further, "Che" Guevera is a descendant of a female Lynch. Spanish surnames often assume the mother's surname.

[143] See http://www.fantompowa.net/Flame/che_guevara_irish_roots.htm

[144] See http://www.thepeerage.com/p10212.htm#i102114

[145] See David Costa's design of *The Beatles Anthology*, published by Chronicle Books in 2000.

INDEX

I

J

William, 448
Lynch's Creek, 349

M

MacLymont
V. H. M., 136
Magnolia Vineyard, 116, 124, 133
Maine
Kittery, 423
Malloch
Dean, 46
Malloch Elementary School, 46, *See*
Dean Malloch
Manheim
E. E., 137
Manigaults, 442, *See* Silk Hope
Margaret of Denmark, 453
Margaret of England, 453
Marion
Francis, 381, 382, 384, 386
General Francis, 346
Mariposa Street, 72
Martin
Ellin, 447
Professor J. M., 78, 79
Martinelli
Giovanni, 28
Mary
Princess of Scotland. *See* Princess
Mary of Scotland
Mary, Queen of Scots, 444
Mason
A. W., 182, 185
Masonic Order, 141
Massachusetts
Boston, 428, 434, 442
Charlestown, 418, 428, 429
Copps Hill, 434
Dorchester, 442
Sudbury, 439
Weymouth, 434, 437, 442
Matthews
Ann, 347
Mattingly
W. T., 153
Maupin
J. B., 136
Maxwell
Mariot, 452
Mayflower, 437, 438

Mayor of Jackson. *See* Rhesa Hatcher
Mayson
C. C., 317
McCabe
Alexander, 192
McCants
Thomas, 371
McCaulley
Mrs., 18
McClain
Mrs. Frank, 203
McClatchy, 16
C. K., 32, 40
Carlos, 33
James, 30
Phebe, 40, *See* Phebe Conley
Susan, 32
William, 33
McCleland
James, 415
McCollouch
Ben, 253
McConnell
Elizabeth, 404
James, 369, 370
Margaret, 405
Mary, 370
McCutchen
Eleanor, 387, 404
Hugh, 370, 405
McFarland
Mr., 265
McGill
David, 346
Dr. Samuel Davis, Jr., 347
Sam, Sr., 346
McGovern
Mr., 99
McIndoo
Ivan C., 134
McKay
Adele May, 208
McKee
Harry M., 199
McKenzie
Fred, 151
W. H., 95, 105
William H., 76
McLymont
V. H. M., 153
McNutt
Alexander G., 318

T

U

V